Votes for Survival

Across the world, many politicians offer benefits in direct exchange for their votes. Scholars often predict the demise of this phenomenon, as it is threatened by economic development, ballot secrecy, and other daunting challenges. To explain its resilience, this book shifts attention to the demand side of exchanges. Nichter contends that citizens play a crucial but underappreciated role in the survival of *relational clientelism* – ongoing exchange relationships that extend beyond election campaigns. Citizens often undertake key actions, including declared support and requesting benefits, to sustain these relationships. As most of the world's population remains vulnerable to adverse shocks, citizens often depend on such relationships when the state fails to provide an adequate social safety net. Nichter demonstrates the critical role of citizens with fieldwork and original surveys in Brazil, as well as with comparative evidence from Argentina, Mexico, and other continents.

SIMEON NICHTER is an assistant professor at University of California, San Diego. He has published articles in the *American Journal of Political Science, American Political Science Review, Comparative Political Studies, Electoral Studies, Review of Economics and Statistics,* and *World Development*. Previously, he served as an academy scholar at the Harvard Academy for International and Area Studies, a postdoctoral fellow at the Center on Democracy, Development, and the Rule of Law at Stanford University, and a postdoctoral fellow at the Center for Global Development. He received a Ph.D. in Political Science from University of California, Berkeley, and an MPA in International Development from Harvard Kennedy School.

Cambridge Studies in Comparative Politics

General Editors
Kathleen Thelen *Massachusetts Institute of Technology*
Erik Wibbels *Duke University*

Associate Editors
Catherine Boone *London School of Economics*
Thad Dunning *University of California, Berkeley*
Anna Grzymala-Busse *Stanford University*
Torben Iversen *Harvard University*
Stathis Kalyvas *Yale University*
Margaret Levi *Stanford University*
Helen Milner *Princeton University*
Frances Rosenbluth *Yale University*
Susan Stokes *Yale University*
Tariq Thachil *Vanderbilt University*

Series Founder
Peter Lange *Duke University*

Other Books in the Series

Christopher Adolph, *Bankers, Bureaucrats, and Central Bank Politics: The Myth of Neutrality*
Michael Albertus, *Autocracy and Redistribution: The Politics of Land Reform*
Ben W. Ansell, *From the Ballot to the Blackboard: The Redistributive Political Economy of Education*
Ben W. Ansell, David J. Samuels, *Inequality and Democratization: An Elite-Competition Approach*
Ana Arjona, *Rebelocracy: Social Order in the Colombian Civil War*
Leonardo R. Arriola, *Multi-Ethnic Coalitions in Africa: Business Financing of Opposition Election Campaigns*
David Austen-Smith, Jeffry A. Frieden, Miriam A. Golden, Karl Ove Moene, and Adam Przeworski, eds., *Selected Works of Michael Wallerstein: The Political Economy of Inequality, Unions, and Social Democracy*
Andy Baker, *The Market and the Masses in Latin America: Policy Reform and Consumption in Liberalizing Economies*

Continued after the index

Votes for Survival

Relational Clientelism in Latin America

SIMEON NICHTER
University of California, San Diego

CAMBRIDGE
UNIVERSITY PRESS

CAMBRIDGE
UNIVERSITY PRESS

University Printing House, Cambridge CB2 8BS, United Kingdom

One Liberty Plaza, 20th Floor, New York, NY 10006, USA

477 Williamstown Road, Port Melbourne, VIC 3207, Australia

314-321, 3rd Floor, Plot 3, Splendor Forum, Jasola District Centre, New Delhi – 110025, India

79 Anson Road, #06-04/06, Singapore 079906

Cambridge University Press is part of the University of Cambridge.

It furthers the University's mission by disseminating knowledge in the pursuit of education, learning, and research at the highest international levels of excellence.

www.cambridge.org
Information on this title: www.cambridge.org/9781108428361
DOI: 10.1017/9781316998014

© Simeon Nichter 2018

This publication is in copyright. Subject to statutory exception and to the provisions of relevant collective licensing agreements, no reproduction of any part may take place without the written permission of Cambridge University Press.

First published 2018

Printed in the United States of America by Sheridan Books, Inc.

A catalogue record for this publication is available from the British Library.

Library of Congress Cataloging-in-Publication Data
NAMES: Nichter, Simeon, author.
TITLE: Votes for survival : relational clientelism in Latin America / Simeon Nichter.
DESCRIPTION: Cambridge ; New York, NY : Cambridge University Press, 2018. |
  SERIES: Cambridge studies in comparative politics | Includes bibliographical references.
IDENTIFIERS: LCCN 2018023422| ISBN 9781108428361 (hardback : alk. paper) |
  ISBN 9781108449502 (paperback : alk. paper)
SUBJECTS: LCSH: Patron and client–Latin America. | Political participation–Latin America. |
  Latin America–Politics and government–1980–
CLASSIFICATION: LCC JL966 .N53 2018 | DDC 306.2098–dc23
  LC record available at https://lccn.loc.gov/2018023422

ISBN 978-1-108-42836-1 Hardback
ISBN 978-1-108-44950-2 Paperback

Cambridge University Press has no responsibility for the persistence or accuracy of URLs for external or third-party internet websites referred to in this publication and does not guarantee that any content on such websites is, or will remain, accurate or appropriate.

To Maysa

Contents

List of Figures	page ix
List of Tables	xi
Acknowledgments	xiii

1	Introduction	1
	1.1 *The Puzzle*	3
	1.2 *The Argument*	5
	1.3 *The Role of Citizens*	6
	1.4 *Relational Clientelism*	7
	1.5 *The Mechanisms*	11
	1.6 *Implications for Clientelism*	14
	1.7 *Why Brazil?*	16
	1.8 *The Plan of the Book*	22

PART I   ELECTORAL CLIENTELISM

2	Challenges for Electoral Clientelism	27
	2.1 *Strategies of Electoral Clientelism*	28
	2.2 *Logic of Electoral Clientelism*	30
	2.3 *Effect of Ballot Secrecy*	33
	2.4 *Effect of Compulsory Voting*	41
	2.5 *Effect of Voter Audits*	49
	2.6 *Effect of Anti-Clientelism Legislation*	53
	2.7 *Summary*	63

PART II   RELATIONAL CLIENTELISM

3	Citizens and Relational Clientelism	69
	3.1 *Definition of Relational Clientelism*	70

	3.2 *Resilience of Relational Clientelism*	70
	3.3 *Vulnerability and Relational Clientelism*	73
	3.4 *Declared Support*	74
	3.5 *Requesting Benefits*	79
	3.6 *Summary*	83
4	Income and Vulnerability	84
	4.1 *Rising Incomes*	85
	4.2 *Income and Clientelism*	92
	4.3 *Vulnerability*	98
	4.4 *Summary*	111
5	Declared Support	113
	5.1 *Prevalence of Declared Support*	114
	5.2 *Declared Support and Relational Clientelism*	117
	5.3 *Quantitative Analysis of Declared Support*	127
	5.4 *Declared Support and Signaling*	139
	5.5 *Voter Calculus of Declared Support*	145
	5.6 *Summary*	147
6	Requesting Benefits	149
	6.1 *Prevalence of Citizen Requests*	150
	6.2 *Requests and Vulnerability*	153
	6.3 *Requests and Relational Clientelism*	156
	6.4 *Requests and Screening*	166
	6.5 *Summary*	176

PART III   EXTENSIONS

7	Citizen Strategies in Comparative Context	179
	7.1 *Mexico*	180
	7.2 *Argentina*	189
	7.3 *Other Countries*	198
	7.4 *Summary*	203
8	Conclusion	205

Appendix A	Description of Qualitative Fieldwork	217
Appendix B	Description of Surveys	220
Appendix C	Signaling Model of Declared Support	235
Appendix D	Regression Tables for Declared Support	241
Appendix E	Regression Tables for Requesting Benefits	254
Appendix F	Regression Tables for Comparative Chapter	265
Bibliography		269
Author Index		287
Subject Index		291

Figures

1.1	Relational clientelism: Defining attributes and citizen mechanisms	page 9
2.1	Strategies of clientelism during elections	29
2.2	a. Map of citizens by political preferences and net voting costs – without electoral clientelism b. Map of citizens by political preferences and net voting costs – with electoral clientelism	32
2.3	a. Turnout in Brazil (1933–2014) – elections for Chamber of Deputies b. Abstention in Bahia (2008)	42
2.4	a. Effect of voter audits (Brazil, 2008) – effect of voter audits on mayoral reelection (regression discontinuity design) b. Effect of voter audits (Brazil, 2008) – heterogeneity of RDD effects by voter transfers	54
2.5	a. Politician removals for clientelism during elections (2000–2008) b. Electoral court documents mentioning clientelism (2000–2013)	60
4.1	Acceptability of hypothetical clientelist offers (2002 and 2007)	94
4.2	Effect of rainfall on willingness to accept clientelist offers (2012)	96
5.1	Declared support and benefits, rural Northeast Brazil (2013)	128
5.2	Declared support and benefits, Brazil (2012–2016)	133
5.3	Declared support and campaign handouts, rural Northeast Brazil (2012)	136
5.4	Declared support and campaign handouts, Brazil (2012 and 2016)	138

5.5	Declared support and voting for mayor, rural Northeast Brazil (2012)	142
5.6	Declared support and perceptions of mayoral candidates, rural Northeast Brazil (2012–2013)	144
6.1	Example of citizen's request to councilor	153
6.2	Citizen requests and private benefits, rural Northeast Brazil (2012–2013)	159
6.3	Citizen requests and relational clientelism, rural Northeast Brazil (2012–2013)	163
6.4	Perception of Councilor in trust game, by fulfilled vs. unfulfilled request, rural Northeast Brazil (2013)	172
6.5	Consistency of voting, by unfulfilled vs. fulfilled request, rural Northeast Brazil (2012)	175
7.1	Mexico: Declared support and clientelism during campaign (2012)	185
7.2	Citizen requests and clientelism during campaigns (2005–2010)	188
7.3	Argentina: Citizen strategies and campaign handouts (2001)	195
A.1	Map of research sites in Bahia, Northeast Brazil	218
B.1	Municipalities in rural clientelism survey, Brazil's semi-arid region, and rainfall levels	221
C.1	Signaling credibility through declared support	238

Tables

6.1	Share of Brazilians requesting help from politicians, 1988–2014	*page* 151
D.1	Declared support and post-election benefits, rural Northeast Brazil, 2013 – Regressions in Figure 5.1, rows 1 and 2	242
D.2	Declared support and post-election benefits, rural Northeast Brazil, 2013 – Regressions in Figure 5.1, rows 3 and 4	243
D.3	Declared support and post-election benefits, rural Northeast Brazil, 2013 – Regressions in Figure 5.1, row 5	244
D.4	Declared support and post-election water delivery, rural Northeast Brazil, 2013	245
D.5	Declared support and post-election benefits, Brazil, online survey, 2016 – Regressions in Figure 5.2, rows 1 and 2	246
D.6	Declared support and post-election benefits, Brazil, online survey, 2016 – Regressions in Figure 5.2, row 3	247
D.7	Declared support and campaign handouts, rural Northeast Brazil, 2012 – Regressions in Figure 5.3	248
D.8	Declared support and campaign handouts, Brazil, online survey, 2012 – Regressions in Figure 5.4, rows 1 and 2	249
D.9	Declared support and perceptions of victorious mayoral candidate, rural Northeast Brazil, 2012–13 – Regressions in Figure 5.6, rows 1–3	250
D.10	Declared support and perceptions of victorious mayoral candidate, rural Northeast Brazil, 2012–2013 – Regressions in Figure 5.6, rows 4 and 5	251
D.11	Declared support and perceptions of defeated mayoral candidate, rural Northeast Brazil, 2012–2013 – Regressions in Figure 5.6, rows 6 - 8	252

D.12	Declared support and perceptions of defeated mayoral candidate, rural Northeast Brazil, 2012–2013 – Regressions in Figure 5.6, rows 9 and 10	253
E.1	Citizen requests and post-election benefits, rural Northeast Brazil, 2013 – Regressions in Figure 6.2, rows 1 and 2	255
E.2	Citizen requests and post-election benefits, rural Northeast Brazil, 2013 – Regressions in Figure 6.2, row 3 (and club goods)	256
E.3	Citizen requests and campaign benefits, rural Northeast Brazil, 2012 – Regressions in Figure 6.2, row 4	257
E.4	Citizen requests and campaign benefits, rural Northeast Brazil, 2012 – Regressions in Figure 6.2, row 5	258
E.5	Correlates of post-election benefits by request, rural Northeast Brazil, 2013 – Regressions in Figure 6.3, row 1	259
E.6	Correlates of post-election requests, rural Northeast Brazil, 2013 – Regressions in Figure 6.3, row 2	260
E.7	Correlates of pre-election benefits by request, rural Northeast Brazil, 2012 – Regressions in Figure 6.3, row 3	261
E.8	Correlates of pre-election requests, rural Northeast Brazil, 2012 – Regressions in Figure 6.3, row 4	262
E.9	Perception of Councilor in trust game, unfulfilled vs. fulfilled request, rural Northeast Brazil, 2013 – Regressions in Figure 6.4	263
E.10	Voting for same mayoral candidate/party in 2008 and 2012, unfulfilled vs. fulfilled request, rural Northeast Brazil, 2012 – Regressions in Figure 6.5	264
F.1	Citizen requests and clientelism during campaigns – Regressions in Figure 7.2 – Africa (Afrobarometer Round 3, 2005–2006)	265
F.2	Citizen requests and clientelism during campaigns – Regressions in Figure 7.2 – Latin America (LAPOP, 2010)	266
F.3	Citizen requests and clientelism during campaigns – Regressions in Figure 7.2 – Argentina (LAPOP, 2010)	266
F.4	Citizen requests and clientelism during campaigns – Regressions in Figure 7.2 – Brazil (LAPOP, 2010)	267
F.5	Citizen requests and clientelism during campaigns – Regressions in Figure 7.2 – Mexico (LAPOP, 2010)	267
F.6	Argentina: Citizen strategies and campaign handouts, 2001 – Regressions in Figure 7.3	268

Acknowledgments

This book has benefited substantially from the support and guidance of many individuals. First, I would like to thank the faculty members of the Political Science Department at the University of California, Berkeley. I am deeply indebted to the generous and thoughtful mentorship of David Collier, whose substantial feedback has profoundly shaped the trajectory of my research and career. Ruth Berins Collier significantly deepened my understanding of Latin American politics and provided many incisive comments about my work on clientelism. Henry Brady and Robert Powell offered important methodological suggestions at key stages of this project. I am also highly appreciative of other UC Berkeley faculty members including Charles Briggs, Pradeep Chhibber, Ernesto Dal Bó, Frederico Finan, Paul Pierson, Alison Post, and Jason Wittenberg. I also learned a great deal from many fellow graduate students at Berkeley, including Taylor Boas, Thad Dunning, Patrick Egan, Candelaria Garay, Sam Handlin, Benjamin Lessing, and Rodrigo Zarazaga.

Much of this book was written under the auspices of the Harvard Academy for International and Area Studies, which generously provided a two-year postdoctoral fellowship. I am especially grateful to participants in my book conference held at Harvard University: Jorge Dominguez, Miriam Golden, Frances Hagopian, Philip Keefer, Herbert Kitschelt, and Steven Levitsky. Each of these scholars not only provided excellent constructive feedback on an earlier version of this manuscript but also has been formative in shaping my broader understanding about clientelism and distributive politics. My work also benefited substantially from input from numerous Senior Scholars (including Robert Bates, Grzegorz Ekeirt, Elizabeth Perry, Susan Pharr, and James Robinson) while presenting at the Harvard Academy, as well as from seminar participants at the David Rockefeller Center for Latin American Studies. It also benefited from discussions with Agustina Giraudy, Sheena Greitens, Nahomi Ichino, Horacio Larreguy, Noora Lori,

Ameet Morjaria, Stanislav Markus, and Harris Mylonas during my time in Cambridge.

I am also extremely grateful to the Center on Democracy, Development and the Rule of Law (CDDRL) at Stanford University. Larry Diamond, who headed CDDRL during my postdoctoral fellowship, shared many insights and provided excellent comments on my research. I was also fortunate to interact with and receive feedback from Beatriz Magaloni, whose work on clientelism and distributive politics has long influenced my own research. I would also like to thank Lisa Blaydes, Elizabeth Carlson, Gary Cox, James Fearon, Francis Fukuyama, Erik Jensen, David Laitin, Natan Sachs, and Kathryn Stoner for helpful input. During my time at Stanford, I also had the opportunity to serve as a nonresident postdoctoral fellow at the Center for Global Development (CGD). I am appreciative of the substantial comments I received during my presentations at CGD, especially from Nancy Birdsall, Michael Clemens, Alan Gelb, Amanda Glassman, Todd Moss, and Justin Sandefur.

I would also like to thank the University of California, San Diego, as insights from many colleagues and graduate students have greatly improved my research. The opportunity to present in the Faculty Research Seminar and in the HALBI Seminar yielded substantial comments incorporated in this book. While I cannot name everyone, I would like to express particular appreciation to Claire Adida, Scott Desposato, Alberto Diaz-Cayeros, Jesse Driscoll, Karen Ferree, Clark Gibson, Stephan Haggard, Seth Hill, Thad Kousser, David Lake, David Mares, Megumi Naoi, Samuel Popkin, Margaret Roberts, Sebastian Saiegh, Christina Schneider, Peter Smith, Susan Shirk, Branislav Slantchev, and David Wiens. In addition, I am grateful for outstanding research assistance from Mariana Carvalho Barbosa, Inbok Rhee, and Henrique Barbosa.

Although the present book significantly extends my past work on clientelism, it has been influenced by and builds on that research. As such, I would also like to express deep appreciation to several of my coauthors. I have learned a great deal from collaborators who were fellow graduate students during my time at Berkeley, including Jordan Gans-Morse, F. Daniel Hidalgo, Sebastian Mazzuca, and Brian Palmer-Rubin. In addition, I have benefited from extensive collaboration with Gustavo Bobonis, Paul Gertler, and Marco Gonzalez-Navarro. Various analyses that I conducted for this book employ a panel survey that we jointly collected in rural Northeast Brazil. That survey involved excellent research assistance from Ridwan Karim, Lisa Stockley, Bárbara Magalhães, Vânya Tsutsui, and Farhan Yahya, as well as survey collection by Márcio Thomé and the BemFam team. Coauthoring with Salvatore Nunnari has yielded many insights; in addition, numerous analyses that I conducted for this book use a dataset that we jointly collected online across Brazil. Moreover, I thoroughly enjoyed my collaboration with Michael Peress, who has shared many excellent insights over the years. Several of these coauthors provided helpful feedback at various stages of this book project, and I am especially thankful to Jordan Gans-Morse, who provided numerous rounds of extensive

Acknowledgments

comments. As discussed in Chapter 1, this book includes brief descriptions of findings from several of my studies with these collaborators.

I would also like to acknowledge the generous support of the National Science Foundation, which provided a Graduate Research Fellowship and a Doctoral Dissertation Improvement Grant, along with the earlier support of a Jacob K. Javits Fellowship from the U.S. Department of Education. Two original surveys employed in this book would not have been feasible without research funding from the Canadian Institute for Advanced Research, the Hellman Foundation, the Social Sciences and Humanities Research Council of Canada, and the Spanish Agency for International Development Cooperation. In addition, I acknowledge the IRB Boards at UC Berkeley, UC San Diego, Innovations for Poverty Action, University of Toronto, and Brazil's Comissão Nacional de Ética em Pesquisa for providing input on and approving the protocol of various components of research in this book.

I will remain forever indebted to the people of Brazil. Hundreds of private citizens in Bahia and Pernambuco welcomed me into their homes and responded to my questions, and many mayors, city councilors, party leaders, and other public officials took time off from their busy schedules to discuss clientelism and related topics. It is not possible for me to thank each of them individually, as given the sensitive nature of clientelism, I promised anonymity to all interviewees. Many others in Brazil also provided important information, guidance, or assistance. I am especially grateful to Màrlon Reis and Douglas de Melo Martins, two Brazilian judges who patiently answered my many questions over the years, as well as to Marcelo Rufino Rodrigues, Thais Antonio, Thais Castilho, David Fleischer, Beatriz de Souza Lima, Beth Lima, Josemar Lima, Emiliano Segatto, and Fernanda Sindlinger. Thank you to the staff members of Movimento de Combate á Corrupção Eleitoral in both Brasília and Salvador for providing a wealth of information and data about various anti-clientelism efforts. At the outset of my fieldwork, I learned a great deal from the intellectual community at Fundação Getulio Vargas, in particular from Marcos Monteiro, Marcelo Neri, and Francisco Costa. I appreciate the time of researchers at the Instituto Brasileiro de Análises Sociais e Econômicas, especially Maurício Santoro, Mariana Santarelli, and Rozi Billo. I thank Claudio Ferraz at the Pontifícia Universidade Católica do Rio de Janeiro, and Alexandre Samy de Castro and Sergei Suarez Dillon Soares at the Instituto de Pesquisa Econômica Aplicada. In addition, I express gratitude to the many staff members in Brazil's electoral governance body who facilitated my research, both in Brasília at the Tribunal Superior Eleitoral and in Salvador at the Tribunal Regional Eleitoral da Bahia.

I thank Cambridge University Press for substantial efforts in publishing this book. In particular, I would like to express gratitude to Robert Dreesen for serving as my editor, to Kathleen Thelen and Erik Wibbels for their roles as editors of the Cambridge Series in Comparative Politics, to Thomas Haynes for serving as content manager, to three anonymous reviewers who provided substantial feedback that greatly improved the book, and to Meera Seth for shepherding me through the publication process.

Last but certainly not least, my deepest appreciation goes to my family. I thank my mother, Mimi Nichter, and father, Mark Nichter, for encouraging my passion for academia and exposing me to fieldwork during my formative years. I would also like to express appreciation to my grandmother Bea Nichter, for always nurturing my intellectual curiosity, and to my brother, Brandon Nichter, for his lifelong friendship. Finally, I dedicate this book to my wife, Maysa Eissa Nichter, whose love and patience are beyond measure. You and our children, Caspian and Acacia, remind me every day of what is most important.

1

Introduction

Many politicians across the world deliver material benefits to citizens in direct exchange for political support. Recent news headlines provide a glimpse of this phenomenon. Nepal's former prime minister warned of politicians who pay citizens as if they are "goats and sheep," thereby "plundering the nation for five years by buying voters for one day."[1] The governing party of South Africa charged that a competitor stooped to "swine politics" by handing out piglets nearly a year before the 2014 elections.[2] Bulgaria's prime minister proclaimed vote buying to be "one of the ugliest phenomena in Bulgaria's recent history" as he spearheaded related investigations and arrests.[3] In Thailand, a Human Rights Watch observer claimed "everyone buys votes," and the *Bangkok Post* blamed vote-buying accusations for "fuelling" antigovernment protests.[4] Meanwhile, Brazil ousted scores of politicians for distributing handouts during campaigns, reaching a staggering 1,000 removals in just over a decade.[5]

Perhaps these reports are just isolated instances? On the contrary, recent surveys of 63,000 citizens across forty-four countries attest to the remarkable prevalence of such exchanges. The Latin American Public Opinion Project conducted surveys in twenty-six countries across the Americas and discovered that nearly 12 percent of citizens "sometimes" or "always" received offers

---

[1] "Madhav Nepal against Vote Buying," *Kantipur*, November 16, 2013.
[2] "Piglets Meant to Pay Off at Polls, Says ANC," *Business Day*, June 11, 2013.
[3] Bulgaria Government Information Service, March 25, 2013. See also: "Bulgarian Prosecutors Investigating 43 Cases of Alleged Electoral Fraud," *Sofia Globe*, May 12, 2013; "Bulgarian Politician Arrested for Vote Buying in Varna," *Sofia News Agency*, July 6, 2013; and "2 Bulgarians Sentenced for Vote Buying," *Sofia News Agency*, May 19, 2013.
[4] "Snap Election Turns the Heat on Watchdogs," *Bangkok Post*, December 15, 2013.
[5] Movimento de Combate á Corrupção Eleitoral (2012).

of benefits in exchange for their votes. This figure exceeded 16 percent in Argentina, Brazil, Mexico, and Paraguay.[6] Likewise, Afrobarometer uncovered that nearly 18 percent of citizens "sometimes" or "often" receive offers for their votes in the eighteen African countries it surveyed. Remarkably, figures surpassed 30 percent in Benin, Kenya, Madagascar, and Uganda.[7] And these findings are likely to be underestimates, because citizens tend to underreport such offers.[8]

This familiar pattern of exchanges – frequently called clientelism or machine politics – is the central focus of this book. Nearly all politicians promise some form of benefits to voters, so what distinguishes clientelism from "politics as usual?" A key distinction is *contingency*: citizens promise to vote for a politician in order to receive clientelist benefits.[9] In return for these promises, citizens may receive handouts during election campaigns or benefits that continue for years. This contingency contrasts sharply with the "programmatic" politics observed in some countries (especially in many but not all advanced democracies), in which citizens do not have to promise to vote for a politician in order to receive benefits.

Over the years, many scholars have been captivated by the question of how clientelism dies in some countries.[10] This book inverts the question and asks how clientelism survives. Fundamental challenges examined next might be expected to undercut machine politics, but the phenomenon remains remarkably resilient in many contexts. A cross-country survey of 1,400 experts by Herbert Kitschelt (2013) confirms that clientelism persists in more than 90 percent of nations, with "moderate" or "major" clientelist efforts in 74 percent of countries.[11] And far from abating, clientelism proves surprisingly durable. According to the study, over the past decade, politicians' clientelist efforts remained constant in half of countries, and even *increased* in another quarter of nations.[12]

---

[6] 2010 Latin American Public Opinion Project. Several other countries reached comparable figures. See also Faughnan and Zechmeister (2011).
[7] Afrobarometer Round 3 Survey (fielded in 2005 and 2006).
[8] Addressing social desirability bias often yields far greater prevalence rates (e.g., Gonzalez-Ocantos et al., 2012).
[9] For a discussion of the key role of contingency, see Kitschelt and Wilkinson (2007, 10–11) and Hicken (2011, 291–292).
[10] Recent examples examining why clientelism declines (either partially or entirely) include Stokes et al. (2013), Hagopian (2014), Weitz-Shapiro (2012), Lyne (2008), Kuo (2013), Montero (2012), Lloyd (2012), and Pasotti (2010).
[11] Expert survey in 2008–2009 of eighty-eight countries (all democratic polities with populations of at least two million citizens). Question: "In general, how much effort do politicians and parties in this country make to induce voters with preferential benefits to cast their votes for them?" Coded as persisting if most of a country's experts indicated "minor," "moderate," or "major" efforts.
[12] Calculated by author using data from Kitschelt (2013). Based on average responses of experts for each country.

1.1 THE PUZZLE

The persistence of clientelism throughout much of the world is striking, given the wide range of challenges that ostensibly threaten its existence. Scholars emphasize that four broad categories of challenges often threaten machine politics: structural changes, institutional reforms, legal enforcement, and partisan strategies. A brief, non-exhaustive overview of such challenges clarifies why the survival of clientelism is an intriguing puzzle.

Structural changes such as economic development may threaten machine politics. Observers long believed that direct exchanges of votes for benefits would wane as countries modernized (cf. Kitschelt and Wilkinson, 2007, 3; Hagopian, 2014). Although its persistence in some wealthy countries tempered such expectations, many contemporary studies contend that economic development undermines clientelism through poverty reduction. Clientelism is most prevalent in low-income countries, and within countries, politicians tend to distribute selective benefits disproportionately to poor citizens (Kitschelt, 2011; Stokes et al., 2013). Microeconomic theory points to one reason why: the diminishing marginal utility of income suggests poor citizens place relatively greater value on material benefits than on ideological preferences (Dixit and Londregan, 1996, 1114; Stokes, 2005, 315). Risk aversion and time preferences are other frequently cited reasons why poor citizens may be most prone to machine politics.[13] Regardless of why poverty and clientelism are linked, the plausible implication is that economic development should hinder machine politics so long as poverty declines. Yet clientelism has survived (and sometimes even thrived) amid a sharp increase in per capita income across the world over the last century (Maddison, 2001), as well as the halving of global poverty since 1990.[14] Similarly, machine politics endured in most of the world amid other structural changes posited to undermine the phenomenon. Examples include urbanization (which may inhibit clientelist monitoring) and population growth (which may raise the relative cost of clientelism).[15] Given economic development and other structural changes, how does clientelism remain so resilient?

Institutional reforms present another reason why the survival of machine politics is perplexing. Although various political and electoral institutions influence politicians' incentives to pursue clientelism (Carey and Shugart, 1995;

---

[13] For a discussion about the role of risk aversion, see Desposato (2007, 104) and Stokes et al. (2013, 163–164). For poor citizens' preference for immediate benefits, see Scott (1969, 1150) and Kitschelt and Wilkinson (2007, 3).
[14] World Bank Poverty Overview. Accessed November 21, 2017 at www.worldbank.org/en/topic/poverty/overview. See also "World Bank Says U.N. Goal of Halving Poverty Met," *Reuters*, February 29, 2012.
[15] Increasing geographic mobility may render clientelist monitoring more difficult (Hicken, 2011, 299–300), while electorate growth may favor programmatic politics over clientelism due to economies of scale (Stokes et al., 2013, chap. 8).

Hicken, 2007),[16] the contemporary literature overwhelmingly identifies one institution as clientelism's biggest threat: the secret ballot. With the introduction of the secret ballot, what prevents citizens from accepting rewards and then voting as they wish? Ballot secrecy may undermine clientelism by making it difficult, if not impossible, to verify how citizens vote. Of course, it is widely known that many politicians violate ballot secrecy; for example, Filipinos distribute carbon paper to copy ballots and Italians lend mobile phones to photograph vote choices (Schaffer and Schedler, 2007, 30–31). Without denying the fallibility of ballot secrecy, most researchers concur that the institution hampers some forms of clientelism by increasing monitoring costs (e.g., Cox and Kousser, 1981; Rusk, 1974; Stokes, 2005). Compulsory voting is another important threat to clientelism because it undermines politicians' ability to use benefits to influence *whether* citizens vote. Beyond influencing vote choices, selective benefits often mobilize supporters and demobilize opposition voters (Cox, 2009; Cox and Kousser, 1981; Nichter, 2008). Abstention penalties hinder such strategies: they shrink the pool of nonvoting supporters who can be targeted and make it tougher to induce opposers to stay home on election day (Gans-Morse, Mazzuca, and Nichter, 2014). Many countries have adopted such institutions that are supposedly inimical to machine politics: the secret ballot is one of the most ubiquitous electoral institutions in the world, and nearly thirty countries have compulsory voting (IDEA, 2009; Przeworski, 2012, 98). Given such institutional challenges, how does clientelism survive?

Heightened legal enforcement poses another key challenge for clientelism. In the case of historic Britain and the United States, Stokes et al. (2013, chap. 8) argue that legal reforms and their enforcement helped eradicate the phenomenon, as did economic development and ballot secrecy. Across the world today, nearly 90 percent of nations prohibit clientelism during campaigns (IDEA, 2012). Although enforcement is often weak, many countries are ratcheting up efforts to identify and punish transgressors, including Colombia, the Philippines, Taiwan, and Thailand (Eaton and Chambers-Ju, 2014; Hicken, 2007; Schaffer, 2008). In tandem with such domestic efforts, international election monitoring dramatically increased over the last half-century: nearly 80 percent of national elections are currently monitored by foreign observers (Hyde, 2011, 356). Heightened legal enforcement may thwart clientelism if politicians are unwilling to stomach the increased risk of punishment. In addition, it may render clientelism costlier for at least two reasons: increased campaign expenditures to evade detection, and higher citizen compensation if receiving benefits is punishable by law. In contexts with heightened legal enforcement, how does clientelism endure?

In some circumstances, party strategies may also threaten the viability of clientelism. Whereas Martin Shefter's (1977) seminal work attributes

---

[16] For a brief overview, see also Kitschelt (2000, 859–862) and Hagopian (2014, 19–20).

parties' adoption of clientelist appeals to their formative years,[17] the dominant paradigm now views party strategies as relatively more adaptable to political incentives and circumstances (e.g., Kitschelt, 2000; Levitsky, 2003b). For example, Phil Keefer (2007) argues that politicians tend to rely on clientelism when they cannot credibly promise to enact policies once elected (see also Keefer and Vlaicu, 2008), implying that politicians may abandon the practice once they acquire such credibility. Moreover, Frances Hagopian (2014, 31) contends that neoliberal reforms motivated some parties to pivot away from clientelism and other distributive strategies – and others to shift toward them – depending on how reforms affected parties' relative competitiveness. A commonality of such studies is that they offer conditions under which parties choose to eschew clientelism. Where such conditions pertain, what explains the perpetuation of clientelism?

This discussion of potential threats to clientelism is not meant to be exhaustive. But a broader point emerges when considering this confluence of structural changes, institutional reforms, legal enforcement, and partisan strategies. As examined extensively in this study, many commonly observed factors might be expected to cripple machine politics. Yet the direct exchange of benefits for political support continues throughout much of the world. Amid so many ostensibly fatal challenges, what mechanisms sustain the patterns of clientelism observed in so many countries?

1.2 THE ARGUMENT

This book argues that citizens play a crucial yet underappreciated role in sustaining clientelism. Despite rising incomes, most of the world's population remains vulnerable to adverse shocks such as unemployment, illness, and droughts. When the state fails to provide an adequate social safety net, this vulnerability motivates many citizens to buttress the stability of "relational clientelism" – ongoing exchange relationships that extend beyond election campaigns. Although relational clientelism is often resilient to many of the challenges discussed earlier, it is especially prone to opportunistic defection, a crucial problem that citizens' actions help alleviate. More specifically, ongoing exchange relationships involve a dual credibility problem: (1) politicians are concerned about whether citizens' promises to deliver political support are credible, and (2) citizens are concerned about whether politicians' promises to deliver benefits are credible. Citizens who depend on these relationships frequently employ two mechanisms to help sustain relational clientelism: they *declare support* to signal their own credibility, and they *request benefits* to screen politician credibility. Citizens who promise to vote for a politician in exchange for material benefits are deemed more trustworthy when they publicly

---

[17] More specifically, Shefter (1977) suggests parties tend to employ patronage if they mobilized a popular base before bureaucratic professionalization, but could not do so otherwise.

declare support by displaying political paraphernalia on their homes, on their bodies, and at rallies. Likewise, politicians who promise assistance during adverse shocks in exchange for political support are deemed more trustworthy when they have a track record of fulfilling their clients' requests. Through both mechanisms, citizens often play an instrumental role in the survival of relational clientelism.

1.3 THE ROLE OF CITIZENS

Clientelism is typically depicted as a top–down phenomenon that is firmly controlled by elites. Citizens involved in exchanges are usually viewed as bit actors who do little more than accept offers and follow instructions from politicians and their representatives. Without denying the importance of elites, I reject the common assumption that citizens are relegated to a passive role in clientelism. Instead, this book argues that the purposive choices of citizens often play a fundamental role in the survival of clientelism.

In much of the world, increased voter autonomy enables citizens to make choices that help sustain clientelism. Traditional literature on the topic examined enduring exchange relationships that were highly asymmetric (e.g., Cornelius, 1977; Powell, 1970), and thus provided few options for citizens to engage in political actions of their volition. In contemporary societies, voters typically have far greater independence within exchange relationships than their historical counterparts, who were often locked into patron–client bonds due to land-tenure arrangements (e.g., Hall, 1974; Scott, 1972, 93). Moreover, many countries have shifted from monopolistic to competitive clientelism (Kitschelt, 2011, 16); when exchanges are no longer dominated by a single machine, the potential scope for citizen choice often increases as voters have alternative sources of handouts. Several analysts of clientelism document a decrease in elite control over citizens (e.g., Archer, 1990; Gay, 2006; Scott, 1972), and others discuss the increased power of voters (e.g., Hilgers, 2012; Piattoni, 2001; Taylor-Robinson, 2010). Nevertheless, the broader literature – including nearly all formal and quantitative research on the topic – tends to give short shrift to the implications of heightened voter autonomy. Studies of clientelism almost invariably focus on the strategies of politicians and their representatives, and generally offer few insights about how the choices of citizens might also influence exchanges. By contrast, the present book puts voter choice into stark relief, and argues that actions chosen by citizens frequently bolster the stability of ongoing exchange relationships.

Across the world, many voters have a powerful motivation for undertaking such actions – elites often help their clients cope with vulnerability. The concept of vulnerability employed in this book encompasses both poverty and risk, given that both low average income and high uncertainty can reduce a citizen's welfare (Ligon and Schechter, 2003).[18] Although poverty has declined in many countries in recent decades, many people remain susceptible to various sources of uncertainty, including unemployment, illness, and drought. Nearly a half-century ago, James Scott linked the survival of patron–client ties in Southeast Asia to a lack of institutionalized ways in which citizens could ensure their livelihood (1972, 101–102). While Scott did not focus on the role of citizen choices, his insights remain relevant. Citizens often strive to sustain relational clientelism if the state does not mitigate their vulnerability; for example, if social policy fails to provide income during bouts of unemployment, health care during illness, or water during droughts. Much of the world's population remains underserved or excluded by social policy, as the welfare systems of both developed and developing countries have embarked on diverse trajectories (Esping-Andersen, 1990, 1996; Haggard and Kaufman, 2008). Although legislation in many countries promises a wide range of social policy benefits, actual delivery to citizens often falls short due to various factors ranging from administrative constraints to political targeting (Mares and Carnes, 2009, 94). And contrary to the notion of a welfare state facilitated by an insulated modern bureaucracy (Esping-Andersen, 1990, 13), evidence from around the world demonstrates that anti-poverty benefits and even health care are frequently allocated on the basis of political criteria (e.g., Cammett, 2011; Diaz-Cayeros et al., 2016). When citizens deem social policy to be inadequate or politicized, they are often motivated to sustain ongoing exchange relationships with politicians who mitigate their vulnerability.

1.4 RELATIONAL CLIENTELISM

Although scholars rarely consider the role of voter choice in clientelism, substantial research emphasizes how some elites provide assistance through ongoing exchange relationships – a phenomenon I term "relational clientelism" (Nichter, 2010). A prominent study by Robert Merton, for instance, argued that political machines (i.e., clientelist parties) in the United States once played an important "social function" by dispensing "all manner of assistance to those in need" (1968, 128; see also Banfield and Wilson, 1963, 126). Drawing analogies between such patterns in the early United States and in developing countries, James Scott similarly explained that the machine's handouts "symbolized its accessibility, helpfulness, and desire to work for the 'little man'" (1969, 1144). Decades later, Judith Chubb emphasized that Italy's Christian Democratic Party doled out clientelist favors as part of "a much more continuous relationship than that produced by the dispensation of benefits just prior to elections" (1982, 174). And along the same vein, Steven Levitsky explored how Argentina's Peronist party frequently delivered assistance to constituents (including the

---

[18] For a more extensive definition and formal analyses of vulnerability, see Ligon and Schechter (2003). Vulnerability is examined thoroughly in Chapter 4.

clientelist disbursement of food and medicine) through an extensive network of "base units" (Levitsky, 2003b, 186–190; see also Auyero, 2001). The present book builds on this influential line of research and demonstrates how citizen actions help sustain such ongoing patterns of relational clientelism.

While my focus on relational clientelism thus rests on considerable precedent, it diverges substantially from the more recent literature's depiction of exchange relations. The vast majority of studies published on the topic over the past decade fixate on "electoral clientelism" – a far more episodic phenomenon that exclusively provides benefits during election campaigns.[19] This strand of research depicts politicians and their representatives as providing campaign handouts to citizens who are unlikely to vote for them in an imminent election, in exchange for promising to act as instructed. A prominent example is Susan Stokes's (2005) work on vote buying in Argentina, which contends that the Peronist party targets weakly opposed voters during campaigns and induces them to switch their votes. Another example is my work on turnout buying, which argues that politicians target nonvoting supporters and induce them to show up on Election Day (Nichter, 2008; see also Cox, 2009). Studies of electoral clientelism are silent about the role (or even existence) of clientelist handouts in the years between election campaigns. As with the overall literature, these studies also generally relegate citizens to a passive role. Citizens only receive clientelist benefits if targeted during campaigns, and their only choice tends to be whether to accept nonnegotiable handouts offered by elites. In sharp contrast to this recent wave of research, the present book considers patterns of clientelism during *and* after campaigns, and argues that citizens' choices play a crucial role in sustaining ongoing exchange relationships.

In order to clarify the distinction between relational clientelism and electoral clientelism, Figure 1.1 describes their key defining attributes. As shown in the upper box, both forms of clientelism share the first attribute: the provision of material benefits is contingent on a citizen's political support.[20] In exchange for benefits, a citizen promises that he or she will provide (or has provided) political support. Next, the lower box shows a second attribute regarding the timing of benefits. A fundamental distinction emerges: only with relational clientelism do these contingent benefits extend beyond election campaigns. By contrast, electoral clientelism distributes benefits *exclusively* during campaigns. With respect to this second attribute, two points deserve emphasis. First, relational clientelism need not suspend assistance to clients during campaigns. Thus, in order to determine whether a campaign handout constitutes electoral or

---

[19] Examples of studies exclusively focusing on electoral clientelism include: Aidt and Jensen (2016), Bratton (2008), Gans-Morse et al. (2014), Gonzalez-Ocantos et al. (2012), Gonzalez-Ocantos et al. (2014), Jensen and Justesen (2014), Larreguy et al. (2016), Morgan and Várdy (2012), Nichter (2008), Rueda (2016), Stokes (2005), and Vicente (2014).

[20] For a discussion of contingency in clientelism, see also Kitschelt (2000, 849–850), Kitschelt and Wilkinson (2007, 10–11, 22), Hicken (2011, 291–292), Robinson and Verdier (2013, 1), and Stokes et al. (2013, 7).

1.4 Relational Clientelism

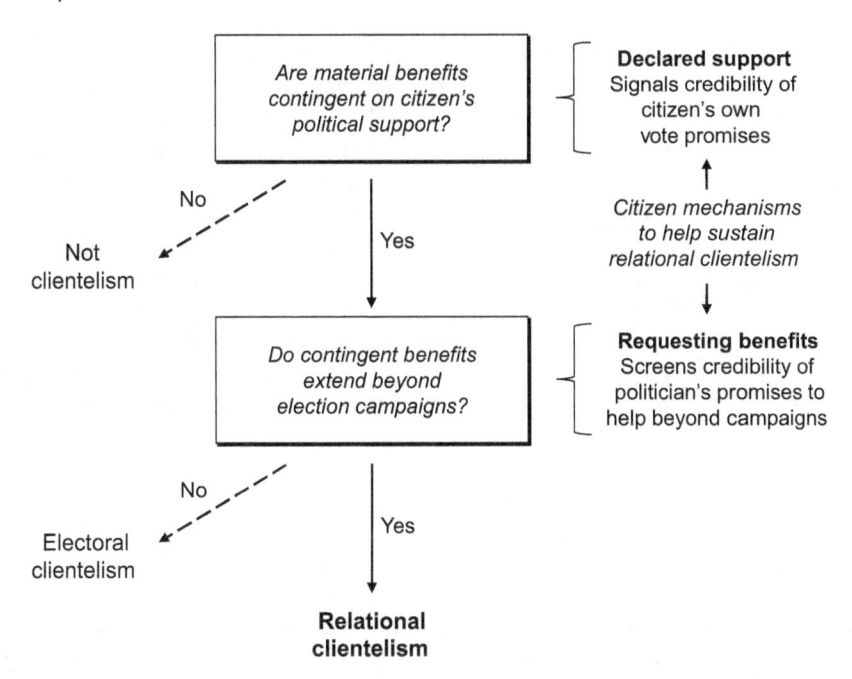

FIGURE 1.1 *Relational clientelism: Defining attributes and citizen mechanisms*

relational clientelism, it is necessary to ascertain whether a citizen's receipt of contingent benefits also extends beyond campaigns. Much of what scholars interpret as electoral clientelism is actually relational clientelism, because most studies fail to make this distinction. And second, relational clientelism does not necessarily provide a steady flow of benefits. As shown extensively in this book, much of relational clientelism involves periodic claims for assistance during adverse shocks, which can strike at any moment, including both election and non-election periods.

Most of the extant literature elides the crucial distinction between relational and electoral clientelism. On the other hand, much research emphasizes important differences between the broader concept of clientelism and other modalities of distributing benefits, such as programmatic politics, pork-barrel politics, and constituency service. Within Figure 1.1, these other forms of distributive politics are situated in the upper box's left branch, as each lacks the contingency that is a hallmark of clientelism. With programmatic politics, parties or candidates offer policy proposals to voters, and employ a codified approach when implementing policies (Kitschelt, 2000, 850). While these policies may favor broad swathes of citizens, benefits are distributed without regards to how or whether a potential recipient voted. With pork-barrel politics, elites target particular geographic districts with non-excludable benefits such as hospitals or roads (Golden, 2003, 200). This non-excludability of benefits inhibits contingent exchange;

residents in targeted districts cannot be precluded from receiving benefits based on their voting behavior. Two other forms of distributive politics similarly lack contingent exchange, and thus should also not be confused with any type of clientelism. With constituency service, politicians provide personalized assistance to residents of their districts, without using any political criteria to favor particular individuals (Fenno, 1978). Finally, with nonbinding favoritism, elites target recipients based on their political stripes, but without requiring votes in return; instead, benefits are distributed to generate goodwill during future elections. Unlike these various forms of distributive politics, citizens involved in relational and electoral clientelism promise political support in exchange for benefits.

The major challenges discussed earlier threaten both of these forms of clientelism – electoral clientelism (in which benefits are limited to campaigns) and relational clientelism (in which benefits extend beyond campaigns). But as explored in Chapter 3, relational clientelism is often more resilient to each category of challenges: structural changes, institutional reforms, legal enforcement, and partisan strategies. For example, even when economic development reduces poverty, continued vulnerability often leaves citizens reliant on ongoing exchange relationships with politicians during adverse shocks. Ballot secrecy fails to cripple relational clientelism because it does not rely on monitoring vote choices of opposing voters; citizens enmeshed in ongoing relationships prefer to vote for politicians who have a proven track record of providing them help. Likewise, relational clientelism is not scuttled by compulsory voting because it does not rely on mobilizing nonvoting supporters (or demobilizing opposition voters). Heightened enforcement of anti-clientelism laws typically focuses on election campaigns, yet much of relational clientelism occurs once the campaign season is over; moreover, benefits are channeled to supporters who are less likely to report their politicians' handouts to authorities. And as demonstrated in the context of Brazil, relational clientelism remained resilient even as some leading parties may have pivoted away from clientelism. Broadening the study of clientelism to consider such ongoing relationships – rather than just campaign handouts – is thus central to understanding how the phenomenon survives major challenges.

Although relational clientelism is more resilient than electoral clientelism to many challenges, it involves more complex – and potentially debilitating – issues pertaining to the trustworthiness of promises. This book argues that citizens buttress the stability of relational clientelism by undertaking actions that alleviate such credibility problems. These voter choices are fundamental to the survival of clientelism, because credibility underpins the viability of contingent exchanges. As discussed earlier, all forms of clientelism involve contingent exchange, in which citizens promise political support in exchange for benefits. Clientelism is effective to the extent that citizens fulfill such promises, so politicians are concerned about the threat of opportunistic defection. Thus, a common feature of both electoral and relational clientelism is that the credibility of a citizen's promises affects the actions of politicians. More specifically, politicians evaluate whether a citizen's promises to provide political support are trustworthy when deciding whether to provide clientelist benefits. The credibility of these promises is affected in part by the extent to which opportunistic defection can be monitored and punished.[21] When citizens cannot credibly promise to provide political support, they are relatively unlikely to receive assistance through ongoing exchange relationships – or even episodic payoffs during elections – from clientelist politicians.

Even though credibility problems plague both forms of clientelism, they prove to be doubly pernicious for relational clientelism. Whereas the credibility of citizens' promises is crucial for all forms of machine politics, relational clientelism also relies on the credibility of *politicians'* promises. Relational clientelism involves promises of benefits beyond campaigns, and citizens may doubt whether a given politician will actually fulfill such promises after an election. In the case of Brazil, a recent national survey found that 82 percent of respondents believe most candidates do not fulfill promises they make during campaigns.[22] Given this risk of opportunistic defection in relational clientelism, citizens' actions are affected by a politician's credibility. Electoral clientelism is fundamentally different because it does not involve promises of favors outside of the election season. Citizens receive all benefits during campaigns *before* voting. Hence, citizens do not face the risk of opportunistic defection and their actions are not affected by a politician's credibility. As explored extensively in this book, the dual credibility problem facing relational clientelism – in which both citizens and politicians are concerned about the trustworthiness of promises – poses a key threat to the viability of ongoing exchange relationships.[23]

1.5 THE MECHANISMS

The choices of citizens play a crucial role in alleviating this dual credibility problem, thereby helping to sustain relational clientelism. This book focuses on two key mechanisms by which citizens can attenuate credibility problems: *declared*

---

[21] For an analysis of how monitoring and punishment can affect credibility (not involving clientelism), see Lupia and McCubbins (1994, 99–100). The effect of monitoring on electoral clientelism is examined in Chapter 2. Other factors also affect credibility, such as information about a citizen's reciprocity (Finan and Schechter, 2012; Lawson and Greene, 2014).

[22] Survey conducted by research firm Vox Populi on behalf of the Associação dos Magistrados Brasileiros in July 2008. Included 1,502 respondents across all regions of Brazil.

[23] To the best of my knowledge, only Nichter (2010) and Hanusch and Keefer (2013) distinguish the credibility issues faced by different forms of clientelism. On the other hand, the general discussion of credibility problems is common in the clientelism literature. Most focus on citizen credibility (e.g., Kitschelt and Wilkinson, 2007; Stokes, 2005) or elite credibility (e.g., Keefer, 2007). Studies by Robinson and Verdier (2013, 1) and Finan and Schechter (2010, 1) mention the "double" credibility problem involving citizens and elites.

support and *requesting benefits*. Declared support mitigates concerns about whether citizens in ongoing exchange relationships are trustworthy. When citizens publicly pledge their political support, they signal the credibility of their vote promises. In addition, citizen requests allay concerns about whether politicians involved in relational clientelism are trustworthy. By requesting benefits and screening out unresponsive politicians, citizens can ameliorate their own concerns about the trustworthiness of politicians' promises to help during adverse shocks. As shown in Figure 1.1, each of these mechanisms alleviates credibility issues stemming from the two defining attributes of relational clientelism discussed earlier. Chapter 3 thoroughly elaborates how and why declared support and requesting benefits mitigate citizens' and politicians' concerns in enduring clientelist relationships. Subsequent chapters provide substantial evidence of both mechanisms in Brazil and in several other countries. Before providing a further synopsis of the logic of these mechanisms, it should be underscored that they are by no means the only ways in which citizens can reinforce ongoing exchange relationships. Nevertheless, evidence of both mechanisms corroborates the central argument of this book – the choices of citizens often play an instrumental role in the survival of relational clientelism.

When citizens declare support, it is commonly assumed that their exclusive motivation is to express political views or to provide free advertising for preferred candidates. Without a doubt, many voters across the world have such objectives in mind when they place campaign flags and banners on their homes, wear partisan paraphernalia, or hold signs at rallies. But for citizens involved in ongoing exchange relationships, declaring support also enables them to convince politicians that their promises of political support are trustworthy. As explained earlier, citizens are relatively unlikely to receive clientelist benefits unless their promises are credible, and they recognize that politicians may otherwise be unsure whether to believe them. They can pledge their support privately to politicians and their representatives, but this action may be interpreted as mere cheap talk. To distinguish themselves from insincere promisers of political support, citizens can signal the credibility of their vote promises through public declarations of support. This mechanism mitigates an important information asymmetry that remains largely unexplored in the clientelism literature: citizens have superior information about their own preferences. By declaring support, citizens transmit information about who they prefer to win in an upcoming election, thereby signaling whether they are likely to fulfill their promises to vote for politicians with whom they have ongoing clientelist relationships. To be sure, citizens in such relationships who prefer that a competitor wins also have an incentive to feign trustworthiness by declaring support. But for these citizens, who are relatively unlikely to fulfill their vote promises, declaration is often too costly: in addition to any material costs, declaring publicly against one's preferences involves expressive costs and may undesirably influence the election. A signaling model elaborated

1.5 The Mechanisms

in Chapter 3 clarifies the logic by which citizens can employ declared support to signal their credibility, thereby alleviating an information asymmetry that undermines relational clientelism.

Declared support, however, mitigates only one side of the dual credibility problem. How do voters in clientelist relationships know whether to trust politicians' promises to provide assistance during illness, drought, and other adverse shocks? The present book argues that citizen requests are a key mechanism that allays such concerns. Although most studies of clientelism focus exclusively on exchanges initiated by elites, many citizens *ask* for benefits. Of course, not all responsiveness to such requests involves clientelism; for example, politicians may engage in constituency service, which provides help to citizens without any contingent exchanges. By contrast, politicians who engage in relational clientelism promise benefits that extend beyond campaigns in exchange for political support. When citizens in clientelist relationships demand help from their entrusted politicians, they not only potentially receive immediate benefits but also elicit information about the trustworthiness of these promises. This mechanism of requesting benefits addresses an important information asymmetry: politicians have superior knowledge about whether they will reliably fulfill their promises of help to clients. For instance, politicians are more informed about discretionary resources available to assist clients, what share of these discretionary resources they will allocate to providing such assistance, and how many voters they have vowed to help. Despite such hidden characteristics, politicians develop reputations based on their track record of fulfilling or denying clients' requests. Within the context of ongoing exchange relationships, citizens screen against politicians based on these reputations. More specifically, they terminate their relationships with politicians who have tarnished reputations, by refusing to vote for them. Chapter 3 elaborates the logic by which citizens can screen politician credibility by requesting benefits, thereby mitigating another information asymmetry that threatens ongoing exchange relationships.

These two mechanisms involving the choices of citizens – declared support and requesting benefits – thus alleviate both sides of the dual credibility problem that threatens the survival of relational clientelism. Both mechanisms can contribute to the often self-reinforcing nature of ongoing exchange relationships: an equilibrium entails an endogenous feedback loop in which citizens and politicians have "self-confirming" beliefs about each other (Spence, 1973, 359–360). On the one hand, citizens have beliefs that politicians who fulfill requests will continue to deliver promised help after an election. Such beliefs are confirmed when citizens discover that such politicians do indeed comply with these promises. On the other hand, politicians have beliefs that citizens who declare support will later provide political support, especially their votes. Even if politicians cannot observe vote choices, their beliefs are confirmed (or at least not disconfirmed) when citizens declare for them again in future campaigns, and in some contexts, when they observe aggregate vote totals in declarers' localities. Overall, the choices of citizens not only mitigate the dual credibility problem in relational clientelism but also provide microfoundations for why in many cases exchange relationships are self-reinforcing over time.

1.6 IMPLICATIONS FOR CLIENTELISM

The choices of citizens not only help to explain the endurance of clientelism but also shed light on an intriguing paradox. Given that many prominent studies depict clientelism as "reward targeting," why do politicians expend scarce campaign funds targeting citizens who are already persuaded and mobilized? Evidence from around the world shows that politicians predominantly distribute campaign handouts to supporters who reliably turn out (Nichter and Peress, 2016; Stokes et al. 2013).[24] This book argues that providing ongoing benefits to supporters is part and parcel of relational clientelism – and moreover, these citizens frequently receive benefits not because they are "targeted," but rather because they initiate requests for them. Politicians have an incentive to fulfill requests of supporters because otherwise they transmit information that their promises of benefits are not credible. This information undermines clientelist relationships that take years to cultivate, as supporters frequently (and credibly) threaten to vote against preferred candidates when their requests are unfulfilled. Citizen requests are thus a mechanism that complements the insightful work of Diaz-Cayeros et al. (2016). Their study, which focuses on party strategies and does not analyze requests, argues that core supporters are targeted with private benefits because otherwise they will become swing voters in the future (what they call "conditional party loyalty").[25] In addition, the present book's focus on citizens provides a different explanation for why supporters receive contingent benefits than that of Stokes et al. (2013). Their important study argues that party leaders intend to target swing voters, but are thwarted by brokers who find it cheaper to distribute benefits to voting supporters. The mechanisms of our studies, which focus on different information asymmetries, are likely to coexist in many settings.[26] Indeed, some unexplored findings in Stokes et al. (2013) underscore the important role of citizens in clientelism; for example, over half of Argentine brokers in their survey reported that they distribute most benefits in direct response to citizen requests (2013, 105).

---

[24] This book primarily provides evidence from Brazil that supporting voters are targeted. It also presents evidence of these patterns in Argentina and cross-nationally in Africa and Latin America (building on Nichter and Peress, 2016). An important contribution by Stokes et al. (2013) demonstrates this pattern in Argentina, India, Mexico, and Venezuela.

[25] The authors also argue that parties employ a portfolio diversification strategy, in which swing districts receive local public goods.

[26] As discussed in Chapter 8, the Brazilian mayors and councilors examined in this book often serve as brokers for higher-level politicians. In Argentina, councilors comprise 300 of the 800 brokers surveyed by Stokes et al. (2013, 268).

1.6 Implications for Clientelism

Although the present book argues that citizens often play an instrumental role in sustaining ongoing exchange relationships, it does not claim that they *always* do so. With regards to demand-side factors, the theoretical argument entails two scope conditions for citizens: *voter autonomy* and *vulnerability*. First, my focus on voter choice presumes that citizens have sufficient autonomy to engage in political actions of their own volition. Citizens may be unable to make independent choices to declare support or demand benefits if elites employ substantial coercion, a key feature in the traditional literature on clientelism that persists in some contexts (Mares and Young, 2016; Piattoni, 2001, 12). As discussed in Chapter 8, voter autonomy may be especially limited in some authoritarian contexts, even if they allow some form of limited electoral politics. Voter autonomy may also be relatively curtailed in some areas with monopolistic clientelism, which in traditional settings often limited citizens' exit options by restricting alternative sources of benefits (Piattoni, 2001, 12). Second, the argument presumes that citizens face vulnerability, a concept that encompasses both poverty and risk (Ligon and Schechter, 2003). If citizens experience neither poverty nor unprotected risk, the allure of contingent benefits may not motivate them to declare support or initiate demands. Thus, welfare states that mitigate adverse shocks through institutionalized channels may obviate citizens' reliance on ongoing exchange relationships with politicians. Chapter 8 explores the implication that relational clientelism (though not necessarily electoral clientelism) erodes as welfare states are introduced, an argument made by influential work that does not analyze the role of citizens (e.g., Banfield and Wilson, 1963; Scott, 1969). In the absence of a welfare state, rising incomes are unlikely to shield citizens from vulnerability, unless citizens can afford to self-insure against risks. These scope conditions – voter autonomy and vulnerability – shed light on why citizens do not always act to bolster relational clientelism.

Just as demand-side factors help to explain why citizens may not exert effort to sustain relational clientelism, so do supply-side factors. Although the objective of this study is to call attention to the undertheorized role of citizens in exchanges, elites obviously also play a fundamental role. The argument of this book – that citizen actions help to sustain relational clientelism – presupposes the existence of ongoing exchange relationships. However, there are numerous conditions under which politicians or parties might not provide benefits during adverse shocks in exchange for political support. On the one hand, they may choose to devote minimal or no resources to clientelism. For instance, Rebecca Weitz-Shapiro (2012) argues that politicians may "opt out" of clientelism when middle-class voters penalize politicians for distributing clientelist benefits.[27] And as mentioned, Phil Keefer (2007) contends that politicians tend to rely on clientelism when they are unable to make credible promises about policy,

---

[27] Weitz-Shapiro (2012) argues this effect pertains given a large middle class and strong political competition.

suggesting they may no longer do so when they achieve such credibility. On the other hand, elites may be unable to engage in clientelism. They may lack resources altogether, or they may not have sufficient discretion over available resources to distribute them in a politicized manner. However, clientelism can thrive on the politics of scarcity, so long as elites have substantial discretion over limited resources (Chubb, 1982, 5–6). Politicians may also lack the dense organizational structure that machines typically use to learn about citizens' preferences, monitor their actions, and deliver benefits (Kitschelt and Wilkinson, 2007, 8–9; Stokes, 2005, 317). Overall, both demand and supply-side factors explain why citizens do not always play an instrumental role in the survival of clientelism.

Even though citizens do not *always* help sustain clientelism, this book argues that in many contexts, they do. To investigate the ways in which citizens take purposive actions to bolster ongoing exchange relationships with politicians, I now turn to Brazil.

1.7 WHY BRAZIL?

This book presents a general argument about how and why many citizens undertake purposive actions to help sustain ongoing clientelist relationships. Given that Kitschelt's 2013 global survey shows the remarkable persistence of clientelism across the world – it continues in over 90 percent of nations – mechanisms could plausibly be investigated in a variety of contexts. I primarily test the argument with empirical materials from Brazil, building on eighteen months of qualitative fieldwork and two original surveys. As discussed next, Brazil presents an especially fortuitous context to examine the survival of clientelism: the phenomenon remains resilient even though many of the challenges discussed earlier are especially daunting. Moreover, the book presents substantial evidence of how citizens buttress the stability of clientelism in Northeast Brazil, which is especially illuminating because much scholarship emphasizes the region's paucity of autonomous voters.

The persistence of clientelism across Brazil's history has long captured scholarly attention (e.g., Andrade, 1997; Hagopian, 1996; Nunes Leal, 1949), with many other influential works also emphasizing its role in Brazilian politics during various periods (e.g., Diniz, 1982; Nunes, 1997; Weyland, 1996).[28] Empirical materials presented in this book suggest that substantial clientelism persists in many parts of contemporary Brazil. For example, a 2010 survey conducted across the nation found that 41 percent of respondents knew someone who had voted in exchange for benefits, though it did not specify

---

[28] Other examples include Cammack (1982), Carvalho (1997), Collier and Collier (1991), Falcón (1995), Mainwaring (1999), Power (2010), Queiroz (1976) and Vilaça and Albuquerque (1965).

1.7 Why Brazil?

when those benefits were received.[29] A brief discussion of campaign handouts – which may involve electoral or relational clientelism, depending on whether benefits also extend beyond campaigns – motivates thorough analyses in later chapters. The nationally representative Brazilian Electoral Panel Study in 2010, for instance, uncovered considerable evidence of campaign handouts: over 16 percent of respondents were reportedly offered favors, food or other benefits in exchange for their political support during recent campaigns.[30] And belying the common misperception that clientelism only remains in certain regions of Brazil, at least a tenth of respondents in *all* regions reported this phenomenon, as did a quarter of those surveyed in the North and Center-West.[31]

Various other sources, including two original surveys described later, also point to the persistence of clientelism in Brazil. In an online survey conducted across the nation in 2016, only a quarter of citizens believed that campaign handouts had decreased in their own municipalities since 2000. By contrast, 36 percent reported an increase and 26 percent reported no change. In fact, nearly a quarter of all participants responded that the distribution of benefits during campaigns had increased "a lot."[32] Findings were similar in a face-to-face surveys conducted across rural Northeast Brazil: less than one-third of citizens believed that campaign handouts had declined since 2000. By contrast, 43 percent reported an increase and 27 percent reported no change.[33] Likewise, findings were comparable in an elite survey conducted in the Northeast state of Maranhão: less than a quarter of judges, prosecutors and activists believed that campaign handouts had declined in the past decade. In contrast, 45 percent of respondents reported an increase, and 29 percent reported no change.[34] And in Herbert Kitschelt's 2013 cross-national survey, only two of thirteen Brazil experts indicated the country's politicians engaged in "much less" efforts

---

[29] Survey conducted by research firm IBOPE on behalf of the Associação dos Magistrados Brasileiros in August 2010. Included 2,002 respondents across all regions of Brazil. The question: "Do you know someone who voted in exchange for a benefit?"

[30] Based on data from Ames et al. (2013). The three-wave survey of 2,669 voting-age Brazilians spanned 60 municipalities in 16 states during the presidential campaign. The question: "In recent years and thinking about election campaigns, did a candidate or someone from a political party offer you something, like a favor, food or any other benefit in exchange for your vote or support?" In Wave 1, 10.4 percent chose "sometimes" and 5.9 percent chose "frequently."

[31] The regional breakdown is 26.4 percent in the North, 24.2 percent in the Center-West, 14.3 percent in the Northeast, 13.6 percent in the South, and 9.5 percent in the Southeast.

[32] Data from the Online Clientelism Survey, which is discussed later and in Appendix B. $N = 1,964$. Findings similar if only including respondents of voting age in 2000. Question: "In your opinion, in the last 10 years, did the practice of politicians distributing money, goods or services during election campaigns increase or decrease in your municipality?"

[33] Data from the Rural Clientelism Survey, which is discussed later and in Appendix B. $N = 2,934$. Findings similar if only including respondents of voting age in 2000. Question: "During which campaign did politicians give more help to voters?"

[34] The author thanks Douglas de Melo Martins (a Brazilian judge) for including this question in his survey, which is discussed in Chapter 2 ($N = 258$). The question is identical to that in the 2016 online survey mentioned earlier.

to provide preferential benefits than a decade earlier.[35] While such evidence suggests the continued existence of clientelism in Brazil, it does not distinguish between electoral and relational clientelism. As explored extensively in this book, campaign handouts are often distributed not in isolation, but as part and parcel of an ongoing relationship in which benefits extend beyond campaigns. Unlike most of the extant literature, the present study examines patterns of clientelism during both election and non-election years, and thus reveals the important role of relational clientelism in Brazil.

More broadly, extensive evidence in this book demonstrates that clientelism is far from extinct in Brazil – much to the contrary, it continues to pervade many parts of the country. The survival of clientelism in Brazil is puzzling: especially since the nation's democratization in 1985, a series of monumental challenges have confronted the phenomenon. These challenges correspond to the four categories of global threats discussed earlier: structural changes, institutional reforms, legal enforcement and partisan strategies. Given that substantial clientelism continues despite such threats, Brazil provides an intriguing laboratory to investigate the mechanisms underlying its survival.

The resilience of clientelism is surprising in part because of Brazil's significant structural changes, which as explained earlier can undermine contingent exchanges. First, economic development is expected to reduce many Brazilians' willingness to vote against their preferences in exchange for benefits. Notwithstanding Brazil's severe recession experienced in 2015–2016 – potentially its worst in over a century[36] – Chapter 4 documents how incomes of the poor have risen dramatically over the past few decades. Growth in income per capita, especially of the poor, had previously reached what some Brazilian economists dubbed a "Chinese rate" of growth.[37] Remarkably, Brazil achieved a UN Millennium Development Goal – halving poverty in a quarter century – in just six years (IPEA, 2013a, 18). Over the past 20 years, the poverty rate fell from 34.7 percent to 5.9 percent (based on $2 PPP per day) (IPEA, 2013a, 18). A contributor is the rapid expansion of Bolsa Família, one of the world's largest conditional cash transfer programs, which reaches a quarter of Brazil's population (IPEA, 2013b; Soares et al., 2010a). Brazil also exhibits two other structural changes predicted to undercut clientelism, urbanization and population growth. Urbanization heightened the mobility of millions of Brazilians in recent decades (IBGE, 2011), which is predicted to undermine clientelist monitoring. And population growth – along with the renewed enfranchisement of illiterates in 1985 – contributed to an over 87 percent rise in the electorate

---

[35] Survey details discussed earlier. Five indicated "somewhat less," three indicated "somewhat greater," and two indicated "about the same." Question: "Do politicians nowadays make the same, greater or lesser efforts to provide preferential benefits to individuals and small groups of voters than they did about ten years ago?"

[36] "Para Meirelles, Brasil terá pior recessão desde 1901," O Globo, August 3, 2016.

[37] "Brasil Retirou 3,5 Milhões de Pessoas da Pobreza em 2012," Instituto de Pesquisa Econômica Aplicada, 10/1/2013.

1.7 Why Brazil?

over the past quarter century, which is predicted to increase the relative costs of clientelism.[38] Given that Brazil's important structural changes are expected to undercut clientelism, its robust survival is perplexing.

As examined in Chapter 2, several institutional reforms might also be expected to extirpate clientelism in Brazil. Over much of the last century, electoral institutions such as open-list proportional representation and presidentialism fostered clientelism and broader personalistic strategies (Ames, 1995; Mainwaring, 1991). Although such institutions continue, a recent major technological shift ostensibly rendered Brazil a much less propitious environment for clientelism. Brazil became the first nation in the world to introduce fully electronic voting in 2000 (Mercuri, 2002, 48), a shift that dramatically improved ballot secrecy. Many previously efficacious tactics to monitor vote choices became useless without paper ballots, making it difficult to verify vote-buying agreements. Brazil also took several steps to strengthen compulsory voting, hindering politicians' ability to influence electoral participation through clientelism. Moreover, the nation instituted voter registration audits to inhibit "voter buying," a clientelist strategy that imports outsiders into municipalities (Hidalgo and Nichter, 2016). Given that this confluence of reforms might be expected to cripple clientelism, its resilience is surprising.

Brazil's impressive enforcement of anti-clientelism laws might also be expected to extinguish the phenomenon. Although over 150 election observers from 36 countries watched its 2010 presidential election,[39] clientelist politicians face a far more serious threat from domestic watchdogs. Formal laws had prohibited campaign handouts for many decades, but until recently politicians delivered them with impunity because prosecutions were rare. Enforcement began ratcheting up after 1999, when over one million Brazilians signed a petition against campaign handouts and thus prodded the enactment of Law 9840, the first popular initiative approved by the national legislature. As explored in Chapter 2, this new law dramatically increased prosecutions for clientelism and is currently the top reason politicians are removed from office in Brazil. Given that such legal enforcement increases the costs and risks of clientelism, why does the phenomenon persist?

Party strategies provide another reason why clientelism's durability is surprising. Several important Brazilian parties have adopted strategies potentially inimical to clientelism. In a new book, Frances Hagopian (forthcoming) argues that increased programmatic competition in Brazil stems from two parties' strategic choices to eschew exchange politics. Briefly summarized, she contends that the Workers' Party (PT) and the PSDB were "distinctly disadvantaged" in distributing patronage and clientelism, so they instead adopted programmatic

---

[38] Electorate growth (1988–2013) calculated by author based on TSE statistics (see also Holston, 2008). Electorate growth increases relative costs of clientelism as programmatic strategies entail more economies of scale (Stokes et al., 2013, chap. 8).

[39] "Mais de 150 Observadores de 36 Países Acompanham as Eleições no Brasil," *Tribunal Superior Eleitoral (TSE)*, October 3, 2010.

policies when faced with neoliberal shocks (Hagopian, 2014, 139). Although the PT's ideological appeals moderated during Luiz Inácio Lula da Silva's presidencies (Hunter, 2010), and have been muddled by major corruption scandals (including Operação Lava Jato) and Dilma Rousseff's impeachment, many studies over the years suggest that the PT is relatively more programmatic than other Brazilian parties.[40] Meanwhile, conservative machines in Northeast Brazil (well-known for doling out clientelist benefits) experienced a considerable erosion of power with numerous gubernatorial defeats (Borges, 2007, 2011; Montero, 2012). Given such developments, how does clientelism persist in Brazil?

Amidst this confluence of challenges, the present book argues that the choices of citizens play a key role in explaining the survival of ongoing clientelist relationships in Brazil. Both qualitative and quantitative evidence are marshaled to test this argument. Qualitative evidence stems from eighteen months of fieldwork, including 110 interviews in Bahia state in 2008–2009 and 22 interviews in Pernambuco state in 2012.[41] I conducted formal interviews with 71 elites (primarily mayors and city councilors) and 61 citizens (both urban and rural residents) in municipalities with populations under 100,000 citizens.[42] Whereas most contemporary research on clientelism focuses on major metropolitan areas, over 45 percent of Brazil's population lives in municipalities under 100,000 citizens, as do over 60 percent of residents in the Northeast region (IBGE, 2010).[43] Additional informal interviews about clientelism were also conducted in Brasília in 2013. Other qualitative materials employed include government documents, court cases, and newspaper articles.

The argument is also tested with two original surveys that build on this fieldwork. First, I collaborated with Gustavo Bobonis, Paul Gertler, and Marco Gonzalez-Navarro to conduct a multiyear, three-wave panel survey of approximately 3,700 rural citizens across 9 states in Northeast Brazil (2011–2013).[44] This "Rural Clientelism Survey" was collected in conjunction with a field

---

[40] The extent to which parties in Brazil are ideologically distinguishable is debated (see Power and Zucco Jr., 2009; and Lucas and Samuels, 2010), but most analysts concur the PT is relatively more programmatic than its peers. For a review of the PT's evolution, see Amaral and Power (2016). Chapter 2 discusses PT efforts against clientelism and recent scandals.

[41] As described in Appendix A, interviews were conducted in Portuguese, lasted an average of seventy minutes, and were nearly all taped and transcribed. I also conducted 350 informal interviews and three focus groups.

[42] Mayors and councilors are elected concurrently in local elections, held nationwide every four years. Mayors are elected by plurality (unless the population exceeds 200,000), can hold office for two consecutive terms, and can be reelected again in later elections. The city council is a municipality's legislative branch. Municipalities have nine to fifty-five councilors (based on population), who are elected without term limits by open-list proportional representation.

[43] Bahia is the most populous state in the Northeast region, with 14 million citizens; Pernambuco is in the same region, with 8.8 million citizens.

[44] There were 3,685 respondents in the 2012 wave, and 3,761 respondents in the 2013 wave. In addition, the 2011 wave gathered baseline data for these and other respondents.

experiment discussed in Chapter 8. Respondents were randomly selected from the federal government's poverty database (Cadastro Único) and, as is common in the rural Northeast, did not have piped water or a water cistern. The survey was conducted in 40 municipalities, selected randomly with geographic stratification.[45] In order to examine patterns elsewhere in Brazil, I then conducted an online survey in collaboration with Salvatore Nunnari in 2016. This survey recruited participants through Facebook advertisements displayed in all municipalities with 250,000 or fewer residents; nearly 60 percent of Brazilians live in such municipalities. Nearly 2,300 citizens participated in the survey, from 1,210 municipalities across the nation. Although online participants were not randomly selected from a sampling frame, their characteristics are fairly representative of Brazil with respect to gender, age, and geographic region. Both surveys are described more extensively in Appendix B.

While the book tests the argument with evidence from across Brazil, its prime focus on the Northeast region is particularly useful for evaluating mechanisms by which citizens help to sustain clientelism. Scholarship on Brazil's Northeast has long emphasized that the region has a paucity of autonomous voters.[46] Indeed, many studies have traditionally discussed its voters using terms such as *votos de cabresto* (halter votes) and *currais eleitorais* (electoral corrals) – both referring to the restraint of animals. One might thus expect the region to offer relatively minimal scope for citizens to undertake actions of their own volition to bolster the stability of ongoing exchange relationships. Yet Part II shows that even in such a context, many citizens declare support and demand benefits from politicians. Such evidence not only demonstrates the mechanisms elaborated in this book, but also challenges the typical assumption that citizens play only a passive role in clientelism.

Overall, this book presents a novel theoretical argument that is primarily tested with unpublished data from two original surveys and interviews. It significantly extends my prior work on the topic, which instead focused predominantly on elite strategies of electoral clientelism. Given Part I's focus on electoral clientelism, a portion of Chapter 2 adapts a typology from Nichter (2008) and discusses findings from Gans-Morse, Mazzuca, and Nichter (2014) and Hidalgo and Nichter (2016). Chapter 3 briefly compares the present book's theoretical contributions with those of Nichter and Peress (2016) and Nichter and Nunnari (2017). Chapter 5, which focuses on declared support, includes a short summary of findings from Nichter and Nunnari (2017). A subset of the comparative evidence in Chapter 7 is adapted from Nichter and Palmer-Rubin (2015) and Nichter and Peress (2016), which both focus exclusively on campaign handouts. In addition, several chapters briefly discuss findings

---

[45] The random sample was stratified geographically by municipality (with probability proportional to families without access to potable water) and by locality (with probability proportional to eligible households).

[46] For instance, see Nunes Leal (1949), Hoefle (1985), Roniger (1987), Bernal (2001), Bursztyn and Chacon (2013) and Moraes (2015).

from a field experiment that reduced vulnerability in Brazil (Bobonis, Gertler, Gonzalez-Navarro and Nichter, 2018).[47]

1.8 THE PLAN OF THE BOOK

This book, which argues that citizens play an instrumental role in the survival of ongoing exchange relationships, is organized in three parts. Part I sets up this argument through juxtaposition, as it examines why more episodic forms of clientelism are under substantial duress in Brazil. More specifically, Chapter 2 demonstrates that electoral clientelism is undermined by the substantial institutional and legal challenges mentioned earlier. First, it presents a typology of distinct strategies of electoral clientelism and introduces a theoretical framework explaining how politicians employ strategies. The chapter shows why two key factors – rigorous ballot secrecy and stringent compulsory voting – pose significant challenges for contingent exchanges during Brazilian campaigns. Given these challenges, many politicians use campaign rewards to import outsiders into their municipalities, but this expensive tactic is also hindered by extensive voter audits. The chapter then turns to yet another major challenge facing electoral clientelism in Brazil, the enactment of a new law against campaign handouts that has ousted over a thousand politicians from office. Amidst such challenges, electoral clientelism has declined in Brazil, though some politicians still employ its risky and unreliable strategies as a secondary measure.

Next, Part II pivots to relational clientelism. Chapter 3 shows that relational clientelism is relatively resilient to the challenges faced by electoral clientelism in Part I, but is threatened by a dual credibility problem. The survival of ongoing exchange relationships is imperiled by the possibility that citizens or politicians may engage in opportunistic defection: citizens may renege on their vote promises, and politicians may renege on their promises of material benefits. As explored in the chapter, voters often undertake purposive actions to mitigate this dual credibility problem, and thereby fortify relational clientelism. Vulnerability frequently motivates clients to do so, as enduring clientelist relationships provide an important form of informal insurance when the state fails to provide an adequate social safety net. To elaborate this argument, Chapter 3 distills the logic and mechanisms by which citizens buttress the stability of relational clientelism. In particular, the theoretical chapter examines two citizen mechanisms introduced earlier – *declared support* and *requesting benefits*. Building on a signaling model, it examines how citizens can declare support to transmit meaningful information about the credibility of their vote promises. In addition, the chapter elaborates the logic by which citizens can

---

[47] Several interview quotes about declared support and citizen requests also appear in Nichter (2009, 2014a) and Nichter and Peress (2016), respectively.

1.8 The Plan of the Book

screen against politicians who are unlikely to follow through on promises of benefits beyond election campaigns.

Subsequent chapters in Part II flesh out and test the argument, building on empirical materials from Brazil. Chapter 4 argues that despite rising income, vulnerability spurs many citizens to sustain ongoing exchange relationships with politicians. First, the chapter examines Brazil's substantial pro-poor income growth, fueled in large part by labor income, social pensions, and a conditional cash transfer program. Analyses show that campaign handouts become less attractive as income increases, as theory predicts. Nevertheless, many Brazilians continue to be vulnerable to adverse shocks, including unemployment, illness, and drought. Given the unemployment insurance system's focus on formal employees and stringent requirements, less than a tenth of Brazilians who lose their jobs receive benefits. Inadequacies in the public health care system often contribute to catastrophic out-of-pocket expenditures, and most citizens cannot afford private health insurance. And recurring droughts threaten many citizens' livelihood, with 40 percent of survey respondents in rural Northeast Brazil facing a water shortage at some point in their lives. The chapter also demonstrates that local politicians have considerable resources and discretion, enabling them to mitigate risks faced by their clients. Overall, vulnerability continues to afflict many Brazilians, providing them an important motivation to help sustain relational clientelism.

Chapter 5 then examines the mechanism of declared support, which enables citizens to signal the trustworthiness of their vote promises. Many Brazilians make public declarations in favor of candidates. While their reasons are multifaceted, evidence points to the role of vulnerability; for example, declarations significantly increase during droughts in rural Northeast Brazil. The chapter demonstrates a substantial link between declared support and relational clientelism. Evidence points to widely shared perceptions that declarations affect whether citizens receive ongoing benefits. Beyond these perceptions, analyses suggest that Brazilians who declare support for victorious candidates are indeed more likely recipients of benefits during election *and* non-election years. Consistent with the logic of signaling elaborated in Chapter 3, qualitative and quantitative evidence suggests that declared support is indeed informative, as citizens overwhelmingly vote and hold perceptions in accordance with their declarations. By allaying politicians' concerns about their trustworthiness, declared support enables many Brazilians to buttress the stability of relational clientelism.

Next, Chapter 6 examines requesting benefits, another key mechanism by which citizens sustain relational clientelism. Even in rural Northeast Brazil, an area not traditionally known for high levels of voter autonomy, the majority of citizens who receive handouts had *asked* politicians for help. Citizens' demands are frequently motivated by vulnerability: most requests involve life necessities, such as water and medicine, and they spike during adverse shocks. Evidence is consistent with both relational clientelism and the logic of screening elaborated in Chapter 3. Analyses suggest that during both election *and* non-election years, requesters disproportionately receive help, with declared supporters as more likely recipients. Interviews provide insight about the screening role of requests in ongoing clientelist relationships, and regressions show that survey respondents often espouse negative perceptions of politicians who deny their requests, and refuse to vote for them. By eliciting information about politicians' trustworthiness, requesting benefits enables citizens to mitigate an important threat to the survival of relational clientelism.

Finally, Part III places the book's argument in comparative context and examines its broader implications. Chapter 7 extends beyond Brazil, focusing primarily on Argentina and Mexico. For both countries, the chapter investigates challenges for clientelism, such as rising income, heightened ballot secrecy, and increased legal scrutiny. Moreover, it documents substantial vulnerability that can motivate citizens to undertake actions to sustain relational clientelism. An analysis of survey data, complemented by qualitative sources, provides evidence of both mechanisms – declared support and requesting benefits – in Argentina and Mexico. Furthermore, patterns consistent with one or both strategies are observed in Ghana, India, Lebanon, and Yemen, and cross-national data from Africa and Latin America suggest a link between requesting benefits and clientelism. Chapter 8 concludes by providing a summary of the overall argument and discussing implications for democracy and development. It emphasizes that relational clientelism is an inferior substitute for an adequate welfare state, but it provides an informal risk-coping mechanism in countries with patchy coverage. The chapter explores why citizens' actions to fortify ongoing exchange relationships may have important consequences for higher levels of political systems, given that the local politicians examined in this book often serve as brokers for state, provincial, and national politicians in various countries. It also discusses when citizens might shift away from sustaining relational clientelism, drawing on findings from a coauthored field experiment in which our team randomly distributed water cisterns to reduce vulnerability in Northeast Brazil.

More broadly, this book suggests important directions for research on clientelism. First, it emphasizes the need to take more seriously the independent role of voters in the survival of clientelism. Second, it underscores the importance of studying how vulnerability, and not just poverty, affects contingent exchanges. And finally, it calls for refocused attention on ongoing exchange relationships, which have been investigated far less than electoral clientelism in recent years.

PART I

ELECTORAL CLIENTELISM

2

Challenges for Electoral Clientelism

Unlike this book's focus on ongoing exchange relationships, most recent research concentrates on electoral clientelism. This episodic phenomenon distributes benefits exclusively during election campaigns. While vote buying is the most commonly studied type of electoral clientelism, other strategies include turnout buying, abstention buying and voter buying. In order to set up the remainder of the book – which explores citizens' role in the survival of relational clientelism – the present chapter examines why electoral clientelism in Brazil is under substantial duress from major institutional and legal challenges. Such factors similarly threaten many contingent exchanges around the world: beyond global evidence discussed in the Introduction, Chapter 7 investigates challenges facing electoral clientelism in Argentina and Mexico. To foreshadow the broader argument, relational clientelism is relatively resilient to various challenges that hinder electoral clientelism, but is especially prone to credibility problems that citizen actions help to mitigate.

To clarify the distinction between different strategies of electoral clientelism, this chapter first presents a typology and theoretical framework. This framework emphasizes that institutional factors in a given society shape the relative costs of different strategies, thereby leading a clientelist party to adapt its mix of electoral clientelism. A confluence of key institutional factors undermines – but by no means eliminates – the use of electoral clientelism in Brazil. First, the nation's adoption of electronic voting heightened ballot secrecy, which undercuts vote buying. Second, strict compulsory voting (despite low fines) inhibits politicians' ability to engage in turnout buying and abstention buying. Given these hindrances, some politicians engage in another, more costly form of electoral clientelism: importing outsiders through voter buying. Yet even this strategy is hamstrung by third institutional challenge: electoral authorities' extensive use of voter audits.[1] Furthermore, the chapter explores a fourth challenge: a remarkably effective new law that prohibits clientelism during elections. Overall, electoral clientelism is buffeted by a multitude of challenges in Brazil.

2.1 STRATEGIES OF ELECTORAL CLIENTELISM

When politicians deliver handouts during campaigns, they have an arsenal of strategies to deploy. Although the vast majority of studies focus exclusively on vote buying, the typology in Figure 2.1 demonstrates several other important strategies of electoral clientelism.[2] These strategies target different types of individuals and induce distinct actions.

Vote buying rewards opposing (or indifferent) voters for switching their vote choices.[3] To provide an illustrative example, an operative in Bahia state recounted to me how he approached rural farmers as they walked towards the polls, inviting each for a drink of *cachaça* (cane alcohol). After a few drinks in a nearby house, he offered each farmer R$10 ($2.50) to switch his vote choice.[4] Such vote buying is the predominant form of electoral clientelism in Brazil, even though, as shown later, the strategy faces considerable challenges. In the Rural Clientelism Survey across Northeast Brazil (described in Appendix B), 15.6 percent of respondents reported that they knew a vote-buying recipient, nearly double the frequency of any other form of clientelism restricted to campaigns. Because this figure reflects citizens' familiarity with vote buying instead of their own experiences, it potentially overstates the strategy's prevalence; nevertheless, the measure is discussed here as the survey includes comparable questions for other strategies of electoral clientelism.

Another form of electoral clientelism, *turnout buying*, rewards unmobilized supporters for showing up at the polls on Election Day. Although most politicians I interviewed in Bahia state suggested this strategy did not exist in their municipalities due to strong compulsory voting, one councilor explained that if a voter "is going to vote for you, but on the day he doesn't have interest in voting ... sometimes you offer something to him."[5] In the Rural Clientelism

---

[1] The point is that some institutional features undercut electoral clientelism in Brazil, not that *all* features do. For example, Brazil's usage of open-list proportional representation for some offices, in conjunction with other electoral rules, is understood to be relatively conducive to clientelism (e.g., Hagopian, 1996, 199; Ames, 2002, 97).

[2] This typology is adapted from my article in the *American Political Science Review* (Nichter, 2008, 20).

[3] Given this chapter's focus on electoral clientelism, rewards are defined here as cash or particularistic goods and services (including food and alcohol) given to individuals before an election. Post-election benefits and transportation to the polls are not considered rewards (Nichter, 2014b).

[4] Author's interview, municipality in Bahia with 10,000 citizens (October 4, 2008). Unless otherwise noted, this book employs the exchange rate on January 1, 2016 (USD$1 = R$3.96).

[5] Author's interview, municipality in Bahia with 15,000 citizens (January 13, 2009).

2.1 Strategies of Electoral Clientelism

	Political Preference of Recipient vis-à-vis Politician Offering Goods	
	Favors Party	Indifferent or Favors Opposition
Inclined to vote — Recipient inclined to vote or not vote	Rewarding loyalists	Vote buying / Abstention buying
Inclined not to vote	Turnout buying	Voter buying / Double persuasion

FIGURE 2.1 Strategies of clientelism during elections
Source: Adapted from Nichter (2008).

Survey across Northeast Brazil, turnout buying was the second-most common form of electoral clientelism: 8.1 percent of citizens reported they knew a turnout-buying recipient.[6]

A third strategy of electoral clientelism, *abstention buying*, rewards opposing (or indifferent) individuals for *not* voting.[7] In Bahia, the vast majority of interviewees proclaimed they had never heard of this strategy. But an illustrative example is provided by a councilor who explained: "The stories that the elderly tell, that someone came to the house with money, took all of the documents … so nobody could vote, because he wasn't certain that if he helped, the person would vote in his favor."[8] In the Rural Clientelism Survey across Northeast Brazil, only 2.5 percent of respondents reported they knew someone who experienced abstention buying.

Voter buying induces citizens in *other* districts to transfer their electoral registration and vote for a specified politician (Hidalgo and Nichter, 2016). Recipients are registered elsewhere before receiving rewards; as such, the typology shows that the strategy targets citizens who neither favor the politician offering goods nor are inclined to vote (in the clientelist politician's district). For example, a councilor candidate in a small municipality in Alagoas state was convicted in 2010 of importing numerous voters and providing each R$50 ($13), food, transportation, and an overnight stay to vote for him.[9] Although usually overlooked by the clientelism literature, voter buying was the third-most common form of electoral clientelism in the Rural Clientelism Survey, with 7.3 percent of citizens reporting they knew a voter-buying recipient.

---

[6] See Nichter (2008) for a more thorough discussion of turnout buying, as well as Cox (2009), Rosas and Hawkins (2008), and Dunning and Stokes (2009).

[7] For example, see Cox and Kousser (1981), Schaffer (2002), Heckelman (1998), Cornelius (2003), and Morgan and Várdy (2012). Abstention buying is often called *negative vote buying*, but the strategy affects turnout instead of vote choices, so *negative turnout buying* would be more accurate as an alternative term.

[8] Author's interview, municipality in Bahia with 15,000 citizens (January 12, 2009).

[9] See Tribunal Regional Eleitoral de Alagoas, Acórdão 7.698 (December 2, 2010) and Tribunal Superior Eleitoral, Andamento do Processo n. 97-88.2010.06.02.0000 (April 24, 2015).

A fifth form of electoral clientelism, *double persuasion*, distributes clientelist benefits to influence vote choices *and* induce electoral participation. The strategy delivers rewards to nonvoters, but unlike turnout buying it targets indifferent (or opposing) voters. Although interviewees rarely mentioned double persuasion, a councilor provided an example when explaining that some rewards target indifferent citizens who say: "I am not going to vote for anyone, I will only vote if somebody gives me something."[10] For simplification, the present chapter does not discuss double persuasion extensively, and the Rural Clientelism Survey did not ask about the strategy.[11]

Finally, *rewarding loyalists* delivers clientelist benefits to supporters who would turn out anyway. By definition, these selective benefits do not influence vote choices or induce turnout in the contemporaneous campaign. Part II of this book argues that delivering assistance to voting supporters facing adversity (regardless whether in the midst of a campaign) is part and parcel of relational clientelism. Given that the present chapter focuses exclusively on electoral clientelism, it restricts attention to other strategies in the typology. As discussed in Chapter 1, Diaz-Cayeros et al. (2016) and Stokes et al. (2013) also provide explanations for why voting supporters receive campaign handouts.

In sum, politicians can choose from a variety of strategies when engaging in electoral clientelism. Survey evidence presented in this chapter suggests that all of these strategies are observed to varying degrees in Brazil. Despite the persistence of electoral clientelism, the phenomenon encounters substantial challenges in the Brazilian context. To clarify the logic, this chapter builds on a theoretical framework that I developed with Jordan Gans-Morse and Sebastian Mazzuca.[12] In contrast to the present book, our collaborative project focused on electoral clientelism, did not examine Brazil, and did not investigate why politicians provide benefits to their own voting supporters. However, its framework proves especially useful for examining challenges to electoral clientelism. The next section, which provides intuition from our formal model, serves two purposes: (1) it clarifies how and why politicians combine several strategies of electoral clientelism, (2) it sheds light on why Brazil's combination of rigorous ballot secrecy and stringent compulsory voting hinders several key strategies.

2.2 LOGIC OF ELECTORAL CLIENTELISM

To provide basic intuition about the logic of electoral clientelism, the present section assumes that only the incumbent political party or group in a given

---

[10] Author's interview, municipality in Bahia with 60,000 citizens (November 6, 2008).
[11] Double persuasion is a hybrid strategy involving both persuasion and mobilization, so it is undermined by both ballot secrecy and compulsory voting. The Rural Clientelism Survey did not inquire about double persuasion because it involves relatively more explanation.
[12] The discussion in Section 2.2 is adapted from our article in the *American Journal of Political Science* (Gans-Morse, Mazzuca, and Nichter, 2014).

2.2 Logic of Electoral Clientelism

municipality distributes contingent benefits during campaigns. While most discussion in this book relaxes this assumption, given the competitive nature of many (but not all) Brazilian municipalities, it is adopted here because it greatly simplifies exposition and conveys generalizable points.

The model in Gans-Morse, Mazzuca, and Nichter (2014) assumes that an incumbent "machine" (M) and an opposition party (O) compete during an electoral campaign, offering policy platforms of x^M and x^O, respectively. A citizen's utility is assumed to equal the difference between her expressive value from voting and her net voting costs.[13] The citizen receives more expressive utility, the closer her ideal point (x_i) is to the platform of the party for which she votes. The citizen's net voting cost (c_i) includes material costs of reaching the polls (such as transportation, lost wages, or child care) less any costs incurred from abstention. Such abstention costs range from social disapprobation to fines and penalties in countries with compulsory voting laws. If a citizen shows up at the polls, she will vote for the machine if doing so provides (weakly) greater utility than voting for the opposition.[14] But a citizen will only vote for her preferred party if doing so provides (weakly) greater utility than abstaining.

When a clientelist party targets citizens with electoral clientelism, the mix of strategies it employs depends on contextual factors as well as citizens' political preferences and voting costs. To provide intuition about how it determines this portfolio, Figure 2.2a presents a map of citizens from the perspective of the machine. Political preferences are on the horizontal axis, with machine supporters on the right. Net voting costs are on the vertical axis; citizens with greater voting costs are higher. Citizens on bolded vertex are indifferent between voting and not voting because they receive the same utility from voting as they do from abstaining.[15] The shape is a vertex because citizens with intense political preferences are willing to incur greater voting costs. All citizens on or below the right section of the vertex (l_1) vote for the machine; those on or below the left section (l_2) vote for the opposition. All citizens above the vertex are nonvoters.

In order to distribute its funds for electoral clientelism most effectively, a machine will target citizens who offer the most net votes per dollar spent. Following this logic, the model determines the most expensive payments the machine is willing to expend on each strategy. An important factor influencing this decision is that vote buying, unlike other strategies, offers two net votes: it provides a vote *and* subtracts one from the opposition. Building on Figure 2.2a, lines are added to Figure 2.2b representing the most a machine is willing to

---

[13] Formally, a citizen of type (x_i, c_i) who votes for party $P \in \{M, O\}$ receives utility: $U^P(x_i, c_i) = -|x^P - x_i| - c_i$.

[14] That is, a citizen votes for the machine if $U_i^M \geq U_i^O$, or equivalently, if $x_i \geq 0$. Thus, citizens with political preferences $x_i \geq 0$ are supporters of the machine, while those with political preferences $x_i < 0$ are opposers.

[15] Formally, these are supporters for whom $-|x^M - x_i| - c_i = 0$ and opponents for whom $-|x^O - x_i| - c_i = 0$. Abstaining yields a reservation utility of 0.

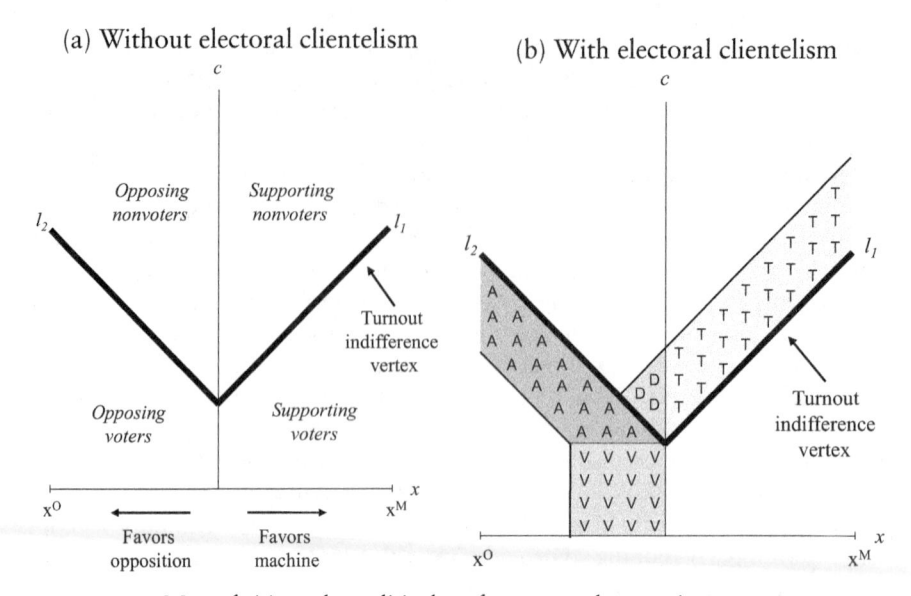

FIGURE 2.2 Map of citizens by political preferences and net voting costs
Note: Figure (a) is a map of citizens, indicating vote choices and turnout before a machine distributes rewards. Figure (b) adds clientelist strategies to this map. Citizens labeled "T" are nonvoting machine supporters who are mobilized due to *turnout buying*. Citizens labeled "V" are opposing voters who switch their votes due to *vote buying*. Citizens labeled "A" are opposing voters who stay home due to *abstention buying*. Citizens labeled "D" are opposing nonvoters who turn out and vote for the machine due to *double persuasion*. The count of letters is illustrative, as the relative prevalence of each strategy depends on numerous factors.
Source: Adapted from Gans-Morse, Mazzuca, and Nichter (2014).

pay for each strategy. As shown by the shaded regions that correspond to each strategy, a machine rewards all citizens who can be bought for these payments or less (see caption). Given the model's focus on electoral clientelism, it provides important insights about four strategies – vote buying, turnout buying, abstention buying, and double persuasion – but does not explore why politicians also provide benefits to supporting voters (a key focus of Part II).

The model predicts that a machine engaging in electoral clientelism will combine all four strategies, and also suggests how numerous contextual factors shape this mix. Particularly relevant to this chapter, it offers important predictions about two institutional features of the Brazilian context examined thoroughly later: rigorous ballot secrecy and strict compulsory voting. Because they alter the vertex in Figure 2.2b, both features raise the costs of specific strategies of electoral clientelism and lead a machine to shift its mix.[16] Ballot secrecy raises the costs of vote buying, leading machines to rely more heavily

---

[16] This point is shown formally in Gans-Morse, Mazzuca, and Nichter (2014) through a comparative statics analysis.

on turnout buying and abstention buying. But the effects of compulsory voting are precisely the opposite: it raises the costs of turnout buying and abstention buying.[17] These countervailing institutional features thus raise the costs of all these strategies, impinging on – but not entirely eliminating – politicians' capacity to use them. Moreover, this chapter shows that voter audits undermine the importation of outsiders through voter buying, and new legislation inhibits all strategies involving campaign handouts. When taken together, this confluence of institutional factors raises the costs of *all* strategies of electoral clientelism.

2.3 EFFECT OF BALLOT SECRECY

Over the last two centuries, the secret ballot emerged as a nearly ubiquitous electoral institution across the world – with only Bhutan and Iran as exceptions in 2000 – but this secrecy can be violated in myriad ways (Przeworski, 2015, 97–101). As this section explores, Brazilian reformers sought to heighten ballot secrecy for over a century with only modest success. However, politicians' ability to observe vote choices fundamentally weakened in 2000, when Brazil became the first country in the world to introduce fully electronic voting. Rigorous ballot secrecy now undermines – but does not eliminate – vote buying in Brazil because it is difficult to ascertain whether a rewarded citizen actually votes for a particular candidate.

At the outset, it should be emphasized that rigorous ballot secrecy does *not* undermine all forms of electoral clientelism. The theoretical framework outlined earlier elucidates its heterogeneous effects. Heightened ballot secrecy renders it more difficult and costly to monitor vote choices, which is important when paying citizens to vote against their preferences through vote buying. But not all forms of electoral clientelism involve monitoring how citizens vote. Strategies that focus on mobilizing or demobilizing citizens only require monitoring *whether* rewarded citizens vote, so their costs are unaffected by ballot secrecy. Hence, electronic voting and other improvements to ballot secrecy are expected to undercut vote buying and lead politicians to shift resources toward turnout buying and abstention buying. But as shown later, compulsory voting hampers these other strategies as well, suggesting that electoral clientelism is hindered by multifaceted challenges.

At least on parchment, electoral laws have ensured ballot secrecy for much of Brazil's history. Although there was already some precedent for secret voting in Brazil, Saraiva Law in 1881 is credited with introducing ballot secrecy (TSE, 2013, 40).[18] An 1896 law affirmed ballot secrecy while simultaneously enabling

---

[17] A similar effect is observed with double persuasion (see Gans-Morse, Mazzuca, and Nichter, 2014).

[18] Brazil's electoral governance body (TSE) credits Saraiva Law with introducing ballot secrecy, but some researchers credit 1875 or 1932 laws instead. Conceptual ambiguity arises to some extent because, as shown later, ballot secrecy laws can employ a continuum of more or less rigorous procedures.

politicians to violate it: after casting their ballots, citizens received vouchers to take home that indicated their vote choices (TSE, 2013, 46).[19] Relative to these laws, two later reforms had a relatively greater effect on ballot secrecy, but as discussed later did not pose insurmountable obstacles to monitoring voting decisions. Getúlio Vargas's 1932 Electoral Code once again called for ballot secrecy, with additional safeguards including official, opaque envelopes and an "impenetrable" voting booth. Another reform that to some extent improved ballot secrecy was the introduction of the Australian ballot in 1955 (Nicolau, 2002a, 52–53). Prior to this reform, parties created most ballots and handed them to Brazilian voters. Chapter 7 discusses how this voting procedure persists in much of Argentina today and facilitates vote buying in that country (Stokes, 2005). In contrast, Brazil's adoption of the Australian ballot meant that electoral officials now produced and distributed uniform ballots (Nicolau, 2015, 6–7). Although such reforms promised ballot secrecy, as shown later, they had only partial success in accomplishing this objective.

Reformers long understood – and were often motivated by – the implications of ballot secrecy for vote buying. During the Old Republic (1889–1930), advocates frequently exhorted publicly for ballot secrecy, often discussing how this electoral institution would curb vote buying.[20] Soon before becoming Brazil's president, Senator Campos Sales argued in 1891 that the secret ballot would curb vote buying because the strategy requires "material, authentic proof" that citizens voted as instructed. With effective ballot secrecy, he explained: "the difficulty of monitoring ... impedes the transaction."[21] Sales's push for ballot secrecy bore no immediate results, but others' efforts soon followed – especially efforts by those seeking to undermine the power of state and local machines.[22] For example, the Nationalist League of São Paulo launched an intense campaign for ballot secrecy (Levi-Moreira, 1984) that frequently railed against vote buying. As part of the campaign, the League handed out over 300,000 fliers calling for heightened ballot secrecy, distributed dozens of publications, and even declared the "week of the secret ballot." Proponents often mentioned vote buying; for instance, a Nationalist League speaker argued in 1922 that with the secret ballot, "certainly no one would

---

[19] See also Nicolau (2002a, 33) and Davalle (2011, 237–238) regarding a 1904 law continuing this mechanism.
[20] To illustrate how politically salient ballot secrecy was in that era, consider that one scholar calls it a "leitmotiv in Rui Barbosa's campaigns" (Sampaio, 1979, 242) and another argues it was a "rallying cry of the Nationalist League, the military rebels of July 1924, the Party of Youth, and the PD [Democratic Party]" (Woodward, 2009, 220).
[21] Annaes do Senado Federal, Congresso Nacional, Volume 3, August 31, 1891, 182.
[22] For many examples, see the compendium by the Democratic Party (Partido Democratico, or PD) discussed later (Partido Democratico, 1927). While Vargas's objectives were clearly multifaceted, Silva (2005, 15) argues he instituted ballot secrecy to curb clientelism by local oligarchies. Vargas did indeed weaken state machines, albeit temporarily (Hagopian, 1996, 50–56).

2.3 Effect of Ballot Secrecy

be so stupid as to fall in the trap of buying votes."[23] Doing so would be like "buying turnips in sacks," he exclaimed using an old adage for buying something without examining it first, and voters might sell votes repeatedly while "deceiving everyone." The Nationalist League influenced the formation of the Democratic Party (Boto, 1994), which continued to pursue ballot secrecy.[24] In 1927, the Democratic Party (PD) published a major book calling for ballot secrecy, replete with arguments about how and why it would reduce vote buying (PD, 1927). A prominent contributor provided an enumerated list of advantages of the secret ballot, with the first being that buying votes would be impossible "because it will be impossible to be sure that the voter voted in this or that manner."[25] In short, Brazil's politicians long recognized ballot secrecy's potential to reduce vote buying.

The introduction of ballot secrecy and early reforms failed to cripple vote buying in large part because their design enabled politicians to observe or infer vote choices. For many years after the enactment of the Saraiva Law in 1881, clientelist politicians could ensure that citizens complied as instructed through the process by which they distributed ballots. Politicians frequently provided envelopes for these ballots distinguishable by shape, color, or size – sometimes even sealing the envelopes to ensure voters did not switch ballots and handing them to voters just steps from the ballot box (Nunes Leal, 1949, 259; Sampaio, 1922, 36–37). One São Paulo legislator argued in 1924 that politicians could monitor vote choices – a practice he deemed the "essence" of vote buying – because Brazil never actually implemented effective procedures to ensure ballot secrecy after importing the rule from other nations: in his words, "We imitate but we don't assimilate adopted institutions."[26] Most researchers concur that ballot secrecy was minimally protected before Getúlio Vargas's ascendancy. While most likely an exaggeration, a senator in 1925 claimed that political operatives knew how nearly all citizens voted: "The proportion of votes, truly secret ... doesn't perhaps reach one percent."[27] To some extent, opponents deliberately introduced design flaws as "poison pills"; rather than overtly oppose further reforms, they could simply claim that existing laws already provided secret voting.[28]

Reforms after the Old Republic yielded relatively stronger ballot secrecy (Nicolau, 2002a, 38–39) but had only modest success in protecting citizens

---

[23] "O Governo do Povo," Conference by Sampaio Doria, June 1922 (PD, 1927, 285–286).
[24] The Democratic Party later participated in the Liberal Alliance, which promised to institute ballot secrecy as part of Vargas's unsuccessful presidential campaign in 1930 (TRE-BA, 2012, 68).
[25] Amadeu Amaral, "A Verdade do Voto" (PD, 1927, 295).
[26] Trajano Machado, São Paulo Congress, December 10, 1924 (PD, 1927, 142, 146).
[27] Senator Thomaz Rodrigues, Senate Judicial Commission, September 9, 1925 (PD, 1927, 80–81).
[28] Sampaio (1922, 23) discusses how secret ballot opponents used an indirect strategy, arguing against reforms by claiming that existing laws already secured ballot secrecy. My use of the term "poison pills" borrows from an intriguing study of judiciaries in contemporary Latin America by Brinks and Blass (2013).

from clientelist monitoring. For instance, some researchers even contend that Vargas's 1932 Electoral Code had "no effect" in rural areas where most Brazilians lived, and only a moderate effect in urban areas (Sampaio, 1979, 242). Parties continued to control the production and distribution of ballots, which played a key role in sustaining clientelism (TRE-BA, 2012, 59).[29] *Jornal do Brasil* (a leading newspaper) reported about the 1950 Electoral Code, which permitted such ballot practices, and claimed that "the public has begun to call [it] the Code of Vote Buying."[30] When electoral officials stripped parties of this role with the Australian ballot's introduction in 1955, they had lofty expectations for its impact on clientelism. The minister of justice argued publicly that "it would impede or make vote buying useless," and in front-page news, the TSE president proclaimed it would "complicate, if not abolish, corruption by vote buying."[31]

These proclamations proved to be overly optimistic. A rigorous study by Daniel Gingerich (2013, 22–23) finds no evidence that the Australian Ballot decreased clientelism in Brazil. Leveraging the reform's gradual implementation, Gingerich compared municipalities with party ballots versus official ballots and found no statistical difference in his clientelism measure.[32] One reason for the circumscribed effects of such reforms was the relative ease of violating secrecy with paper ballots, leading the military regime to impose a draconian penalty – up to five years' imprisonment – for providing prefilled or marked ballots.[33] Such ballots played a central role in politicians' strategies to outfox the Australian ballot, including the infamous *formiguinha* (little ant) method. With this tactic, known as the "Chain of Love" in the Philippines and the "Tasmanian Dodge" in Australia (Cox, 2009), a politician gives a voter a prefilled ballot to smuggle into the voting booth. Instead of filling out the blank ballot given by election officials, the citizen casts the prefilled ballot and smuggles the blank ballot to the politician. The politician then uses this fresh ballot to repeat the scheme with another voter. The particular modalities aside, the broader point is that problems with ballot secrecy facilitated vote buying during much of Brazil's history.

Electronic voting greatly reduced politicians' ability to monitor vote-buying transactions. This impact was by no means accidental. Much to the contrary, improving ballot secrecy and reducing vote buying were key parts of the debate

---

[29] See also: "A Reforma da Legislação Eleitoral," *Jornal do Brasil*, May 13, 1955.
[30] "Para Evitar a Plutocracia," *Correio da Manhã*, October 20, 1954.
[31] "Reconhecendo a Premente Necessidade de uma Reforma da Lei Eleitoral," *Jornal do Brasil*, March 18, 1955 and "Impossível a Tinta Indelével nas Próximas Eleições," *Jornal do Brasil*, August 6, 1955.
[32] The study's differences-in-differences design employs the Herfindahl-Hirschman index of vote concentration for federal deputy elections as a clientelism proxy. The proxy, while not ideal, is suggestive given limited historical data. Gingerich argues that while the reform did not reduce clientelism, it disenfranchised some voters through an increase in invalid votes (2013, 23–24).
[33] Such a penalty was included in the 1965 electoral code (which is still in effect today), but not in the first four electoral codes (1932, 1935, 1945, and 1950).

2.3 Effect of Ballot Secrecy

over its introduction, even though its ability to curb fraud received more public attention. Decades of debate preceded the gradual rollout of electronic voting during the 1996 and 1998 elections and its comprehensive adoption during the 2000 municipal elections.[34] During this time, the TSE frequently promoted the concept of electronic voting by arguing that it would improve ballot secrecy and thereby prevent clientelism (Brunazo Filho and Cortiz, 2006, 55). Moreover, the TSE raised concerns about vote buying when arguing to legislators and the public that printed voting receipts were undesirable (Brunazo Filho and Cortiz, 2006, 55). Many Brazilian observers had complained that a lack of printed receipts for citizens' electronic vote choices inhibited recounting.[35] During a 2013 press interview arguing against such procedures, a top TSE official repeatedly mentioned risks of ballot-secrecy violations and vote buying.[36] Similarly, when ruling in 2013 that vote receipts were unconstitutional, TSE President Cármen Lúcia argued that a voter is better off without one: "Nothing can be exacted of him, proof can't be required of what was done" in the ballot booth.[37] Despite such objections, legislative pressure eventually culminated in a 2015 electoral reform that required printed receipts starting in the 2018 elections.[38] However, the TSE has adapted its electronic voting machines in a manner that ensures receipts cannot be used to violate ballot secrecy. Voters will view their printed receipts – located behind a sealed display window within the electronic voting machine – before leaving the voting booth. Overall, an objective of electronic voting in Brazil is diminishing the observability of vote choices, a key mechanism of vote buying.

Evidence suggests that electronic voting achieved this objective to a remarkable degree. Even in rural Northeast Brazil, a region not typically credited with quickly implementing formal rule changes, the Rural Clientelism Survey found that 87 percent of respondents believe their vote is secret (9 percent believed it was not secret and 4 percent did not know).[39] Likewise, during my extensive interviews in Bahia, over 80 percent of citizens and *every* politician I asked

---

[34] For example, the TSE rejected an initial project in the 1960s as well as a prototype by the state electoral court of Minas Gerais in 1978 (Tavares and Moreira, 2011, 15).

[35] Despite some criticisms, electronic voting in Brazil is generally viewed by experts as well-insulated from fraud. Even before the reform discussed later, a receipt was printed per machine (not per voter), which facilitated inspection and recounting. In addition, the TSE invites party representatives, international experts, and even hackers to inspect and test the integrity of voting machines. See "How Electronic Voting Could Improve Voters' Trust," *Christian Science Monitor*, October 13, 2015.

[36] Interview with the TSE Secretary of Information Technology Giuseppe Dutra Janino. "Secretário de TI do TSE Comenta Segurança de Urnas Eletrônicas," *Tecmundo*, September 30, 2013.

[37] "Norma que Institui Voto Impresso a Partir de 2014 é Inconstitucional, Decide STF," TSE, November 7, 2013.

[38] "Regra Aprovada pela Câmara Prevê Comprovante Impresso do Voto em 2018," *O Globo*, October 6, 2017.

[39] $N = 3,654$. This survey shows that citizens who believe voting is secret are no more or less likely to receive campaign handouts or know recipients of each form of electoral clientelism.

reported that discovering vote choices is impossible.[40] As explored extensively in this book, many voters express their vote choices to others, and politicians sometimes employ weakly effective (or short-lived) tactics to try to infer how citizens voted. But violating ballot secrecy is largely deemed implausible. Even in the smallest municipalities I visited, citizens tended to express views like "It's secret! The vote is secret!"[41] or "Now with these electronic ballots, I think there is no way to discover [my vote choice]."[42] Likewise, in the words of a councilor: "There is no way for anyone to know who voted for whom. The vote in Brazil is secret."[43] The mass media likely contributes to such perceptions, as television and radio stations continue to air segments during election years emphasizing that ballot secrecy is inviolable with electronic voting.[44] Beyond Northeast Brazil, a nationally representative survey in 2008 found that only 21 percent of Brazilians agreed with the statement that candidates could find out who citizens voted for, while 56 percent disagreed (14 percent neither agreed nor disagreed, and 9 percent did not respond).[45] While such evidence suggests that a minority of Brazilians still harbor doubts about ballot secrecy, it is useful to put these figures in perspective by comparing ballot-secrecy perceptions in the United States. In a recent study by Gerber et al. (2013, 87), 25 percent of US respondents did not believe that their votes are kept secret, and in a separate question, 40 percent thought it would not be difficult for politicians to discover their vote choices.[46] Though such figures suggest there may well be a disconnect between perceptions and actual ballot secrecy, perceptions are nevertheless important because they can deter opportunistic defection in contexts with clientelism (Weitz-Shapiro, 2014, 43–44). And given that perceptions are not too different from the US context, it is reasonable to conclude that Brazilians – especially those living in the rural Northeast – have strong perceptions of ballot secrecy.

As reformers predicted, electronic voting undermined politicians' ability to buy votes. Many effective techniques under paper balloting, such as the *formiguinha* method discussed earlier, became "obsolete" with the electronic

---

[40] Of fifty-two citizens responding, forty-two (81 percent) believed voting is secret. None of the thirty-eight elites asked thought it was possible for a politician to observe how a citizen voted. These figures correspond to violations of ballot secrecy, not inferences through declarations (see Chapter 5) or word-of-mouth.
[41] Author's interview, municipality in Bahia with 15,000 citizens (January 15, 2009).
[42] Author's interview, municipality in Bahia with 10,000 citizens (October 1, 2008).
[43] Author's interview, municipality in Bahia with 15,000 citizens (January 12, 2009).
[44] For example, see "Regras Criadas pela Justiça Eleitoral Garantem Sigilo do Voto," *TV Globo*, October 1, 2016.
[45] Survey conducted by research firm Vox Populi on behalf of the Associação dos Magistrados Brasileiros in July 2008. Included 1,502 respondents across all regions of Brazil.
[46] The authors corroborated these findings from the Cooperative Congressional Election Study ($N = 804$) with two other surveys ($N = 573$ and $N = 903$). The 40 percent statistic refers to citizens indicating it would be "not difficult at all" or "not too difficult" for "politicians, union officials, or the people you work for" to discover their vote choices (87).

2.3 Effect of Ballot Secrecy

ballot (Gastaldi and Rosendo, 2012, 82; Speck, 2003, 157). Electronic voting decreased the sanctioning capacity of vote buying. As one councilor complained: "There's no guarantee at all … voters started to become clever. They started to gain from everyone and then vote for whomever they wanted."[47] The Rural Clientelism Survey identified that some respondents are readily willing to admit that they would renege on vote-buying offers: 43 percent of those familiar with vote buying said they would take the money and vote against the politician.[48] The nationally representative Brazilian Electoral Panel Study suggests why, given politicians' inability to sanction recipients under electronic voting, vote buying is an especially risky endeavor: 44 percent of those receiving offers reported being *less* inclined to vote for the candidate, while only 18 percent said they were more inclined and 38 percent said they were equally inclined (Ames et al., 2013). Thus, vote buying in Brazil encounters considerable opportunistic defection, which is far more challenging to detect now that electronic voting has enhanced ballot secrecy.

Electronic voting undercut vote buying, though it has by no means extinguished this form of electoral clientelism. After all, evidence earlier from the Rural Clientelism Survey reveals that 15.6 percent of respondents indicated they knew a vote-buying recipient. Two other surveys also point to the existence of vote buying, though they do not indicate how often politicians employ this strategy.[49] In the Online Clientelism Survey conducted across Brazil (described in Appendix B), 63.7 percent of respondents reported that it is "common" or "very common" for there to exist politicians in their municipalities who engage in vote buying during local elections. Furthermore, a 2015 elite survey conducted in the Northeast state of Maranhão found that 96.9 percent of judges, prosecutors and activists indicated that it is "common" or "very common" for such politicians to exist.[50] While vote buying persists, numerous elites suggest that opportunistic defection now renders this strategy as nothing more than a gamble. One councilor, for instance, compared vote buying to poker and explained that it is "a bet. Sometimes it works, sometimes it doesn't."[51] To be sure, some recipients may follow through due to feelings of reciprocity (Finan and Schechter, 2012; Lawson and Greene, 2014). However, some interviewees complained it was tougher today to trust voters' promises of votes in exchange of benefits; as one councilor explained, a citizen's "word was

---

[47] Author's interview, municipality in Bahia with 60,000 citizens (November 6, 2008).
[48] Citizens were coded as familiar with vote buying if they knew any vote-buying recipients. Across all citizens, 28 percent said they would break the deal.
[49] Surveys discussed in this chapter focus specifically on strategies of electoral clientelism.
[50] Online survey by Judge Douglas de Melo Martins, who emailed in September 2015 all state judges and prosecutors in Maranhão, and activists in his professional network. Respondents include 80 judges (28 percent of 281 total judges), 43 prosecutors (16 percent of 269 total prosecutors), and 135 activists. Several questions were included at my recommendation.
[51] Author's interview, municipality in Bahia with 60,000 citizens (November 4, 2008).

worth a lot in the past. And today, no."[52] Interviewees suggested that aggregate vote monitoring, an approach observed elsewhere (e.g., Chandra, 2004; Rueda, 2014), is mostly ineffectual because vote buying aims to influence and monitor individuals' votes. If a candidate obtains no votes in the rewarded citizen's precinct, which have on average 316 voters across Brazil,[53] then the recipient obviously defected. But given that mayoral elections have only a few candidates, it is exceedingly rare to have no votes in a precinct.[54]

Unable to rely on traditional monitoring mechanisms, politicians have achieved temporary successes through innovation. A team of operatives revealed to me how they check whether recipients vote as instructed. Electronic voting machines show a candidate's picture only if selected as the vote choice. Therefore, the operatives would ask recipients what color shirt the candidate wore in the displayed picture: "If he voted for the guy, he knows. White shirt, striped."[55] This tactic has also been reported in Mato Grosso state (Reis, 2006, 25), and a TSE Minister once described to David Fleischer how some politicians wore bowties or shaved their mustaches for the same testing purpose.[56] But my informants suggested this technique is now much less effective and only works to a limited degree with poor, rural voters: citizens realized they could view the picture and then push buttons to change their vote choices. Using a more reliable approach, politicians began to lend camera phones and ask rewarded voters to take pictures of their vote choices, a strategy also observed in countries such as Italy and Mexico (Schaffer and Schedler, 2007, 23). But the TSE soon caught on and banned cell phones in polling places – with the "target of vote buying," explained one newspaper – and even established imprisonment as a potential penalty.[57]

Overall, vote buying is now far more challenging for politicians than it was in the past. Reforms over the past century strived to enhance ballot secrecy, and the introduction of electronic voting hobbled politicians' ability to monitor vote choices when buying votes. No longer can they ensure that citizens follow through with their end of the bargain, so it remains highly uncertain whether vote-buying recipients will actually vote against their preferences. The theoretical framework suggests that rigorous ballot secrecy drives up the cost

---

[52] Author's interview, municipality in Bahia with 15,000 citizens (January 14, 2009).
[53] Calculated from 2014 TSE data.
[54] A few elites said the tactic could plausibly work for some councilors in small municipalities (only for those who receive low votes). Electronic voting also complicates aggregate vote monitoring in Brazil. For example, at the time of Chandra's (2004, 139) research in India, aggregate monitoring was facilitated by opening ballot boxes "carefully" to glean the general order in which votes were cast. This technique is impossible with Brazil's electronic voting.
[55] Author's interview, municipality in Bahia with 10,000 citizens (October 4, 2008).
[56] See "Notas Taquigráficas," Câmara do Deputados, May 4, 2004. Scott Desposato (2002, 17–18) provides additional examples.
[57] Quote from "Levar Celular Para a Cabine de Votação Pode dar Cadeia," *Diario do Vale*, July 14, 2012. See also "TSE Decide Proibir Celulares e Câmaras na Cabine de Votação," *Estadão*, October 2, 2008.

of vote buying and leads politicians to shift resources towards turnout buying and abstention buying. But as explored next, strict compulsory voting impinges on politicians' ability to employ these alternative strategies.

2.4 EFFECT OF COMPULSORY VOTING

Although this rigorous ballot secrecy would be expected to motivate clientelist politicians to shift towards mobilization, compulsory voting has an important countervailing effect in Brazil. This electoral institution severely constrains – but does not altogether eliminate – Brazilian politicians' ability to influence turnout through electoral clientelism. Substantial evidence demonstrates that the country has strict mandatory voting, belying the common misperception that its impact is minimal just because monetary fines are low.

Before turning to evidence about compulsory voting in Brazil, why is this institution expected to undermine turnout buying and abstention buying? Returning to the theoretical framework, higher abstention costs boost turnout and shift the turnout indifference vertex in Figure 2.2b upwards. Abstention penalties shrink the pool of nonvoting supporters who can be targeted and make it tougher to induce opposers to stay away from the polls. The relative costs of turnout buying and abstention buying increase, leading politicians to reduce expenditures on both strategies.[58] In other words, compulsory voting deals another blow to electoral clientelism in Brazil by impairing the very strategies that would otherwise be most effective in a context with rigorous ballot secrecy.

Compulsory voting has increasingly become an impediment to electoral clientelism in Brazil as its coverage expanded and as officials ratcheted up its enforcement. Although such regulation existed for much of Brazil's history, most of the electorate long remained outside its purview. Getúlio Vargas introduced compulsory voting to republican Brazil in 1932, though a small fraction of citizens also faced voting requirements in imperial Brazil. As shown in Figure 2.3a, the initial impact of Vargas's reform was minimal; only 3.3 percent of the overall population voted during the next year's legislative elections (Nicolau, 2002b, 23). One reason is that although his 1932 Electoral Code instituted women's suffrage, compulsory voting for all females followed only in the 1946 Constitution.[59] Illiterate Brazilians remained disenfranchised for over a century, and to this day are exempted from mandatory voting. The 1988 Constitution compels all Brazilians aged eighteen to sixty-nine years to vote, unless they are illiterate. Voting is optional for illiterates and citizens who are sixteen, seventeen, or at least seventy years of age.

---

[58] This point is also shown formally in Gans-Morse, Mazzuca, and Nichter (2014) through a comparative statics analysis.
[59] The second electoral code (in 1935) exempted all women except public employees from compulsory voting, and the third (in 1945) exempted women without remunerated employment.

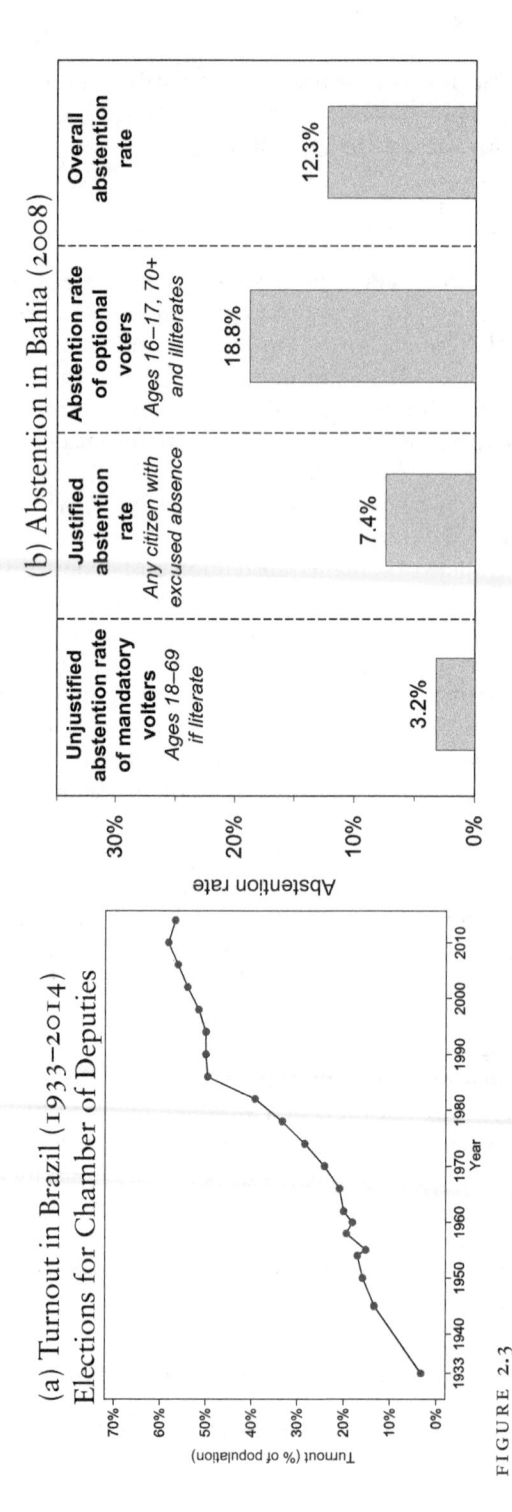

(a) Turnout in Brazil (1933–2014) Elections for Chamber of Deputies

(b) Abstention in Bahia (2008)

FIGURE 2.3

Note: Figure 2.3a extends Nicolau (2002a, 46), using more recent TSE electoral data and IBGE population data. Population is employed as the denominator, to reflect trends in the share of Brazilians obligated to vote (turnout as a share of registered voters is higher). Figure 2.3b is calculated by the author using data from Bahia's state electoral court (TRE-BA). Figures reflect unweighted means of 267 municipalities for which TRE-BA data match TSE aggregate abstention rates within one percent. These included municipalities correspond to 77 percent of Bahia's electorate and 64 percent of its total municipalities. If using weighted means, the figures are: unjustified (4.7 percent), justified (7.4 percent), optional (27.9 percent) and overall (14.5 percent). Citizens subject to mandatory voting who submit excuses constitute the vast majority of "justified abstention," but this category also includes some optional voters who voluntarily justify their absence.

2.4 *Effect of Compulsory Voting*

Broadened coverage of compulsory voting was a key determinant of Brazil's dramatic rise in turnout. Figure 2.3a demonstrates that turnout as a share of population increased to 20 percent in 1962, 50 percent in 1986, and 57 percent in 2014.[60] Both gender and literacy played important roles in this expanded coverage. When compulsory voting extended to women in 1946, the share of Brazilians subject to compulsory voting nearly doubled; women comprised over half the electorate in 2014.[61] As for literacy, its impact on mandatory voting far preceded 1985, when a constitutional amendment enfranchised illiterates. For much of the last century, steeply declining illiteracy rates increased the share of Brazil's population subject to compulsory voting (Nicolau, 2002b, 25). The percentage of illiterate Brazilians aged fifteen or over was 61 percent in 1930, 40 percent in 1960, 21 percent in 1990, and 9 percent in 2012.[62] Coverage of compulsory voting laws increased dramatically during the country's latest bout of authoritarianism (1964–1985), when elections continued in part to signal supposed legitimacy.[63] A 1975 law required teachers and others providing literacy courses to notify electoral judges when someone became newly literate and thus eligible to vote, in order to expedite registration. After Brazil became the last Latin American country to grant illiterates the right to vote, growing literacy continued to extend the coverage of mandatory voting, as analphabets are excused from the regulation. Citizens inform electoral officials of their literacy status upon registration and if they later learn to read, they are legally obliged to self-report their accomplishment to officials.[64] While TSE officials openly state that they take citizens' literacy assessments at their word, the stigma surrounding illiteracy may motivate compliance (Power, 2009, 105–106). In addition, an electoral official in Bahia suggested that citizens could face legal complications if they claim to be illiterate but later fill out and sign other official documents.[65] Overall, factors related to both gender and literacy contributed to Brazil's increasing coverage of compulsory voting.

Along with broadened coverage, increased enforcement also heightened the impact of compulsory voting laws. The 1955 reform that introduced the Australian ballot also created "voting folders" for each individual, located in each electoral office, which in conjunction with voter documents facilitated record keeping about whether a citizen had voted in each election. These folders hindered both turnout buying and abstention buying by making it more likely

---

[60] Population is employed as the denominator in order to reflect changes in the share of Brazilians obligated to vote. Turnout as a share of registered voters is higher, e.g., nearly 81 percent in the first-round election of 2014. Elite mobilization also influenced turnout (Limongi et al., 2018).
[61] Data from TSE.
[62] Data from Thorp (1998, 374) and "Pesquisa Nacional por Amostra de Domicílios – PNAD 2012," Presentation by Ministério da Fazenda, September 2013.
[63] For a discussion of the role of elections in authoritarian Brazil, see Lamounier and Duarte (1980) and Hagopian (1996).
[64] TSE Resolution 21.538 (2003).
[65] Interview by author in state electoral court of Bahia, May 28, 2008.

that citizens would be caught for disobeying compulsory voting. Furthermore, as the TSE President explained in 1957, the folders made abstention buying "inoperable" because obtaining an opposer's voting document no longer ensured abstention.[66] Even without her voting document, the reward recipient could still vote because the office folder provided a photograph and other information to verify her identity. Starting less than a decade later, the authoritarian regime undertook "stringent efforts" to enforce compulsory voting, further contributing to Brazil's sharp increase in electoral participation (Holston, 2008, 106–107; Nicolau, 2002a, 57–58). Given that recent inflationary bouts quickly diminished the level of fixed abstention penalties, the 1965 Electoral Code enacted indexed penalties.[67] Voters who failed to show up at the polls (or justify their absence to a judge) had to pay fines of up to 10 percent of their region's minimum monthly salary, or else they faced numerous bureaucratic hassles similar to those currently in effect.[68] Compulsory voting's enforcement was streamlined after democratization with the 1986 digitization of voting rolls and the advent of electronic voting a decade later. Currently, the TSE oversees a national database (managed by each state's electoral court) that automatically reports whether a citizen voted, along with exemptions (due to age or illiteracy) and justified absences. This confluence of factors facilitated enforcement and thereby sharpened the effect of compulsory voting.

The common misperception that compulsory voting is lax in contemporary Brazil stems from its low monetary fine. The abstention fine – R$3.50, which is about $1 – might appear to suggest that mandatory voting can be ignored by all but the most destitute.[69] But this monetary penalty is misleading. As a politician explains, "Everyone knows that if you don't vote, you harm yourself ... your voting document becomes irregular."[70] When unexcused abstention leads to the suspension of voting documents (i.e., they become "irregular"), Brazilians cannot obtain identification cards, work in the public sector, qualify for government loans, or enroll in public educational institutions. Although poor or less-educated Brazilians are relatively less affected by some of these regulations (Cepulani and Hidalgo, 2015, 4), the "vast majority" of Brazilians need an identity card for various purposes ranging from boarding interstate buses to cashing checks (Power, 2009, 107), and in some instances even for the elderly to buy alcohol.[71] And many citizens have concerns about what may

---

[66] "Ainda os Homenagens na Despidida do Ministro Edgard Costa, Realizada na Sessão de 4a-feira," *Jornal do Brasil*, February 3, 1957. See also: "Todos os Eleitores Terão de Alistar-se Novamente," *Jornal do Brasil*, July 11, 1956.

[67] Regarding high inflation under Kubitschek, see Mesquita (2010, 2).

[68] This fine corresponds to Law 4961 of 1966, which amended fines in the 1965 Electoral Code.

[69] Judges can increase fines up to tenfold based on voters' income, but fines applied are typically affordable even for the poor (Power, 2009, 107).

[70] Author's interview with a councilor in a Bahia municipality with 15,000 citizens, January 13, 2009.

[71] "Supermercados Já Exigem RG Até de Idosos Antes de Vender Bebida Alcoólica," *Estadão*, August 7, 2012.

2.4 Effect of Compulsory Voting

happen if they fail to vote: the Rural Clientelism Survey, for instance, found that over 71 percent of respondents believe it would be more difficult to receive a pension or Bolsa Família if they do not vote.[72] With regards to pensions, this concern is not entirely misplaced.[73] With regards to Bolsa Família, Ministry of Social Development (MDS) officials have attempted to quell such erroneous concerns by publicly announcing that program eligibility does not require turnout or voter registration.[74] In order avoid actual punishments, citizens whose abstention is not justified (discussed below) must undergo a time-consuming procedure to avoid punishments: they obtain paperwork about their outstanding fines at an electoral office, travel to a nearby bank and wait in line to pay the fine, and then return to the electoral office with proof the fine has been paid (de Figueiredo et al., 2013, 11). All in all, substantial abstention costs – primarily non-pecuniary – heighten the effectiveness of compulsory voting.

In contemporary Brazil, the prevalence of a phenomenon called "justification" shows just how much effort citizens exert to avoid abstention penalties. If voters are out of town or otherwise cannot report to their designated polling places, they can report to other locations outside their municipalities on Election Day to fill out justification forms (or can do so within sixty days).[75] Although voters cannot cast ballots while away (absentee voting is generally forbidden), they avoid all abstention penalties by submitting valid forms. Over 7.6 million voters took the time to justify their absence in the 2012 election, even though this considerable time investment did not allow them to vote. These justifiers accounted for one-third of all citizens who failed to turn out in 2012; just after democratization, justifiers had accounted for as much as two-thirds of abstention (Nicolau, 2002b, 30).[76] Justification patterns suggest abstention is often due to geographic distance: nearly half of justifications in 2012 were conducted in a different state than where the citizen was registered to vote.[77] One might expect that only citizens required to vote would go through the hassle of justifying their absence. But much to the contrary, over 230,000 citizens exempted for illiteracy still justified their absence in 2008,

---

[72] $N = 3,650$.
[73] With pensions, abstention can create indirect problems. For example, a CPF (similar to a social security card) is required to start receiving a public pension. To receive a CPF, or to rectify any problems arising with a CPF, citizens aged eighteen to sixty-nine must present voting documents or proof of exemption. But voting documents are canceled after failing to vote or justify for three consecutive elections – and each missed round counts as an election.
[74] For instance, see "Título de Eleitor não é Obrigatório para Manter Bolsa Família, Diz MDS," *Globo*, October 7, 2013.
[75] Since 2010, these forms can be filled out online, but they still need to signed by a poll worker or mailed for a judge's review after the election.
[76] TSE data for 2012 municipal elections reflect the first round, in which 22.7 million of 138.5 million eligible voters abstained.
[77] Substantial geographic variation is observed (likely due to migratory patterns): four-fifths of justifiers from the relatively poor states of Alagoas and Piauí submitted forms out-of-state, versus just one-third of justifiers from the wealthier states of Rio de Janeiro and São Paulo.

either because they remained concerned about abstention consequences or because they were misinformed.[78] Overall, efforts to justify abstention suggest that voting is indeed considered obligatory in Brazil.

A closer examination of abstention rates also suggests that compulsory voting requirements are binding for many Brazilians. Abstention rates, to a substantial degree, do not reflect citizens wantonly disobeying rules. Instead, most abstention involves justified absences and optional voters. Although Brazil has the most citizens subject to compulsory voting in the world, at least ten million Brazilians may choose whether to vote (Power, 2009, 97, 117). This option is because they are illiterate, or because they are sixteen, seventeen, or at least seventy years of age.[79] A rigorous study by Cepaluni and Hidalgo (2016) suggests that abstention rates rise for the elderly who reach the age at which voting is optional. Their regression discontinuity design compares literate Brazilians just before and after they reach their seventieth birthday, demonstrating that 2012 abstention rates jumped by 4.4 percentage points among citizens who surpassed this threshold and are thus no longer compelled to vote (2015, 9).[80] Although their study is restricted to narrow age ranges and does not consider illiterates or justification, evidence I collected from Bahia's state electoral court also points to the effects of compulsory voting across a broader population in that state.[81] As shown in Figure 2.3b, 18.8 percent of exempt Bahians failed to show up at the polls in 2008 (i.e., optional abstention). By contrast, just 3.2 percent of mandated Bahians failed to show up *and* failed to take efforts to justify their absence within sixty days of the election.[82] In Bahia, such scofflaws were far rarer than justifiers, who reached 7.4 percent of mandated citizens.[83] To some extent, this finding corroborates

---

[78] Unlike mandatory voters, optional voters are not removed from the rolls if they miss three elections without justifying. Over 96,000 citizens exempted due to age still justify; however, some of these non-required justifiers overlap with the 230,000 illiterates. Both figures from TSE for first round in 2008 municipal elections. See also Justiça Eleitoral (2007, 5).

[79] Of Brazil's electorate, 5.5 percent is illiterate, 1.7 percent is sixteen to seventeen years old, and 7.3 percent is at least seventy years old. This suggests an upper bound of 14.5 percent of the electorate not subject to compulsory voting. However, the true figure is likely several percentage points lower because of high overlap in the elderly and illiterate categories. Data from TSE web site in February 2014.

[80] Effects are greater for more educated citizens, though findings are also significant for lower-educated citizens (8). Cepaluni and Hidalgo also find significant effects when examining the threshold at eighteen years old, but interpretation is less clear as passing this threshold also influences registration (7).

[81] The analysis examines data used to allocate compulsory voting fines (for each municipality, how many citizens fall into each code category).

[82] One reason for low unexcused abstention: periodically, the TSE culls voter rolls of all voters who have missed three consecutive elections without justification.

[83] As explained earlier, in some cases, optional voters voluntarily justify their absence; such instances are coded as justifiers in the data. Estimating such cases is imprecise, but using reasonable assumptions based on Bahian data, the maximum possible effect would be to decrease the justified abstention rate shown to 7 percent.

2.4 Effect of Compulsory Voting

an intriguing ecological analysis by Timothy Power, who finds that states with more registrations of exempt-aged citizens have lower turnout (2009, 114–116).[84] Although it is important to keep in mind that Figure 2.3b only includes data from one state, the takeaway is that the vast majority of citizens subject to compulsory voting comply with the law – either by showing up at the polls, or by undertaking efforts to justify their absence.

Just as the theoretical framework predicts, Brazil's rigorous compulsory voting hinders the use of campaign handouts to influence turnout, though it does not stamp it out entirely. First, with respect to turnout buying, recall that only 8.1 percent of respondents in the Rural Clientelism Survey across Northeast Brazil knew anyone who had experienced the practice – half the corresponding percentage for vote buying. Other surveys confirm the existence of turnout buying, though they do not shed light on its prevalence. Approximately 57.6 percent of citizens in the Online Clientelism Survey and 64.3 percent of elites in the Maranhão survey reported that it is "common" or "very common" for there to exist politicians in their municipalities who engage in turnout buying during local elections. With respect to qualitative evidence, many interviewees in Bahia said that they had never heard of turnout buying; several who had suggested it focused on the elderly (for whom voting is optional) or those with suspended voting documents. Among citizens, the vast majority indicated no familiarity. Of those who said turnout buying occurs, one citizen indicated that "only the elderly" receive benefits for turnout, and another suggested that cash is occasionally distributed to elderly voters who have difficulty reaching the polls.[85] Politicians I interviewed in Bahia overwhelmingly indicated that only a small fraction of resources, if any, were channeled towards stimulating turnout – clientelism or otherwise – because voting is mandatory and citizens already "fear" the official consequences of noncompliance.[86] Unlike for vote buying, nearly 40 percent of interviewed politicians had never heard of a single case of turnout buying. One councilor answered: a voter "receive something to go vote? No ... this doesn't happen, because people insist on voting."[87] Those who had heard of turnout buying emphasized its rarity, typically mentioning past elections or isolated reports in other municipalities. An exception was a councilor who explained that politicians may provide as much as R$50 for "expenses" so that citizens can rectify voting documents suspended due to repeated abstention.[88] Though such evidence is consistent with predictions that

---

[84] Power's analysis builds on Figueiredo (1991), who posited that mandatory voting affects formal workers more than others. The results here cannot speak to Power's unexpected finding that states with higher illiteracy have higher turnout.

[85] Author's interviews, municipalities in Bahia with 50,000 and 10,000 citizens, respectively (November 11, 2008 and October 4, 2008).

[86] Author's interview, municipality in Bahia with 30,000 citizens (December 3, 2008).

[87] Author's interview, municipality in Bahia with 10,000 citizens (November 26, 2008).

[88] Author's interview, municipality in Bahia with 100,000 citizens (December 18, 2008). These rewards were described as responses to voter demands – beyond abstention penalties, a citizen

Brazil's stringent compulsory voting undermines turnout buying, it should be underscored that the strategy nevertheless persists.

Also consistent with theoretical predictions about rigorous compulsory voting, evidence suggests that abstention buying is relatively rare in Brazil. Recall that only 2.5 percent of respondents in the Rural Clientelism Survey knew anyone who had experienced the practice – one-sixth the corresponding percentage for vote buying. Other surveys also suggest the existence of abstention buying in Brazil, with more limited evidence than for other strategies of electoral clientelism. Less than 16.4 percent of citizens in the Online Clientelism Survey, and 30.6 percent of elites in the Maranhão survey, indicated that it is "common" or "very common" for there to exist politicians in their municipalities who engage in abstention buying. Again, these surveys inquired about the existence of different forms of electoral clientelism during local elections, not about how frequently they are used. In terms of qualitative evidence, interviewees in Bahia overwhelmingly (but not universally) proclaimed the nonexistence of abstention buying. Some citizens provided short responses such as "No, that doesn't exist here,"[89] while others offered further explanation such as: "No ... you will pay a fine. If you go to get a pension, you won't get it because you ... have to have proof of voting."[90] Likewise, less than 15 percent of elites I interviewed in Bahia indicated that abstention buying occurs, often pointing to other municipalities instead of their own.[91] A mayor responded that he didn't know of any cases, and that such a strategy would be difficult "because here the vote is obligatory, and if a citizen doesn't go vote, afterwards he is going to have to justify himself, a series of things."[92] Some other politicians were particularly incredulous that such a strategy would ever be tried. When I asked one mayor, who had already discussed the use of clientelism in his municipality, about abstention buying, he replied: "I can't even conceive that someone would think in this manner."[93] Similarly, a councilor exclaimed that the strategy was "impossible."[94] Overall, while both abstention buying and turnout buying are observed to a limited degree in Brazil, evidence suggests that their usage is undermined by effective mandatory voting. One likely reason for their continued use is the exemption of some Brazilians from compulsory voting, based on age and illiteracy. Their continued use also conforms with theoretical expectations; the model summarized in Section 2.1 predicts that a

---

might request money to reissue a lost ID card and birth certificate, to pay for a required photo, and to buy lunch during registration.

[89] Author's interview, municipality in Bahia with 15,000 citizens (January 15, 2009).
[90] Author's interview, municipality in Bahia with 10,000 citizens (October 4, 2008).
[91] Some other interviewees mentioned the strategy was used in the past (e.g., a councilor said he knew of cases fifteen years ago).
[92] Author's interview, municipality in Bahia with 50,000 citizens (November 12, 2008).
[93] Author's interview, municipality in Bahia with 100,000 citizens (December 18, 2008).
[94] Author's interview, municipality in Bahia with 100,000 citizens (December 18, 2008).

machine engaging in electoral clientelism is most effective when it combines *all* of the strategies analyzed.

Stepping back, the two institutional features just investigated jointly pose a substantial challenge for electoral clientelism in Brazil. Rigorous ballot secrecy renders vote buying more difficult, and formal analysis predicts politicians would mitigate this challenge by shifting resources towards strategies that influence mobilization. But such strategies are also under duress, because stringent compulsory voting undercuts turnout buying and abstention buying. Thus, the coupling of both institutional factors in Brazil is especially daunting for electoral clientelism, though the phenomenon is not eliminated altogether. The interplay between ballot secrecy and compulsory voting was by no means unforeseeable to anti-clientelism advocates; in fact, a prescient politician warned publicly in 1922 that with heightened ballot secrecy, voters could simply be "paid to not go to the polls. The secret ballot law ... should, therefore, contain arrangements that lead to compulsory voting" (Sampaio, 1922, 43).[95] Given the challenges posed by both factors, politicians also turn to voter buying, a relatively expensive form of electoral clientelism that is under assault by yet another unfavorable institutional feature of Brazil – voter audits.

2.5 EFFECT OF VOTER AUDITS

Although typically overlooked by the literature on clientelism, voter buying is another important form of electoral clientelism that politicians can employ during campaigns. Recall that this tactic induces citizens in other districts to transfer their electoral registration and vote for a specified candidate. As discussed in Section 2.1, the Rural Clientelism Survey across Northeast Brazil suggests that voter buying is the third-most common strategy of electoral clientelism, with 7.3 percent of citizens reporting they knew a voter-buying recipient. In addition, other surveys confirm its use in Brazil. Nearly 41.4 percent of citizens in the Online Clientelism Survey, and 81 percent of elites in the Maranhão survey, responded that it is "common" or "very common" for there to exist politicians in their municipalities who engage in voter buying during local elections.[96] As my collaborative work with F. Daniel Hidalgo (2016) demonstrates, voter buying not only exists but also has substantial effects on many local Brazilian elections.[97] But analogous to other strategies of electoral clientelism, voter buying is also undercut by an institutional feature

---

[95] Sampaio served in a variety of positions including judge, federal and state deputy, and councilor in São Paulo.
[96] As noted earlier, these surveys inquire about the existence, but not the prevalence, of each strategy of electoral clientelism.
[97] Section 2.5 is adapted from our article on voter buying in the *American Journal of Political Science* (Hidalgo and Nichter, 2016). Full citations, as well as further evidence and analyses, are provided in that article.

of Brazil: extensive voter audits that electoral officials employ to extirpate the phenomenon.

One might expect voter buying to be an unlikely strategy due to its cost, as politicians incur substantial transportation expenses in addition to any rewards. Given that Brazilians cannot vote outside their registered municipality, voter buying involves registration transfers, in which citizens submit paperwork in the new municipality while attesting to at least three months of residency.[98] Why not simply pay citizens to switch their vote choices through vote buying, which would yield twice as many net votes (by also reducing their local competitor's vote tally)? And why not draw nearby unmobilized supporters to the polls through turnout buying, which would involve lower transportation costs? Indeed, the very existence of voter buying is a testament to the severity of challenges facing these other strategies. Brazil is a propitious environment for voter buying in part because the strategy is relatively resistant to ballot secrecy and compulsory voting. Monitoring vote choices is unnecessary because imported citizens do not have a stake in the destination municipality's election, and compulsory voting is not a deterrent because reward recipients still turn out to vote (but do so elsewhere).

This section provides direct evidence of voter buying and indirect evidence of how this strategy is fundamentally weakened by voter audits. To guide the discussion, consider several predictions about the conditions under which this form of electoral clientelism is most effective. First, voter buying is most likely in small districts, where fewer outsiders must be imported to influence the election and it is easier to monitor that reward recipients transfer and turn out.[99] Second, in order to economize on transportation costs, politicians are likely to import citizens from neighboring districts.[100] And third, incumbents are more likely than challengers to employ voter buying because they typically have greater access to resources.[101] In Hidalgo and Nichter (2016), these predictions are expounded and corroborated with both qualitative and quantitative evidence.

Consistent with these predictions, politicians in small municipalities frequently import citizens from neighboring districts. For instance, a newspaper in the state of Amazonas reported in 2011 that municipal elections are "historically marked by fraudulent transfers of voters on the periphery of Manaus [the state's capital] to neighboring towns," which typically "involve

[98] In Brazil, some voter buying physically transports voters (costing fuel and labor), while some compensates voters for transportation. Citizens self-declare their residency in the new municipality, typically without verification. For more details, see Hidalgo and Nichter (2016).
[99] As discussed in Hidalgo and Nichter (2016), this prediction builds on Fukumoto and Horiuchi (2011, 593–594), Nichter (2008, 28), Stokes (2005, 322–323), and Stokes et al. (2013, 181–182).
[100] This logic builds on Ichino and Schündeln (2012, 295).
[101] Hidalgo and Nichter (2015) provide logic and evidence, building on Gallego and Wantchekon (2012, 185) and Stokes (2009, 14–15).

2.5 Effect of Voter Audits

free transport on Election Day, cash payments, and promises of work."[102] The state electoral court investigated and found that many citizens are indeed induced with "money, gifts and transportation" to transfer from Manaus to small neighboring municipalities during local elections.[103] In the state of Rio Grande do Norte, federal prosecutors filed over 100 cases regarding illegal registrations in Timbaúba dos Baptistas (2,295 citizens), many of which involve induced transfers from the neighboring municipality of Serra Negra (twenty-three miles away).[104] And in Pernambuco, prosecutors discovered that operatives in Santa Cruz do Capibaribe (87,582 citizens) had imported citizens from the nearby capital city of Recife using monetary rewards.[105] Overall, these examples provide a glimpse into how some Brazilian politicians employ voter buying.[106]

Incumbent politicians have a competitive advantage at voter buying in Brazil because the strategy often involves local officials and public programs. The complicity of local officials is not necessary but can facilitate voter buying.[107] Mayors frequently appoint workers into the offices that handle voter transfers, even though such documentation may legally only be processed by the judiciary's civil service employees.[108] For instance, during the trial to remove the mayor of Caracol (Piauí) for clientelism during his 2008 reelection campaign, a municipal worker in the electoral office reportedly testified to "suffering pressure from the mayor" to process illegal transfers from neighboring municipalities.[109] Another advantage enjoyed by incumbent mayors (and councilors in their coalitions) is that they can often more easily divert funds from public programs. For example, a incumbent councilor in Nova Ipixuna, Pará (14,645 citizens) faced charges for diverting funds from a federal fishing program for the purposes of voter buying, providing rewards to outsiders who didn't even fish.[110] All in all, incumbents' power over municipal employees and public programs afford them a competitive advantage at voter buying.

Analogous to other strategies of electoral clientelism, voter buying is undercut by an institutional feature of Brazil. A substantial threat to voter buying

---

[102] "Juízes Apertam o Cerco Contra Fraudes Eleitorais no AM," *A Crítica*, December 9, 2011.
[103] "Corregedor Flávio Pascarelli Anuncia Medidas para Sanear Pendências no Eleitorado de Silves e Manacapuru," *A Crítica*, September 4, 2011.
[104] "As Fraudes da Migração Eleitoral," *Correio Braziliense*, July 4, 2010.
[105] "Fraude Eleitoral é Descoberta," Ministério Público de Pernambuco, March 14, 2008.
[106] For many other examples, see Hidalgo and Nichter (2016).
[107] For example, it can help with circumventing residency requirements.
[108] Insufficient staffing is one reason why some local electoral offices depend on help by workers loaned by the municipality. Author's interview with Judge Marlon Reis (August 9, 2013).
[109] The population of Caracol is 10,212. "Diário da Justiça Eletrônico," Tribunal Regional Eleitoral-Piauí, January 15, 2010 and "Tribunal Superior Eleitoral Mantém Cassaçao do Prefeito de Caracol," *Saraiva Reporter*, May 17, 2011.
[110] "Vereador de Nova Ipixuna é Denunciado por Fraude no Seguro-Defeso," Ministério Público Federal no Pará, July 15, 2011.

is the TSE's extensive use of voter audits – formally known as "electoral revisions" – which inspect a municipality's electorate and remove all ineligible voters.[111] Electoral rules instituted by the TSE trigger an audit if a municipality meets three criteria; by far the most important criterion is that its electorate exceeds 80 percent of its population.[112] Remarkably, electoral officials audited over one-fifth of Brazil's municipalities between 2007 and 2008.[113] The goal of these audits, which involve reregistering all voters in a municipality, is to cull the voter rolls of fraudulent registrations. Because duplicate and phony registrations "became almost impossible" after Brazil implemented a digitized registry in the mid-1980s (Nicolau, 2002a, 68), fraudulent registrations stemming from illegal voter transfers (typically induced) are a pressing concern. In the words of the president of Minas Gerais's state electoral court, "what justifies a revision is the existence, in the electoral rolls, of voters who don't have links with a municipality. ... In municipal elections, one vote determines the selection of the mayor."[114] Likewise, a Mato Grosso state deputy contended that mayoral elections will be improved by voter audits because they ensure that "only people who actually live there" will vote.[115]

Voter audits fundamentally undercut the reelection prospects of incumbent mayors, in large part because many substantial voter-buying efforts came to naught.[116] In Hidalgo and Nichter (2016), we employ a regression discontinuity design (RDD) to examine these effects rigorously. The RDD analysis takes advantage of the fact that municipalities are audited if they exceed the arbitrary 80 percent threshold discussed earlier; a standard "fuzzy" RDD is employed given the audit trigger is not fully deterministic.[117] By comparing mayoral reelection rates of municipalities just below and above this threshold,

---

[111] The TSE performed audits for decades but were more limited due to funding constraints. These constraints were alleviated during the 2007–2008 wave, which was the most extensive in decades. Law 9504 in 1997 indicated specific criteria for audits.

[112] The other two criteria are: (a) electorate is at least twice the summed population of citizens aged 10–15 and over 70 years, and (b) voter transfers grew at least 10 percent in last year. Of Brazil's municipalities, 27 percent meet the 80 percent criterion, while over 99 percent meet (a) and over 60 percent meet (b). Three-fourths of municipalities that meet the 80 percent threshold also meet both other criteria.

[113] The TSE orders most audits before it finalizes the electoral rolls for each upcoming election. Audits target small municipalities, so only 5.4 percent of the nation's electorate (6.8 million voters) had to reregister during the 2007–2008 wave.

[114] "Presidente do TRE Acompanha Início da Revisão com Biometria em Itaguara," *TRE-Minas Gerais*, September 1, 2011.

[115] "Rezende Acredita que Correição Garante Eleições Mais Transparentes," *Várzea Grande*, August 10, 2004.

[116] Mayors may only serve two consecutive terms in Brazil; subsequent reelection is also permitted.

[117] McCrary (2008) density tests reveal no manipulation to remain below the threshold. Hidalgo and Nichter (2016) show that politicians cannot precisely control their electorate or population, so sorting would not bias RDD estimates (Lee, 2008). Some municipalities exceed the threshold without voter buying, given their demography and compulsory voting.

2.6 Effect of Anti-Clientelism Legislation

regressions estimate the causal effects of voter audits.[118] As shown graphically in Figure 2.4a, voter audits – which undermined voter buying – decreased the likelihood of mayoral reelection by 18 percentage points. Analyses suggest audits undermined incumbents' continuity of power through two channels: (a) reducing the probability that incumbents run for reelection, and (b) worsening the electoral performance of those incumbents who decide to run.

Evidence suggests voter audits cut mayoral reelection rates in large part because they undermined voter buying. As shown in Figure 2.4b, in line with voter-buying predictions, the negative effect on incumbent reelection is far greater if many voters recently transferred away from neighboring municipalities.[119] Moreover, the figure also shows that the negative effect on incumbent reelection is magnified in municipalities recently experiencing large voter inflows. Also observe that in those municipalities with low voter inflows or low outflows from neighbors – i.e., without much or any voter buying – no significant effect on mayoral reelection is observed. Tests show that alternative explanations such as emigration cannot explain results, and findings are robust to an alternative research design employing a distinct dataset. Fixed-effects specifications indicate that within audited municipalities, mayors perform more poorly in precincts with many removed voters, particularly if those precincts recently imported many voters from surrounding municipalities. In sum, voter audits' effects on mayoral reelection are in large part attributable to their impact on voter buying.[120]

The broader point is that voter buying, similar to other strategies of electoral clientelism, encounters substantial challenges due to Brazil's institutional context. Electoral laws trigger voter audits in many municipalities, and these audits undermine the effectiveness of voter buying. Although survey evidence presented earlier suggests that voter buying persists in many parts of Brazil, audits have to a large degree deprived many politicians from taking full advantage of this innovative tactic.

2.6 EFFECT OF ANTI-CLIENTELISM LEGISLATION

Beyond the challenges examined thus far, electoral clientelism faces yet another formidable obstacle in Brazil. A monumental law enacted in 1999 significantly

---

[118] Analyses use both differences-in-means and local-linear estimators. The latter employs linear regressions on each side of the threshold to account for differential slopes within specified bandwidths. The paper demonstrates covariate balance and shows numerous robustness checks including the use of various bandwidths, McCrary density tests and placebo threshold tests.

[119] Heterogeneity analyses conducted by splitting the sample by: (a) median number of transfers out of neighboring municipalities, and (b) median number of transfers into the municipality.

[120] See Hidalgo and Nichter (2016) for further analysis. Broader patterns are also consistent with voter-buying predictions. For example, audits are disproportionately triggered in small municipalities: of over 1,100 audits performed in 2007–2008, only two took place in municipalities with populations over 90,000 citizens.

(a) Effect of voter audits on mayoral reelection
(regression discontinuity design)

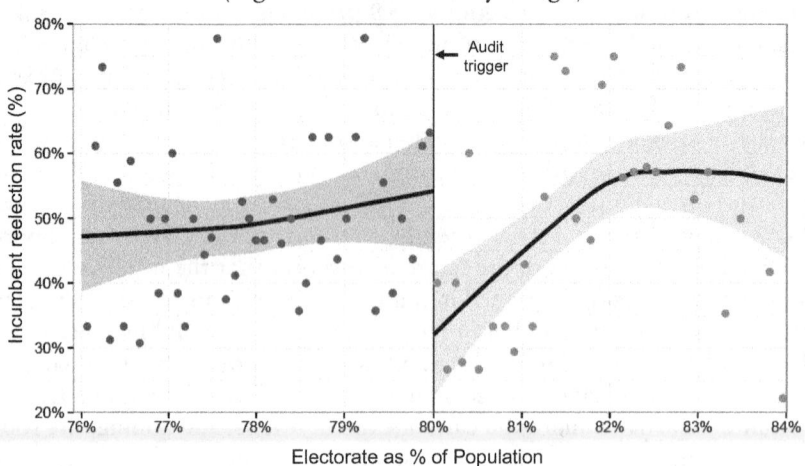

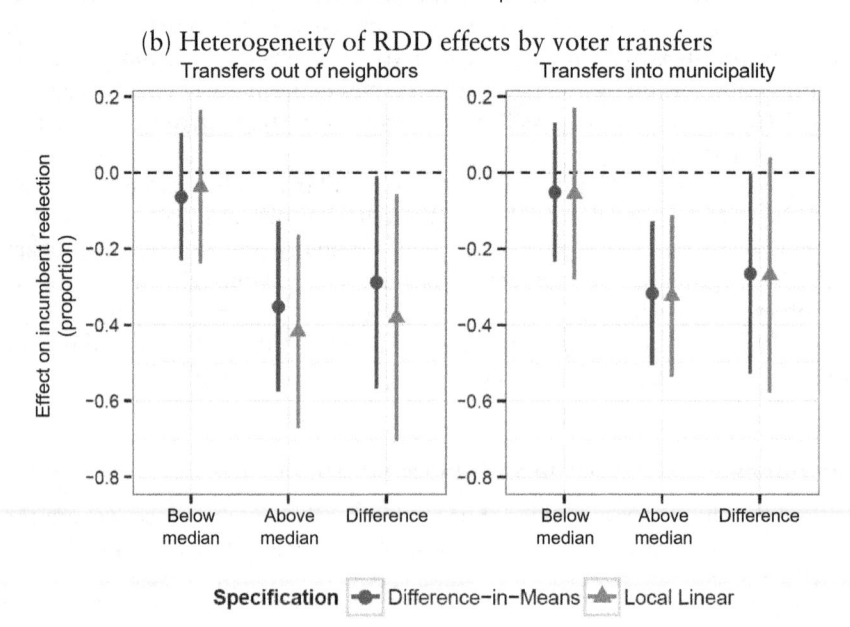

(b) Heterogeneity of RDD effects by voter transfers

FIGURE 2.4 Effect of voter audits (Brazil, 2008)
Note: Figure 2.4a shows the effect on mayoral reelection in 2008 of surpassing the 80 percent trigger for voter audits. Each dot represents the reelection rate within a bin containing 20 municipalities. Conditional average (black lines) and 95 percent confidence intervals (shaded region) are loess regression estimates. Consistent with voter buying, Figure 2.4b shows how the effect of audits (employing a regression discontinuity design) varies by whether municipality has above-median voter transfers (1) out of neighboring municipalities and (2) into the municipality. The difference between strata effects is also shown. As a robustness check, two specifications are provided. Vertical lines represent 95 percent confidence intervals.
Source: Hidalgo and Nichter (2016).

2.6 Effect of Anti-Clientelism Legislation

increased the threat of prosecution facing politicians who distribute benefits during campaigns. Although the practice continues, the country now ranks as a world leader in swiftly ousting politicians for the provision of campaign handouts. As explored, this legislation is remarkable because it entailed a striking turnaround. Although Brazil had long prohibited campaign handouts, many politicians distributed them with impunity. But in the late 1990s, popular pressure mounted as over one million Brazilians signed a petition against clientelism during campaigns. This effort culminated in legislation that has removed over a thousand politicians from office, rendering clientelism the top reason why politicians are ousted in Brazil.[121]

Although formal rules against clientelism during campaigns have long been on the books, until recently they were rarely enforced. When Getúlio Vargas codified the electoral process soon after the Revolution of 1930, candidates were explicitly prohibited from distributing benefits during campaigns in exchange for political support. The first Electoral Code (Law 21076 of 1932) enacted a substantial punishment for this crime – from six months to two years in prison.[122] And the most recent Electoral Code of 1965 imposes an even more severe punishment: up to four years of imprisonment as well as fines. Rather than simply prohibiting vote buying, the laws covered a broad range of actions, including turnout buying and abstention buying, and even promises and refused offers. In particular, the 1965 Electoral Code proclaims that it is punishable by criminal law "to give, offer, promise, solicit or receive, for oneself or for another, money, gifts, or any other benefits, in order to obtain or give a vote, or to obtain or promote abstention, even if the offer is not accepted."[123]

Despite these strong words, prosecutions were rare. While legislation criminalized the distribution of campaign handouts, the crime remained almost entirely unenforced (Câmara dos Deputados, 1999; CBJP, 2000, 13). Until recently, politicians rarely faced charges for clientelism and even fewer were successfully prosecuted.[124] One reason involved delays and backlogs in the court system (Câmara dos Deputados, 1999). As one of Brazil's most influential judges explained with regards to vote buying before Law 9840, "the famous slowness of the judiciary … facilitated impunity" (Delgado, 2010).[125] Many observers consider the country's judicial system to be highly inefficient due to various factors including procedural problems and resource constraints.

If prosecuting clientelist politicians was difficult, removing them from office was even tougher. Convicted politicians would file so many appeals that they managed to finish their mandates (Reis, 2006, 17), a phenomenon that more generally slows Brazil's judicial process (Yeung and Azevedo, 2011, 2). Unlike many other countries, Brazil long presumed that defendants were innocent

---

[121] "Compra de Voto Ainda é o que Mais Cassa Políticos no Brasil," *O Globo*, July 25, 2010; Movimento de Combate á Corrupção Eleitoral, 2012.
[122] Article 107/21 of the 1932 Electoral Code.
[123] Article 299 of the 1965 Electoral Code.
[124] Author's interview of Judge Marlon Reis (October 20, 2011).
[125] José Augusto Delgado served as a judge for forty-three years, including thirteen years on the *Superior Tribunal de Justiça* (STJ), Brazil's highest appellate court for non-constitutional cases.

until proven guilty *and* all appeals had been exhausted.[126] Lengthy appeals, combined with minimal prosecutions, enabled many politicians to distribute campaign handouts with impunity. For example, Federal Deputy Eduardo Paes argued in 1999 that of all "criminalized behavior" in Brazil, vote buying was "one of the most practiced with almost no punishment" – a problem he blamed on delays in criminal prosecution.[127]

In contrast to such impunity, Law 9840 now imposes a substantial risk of prosecution. Before investigating consequences, the momentousness of this legislation is emphasized by discussing the substantial efforts undertaken to achieve its popular initiative. According to Article 61 of the 1988 Constitution, citizens can introduce legislation by gathering signatures from at least 1 percent of the national electorate. To demonstrate a breadth of support, signatures must include at least 0.3 percent of voters in five states. Obtaining over a million signatures presented a massive challenge, and before Law 9840, no popular initiative had ever been approved by Brazil's legislature.[128]

Civil society spearheaded the popular initiative against clientelism during campaigns. Over 60 non-governmental organizations joined forces to collect enough signatures to put forward the initiative for voting by national congress. Their eighteen-month effort, with activities ranging from grassroots campaigning to collective news conferences, was launched and coordinated by Brazil's Justice and Peace Commission (Comissão Brasileira de Justiça e Paz, or CBJP). This religious organization extends an eponymous Vatican effort to improve social justice and reduce poverty across the world. During the anti-clientelism initiative, the CBJP collaborated closely with its influential sister organization, the Conferência Nacional dos Bispos do Brasil (National Conference of Brazilian Bishops, or CNBB), which has been historically described as "the ultimate authority of the Catholic Church in Brazil" (Mainwaring, 1986, 84).[129] Over 40 percent of the NGOs involved in the popular initiative were religious organizations, of which at least three-fourths were closely linked to the CNBB.[130] The involvement of these organizations, and the Catholic Church more broadly, builds on their long history of social and political action in

---

[126] Article 5 of Brazil's Constitution states that "no one shall be guilty until a final sentence of condemnatory sentence has passed." However, the Supreme Court ruled in 2016 that a sentence can be imposed after the first appeal confirms a criminal conviction. See "STF Muda Entendimento e Passa a Permitir Prisão depois de Decisão de Segundo Grau," *Consultor Jurídico*, February 17, 2016.

[127] Câmara dos Deputados, Sessão da Comissão de Constituição e Justiça de Redação, September 8, 1999; "Aprovada Lei de Iniciativa Popular Contra Corrupção," *O Estado de São Paulo*, September 24, 1999.

[128] "Ficha Limpa é o Quarto Projeto de Iniciativa Popular a Se Tornar Lei," *Globo*, May 20, 2010; "Iniciativa Popular: Em 11 Anos, Nenhum Projeto Feito Pelo Povo," *A Gazeta*, July 5, 2015.

[129] Illustrating their role in the efforts, transcripts of congressional deliberations over the popular initiative mentioned the CBJP twenty-five times (by name) and the better-known CNBB 101 times (by acronym). Calculated by author using Câmara dos Deputados (1999) transcripts.

[130] Author's analysis of each organization's website.

2.6 Effect of Anti-Clientelism Legislation

Brazil.[131] Other prominent organizations participating in the popular initiative included Brazil's largest labor union (Central Única dos Trabalhadores) and its national bar association (Ordem dos Advogados do Brasil).

By August 1999, civil society organizations had gathered the required signatures and delivered them by the truckload to the national congress. While signatories resided in all states, they were concentrated in the wealthier South and Southeast regions. Four states in those regions – São Paulo, Minas Gerais, Paraná and Espírito Santo – represented 68.7 percent of signatures but only 41.1 percent of the national electorate.[132] By contrast, only 16.7 percent of signatures were collected in the poorer North and Northeast regions, where 33.4 percent of voters resided. One plausible reason for such patterns is a greater aversion to clientelism among wealthier citizens; however, some relatively wealthy states such as Rio de Janeiro had disproportionately few signatures.[133] An additional reason is likely the heterogeneous institutional capacity of civil society organizations across Brazil.[134]

The judiciary also facilitated the enactment of Law 9840. It served as a valuable ally for civil society in the anti-clientelism initiative, because electoral governance in Brazil is highly centralized in the judiciary and relatively insulated from political interference.[135] Top judicial executives such as the TSE President publicly supported the initiative. Furthermore, an anti-clientelism task force that played a central role in this effort was led by a recent attorney general of Brazil and included several prominent judges (Câmara dos Deputados, 1999; CBJP, 2000). Armed with this judicial experience, the task force designed an innovative way to tackle politicians' impunity while circumventing the legal quagmire surrounding clientelism prosecutions. The sanctions imposed through Law 9840 – removal from office and fines – do not substitute for or involve criminal charges, but are instead levied through a parallel process (Reis, 2006; Tozzi, 2008, 43). More specifically, the distribution of benefits during campaigns also became an electoral infraction, thereby adjudicated by electoral courts. This approach avoided the delays and inefficiencies of criminal courts, allowing for the expedited removal of politicians.

Legislators from left-of-center parties also helped to enact Law 9840. Although mobilized by signatures, the popular initiative was then "adopted"

---

[131] The CBJP played a key role in the Catholic Church's campaign against human rights abuses during the authoritarian period (Mainwaring, 1986, 106–107), and provided support "to virtually all the campaigns and movements for the redemocratization of Brazil" (Pope, 1985, 439).

[132] Calculations by author based on data from TSE and Câmara dos Deputados (1999). São Paulo represented 37.9 percent of signatures, versus 22.1 percent of Brazil's electorate.

[133] Rio de Janeiro – the state with the second highest income per capita in 1998, after São Paulo (IBGE 1998) – had 3.1 percent of all signatures but 9 percent of Brazil's electorate.

[134] Author's interview with Judge Márlon Reis, October 20, 2011.

[135] See Marchetti (2008, 882–883), Hartlyn et al. (2008) and Rosas (2010). As one example, lower-level judges in the overall legal system, who form the corps of first-instance electoral judges, are selected by rigorous competitive examination.

by legislators to expedite the process.[136] At first glance, it might appear that legislators across the political spectrum advocated equally for the measure. The bill adopting the initiative had 11 coauthors from distinct parties, which held 93.7 percent of seats in the lower house. It passed the Chamber of Deputies unanimously amidst applause and then passed the Senate just two days later with minimal resistance.[137] However, closer analysis suggests that left-of-center parties were especially keen advocates. Consider that the bill quickly reached the full plenary session of the Chamber of Deputies, in part because it obtained signatures from at least 10 percent of deputies (i.e., 52 of all 513 deputies). A striking pattern emerges when examining which deputies signed: over half of the 53 signatories were members of the Workers' Party (Partido dos Trabalhadores, or PT), which held less than 12 percent of all seats in the Chamber. And nearly three-quarters of signatories were from five left-of-center parties, which represented only 21 percent of all federal deputies.[138] Moreover, the PT and other left-of-center parties also disproportionately spoke in favor of the bill during legislative debates.[139]

What accounts for the PT's outsized advocacy for Law 9840? Established relationships provide one explanation: the CBJP's leader during the initiative (Francisco Whitaker) is often deemed to have been a *founder* of the PT (MPPD, 2006, 7), and more broadly the party has traditional ties to the Catholic Church.[140] Second, Law 9840 dovetailed with the PT's ideological bent: the party had long envisioned itself as an "ethical alternative to politics as usual" (Hochstetler, 2008, 38), and its leaders "opposed vehemently the clientelistic and personalistic orientation of Brazilian politics" (Hunter, 2010, 27). The point is not that the PT has always lived up to these standards; after all, Baker et al. (2016, 200) argue that the PT's brand as "the party of clean government ... imploded in mid-2005 with the revelation of the *mensalão* scandal," which involved buying votes of federal legislators, and the party became embroiled in further prominent scandals such as *Operação Lava Jato*.[141] Notwithstanding

---

[136] All successful initiatives to date ended up being adopted. Law 9840 is considered the first law by popular initiative adopted by the national legislature. See Câmara dos Deputados (1999), "Deputado 'Adota' Projeto de Iniciativa Popular," *G1*, October 4, 2007, and "Iniciativa Popular: Em 11 Anos, Nenhum Projecto Feito pelo Povo," *A Gazeta*, July 5, 2015.

[137] From Chamber of Deputies and Senate records, and "Aprovada Lei de Iniciativa Popular Contra Corrupção," *O Estado de São Paulo*, September 24, 1999.

[138] These parties were PCdoB, PDT, PPS, PSB and PT, using Power and Zucco's (2009) ideological scale.

[139] Of those who spoke about the bill on the floor, left-of-center parties accounted for 23 of 42 deputies, and 8 of 16 senators (most from the PT). These parties held 21 (20) percent of deputy (senator) seats. Calculations by author using transcripts in Câmara dos Deputados (1999).

[140] Whitaker also served twice as a PT councilor for the city of São Paulo (1989–1996). The Church and its grassroots organizations, especially Ecclesial Base Communities (CEBs), contributed to the PT's early expansion (Keck, 1992, 78–79; Trejo and Neto, 2014, 2).

[141] This major corruption probe ("Operation Car Wash") implicated many politicians from the PT and other parties. Another major scandal involved budget law violations, culminating in ex-President Dilma Rousseff's impeachment. For insights about the PT's evolution, see for

2.6 Effect of Anti-Clientelism Legislation

such developments, during Law 9840's enactment in the late 1990s, the PT had a reputation for being a "clean" party and for fighting clientelism.[142] Third, Law 9840 aligned with the PT's electoral incentives. Traditional elites in Brazil had long employed clientelism to help maintain political control (Hagopian, 1996), and conservative parties historically tended to employ clientelism more than parties on the left (Mainwaring et al., 1999, 48). Undercutting such practices could boost PT votes by the poor and weaken conservative machines' domination of some localities.[143] And indeed, Law 9840 disproportionately harmed its competitors: the PT comprised less than 3 percent of ousted politicians.[144] However, beyond advocacy within the legislature, no available evidence suggests that the PT (or any other party) influenced the collection of signatures or the law's implementation.

Since its enactment in 1999, Law 9840 has increasingly posed a formidable challenge for electoral clientelism. The sheer magnitude of prosecutions under this law suggests that politicians who distribute campaign handouts face substantial risks. The Movimento de Combate á Corrupção Eleitoral (Movement against Electoral Corruption, or MCCE), an umbrella network of civil society organizations against clientelism, identified nearly 700 politicians who had been ousted by 2009 for violating Law 9840. Furthermore, it estimated that the number surged to at least a thousand by 2011.[145] As shown in Figure 2.5a, these removals span Brazil. The vast majority of these prosecutions involve municipal-level politicians: 667 mayors, vice-mayors, and councilors were ousted, versus only 31 state and federal politicians. One reason for this distribution of figures is simply that local politicians constitute the vast majority of Brazilian politicians.[146] But beyond this obvious reason, citizens and politicians interviewed in Bahia also suggest that clientelism is more prevalent during municipal than national elections. Over two-thirds of local politicians removed from office are mayors and vice-mayors (who are removed together); the remainder are councilors. Court records from Law 9840 prosecutions reveal a wide range of benefits used for clientelism, including food, medicine, water, building materials and money.

Law 9840's threat to electoral clientelism has intensified, as evidenced by a growing number of politician removals. Consider this upward trend during local elections: 95 removals of politicians elected in 2000, 215 removals of

---

instance Alves and Hunter (2017, 451), who argue more generally that its success in some subnational contexts "required actions that were increasingly at odds with its earlier principles and methods."

[142] Regarding this reputation, see Hunter and Power (2005, 129) and Abers (2000, 53).
[143] In the late 1990s, the PT underperformed in the *grotões* – small municipalities in Brazil's interior that were voting overwhelmingly for conservative parties (Zucco, 2008, 42).
[144] Employs data about 2000–2007 prosecutions from MCCE (2007).
[145] Data in this paragraph are from MCCE (2007, 2009, 2012).
[146] In 2012, 5,568 mayors and 57,409 councilors were elected. By contrast, there are just 81 senators, 513 federal deputies, 1,059 state deputies, as well as the president and 27 governors.

(a) Politician removals for clientelism during elections (2000–2008)

Prosecutions
· 1–2
• 3–4
● 5+

(b) Electoral court documents mentioning clientelism (2000–2013)

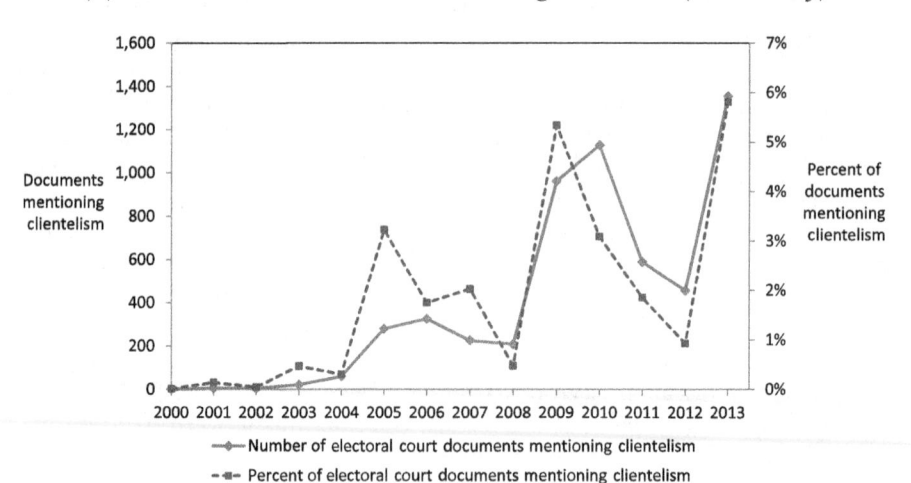

→ Number of electoral court documents mentioning clientelism
--■-- Percent of electoral court documents mentioning clientelism

FIGURE 2.5
Note: In Figure 2.5a, the map indicates state boundaries. Dots reflect the location of first-instance electoral courts that issued at least one verdict to remove a politician from office for an infraction of Law 9840 – which prohibits campaign handouts – in municipal elections from 2000 to 2008. Size of dots represents the number of politicians for whom removal verdicts were issued. In Figure 2.5b, vertical axes represent the number and percent of electoral court documents – i.e., all judgments and resolutions at the federal (TSE) or state (TRE) level – in each year mentioning "*captação ilícita de sufrágio*" (i.e., "illicit capture of suffrage"), the term used for clientelism during campaigns as codified in Law 9840.
Source: Author's analysis of data from Movimento de Combate á Corrupção Eleitoral and TSE.

2.6 Effect of Anti-Clientelism Legislation

politicians elected in 2004, and 357 removals of politicians elected in 2008 (MCCE, 2009).[147] Remarkably, one newspaper calculated that during the first few months after the 2008 election, a mayor was removed from office for clientelism every sixteen hours.[148] And it should be emphasized that these data only reflect guilty verdicts – the number of clientelism charges filed is far greater. A TSE analysis found that of 4,000 legal proceedings to remove local politicians during the 2008 elections, approximately 3,000 mentioned "vote buying."[149]

Further confirming Law 9840's threat to electoral clientelism, court activity pertaining to the legislation is substantial and has surged in recent years. To measure such activity, I conducted a text search of over 320,000 documents – more specifically, the entire contents of all electoral court judgments and resolutions from 2000 to 2013 at the federal and state level available in the TSE database. The search term employed was the actual terminology codified in Law 9840 for the prohibited activity: "*captação ilícita de sufrágio*" (i.e., "illicit capture of suffrage"). Although often translated in the vernacular as "vote buying," this term also includes campaign handouts distributed without an explicit exchange for vote choices (Reis 2006, 59–60) and has been ruled to include other strategies of electoral clientelism such as abstention buying (Prado 2014, 55–56). From 2000 to 2013, 6,557 documents included this search term, constituting 2 percent of all documents. As shown in Figure 2.5b, the number and share of documents mentioning *captação ilícita de sufrágio* has increased substantially since 2000 – reaching 5.8 percent of documents in 2013. It also reveals especially high court activity pertaining to Law 9840 after municipal elections (held in October of 2004, 2008, and 2012), which are considered to involve the most clientelism and have the most political candidates.[150]

The extent of Law 9840 prosecutions might be surprising, given that electoral clientelism was practiced with impunity for generations. Civil society has heightened the threat to politicians who violate the new legislation. Just after its enactment, the CBJP issued a detailed guidebook urging communities to form "9840 Committees." These committees, which soon mushroomed across Brazil, collect evidence against politicians who distributed campaign handouts and monitor local electoral courts to ensure they prosecute the law's transgressors. By the 2002 national election, 130 anti-clientelism committees operated in 17 states, with approximately 1,600 people participating (MCCE, 2007). And by 2013, there were 329 committees operating in every Brazilian state (MCCE, 2013). Whereas signatures for the popular initiative had been disproportionately collected in wealthier regions, relatively more 9840 Committees were formed in *poorer* regions. In 2013, over 44 percent

---

[147] Figures may change after appeals and are unavailable for the 2012 election.
[148] "Um Prefeito é Cassado a Cada 16 Horas no País," *Globo*, May 5, 2009.
[149] "Um Prefeito é Cassado a Cada 16 Horas no País," *Globo*, May 5, 2009. Analysis conducted in December 2008 and based on 21 states that provided data.
[150] These documents lag the first adjudication of cases, as they are from state (*TRE*) and federal (*TSE*) electoral courts, which serve as appellate courts for municipal politicians.

of committees were in the poorer North and Northeast regions, where 33 percent of voters resided. By contrast, approximately 47 percent of committees were in the wealthier South and Southeast regions, where 60 percent of voters resided.[151]

The judiciary has also magnified the threat to electoral clientelism posed by Law 9840. First, it removed a major obstacle by ruling against challenges to the law's constitutionality. Second, the judiciary's interpretation of the new legislation has facilitated the removal of politicians who distribute campaign handouts. For example, the TSE has ruled that politicians can be punished for clientelism even if there is no effect on an election outcome. In addition, the TSE has ruled that politicians can be prosecuted when intermediaries distribute campaign benefits on their behalf (da Costa, 2009, 212; Reis, 2006, 57). This interpretation was important because legislators had stripped the explicit prohibition of indirect transactions from earlier drafts of the law. Third, the judiciary has expedited the execution of Law 9840 by permitting the ouster of politicians immediately after lower-level courts issue guilty verdicts. This swift action, which is accompanied by an efficient appeals process, contrasts sharply with the relatively glacial pace of criminal charges against clientelism.[152] Fourth, the judiciary has facilitated prosecutions by broadening the scope of prohibited handouts: in 2006, it banned "campaign gifts" such as T-shirts, key chains, hats and pens. And fifth, the TSE heightens public awareness of the anti-clientelism law through efforts such as many public service announcements on radio and television. In part due to such actions, a 2008 survey found that 72 percent of Brazilians were familiar with Law 9840.[153]

Another reason for this familiarity is substantial coverage by the mass media, which helps to inform Brazilians about electoral clientelism. Especially during election years, television and radio stations frequently discuss campaign handouts, emphasizing their illegality, ways to report transgressors, and the ouster of politicians. For example, Rede Globo's prominent television show *Fantástico* aired a lengthy segment in 2014 focused on vote buying, with interviews of the TSE President, prosecutors, accused politicians and purported recipients.[154] Another local television station covered the launch of a 9840 Committee, underscoring that it would enable voters to report clientelism during elections.[155] Moreover, *telenovelas* have broached the topic of clientelism

---

[151] Eight and a half percent of committees were in the Center-West region.
[152] To illustrate, second-instance courts have just three days to rule if these appeals have merit for hearings (Cureau, 2010). Some politicians have returned to office by successful appeal. As an exception, courts may issue injunctions for politicians to remain in office pending appeal.
[153] Study by TSE in collaboration with the Associação dos Magistrados Brasileiros, 2008.
[154] "Prática de Compra de Votos é Investigada em Mais de Mil Municípios Brasileiros," *Fantastico*, September 7, 2014. Another example discussing anti-clientelism laws is: "Compra de Votos é Crime Eleitoral e Já Causou a Cassação de Prefeitos," *EPTV*, September 26, 2012.
[155] "Comitê 9840 em Foz vai Orientar os Eleitores a Denunciar a Compra de Votos," *Parana RPC*, July 25, 2012.

2.7 Summary

over the years, and media coverage fueled the collection of signatures for the popular initiative culminating in Law 9840 (MPPD, 2006, 89).[156]

Overall, Law 9840 poses yet another challenge for electoral clientelism in Brazil. Politicians can no longer distribute benefits during campaigns with impunity, as they now face the substantial risk of punishment. Although vote buying and other strategies continue, Law 9840 has removed over a thousand clientelist politicians from office. Amplifying the effects of such removals, a subsequent popular initiative – *Lei da Ficha Limpa* (Clean Slate Law) in 2010 – layered on yet another severe punishment. Politicians ousted for violating Law 9840 or convicted of various crimes are now ineligible to run for office for eight years, a potentially devastating setback for their political careers.[157]

2.7 SUMMARY

Most contemporary research on clientelism focuses on strategies that exclusively deliver benefits during election campaigns. Such "electoral clientelism" involves not just vote buying, but also several other important strategies. Evidence suggests that all forms of electoral clientelism exist in Brazil but are undermined by significant challenges.

The theoretical framework presented in this chapter elaborates how institutional factors in a given society shape the relative costs of different strategies, thereby leading a machine to adapt its mix of electoral clientelism. But a combination of several institutional features in Brazil means that *all* these strategies face daunting challenges, thereby undercutting the overall effectiveness of electoral clientelism. First, the nation's adoption of electronic voting heightened ballot secrecy, making vote buying more difficult. Second, strict compulsory voting (despite low fines) hinders politicians' ability to engage in turnout buying and abstention buying. Given these hindrances, some politicians engage in another, more costly form of electoral clientelism: importing outsiders through voter buying. Yet even this strategy is hamstrung by third institutional challenge: electoral rules that trigger voter audits in many municipalities. Moreover, Law 9480 has impinged on all forms of electoral clientelism, because it has substantially heightened the risk of punishment when distributing campaign handouts.

Although this book argues that many Brazilian politicians assist clients during both campaign and non-campaign periods, such challenges have decreased electoral clientelism – that is, the use of episodic strategies that *exclusively*

---

[156] For a historical discussion of clientelism in *telenovelas* (soap operas), see Matos and Ferreira (2015) and Fernandes (2015).

[157] An additional constraint on handouts is Brazil's 2015 campaign finance law, as it bans corporate donations for campaigns and thus reduces available funds. See "STF Publica Acórdão que Proíbe Financiamento Eleitoral por Empresas," *Consultor Jurídico*, March 5, 2016.

provide campaign handouts. The cross-national Varieties of Democracy dataset is particularly illuminating as it provides longitudinal evidence and explicitly hones in on electoral clientelism: it reports the level of vote buying and turnout buying during national elections since 1900. For each Brazilian election, five country experts independently coded this level using a scale ranging from zero ("no evidence of vote/turnout buying") to four ("systematic, widespread, and almost nationwide vote/turnout buying by almost all parties and candidates"). According to these experts, electoral clientelism fell substantially in Brazil over the past century, with ratings of 3.73 in 1902, 3.33 in 1930, 2.53 in 1958, 2.24 in 1986, and 1.99 in 2014.[158] Further insight is gleaned by comparing Brazil's ratings with those of other countries in the same dataset. In the first half of the twentieth century, Brazil was rated as having the most electoral clientelism of any nation in the world. By contrast, Brazil is now rated as having less electoral clientelism than half of all countries – and two-thirds of all non-OECD countries.[159]

Notwithstanding this decline, electoral clientelism persists in Brazil. Given the competitiveness of local elections – about a quarter of mayoral elections are decided by five percentage points or fewer (Klasnja and Titiunik, 2017, 145)[160] – some politicians take risks to employ these unreliable strategies as a secondary measure. As described earlier, numerous interviewees perceived vote buying to be nothing more than a gamble; however, some elites noted that candidates in close elections may still devote limited resources to this strategy in a final push to obtain additional votes. For example, a councilor explained that although it is impossible to monitor how citizens vote: "You have to take chances ... when the final hour arrives, it's do or die."[161] While campaign benefits are no longer distributed as openly or widely as in the past, surveys described in this chapter suggest that many contemporary Brazilians believe that electoral clientelism exists.[162] And in the Rural Clientelism Survey, some respondents indicated that they personally knew a recipient: 15.6 percent for vote buying, 8.1 percent for turnout buying, 7.3 percent for voter buying,

---

[158] Data from Coppedge et al. (2017); original scale is inverted. V-Dem employed inter-coder reliability tests, and a measurement model to convert from ordinal to interval scale. Question: "In this national election, was there evidence of vote and/or turnout buying?" Scale also includes: (1) "almost none," (2) "restricted," and (3) "some" evidence of vote and/or turnout buying.
[159] For each nation, comparisons average ratings of all national elections in a period. Brazil had the highest rating for electoral clientelism of all thirty-three (forty-four) countries rated between 1900 and 1925 (1950). Contemporary comparison of sixty-eight nations averages ratings from 2000–2016.
[160] This figure is based on elections from 1996 and 2012.
[161] Author's interview, municipality in Bahia with 100,000 citizens (December 17, 2008).
[162] For discussion of how openly and widely benefits were once distributed, see: "O Momento Politico," *O Imparcial*, March 2, 1922, p. 1; "Scepticismo Infundado," *Diario Nacional*, June 24, 1930, 3; and "Ministro da Justiça Comprova: Dinheiro para Compra de Votos," *Jornal do Brasil*, October 2, 1958, 4.

2.7 Summary

and 2.5 percent for abstention buying. More broadly, nearly 10.7 percent of Brazilian LAPOP respondents indicated that they were offered benefits for their votes during the 2014 campaign, though like most surveys it did not distinguish between electoral and relational clientelism.[163]

Despite the continued existence of electoral clientelism, many campaign handouts are distributed not in isolation, but rather as part and parcel of ongoing exchange relationships in which benefits extend beyond campaigns. As argued by this book, such relational clientelism is relatively resilient to the institutional challenges explored in the present chapter, but involves a dual credibility problem that citizen actions help to mitigate.

---

[163] LAPOP's 2014 AmericasBarometer surveyed 1,500 Brazilians in 107 municipalities.

PART II

RELATIONAL CLIENTELISM

3

Citizens and Relational Clientelism

Although a recent wave of research focuses centrally on electoral clientelism – a phenomenon that exclusively distributes benefits during campaigns – this fixation contrasts sharply with most traditional literature on the topic. Generations of scholars depicted clientelism not as episodic or time-bound transactions, but rather as enduring relationships providing material benefits well beyond election periods. The remainder of this book refocuses attention on these ongoing exchange relationships – which I term "relational clientelism" – and argues that citizens often play a fundamental role in their survival. As explored in this chapter, relational clientelism is relatively resilient to numerous challenges that often undercut electoral clientelism, including those discussed in the preceding chapter. Nevertheless, the viability of long-term relationships is threatened by the possibility that citizens or politicians may engage in opportunistic defection: citizens may renege on their vote promises, and politicians may renege on their promises of material benefits. Across the world, citizens often undertake purposive actions to mitigate this dual credibility problem, and thereby buttress the stability of relational clientelism. Vulnerability frequently motivates clients to do so, as ongoing exchange relationships provide an important form of informal insurance when the state fails to provide an adequate social safety net. Despite widespread efforts to develop and expand social programs, many citizens remain vulnerable to shocks such as illness, unemployment, and drought, and they often rely on clientelist relationships with politicians who render assistance when adversity strikes.

To elaborate this argument, the present chapter distills the logic and mechanisms by which citizens fortify relational clientelism. Subsequent chapters in Part II flesh out and test the argument, building on empirical materials from Brazil. Chapter 4 reveals why vulnerability provides a powerful motivation for Brazilians to reinforce ongoing exchange relationships: many citizens are vulnerable to adverse shocks, and local politicians have both resources and discretion to provide preferential assistance to clients during times of need. After establishing their motivation, the following two chapters demonstrate how voters' choices alleviate credibility issues in relational clientelism. Chapter 5 examines how Brazilians *declare support* to signal their own credibility, and Chapter 6 investigates how they *request benefits* to screen politician credibility. As explored in Part III, these two mechanisms – by which citizens help to sustain relational clientelism – are also observed in various other countries.

3.1 DEFINITION OF RELATIONAL CLIENTELISM

Before elaborating how and why citizens sustain relational clientelism, it is essential to clarify the concept. As discussed more extensively in Chapter 1, relational clientelism has two key defining attributes: (1) it involves contingent exchange; and (2) its benefits extend beyond election campaigns. With regards to the first attribute, all forms of clientelism involve contingent exchange (Hicken 2011, 291–292; Kitschelt and Wilkinson, 2007, 10–11, 22) in which a citizen promises that he or she will provide (or has provided) political support. Various other modes of distributive politics, including programmatic politics, pork and constituency service, lack such contingency. With regards to the second attribute, relational clientelism delivers at least some of its material benefits during non-election periods. This timing of benefits contrasts with electoral clientelism, which distributes benefits *exclusively* during election campaigns. Two points raised in Chapter 1 regarding the second attribute deserve emphasis. First, relational clientelism need not suspend assistance to clients during campaigns. As such, to ascertain whether a campaign handout involves electoral or relational clientelism, it is necessary to investigate whether the citizen also receives contingent benefits outside of campaigns. Second, relational clientelism often involves periodic claims of assistance during adverse shocks rather than a continuous flow of benefits. Although understudied in the contemporary literature, a wide range of analyses in this book reveal patterns of relational clientelism, in which contingent benefits extend beyond campaigns.

3.2 RESILIENCE OF RELATIONAL CLIENTELISM

This book argues that citizens play an important role in the resilience of relational clientelism, because they mitigate severe threats to its survival. As described in Chapter 1, the phenomenon faces major challenges pertaining to the trustworthiness of promises, which stem from the fact that its contingent exchanges extend beyond campaigns. Both citizens and politicians in ongoing exchange relationships make promises to each other: citizens promise to provide political support, and politicians promise to help when adversity strikes. The viability of relational clientelism depends on whether these promises are trustworthy, raising bilateral concerns about the threat of opportunistic defection. More specifically, a dual credibility problem ensues: politicians may be concerned about whether citizens' vote promises are credible, and citizens may be concerned about whether politicians will follow through on promises of assistance after they cast their votes. As explored in the present chapter, citizens in long-term exchange relationships often undertake actions that alleviate these credibility issues.

Citizens' actions are fundamental to the survival of relational clientelism, because the credibility issues just mentioned are especially complex. By comparison, electoral clientelism involves only a unilateral risk of opportunistic defection. Although politicians who engage in strategies such as vote buying may be concerned about whether citizens' vote promises are credible, citizens need not be concerned about whether politicians will follow through on their side of the exchange. The reason is that recipients receive rewards *before* they cast their ballots; by definition, electoral clientelism provides no benefits beyond campaigns. Aside from these credibility issues – which citizens help to surmount – relational clientelism is relatively resilient to numerous threats that often undercut electoral clientelism. The phenomenon is often able to withstand four broad threats to clientelism presented in Chapter 1: structural changes, institutional reforms, legal enforcement, and partisan strategies.

First, relational clientelism is relatively robust to a major structural change that has undermined electoral clientelism in recent years: economic development. Despite rising incomes in much of the world, continued vulnerability often leaves citizens reliant on ongoing exchange relationships to overcome adverse shocks. With respect to Brazil, the next chapter shows that although higher income reduces citizens' willingness to accept vote-buying offers, much of the population remains unprotected from illness, unemployment, and drought. Many residents are unable to self-insure against such shocks, and thus depend on relationships with politicians and other elites to cope with their vulnerability. Beyond Brazil, Chapter 7 examines how much of the world remains exposed to dire risks, even in countries where the standard of living has improved markedly. Although relational clientelism is not entirely immune to rising incomes, it helps citizens cope with this continued vulnerability and thus withstands pressure from economic development, a factor often corrosive for clientelism.

Second, relational clientelism is relatively resilient to institutional reforms – such as the secret ballot and compulsory voting – that have undercut electoral clientelism in many countries. As explored in Chapter 2, rigorous ballot secrecy hinders vote buying in Brazil, especially after the advent of electronic voting. But unlike many vote-buying transactions, relational clientelism does not hinge on monitoring vote choices to enforce compliance. Instead, it is often sustained in part by declared support, a mechanism in which citizens publicly display political paraphernalia during campaigns. With this action, clients transmit a costly signal that they will vote for a politician, thereby helping politicians distinguish whose promises of political support are credible. By observing declarations, politicians who provide their clienteles with long-term assistance during adverse shocks can be more confident that these citizens are indeed delivering their promised votes. Relational clientelism is also insulated from compulsory voting, an institution that undermines turnout buying and abstention buying, because ongoing exchange relationships can flourish even where few nonvoters exist or where it is difficult to induce abstention. Moreover, the phenomenon is robust to institutional reforms that protect electoral rolls, including digitization and audits in Brazil. While such reforms inhibit voter buying, relational clientelism remains resilient because it does not employ rewards to distort voter registration.

Third, relational clientelism is able to withstand the heightened enforcement of anti-clientelism laws, which have undercut electoral clientelism in various countries. Whereas such laws typically focus on election campaigns, much of relational clientelism occurs once the campaign season is over. With respect to Brazil, the preceding chapter explored how Law 9840 led to a dramatic surge in legal enforcement against campaign handouts, with continuing reverberations after the ouster of over a thousand politicians. But regulations imposed by that legislation only take effect during election campaigns. Thus, while Law 9840 always hinders electoral clientelism (which is exclusively a campaign phenomenon), it hinders relational clientelism (which extends beyond campaigns) only a fraction of the time. Around the world, another reason for the relative resilience of relational clientelism is that it channels benefits to supporters. Citizens in ongoing exchange relationships with politicians tend to prefer that their benefactors win. Hence, unlike forms of electoral clientelism that target opposers, relational clientelism involves less risk that recipients will turn in politicians who transgress anti-clientelism laws by providing them benefits.

Fourth, relational clientelism can remain robust even if partisan strategies involve a shift towards programmatic politics. In the case of Brazil, Hagopian (2014) argues that the PT and PSDB heightened programmatic competition at the national level and adopted major reforms that reduced the supply of resources for patronage. When considering potential effects on clientelism in municipal politics, it is important to recognize that the PT and PSDB jointly constitute less than a quarter of mayors – and less than one-fifth of city councilors – across Brazil.[1] The PT won mayoral races in 11.8 percent of Brazil's municipalities in 2012, falling to just 4.6 percent in 2016 in the wake of Dilma Rousseff's impeachment and major corruption scandals (most prominently, Operação Lava Jato, or Operation Car Wash). The PSDB won just 12.9 and 14.2 percent of mayoral races in 2012 and 2016, respectively.[2]

---

[1] As mentioned in Chapter 1, councilors serve on the city council, the municipality's legislative branch. Each municipality has between nine and fifty-five city councilors, depending on population. Councilor and mayor elections are concurrent.

[2] Data on Brazil's municipal elections from David Fleischer's "Brazil Focus" (October 3, 2016).

And while less pork from federal and state governments might arguably reduce the pot of funds available to dole out during campaigns, relational clientelism thrives on scarcity. As discussed in the next chapter, local politicians often have substantial discretion over resources. If a mayor can only afford to provide coffins to a fraction of indigent families instead of all of them, the issue of preferential access becomes all the more salient. In line with this point, Chubb (1982, 5–6) found that the Christian Democratic machine in Palermo, Italy, continued to thrive despite resource scarcity, in large part because it distributed limited public resources to supporters in a discretionary manner. As explored in the present book, relational clientelism is alive and well in many contexts with scarce resources.

In sum, relational clientelism is relatively resilient to numerous fundamental challenges facing electoral clientelism. However, the viability of ongoing exchange relationships is threatened by a dual credibility problem, as both citizens and politicians are concerned about whether each other's promises are trustworthy. As discussed next, vulnerability motivates many citizens to undertake two important actions – declared support and requesting benefits – that alleviate these issues and thereby buttress the stability of relational clientelism.

3.3 VULNERABILITY AND RELATIONAL CLIENTELISM

Vulnerability afflicts much of the world's population, providing many citizens a powerful motivation to sustain long-term clientelist relationships that help them cope with adversity. This book's focus on vulnerability – a concept that encompasses both poverty and risk – emphasizes that both low average income and high uncertainty are detrimental to a citizen's welfare (Ligon and Schechter, 2003). Despite substantial improvements in the standard of living observed in most nations, the majority of citizens across the globe continue to face pronounced uncertainty as they remain susceptible to various adverse shocks including illness, unemployment and drought. Notwithstanding efforts to introduce and expand social insurance in many countries, programs rarely shield residents adequately from all sources of risk. A common problem is that a significant share of citizens, including informal and self-employed workers, is often excluded altogether from coverage. Furthermore, the delivery of social policy benefits frequently falls far short of what is enshrined in law, for reasons ranging from administrative constraints to political targeting (Mares and Carnes, 2009, 94). In contexts where the state fails to protect its population from adverse shocks, many citizens rely on ongoing exchange relationships with politicians as a risk-coping mechanism. In return for their political support, these relationships provide favored access to material benefits during bouts of acute deprivation. Because relational clientelism mitigates their vulnerability, these citizens are often motivated to undertake actions that bolster the survival of their long-term relationships with politicians.

To explore this important point, the next chapter focuses on vulnerability in Brazil. As a lens into the broader phenomenon of vulnerability, it examines the specific domains of healthcare, employment, and water. Many Brazilians experience shocks including catastrophic health expenditures, involuntary job loss, and recurring droughts. While the nation has expanded programs to tackle these sources of insecurity, most of the population continues to be inadequately protected from risk. To cope with vulnerability, many citizens rely on ongoing exchange relationships with local politicians, who often have resources and discretion to provide selective benefits to their clients when adversity strikes. For this reason, vulnerability often motivates Brazilians to buttress the stability of relational clientelism. As explored in Chapter 7, this pattern is by no means limited to Brazil. Across the world, many citizens experience pronounced vulnerability, and are thus similarly motivated to sustain ongoing exchange relationships.

Given that vulnerability motivates many citizens to shore up their long-term clientelist relationships, how can they achieve this objective? The present book argues that they undertake two key actions to mitigate the dual credibility problem faced by relational clientelism: citizens *declare support* to signal the trustworthiness of their own vote promises, and they *request benefits* to screen the trustworthiness of politicians' promises to help during adverse shocks. Both mechanisms are discussed in the present chapter and tested extensively in the remainder of the book. Further emphasizing the link between vulnerability and these mechanisms, Chapters 5 and 6 also show that citizens are more likely to engage in both actions when exposed to adverse shocks.

3.4 DECLARED SUPPORT

Citizens in ongoing exchange relationships often publicly declare support for politicians, and thereby alleviate an important threat to the survival of relational clientelism. These relationships involve contingent exchange, in which citizens promise to provide political support in exchange for material benefits. A crucial concern emerges: how do politicians know whether to trust citizens' vote promises, given that nearly all countries employ the secret ballot? Declared support is a key mechanism by which citizens mitigate this fundamental concern. They recognize that clientelist politicians are unlikely to provide preferential assistance during adverse shocks unless their vote promises are credible. While clients can pledge their votes privately during campaign visits, this communication may be deemed as cheap talk. After all, untrustworthy voters can make such promises insincerely to one or more candidates, even as they cast ballots for competitors. By contrast, public declarations of support enable citizens in ongoing exchange relationships to signal the credibility of their vote promises. Such declarations include placing campaign posters and flags on their homes, wearing political paraphernalia, and holding signs at rallies. To be sure, citizens who prefer that a competitor

3.4 Declared Support

wins also have an incentive to feign trustworthiness by declaring support. But for these citizens, who are relatively unlikely to fulfill their vote promises, declaration is often too costly: beyond any material costs, declaring publicly against one's preferences involves expressive costs, and might even undesirably influence the election. To clarify why declared support transmits meaningful information to politicians – and thus mitigates a substantial challenge to the viability of relational clientelism – this section provides the intuition behind a signaling model developed in Appendix C. With reasonable assumptions, its game-theoretical analysis demonstrates the conditions under which public declarations reveal the trustworthiness of citizens' promises of political support.

Before elaborating this mechanism, it deserves emphasis that the logic of declared support in no way suggests that all citizens who display political paraphernalia are involved in clientelism. To be sure, many citizens across the world are motivated to express political preferences for purely non-clientelist reasons; for instance, voters with strong programmatic preferences may wish to provide free advertising on behalf of their candidates. Moreover, various studies of American politics have explored how actions such as displaying campaign posters and lawn signs are important forms of democratic participation, allowing voters to convey preferences and possibly influence election outcomes (e.g., Huckfeldt and Sprague, 1995; Verba, Nie, and Kim, 1978). But for a substantial share of the population in many countries, relational clientelism provides an additional motivation, as declarations enable citizens to signal the credibility of their vote promises. Given that this section aims to elaborate the logic by which declared support reinforces ongoing exchange relationships, it focuses squarely on citizens who are in such relationships with politicians. For brevity, such citizens are referred to as "promisers"; by definition, they promise to vote for a politician in exchange for future benefits.

Asymmetric information fuels politicians' concerns about whether to trust these promises. Within the context of long-term clientelist relationships, citizens are privy to their own political preferences and vote choices, whereas politicians have inferior knowledge about these aspects of their clients. To simplify the discussion, assume there are two types of citizens involved in relational clientelism: *supporting promisers* and *opposing promisers*. Both types promise to vote for politician P in an upcoming election, in exchange for future benefits if she wins. But whereas supporting promisers prefer to vote for P, opposing promisers prefer to vote against her. These preferences may stem from some combination of partisanship, programmatic appeals, gratitude toward help received in the past, and other factors. As discussed extensively in Chapter 6, citizens in ongoing exchange relationships often prefer politicians who have longstanding track records of providing them help during bouts of adversity. In the context of Brazil, the weight of partisanship should not be overstated when examining municipal-level politics, especially given that only a minority of citizens express a preference for any party and that local groups are often deemed more important.[3] The present analysis brackets such considerations, as it does not require identifying the nature of underlying preferences of citizens who promise votes in exchange for clientelist benefits.

To evaluate the logic of declared support, the signaling model in Appendix C makes several assumptions. Politician P cannot observe a citizen's vote choices and preferences, but she can observe whether the citizen publicly declares support for her during the campaign. As discussed later, extensive networks of political operatives are often employed to monitor declarations. The citizen receives expressive utility from declaring support publicly in accordance with his preferences. That is, he gains utility by declaring for his preferred candidate, but loses utility by declaring for a candidate he disfavors. By assumption, the citizen's declaration has no effect on the election outcome.[4] He incurs a material cost if he declares support. This cost includes both expenses (e.g., transportation and childcare) and opportunity costs (e.g., foregone wages) incurred when traveling to obtain declaration materials from campaign offices or to display paraphernalia at rallies. Moreover, it includes any costs of placing or removing displays of support from his residence or mode of transportation.[5] On Election Day, the citizen votes in accordance with his type. By assumption, the citizen receives expressive utility from voting, but his vote does not affect the election outcome.[6] If elected, politician P chooses whether to provide benefits to the citizen in exchange for having declared support for her during the campaign. It is assumed that she only has resources to provide these benefits if she wins the election. Although the logic of declared support does not require the existence of punishments, the analysis considers an additional possibility: if politician P loses, the elected opposition candidate punishes citizens who declared for P during the campaign.

Given these assumptions, the signaling model suggests that under reasonable conditions, declared support provides meaningful information about whether

[3] A third of respondents expressed a preference for any party in the Brazil 2010 Panel Study, as did one-tenth of citizens in the Rural Clientelism Survey. Most politicians I interviewed in the interior of Bahia indicated their party was not important to them; the vast majority said they received no help from their party during municipal campaigns, with many saying they simply needed a party label to run and did not know about their party's ideology. The PT was an exception but, as noted earlier, won just 4.6 percent of mayoral seats across Brazil in 2016.

[4] As with expressive utility, such an election influence would increase the cost of declaring against one's preferences. While only expressive utility is examined formally, both factors can render declaration a more informative signal.

[5] For example, a computer technician in Bahia explained he avoided attending or declaring at rallies because "my time is sacred," and a temporary worker noted difficulties in removing campaign bumper stickers and repainting his home's wall. Author's interviews, municipalities in Bahia with 80,000 and 10,000 citizens, respectively (November 20, 2008, and October 22, 2008).

[6] This assumption follows other models of clientelism (e.g., Gans-Morse et al., 2014; Morgan and Várdy, 2012; Nichter, 2008; Stokes, 2005). Morgan and Várdy (2012) provide a formal defense of focusing only on expressive utility. Relaxing this assumption yields a similar logic of declared support with added complexity.

3.4 Declared Support

a citizen in an ongoing exchange relationship will fulfill his vote promises. More specifically, it reveals the contextual conditions needed for "separating equilibria," in which only promisers who actually prefer that politician P wins will declare support. The underlying intuition is that for declarations to play an effective signaling role, supporting promisers should declare and opposing promisers should *not* declare. A supporting promiser will declare for politician P if the utility of declaring (in which case P provides a reward if elected) is weakly greater than the utility of not declaring (in which case P does not provide a reward). In addition, an opposing promiser will decide *not* to declare for P if the utility of not declaring is weakly greater than the utility of declaring. In such settings, declarers' vote promises are credible – even with rigorous ballot secrecy – whereas non-declarers' vote promises are not.

Beyond showing how declared support can transmit information about the trustworthiness of vote promises, the signaling model also unpacks effects of several factors. First, it shows that citizens' political preferences drive the separation between types: whereas declaring for politician P yields expressive utility for a supporting promiser, it yields expressive disutility for an opposing promiser. Furthermore, it suggests when declaration is a more informative signal. If the politician observes a citizen declaring, more information is conveyed about the citizen's type when the clientelist reward is small, when the declaration cost is large, when the politician's probability of victory is small, and when any clientelist punishments are large. Overall, the game-theoretic analysis in Appendix C reveals the conditions under which declared support enables citizens to signal the credibility of their vote promises, thereby mitigating a key threat to the viability of relational clientelism.[7] As discussed earlier, these declarations serve as a costly signal: citizens lose utility by declaring for candidates they disfavor, they incur expenses and opportunity costs, and in some settings they may undesirably affect the election or face punishments if their declared candidate is defeated.

This book examines the logic of declared support extensively, building on empirical materials from various countries. Chapter 5 focuses on the mechanism in Brazil, where many interviewed politicians expressed concerns about the credibility of citizens' vote promises. Declarations enable many Brazilians in long-term clientelist relationships to assuage such concerns. Consistent with the signaling model, qualitative and quantitative evidence suggests that declared support conveys meaningful information, as Brazilians overwhelmingly vote and hold perceptions in accordance with their declarations. Furthermore, analyses show a robust link between declared support and relational clientelism: for example, citizens who display support publicly for victorious candidates are significantly more likely to receive benefits during

---

[7] The model also reveals that the mechanism is ineffective if the conditions just described are too extreme, as a "pooling" equilibrium is expected in which nobody declares. It would also be uninformative in a pooling equilibrium in which all citizen types declare.

both election and non-election years. Evidence from Brazil also sheds light on the dense networks of operatives that facilitate the monitoring of citizens' public displays of political paraphernalia. In the Rural Clientelism Survey, citizens received an average of 4.6 visits to their homes by politicians and their representatives during the 2012 municipal campaign, with 81.3 percent of respondents receiving at least one such visit.[8] Candidates for city council, who tend to have especially frequent interactions with voters, often monitor declarations on behalf of allied mayoral candidates. Overall, nearly two-thirds of survey respondents believed others would remember who declared support with flags during the 2012 campaign – as did almost three-fourths of citizens who declared support in that manner.[9] In Chapter 7, further evidence from Argentina, Mexico, Ghana, Lebanon, and Yemen suggest that the mechanism of declared support is observed well beyond Brazil.

The signaling logic of declared support just described is an important mechanism by which many citizens help to sustain relational clientelism. Another important consideration is the influence of numerous factors, including politicians' monitoring ability and likelihood of electoral victory, on citizens' choices to declare support. To explore such effects, I developed a complementary model in collaboration with Salvatore Nunnari. Unlike the signaling model's use of game theory to investigate asymmetric information, Nichter and Nunnari (2017) employ decision theory with perfect information to analyze the effects of various factors. Our model assumes that voters' declaration choices are based on expected utility, which is shaped by: their political preferences towards the victorious candidate; any post-election rewards or punishments for declaring; material and social costs of declaring; expressive utility from declaring; and any effect of declarations on the election outcome.[10] Given such assumptions, formal analysis yields predictions about when more citizens will choose to declare support for clientelist politicians; for example, when such politicians offer larger material rewards, can monitor declarations effectively, and are preferred on programmatic or ideological grounds. These conditions also decrease the number of citizens who remain undeclared or declare support for non-clientelist candidates. The model also offers various other predictions regarding electoral competition, competitive clientelism, and punishments. For example, more citizens are expected to declare for a clientelist candidate who is heavily favored to win the election.[11] As discussed in Chapter 5, evidence not only corroborates the signaling logic presented earlier but is also largely

[8] $N = 3,107$.
[9] $N = 3,476$ for overall citizens.
[10] Theoretical predictions in Nichter and Nunnari (2017) are identical if declarations have no effect on the election outcome.
[11] With this factor, effects on non-declarations and declarations for non-clientelist candidates depend on parameter values. As with signaling, the complementary model suggests that under specific conditions, some declarations would not represent genuine political preferences (e.g., if a clientelist candidate is heavily favored to win or provides very large post-election rewards).

consistent with this complementary model's predictions about how numerous contextual factors affect declared support.

While voters' choices are thus multifaceted, the overarching point is that declared support is a citizen mechanism that helps to sustain relational clientelism. Even with rigorous ballot secrecy, citizens can signal the credibility of their vote promises through public displays of political support. By declaring support, citizens who rely on ongoing exchange relationships to cope with vulnerability mitigate politicians' concerns about their trustworthiness.

3.5 REQUESTING BENEFITS

Beyond declared support, citizens in ongoing exchange relationships also request benefits, an action that mitigates another fundamental threat to the survival of relational clientelism. Within these long-term relationships, politicians vow to their clients that they will provide help during bouts of hardship, and thereby alleviate their vulnerability. But such promises of post-election benefits raise the specter of opportunistic defection, as unscrupulous politicians can renege after citizens cast their votes. How do voters in clientelist relationships know whether to trust politicians' promises to provide assistance during adverse shocks? Citizen requests are a key mechanism to alleviate such concerns about politician credibility. Voters in ongoing exchange relationships glean valuable information by observing whether entrusted politicians fulfill their own requests. Given that these politicians had vowed to provide assistance, denying clients' requests conveys that such promises are untrustworthy. Within relational clientelism, citizens thus observe politicians' responsiveness to their own demands and terminate relationships with those who reveal – through denied requests – that they are unlikely to help when adverse shocks strike. In other words, citizens screen politicians based on their track record of fulfilling requests.

This focus on citizen requests warrants discussion, as it contrasts starkly with the literature's predominant focus on elite offers of clientelist benefits. As examined in Chapter 1, increased voter autonomy in much of the world has heightened citizens' ability to influence clientelism, with many contingent exchanges now initiated by bottom-up demands. Even in rural Northeast Brazil, an area not traditionally known for substantial voter autonomy, Chapter 6 shows that the majority of citizens who receive handouts had *asked* politicians for help. And citizen requests are widely observed across the world, as explored in Chapter 7. Although relatively understudied, this book argues that such demands have important consequences because citizen requests alleviate the problem of politician credibility that otherwise threatens the viability of relational clientelism.

Citizens' concerns about politician credibility are fueled by an important information asymmetry inherent in ongoing exchange relationships. Politicians are more informed than citizens about whether they are the "type" of politician who will fulfill requests reliably. An established literature demonstrates how individuals or firms can learn about the qualities of others in contexts with such asymmetric information (e.g., Spence, 1973; Stiglitz, 1975). Whereas signaling (e.g., through declared support) involves an informed party as the first mover, citizen requests involve screening in which an uninformed party moves first. In the present discussion, the citizen is referred to as "uninformed" because he lacks information about the politician's type, which the politician herself knows. The uninformed citizen can acquire private information and combat adverse selection by employing a "screening device," which sorts politicians of different qualities because they respond in distinct ways (Stiglitz, 1975, 283).

At the outset, it deserves emphasis that while screening politicians is an important function of citizen requests, it is by no means their exclusive function. When a citizen asks a politician for medicine for a sick child or for water during a drought, acquiring information can hardly be considered the primary objective. Nevertheless, the politician's response transmits information to the requester; that is, requests play a screening role as a "by-product" of their principal activity of obtaining needed goods and services. The logic is analogous to Stiglitz's (1975, 294) argument about the screening role of education: it reveals characteristics of citizens that affect productivity, as "a natural by-product" of its principal activity of teaching and guiding students.

The present discussion of citizen requests builds on existing formal work, which suggests that *reputation* can serve as a screening device in a variety of contexts ranging from credit to employment (Stiglitz and Weiss, 1983; Weigelt and Camerer, 1988).[12] When an uninformed party moves first, it can screen others by refusing to participate with individuals who have poor reputations.[13] For example, a bank does not know whether an entrepreneur is an honest type who repays debts, but it can refuse credit to borrowers who previously reneged on its loans. In turn, this threat that misbehavior will terminate a relationship motivates borrowers to repay their loans (Stiglitz and Weiss, 1983, 912; Weigelt and Camerer, 1988, 451; Hoff and Stiglitz, 1990, 240).

The logic of reputation as a screening device also extends to citizen requests, which provide (imperfect) information about politicians' hidden characteristics. Consider an ongoing exchange relationship in which a politician promises to provide assistance to her client during adverse shocks. As mentioned, an information asymmetry arises because the politician has private information about whether she will reliably fulfill that promise. First, the politician has superior information about discretionary resources available to assist clients, which may stem from both official and unofficial sources. Second, she is

---

[12] An individual's reputation can be defined formally as "the probability that she has a certain privately observed type or will take a certain action" and can be inferred from previous actions (Camerer, 2003, 445; Weigelt and Camerer, 1988, 443).

[13] Weigelt and Camerer (1988) expound on how reputations can serve as a screening mechanism. Their work builds on Stiglitz and Weiss (1983), which focuses primarily on identical types of agents but emphasizes findings are strengthened when examining different types.

3.5 Requesting Benefits

more knowledgeable about what share of these available discretionary funds she will allocate to providing such assistance, as opposed to alternative uses including her own consumption. And third, the politician is more informed about the number of citizens she has promised to help after the election. For sake of exposition, assume there is a "trustworthy" type of politician, who only promises as much future assistance as she can reliably fulfill, and an "untrustworthy" type of politician, who makes empty promises of future help in order to attract political support. Although the politician knows her own type, the citizen is uncertain about this private information. Adverse selection is a concern because untrustworthy types are especially likely to promise future assistance, given that they do so without considering the feasibility of fulfilling promises. Despite a politician's hidden characteristics, she may have a reputation for acting "trustworthy" in the eyes of a particular citizen if she always fulfills that citizen's requests – and in turn, the citizen may infer her type based on this history of actions (Weigelt and Camerer, 1988, 444). Part of a politician's reputation is specific to a given citizen, as it is established through years of providing private help during shocks, often in a discreet manner given scarce resources and the risk of stoking others' demands. In addition, there is also a collective element of a politician's reputation, given that voters may report to their family and friends about help they receive during times of need.

Within the context of ongoing exchange relationships, citizens screen politicians based on their reputations for fulfilling requests. More specifically, they terminate their relationships with politicians who have tarnished reputations, by refusing to vote for them. Citizens deem such politicians to be untrustworthy types, as they reneged on past promises to provide assistance during adverse shocks. In light of the asymmetric information described earlier, citizens use a politician's reputation for fulfilling requests as a screening device to differentiate between trustworthy and untrustworthy types. In turn, the threat of losing political support induces politicians to fulfill requests of citizens with whom they have ongoing relationships. This form of screening can be understood as an analogue to reputation screening in credit markets, by which some lenders "use the threat of cutting off credit to induce desired borrower behavior ... borrowers want to avoid defaulting on loans because to do so tarnishes their reputation and curtails their access to future loans" (Hoff and Stiglitz, 1990, 240; see also Stiglitz and Weiss, 1983).

This important screening role of requests is observed over the course of long-term clientelist relationships. Requests are common when clients experience adverse shocks, such as unemployment, illness, or drought, which can strike at any moment. During such bouts of acute deprivation, politicians who fulfill their clients' requests provide crucial sustenance and also transmit valuable information about their own credibility. In the absence of shocks, citizens involved in relational clientelism typically refrain from making clientelist requests. A key reason is that politicians have limited resources, so even trustworthy types are constrained in their cumulative responsiveness to each client's demands. Voters thus face intertemporal tradeoffs between clientelist assistance received in the present and in the future. By conserving requests until they experience shocks, citizens heighten the extent to which relational clientelism can mitigate their vulnerability in situations of dire need. However, if citizens in clientelist relationships do not request help for years, they face a countervailing incentive to initiate demands more promptly. Their confidence in politicians' responsiveness gradually erodes, as reputations for fulfilling requests decay over time if no demands are made. For screening purposes, clients in such circumstances are thus motivated to test the continued responsiveness of their politicians, especially at times when they are expected to provide political support. As such, some citizens in ongoing exchange relationships demand small favors during electoral campaigns, even in the absence of adverse shocks.

The screening logic of citizen requests also provides an explanation for an intriguing paradox discussed in Chapter 1. If clientelism is merely a top-down phenomenon involving elite targeting, as most studies suggest, then why do politicians expend scarce resources to target citizens who are already persuaded and mobilized? The present book argues that voting supporters often receive benefits not because they are targeted, but instead because they demand them. As described earlier, politicians who employ relational clientelism face pressure to fulfill clients' requests – during both election and non-election periods – because otherwise these citizens will terminate the relationship and refuse to vote for them. Within the context of relational clientelism, denying supporters' requests tarnishes a politician's reputation, and thereby undermines ongoing exchange relationships that take years to cultivate.

A complementary model that I developed with Michael Peress provides further insight into why clientelist politicians are especially responsive to their own supporters' requests. While the model adopts a distinct focus and different assumptions, its key predictions are consistent with the logic of screening. Unlike the discussion earlier, Nichter and Peress (2016) focus exclusively on campaigns, assume perfect information, and assume without elaboration that citizens vote against politicians who deny their requests. Instead, we examine a two-stage model: citizens first request benefits from a clientelist politician, who then decides which requests to fulfill. Using backward induction, the analysis first evaluates how the politician responds to requests. Given limited resources, fulfilling the cheapest requests secures the most votes. Foreseeing this logic, citizens recognize that the politician will fulfill demands that are sufficiently small. The politician's supporters thereby submit relatively small requests because they are easily placated, whereas opposers are unwilling to vote for the politician unless their larger demands are met. As a consequence, our model predicts that the clientelist politician will predominantly fulfill her own supporters' demands. This key prediction accords with the screening logic elaborated in the present chapter, which provides an underlying explanation for the responsiveness of clientelist politicians to supporters' requests. In addition, Nichter and Peress (2016) predict that politicians fulfill more requests when citizens place greater weight on handouts relative to ideological preferences, which may be especially likely in contexts with substantial vulnerability.[14]

Stepping back, requesting benefits provides another important mechanism by which citizens buttress the stability of relational clientelism. Citizens involved in ongoing exchange relationships are often concerned about the trustworthiness of their politicians' promises to help during adverse shocks. Clients' demands not only solicit crucial sustenance, but also provide valuable information about politicians' responsiveness. Politicians who promise to provide assistance, only to deny requests when adversity strikes, tarnish their own reputations. Clients often sever ties with such politicians and refuse to vote for them. By screening out those with poor track records of fulfilling their requests, citizens alleviate concerns about whether their political patrons will follow through on promises to provide benefits during future shocks.

3.6 SUMMARY

Citizens play a crucial role in the survival of relational clientelism. Unlike vote buying and other forms of electoral clientelism, these ongoing exchange relationships provide contingent benefits that extend beyond campaigns. The remainder of this book expounds on how and why citizens help to sustain relational clientelism, fleshing out and testing the logic and mechanisms distilled in this chapter. To this end, the next three chapters of Part II analyze evidence from Brazil. Chapter 4 examines why vulnerability motivates many Brazilians to undertake actions to fortify their long-term clientelist relationships. Much of the nation's population remains exposed to various adverse shocks, and many local politicians have substantial resources and discretion to smooth these shocks by providing selective benefits to clients. Having established citizens' motivation, Chapter 5 then explores declared support, an important mechanism by which clients in ongoing exchange relationships alleviate concerns about whether their own vote promises are trustworthy. Next, Chapter 6 investigates citizen requests, a key mechanism by which many Brazilians mitigate their own concerns about whether to trust politicians' promises to help during adverse shocks. This important role of citizens in the survival of relational clientelism is by no means limited to Brazil. As shown in Part III, vulnerability is dire across most of the world, and many citizens in various countries engage in both of these mechanisms that bolster ongoing exchange relationships. The book's concluding chapter emphasizes that relational clientelism is an inferior substitute for an adequate welfare state, and underscores that citizens' purposive actions to sustain the phenomenon have important implications for both democracy and development.

---

[14] The model also predicts that clientelist politicians with larger budgets fulfill more requests.

4

Income and Vulnerability

In recent decades, income per capita has increased sharply across the world (Maddison, 2001), and global poverty has fallen substantially (Dollar, 2005). Brazil has similarly experienced impressive income gains and poverty reduction, though these achievements are at times clouded by lackluster economic growth. As discussed in Chapter 1, many scholars view such economic development to be a catalyst for the decline of clientelism. Rising incomes are commonly understood to tarnish the allure of clientelist rewards, not least because a citizen who escapes poverty may be less willing to exchange his or her political preferences for a small payoff. This chapter examines various sources of income gains in Brazil and provides evidence that campaign handouts do indeed become less attractive as livelihoods improve. Unlike the challenges examined in Part I, which predominantly undercut electoral clientelism, rising incomes undermine *both* electoral and relational clientelism.

Despite rising incomes, many voters across the world have a powerful motivation to fortify their long-term clientelist relationships: elites often help their clients cope with vulnerability. In many countries, the state fails to protect residents from various sources of risk, either because social programs are nonexistent, exclude major groups from coverage, or are poorly implemented (ILO, 2015, 73). In the case of Brazil, much of its population remains vulnerable to a multitude of adverse shocks. Although the state has taken considerable strides to address such risks, yawning gaps in public services and social insurance remain. Many families suffer from catastrophic health expenditures, nine of ten Brazilians who lose their jobs receive no unemployment benefits, and many citizens' economic and even physical livelihood is imperiled by recurring droughts. The present chapter documents the insecurity facing many citizens in these three spheres – health care, unemployment and water – to illustrate the broader phenomenon of vulnerability in Brazil. Moreover, it examines why this vulnerability motivates many Brazilians to help sustain relational clientelism: local politicians often have resources and discretion to help their clients smooth shocks through the provision of selective benefits. After exploring this vulnerability, subsequent chapters in Part II investigate two mechanisms – declared support and requesting benefits – by which citizens enhance the survival of clientelist relationships with politicians who mitigate their exposure to various risks.

4.1 RISING INCOMES

Before turning to vulnerability in Brazil, it is important to consider the nation's significant income gains and related consequences for clientelism. Notwithstanding Brazil's severe economic crisis in 2015–2016, broader trends show that its overall population, and especially poor Brazilians, experienced substantial income growth over the past few decades. According to the World Bank, Brazil exhibited faster growth in median income than any other Latin American country between 1990 and 2009 (Ferreira et al., 2013, 101). Most of this growth occurred after Brazil's 2003 recession; incomes did not rise considerably from 1995 to 2003 and even declined in several of those years (IPEA, 2010a, 46). Between 2004 and 2013, the average monthly income of Brazil's economically active population grew from R$846 to R$1,205, even after adjusting for inflation.[1] This 42 percent cumulative increase in real incomes in just nine years corresponds to an annual growth rate of over 4 percent.[2] Brazil experienced uneven growth during this period, with incomes in the relatively poor Northeast region expanding over 57 percent (over 5.1 percent annual growth). In addition, income growth has been especially pronounced for poor Brazilians, the subset of the population most predisposed to accept clientelist offers (as shown later). The average real incomes of the poorest decile of Brazilians far outstripped that of the richest decile, growing at nearly five times the rate and more than doubling between 2001 and 2012.[3] In the words of prominent economist Ricardo Paes de Barros, incomes of the poorest decile of Brazilians grew at a rate rivaling China's, whereas incomes of the richest decile grew at a rate rivaling Germany's.[4] Faster income growth of the poor coincided with falling income inequality: although Brazil remains one of the most unequal countries in the world, its income inequality fell continuously since 1998 to reach a record national low of 0.501 in 2013.[5]

---

[1] In constant 2013 terms, when R$1 = $2.05. PNAD Síntese de Indicadores 2013 (IBGE).
[2] PNAD Síntese de Indicadores 2013 (IBGE).
[3] According to household surveys, the bottom decile grew 120.2 percent, while the top decile grew 26.4 percent. Presentation by Marcelo Neri, Fábio Vaz and Pedro Souza, "O Bolsa Família e a Economia," IPEA, 2013.
[4] "Sobre a Evolução Recente da Pobreza e da Desigualdade," IPEA Presentation, September 2009. Based on PNAD data from 2001–2008.
[5] Lustig et al. (2013, 134–135) and 2013 PNAD, IBGE, Table 7.1.7.

Rising incomes facilitated a dramatic decrease in Brazilian poverty. Brazil has been one of Latin America's leaders in poverty reduction (Barros et al., 2010, 4–5), with an estimated twenty-five million Brazilians exiting moderate or extreme poverty in 1990–2009 (Cord et al., 2015, 77). The nation achieved the key target of the first Millennium Development Goal – halving the extreme poverty rate – nearly a decade early (Barros et al., 2010, 1). According to international poverty lines, moderate poverty fell from 43.0 to 20.8 percent between 1999 and 2012, while extreme poverty fell from 26.0 to 9.6 percent (Cord et al., 2015, 79).[6] While Brazil does not have official poverty lines, measures employed by the government's Brasil Sem Miséria (Brazil without Extreme Poverty) program suggest comparable trends and even lower poverty rates – 9 percent in moderate poverty and 3.6 percent in extreme poverty in 2012 (Cord et al., 2015, 81, 85).[7] Poverty levels had been relatively stagnant for eight years up to Brazil's 2003 recession and then fell sharply thereafter (IPEA, 2010a, 50). Poverty declines continued even during the 2009 global economic crisis (Neri, 2010, 12), though a slight uptick was observed in 2012–2013 (IPEA, 2015, 59). As with income growth, poverty reduction was also uneven. Poverty fell substantially more in the relatively less-developed North and Northeast regions than elsewhere in Brazil (Cord et al., 2015, 80), and urban citizens were up to 50 percent more likely to exit poverty than their rural counterparts (Ferreira et al., 2013, 110).

Much of the world has experienced a tremendous expansion of the middle class in recent years (Ferreira et al., 2013, 145; Ravallion, 2010, 452), and Brazil is no exception. Rising income has catapulted many Brazilians into the middle class, which has the potential to play an important role in curbing clientelism (Fukuyama, 2013, 30; Weitz-Shapiro, 2012). Whereas only about 15 percent of Brazilians were in the middle class in the early 1980s (Ferreira et al., 2013, 144), some prominent analysts contend it now contains the majority of Brazilians. Marcelo Neri estimates that 42.2 million Brazilians entered the "new middle class" between 2003 and 2012, such that its share of the overall population increased from 37.5 to 55.3 percent during this period (Neri, 2014, 29).[8] The middle class is far larger in the South and Southeast regions: three-quarters of citizens there are in the middle class or above, compared to significantly less than half of residents in some North and Northeast states (Neri, 2014, 16). Just as they are more likely to exit poverty, urban residents are also substantially more likely to enter the middle class than those in rural Brazil

---

[6] This ECLAC study employs a common international metric of $4 a day for moderate poverty and $2.50 for extreme poverty (2005 US dollars adjusted for purchasing power parity).
[7] The program established an extreme poverty line of R$70 per month (equal to PPP-adjusted $1.25 per day) and a moderate poverty line of R$140 per month ($2.50 per day) in 2011, with subsequent inflation adjustments.
[8] This class corresponds to "Class C," which had between R$1,126 and R$4,854 from all sources in constant 2010 reais (Neri, 2010, 32, 37). Neri (2014) extends his expansive 2010 analysis through extrapolation of 2003–2009 data.

4.1 Rising Incomes

(Ferreira et al., 2013, 110). All in all, Brazil's middle class is typically viewed as having expanded dramatically in recent years amidst rising incomes.[9]

Overall growth of the economy offers a partial explanation for rising incomes. Although Brazil's economic growth is in many years deemed to be lackluster – often earning the diminutive nickname "*PIBinho*," or "little GDP" – it actually expanded relatively quickly at the start of the twenty-first century. From 2000 to 2014, Brazil's real GDP per capita grew at an annual rate of 2.2 percent, compared to just 0.1 percent growth in the 1980s and 0.8 percent growth in the 1990s (World Development Indicators, 2017).[10] When the 2009 global economic crisis battered much of the world, Brazil emerged relatively unscathed and economic output did not contract for the overall year (Neri, 2010, 15). But in 2015–2016, the nation suffered a severe recession – potentially its worst in over a century.[11] Notwithstanding the recent crisis, Brazil's economic growth over the longer term has contributed to rising incomes. But it by no means provides a complete explanation: as Marcelo Neri emphasizes, household surveys reveal a "complete dissonance" between GDP growth and the income growth experienced by citizens in Brazil.[12] For example, whereas real GDP per capita grew 2.7 percent annually between 2003 and 2012, real income per capita for the median household grew 6.6 percent annually during the same period (Neri, 2014, 19). While household income stems from various sources, examining three of its components – labor income, pensions, and conditional cash transfers – sheds substantial light on why many Brazilians' incomes have risen significantly. As discussed later, these income gains pose an important challenge for all forms of clientelism, but persistent vulnerability motivates many citizens to help sustain long-term clientelist relationships with politicians.

4.1.1 Labor Income

Labor income plays a central role in the sharp income growth experienced by many Brazilians in recent years. Indeed, it grew just as quickly as – and accounted for 76 percent of – household income: whereas income growth was 4.7 percent annually between 2003 and 2009, labor income growth was 4.6 percent (Neri, 2010, 18). Rising employment provides one explanation. For example, the number of formal workers increased from 23.8 million in 1995 to 47.6 in 2012, roughly doubling in seventeen years and representing an annual growth rate of 4.2 percent (Amitrano, 2015, 29). After 2004, the

---

[9] Fukuyama (2013, 28) notes Brazil's middle class expansion is less impressive with an educational definition: only 2 percent of the population is university-educated. For various income definitions of the middle class, see Ferreira et al. (2013, 32).
[10] Compounded annual growth rate based on constant 2010 dollars.
[11] "Para Meirelles, Brasil terá pior recessão desde 1901," *O Globo*, August 3, 2016.
[12] "PNAD Mostra que Brasil Cresceu em Ritmo Chinês, Diz Ministro de Assuntos Estratégicos," *Agência Brasil*, September 27, 2013.

rate of formal job creation approximately doubled its prior rate (Neri, 2010, 16). More broadly, the unemployment rate in metropolitan areas fell to 4.8 percent in 2014, before rising to 6.9 percent in 2015.[13] These rates marked a strong improvement: unemployment had risen in the late 1990s and early 2000s, reaching 13 percent in 2003.[14]

In addition to growing employment, minimum wage increases substantially boosted incomes, especially but not exclusively of the poor. Minimum wage hikes have widespread effects in Brazil because the incomes of 46.7 million Brazilians are directly tied to its level (DIEESE, 2015, 5). Across the nation, 28.6 percent of workers receive the minimum wage or less, a figure ranging from 16.9 percent in the South to 54.4 percent in the Northeast (DIEESE, 2015, 8). For many years, Brazil's minimum wage had failed to keep up with inflation; for example, its real monthly value fell from R$361 to below R$131 between July 1982 and August 1991 (IPEA, 2009, 54).[15] But under legislation introduced during Luiz Inácio Lula da Silva's presidencies, the minimum wage now increases automatically each year to adjust for inflation as well as GDP growth. As a consequence, the minimum wage has since increased substantially more than inflation in recent years, heightening income growth. Between 2002 and 2015, the nominal minimum wage nearly quadrupled from R$200 to R$788 per month, which represents a cumulative increase of 76.5 percent when adjusting for inflation (DIEESE, 2015, 2–3). In fact, Brazil's Central Bank reported that the purchasing power of the minimum wage in 2015 – R$788 per month – exceeded that of any time since 1965.[16] All in all, both minimum wage hikes and higher employment boosted labor income, which in turn propelled overall income growth.

While labor income comprises over three-quarters of household income, government transfers are also important, as approximately 45 percent of Brazilians live in households with transfer income (Barros et al., 2010, 16). Two types of transfers that played an especially important role in income growth are now considered: pensions and conditional cash transfers.

4.1.2 Pensions

Along with labor income, pensions have also been an important source of rising income in Brazil, with increased benefits as well as expanded coverage. A first key point is that minimum wage increases did not just raise the floor on wages for unskilled labor – they also ratcheted up pensions for many

---

[13] Pesquisa Mensal de Emprego (IBGE), June 2015. All unemployment figures for June and reflect six major cities.
[14] Pesquisa Mensal de Emprego (IBGE), June 2015; "Taxa de Desemprego Cai para 5.4% na Média de 2013, Menor da História," *Estado de São Paulo*, January 30, 2014.
[15] Values in constant 2008 reais. Brazil's minimum wage is defined in terms of a monthly salary.
[16] "Poder de Compra do Salário Mínimo é o Maior Desde 1965, Diz Banco Central," *O Globo*, February 2, 2015.

4.1 Rising Incomes

Brazilians (Barros et al., 2010, 33). As enshrined in the 1988 Constitution, nearly all public pension benefits meet or exceed the minimum wage; by means of comparison, two-thirds of pension benefits fell below the minimum wage in 1987 (IPEA, 2009, 74). When the minimum wage rose from R$724 to R$788 in January 2015, the incomes of nearly twenty-two million pension beneficiaries grew in lockstep (DIEESE, 2015, 5). And the impact of such increases often extends beyond the elderly, because many Brazilians live in multigenerational households. Amongst the poorest quintile of Brazilians, 85 percent of citizens aged 60 years or older live with family members other than a spouse (OECD, 2014, 24). Given the prevalence of multigenerational households, 31 percent of all Brazilians live in families with pension income (Medeiros and de Souza, 2013, 14).

Not just increased benefits, but also expanding coverage of pensions contributed to rising income in Brazil. In recent years, social pensions – for which benefits are not conditional on making contributions – have proliferated in Latin America and elsewhere, and Brazil is no exception (OECD, 2014, 28). As with most countries in the region, Brazil's pensions and other forms of social insurance had long followed a Bismarckian approach, privileging formal-sector employees while providing relatively scant coverage to informal and rural workers (Haggard and Kaufman, 2008, 4; Weyland, 1996, 131–136). The 1988 Constitution ameliorated this problem by universalizing pension benefits, as well as undertaking actions such as doubling rural pensions, ensuring pensions would not fall below the minimum wage, and indexing pensions to inflation (Matijascic and Kay, 2008, 286). Later reforms also helped to lower inequities (Brooks, 2009, 144). Brazil now has amongst the widest coverage and most generous benefits of social pensions in Latin America (OECD, 2014, 10, 31). As a result, poverty rates of the elderly are only a fraction of those for other Brazilians (OECD, 2014, 25–26). The non-contributory nature of social pensions is particularly important for universalizing coverage – and thereby increasing incomes of the poor – because many Brazilians cannot afford to make consistent contributions (Weyland, 1996, 136). Recent surveys show that 68 percent of informal workers contribute to neither public nor private pension plans, and the top reason provided is by far insufficient income to pay contributions (SIPS, 2011d, 24–25).

The key component of social pensions in Brazil is Benefício de Prestação Continuada (BPC, or Continued Payment Benefits), which provides a monthly cash benefit equivalent to the minimum wage. Brazilians at least sixty-five years old, as well as disabled citizens of any age, are eligible to receive BPC if their monthly household income per capita is less than one-fourth the minimum wage. As of June 2015, BPC provided R$786 each month to 4.2 million citizens, of which 1.9 million were elderly and 2.3 million were disabled.[17]

---

[17] Data from Ministério do Desenvolvimento Social: http://mds.gov.br/assuntos/assistencia-social/beneficios-assistenciais/bpc.

This coverage is far less than that of Bolsa Família, a program discussed next, but BPC's benefits are substantially more generous: among recipient households, the per capita value of BPC payments was R$107 in 2007, over six times the per capita value of Bolsa Família payments (Barros et al., 2010, 17). The income provided by BPC, as well as contributory rural pensions, play a key role in reducing poverty (Matijascic, 2015, 16). Overall, the primary takeaway is that the expanded scope and increased benefits of pensions have contributed significantly to rising income in Brazil, which as discussed later presents a challenge for clientelism.

4.1.3 Conditional Cash Transfers

Bolsa Família, Brazil's conditional cash transfer (CCT) program, has also substantially increased incomes of the poor. In the mid-1990s, Brazil and Mexico pioneered CCTs, which distribute money to poor families that undertake designated actions such as sending their children to school and medical appointments. By 2014, sixty-four nations across the globe had implemented CCT programs, including nearly every nation in Latin America (World Bank, 2015, 10).[18] Bolsa Família is currently the second-largest CCT in the world, trailing only India in terms of beneficiaries (World Bank, 2015, 12). As of May 2015, Bolsa Família provided benefits to about a quarter of Brazil's population: 13.7 million families, or about 47.7 million citizens.[19] The program was formed in October 2003 during Lula's first presidency, integrating four existing cash transfer programs: Bolsa Escola (a CCT for education), Bolsa Alimentação (a CCT for health and nutrition), Cartão Alimentação (a CCT for food consumption), and Auxilio Gás (compensation for removed cooking gas subsidies).

Bolsa Família provides a modest but important source of income for many lower-income citizens. It provides a monthly base stipend of R$77 – regardless of whether they have children – to extremely poor families (i.e., those with monthly incomes up to R$77 per capita). In addition, Bolsa Família provides variable benefits to families in both moderate and extreme poverty (i.e., those with monthly incomes up to R$154 per capita). Within specified limits, families receive R$35 monthly for each child fifteen years or younger, an extra R$35 monthly for pregnant mothers and infants, and R$42 monthly for each child sixteen or seventeen years old.[20] When considering all of these benefits, the average monthly Bolsa Família benefit per recipient household was R$168 in May 2015, just over one-fifth of the minimum wage. In addition to this

---

[18] See also a map of CCTs at devex.com.
[19] Calculations based on World Bank (2015, 14), using the average household size of 3.47 and population estimates from IBGE. See also "Bolsa Família tem Menor Número de Beneficiários dos Últimos Dois Anos," *Veja*, June 2, 2015.
[20] In part to avoid stimulating increased fertility, families can receive only up to five of these R$35 variable benefits and two of these R$42 variable benefits.

4.1 Rising Incomes

payment, the Brasil Carinhoso program has delivered supplementary funds to extremely poor families since 2012. This program supplements Bolsa Família to ensure that the overall per capita income of beneficiaries exceeds the extreme poverty line. As of December 2014, 5.3 million families received an average supplement of R$89 to their Bolsa Família benefit.

Benefit payments in the Bolsa Família program are directed towards women, who comprise 93 percent of account holders (Campello and Neri, 2013, 18). Families must comply with education and health conditionalities to continue receiving payments. With regards to education, children aged six to fifteen must achieve at least 85 percent school attendance, while sixteen- and seventeen-year-olds must achieve 75 percent attendance. With regards to health, for example, children up to age six must receive vaccinations and checkups, while mothers must receive pre- and post-natal medical attention. Fiszbein and Schady (2009) indicate that although Bolsa Família has relatively frequent monitoring, its noncompliance penalties are "light" when compared to other countries with CCTs.

Careful design of the Bolsa Família program enables it to boost incomes of poor Brazilians with relative insulation from clientelist influence. Safeguards restricting municipal discretion are integral to the design. The Ministry of Social Development and the Fight against Hunger (Ministério do Desenvolvimento Social e Combate á Fome, or MDS) – a federal agency – established quotas for the maximum number of families per municipality that could receive benefits, using poverty estimates from household survey data. Municipalities interview potential beneficiaries and input data into a national registry (Cadastro Único), which the MDS uses to calculate self-declared income and select eligible households. Although beneficiary selection thus occurs at the federal level, some analysts contend local registration involves the largest influence over who obtains program benefits (cf. Barrientos, 2013, 139).[21] Evidence occasionally surfaces about clientelist manipulation of the Bolsa Família program, but such abuse is not systematic.[22] A survey by Sugiyama and Hunter (2013, 50) finds that only 14.9 percent of respondents believe Bolsa Família is used for vote buying.[23] During my interviews in Bahia, some politicians and citizens provided examples of how local officials could manipulate the program, such as intentionally neglecting to input opposition voters' data into the Cadastro

---

[21] As an example of this influence, Frey (2017) suggests that mayors eligible for reelection are more likely to allow the poor to underreport their income so as to be eligible for the program.

[22] Examples include a *Folha de São Paulo* investigation into its use for vote buying during the 2008 municipal elections (Sugiyama and Hunter, 2013, 47), and a 2015 investigation by the Federal Police into a federal deputy and a state deputy who allegedly used Bolsa Família and other benefits for vote buying. See "PF Pede a Procurador Investigação de Crime Eleitoral Contra Deputados," *Hoje em Dia*, April 2, 2015.

[23] The survey of 1,100 respondents in three municipalities in Northeast Brazil was not representative of the overall population, as it employed quota sampling to ensure 80 percent of respondents were Bolsa Família recipients.

Único, or pressuring teachers and health officials to avoid reporting supporters' noncompliance with conditionalities. Nevertheless, compared to other programs in which municipal officials have far greater discretion, Bolsa Família is relatively robust against clientelism. More broadly, most analysts agree with Borges's (2007, 133) conclusion that the program "cannot be considered an instance of clientelism, for the selection of beneficiaries is based on universalistic criteria."

Bolsa Família is globally recognized as improving the standard of living of many Brazilians. For instance, the International Social Security Association granted Brazil its 2013 ISSA Award for Outstanding Achievement in Social Security, given every three years.[24] Bolsa Família is one of the better targeted CCTs in the world, with 55 percent of benefits received by the poorest quintile of Brazilians (World Bank, 2015, 50). Although the program accounted for less than a percent of household income across the overall population, it comprised 60.9 percent of household income of the extreme poor in 2011, as well as 17.6 percent of household income of the poor (de Souza and Osorio, 2013, 145). Extreme poverty would be substantially greater in Brazil without Bolsa Família: over a quarter of the nation's reduction in extreme poverty between 2008 and 2012 can be attributed to the program.[25] Moreover, it was responsible for approximately 15 percent of Brazil's substantial decline in income inequality between 1999 and 2009 (Soares et al., 2010b, 49).

More broadly, labor income, pensions and conditional cash transfers have all contributed substantially to the impressive income growth experienced by poor Brazilians. As the next section examines, higher income reduces citizens' propensity to exchange their vote choices for clientelist payoffs. Despite rising incomes, however, the remainder of this chapter argues that many Brazilians continue to be highly vulnerable to risks such as illness, unemployment, and drought. This vulnerability motivates many citizens to sustain ongoing patterns of relational clientelism as a risk-coping mechanism.

4.2 INCOME AND CLIENTELISM

What is the impact of rising incomes on clientelism in Brazil? The link between income and clientelism has captivated the attention of generations of researchers. As discussed in Chapter 1, poor citizens are often viewed as more responsive to contingent benefits, and many scholars view economic development as a catalyst for the decline of clientelism. One reason is that the diminishing marginal utility of income suggests poor citizens place relatively greater value on material benefits than ideological preferences (Dixit and Londregan, 1996, 1114; Stokes, 2005, 315). In addition, risk aversion and time preferences

---

[24] See www.issa.int/-/issa-award-presented-to-brazil-during-world-forum.
[25] Marcelo Neri, Fabio Vaz and Pedro de Souza, "O Bolsa Família e a Economia," IPEA Presentation, 2013.

4.2 Income and Clientelism

are other frequently cited reasons why poor citizens may be most prone to clientelism.[26] To what extent has income growth in Brazil diminished citizens' willingness to accept rewards in exchange for their vote choices? Although a direct test is unavailable, this section gains purchase on this question in two ways: (1) examining attitudes and behaviors across income levels; and (2) analyzing how rainfall shocks – an exogenous source of variation in agricultural income – affect rural citizens' willingness to exchange votes for rewards.

Consistent with theoretical predictions and empirical evidence from many other countries, poor Brazilians are more willing accept clientelist handouts in exchange for vote choices than their wealthier counterparts. This pattern is observed in citizens' answers about hypothetical scenarios as well as responses about actual clientelist experiences. First, consider two national surveys that inquired about vote buying. Both the 2002 Brazilian Electoral Study (ESEB) and the 2007 LAPOP AmericasBarometer survey included identical questions involving hypothetical citizens with unmet needs who received offers of various material benefits from a candidate.[27] To gain insight on respondents' willingness to exchange votes for handouts, of particular interest are their beliefs about what the hypothetical citizens "should do" when offered benefits.[28] The survey provided respondents just two answer choices: (1) the citizen should accept the benefit and vote for the candidate, or (2) the citizen should reject the benefit and vote for another candidate.[29] Such hypothetical questions are advantageous because they can be asked of everyone rather than just citizens receiving offers, but they raise important concerns about whether answers correspond to how respondents would act if faced with similar situations. Notwithstanding this caveat, insights can be drawn from the systematic variation in answers across income levels of respondents. As shown in Figure 4.1, poorer respondents are disproportionately likely to answer that the citizen should accept the benefit and vote for the candidate who offered it. This difference is observed in both years and in scenarios involving urgent needs – such as a medical treatment for a sick child – as well as with all other benefits offered such as bricks or a child's bicycle.[30] Moreover, the percentage of respondents sharing this view

---

[26] As mentioned in Chapter 1, for a discussion about the role of risk aversion, see Desposato (2007, 104) and Stokes et al. (2013, 163–164). For poor citizens' preference for immediate benefits, see Scott (1969, 1150) and Kitschelt and Wilkinson (2007, 3).

[27] The LAPOP survey included 1,214 urban and rural respondents. It used a national probability design, stratified by region with 122 sampling units.

[28] The survey also asked separate questions about what respondents thought hypothetical citizens "would do," but this formulation is suboptimal to test respondents' propensity for clientelism. With that question, similar patterns across income are observed, but findings are less robust.

[29] The survey did not allow respondents to take the benefit and vote for another candidate; citizens who insisted on such answers would be coded as "no response" (NR). Among questions analyzed here, the highest non-response rate was 6 percent.

[30] The wording of each scenario varied, but most mentioned that the offer recipient was poor or otherwise needed the benefit. Such framing in part explains the relatively high affirmative responses across all income categories.

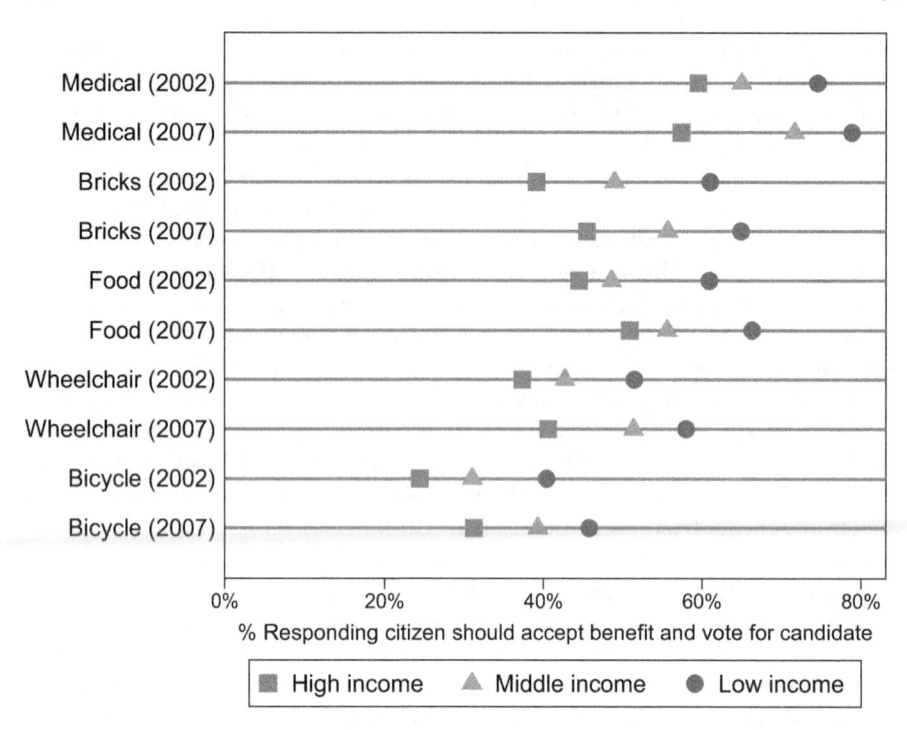

FIGURE 4.1 Acceptability of hypothetical clientelist offers (2002 and 2007)
Note: Respondents asked what a hypothetical citizen "should do" when offered the benefits listed on the vertical axis, providing two options: (1) accept the benefit and vote for the candidate, or (2) reject the benefit and vote for another candidate. Number of observations is 2,178 in 2002 and 1,134 in 2007. Income based on ordinal ranges of total household income provided in 2007 survey, categorized as follows: "Low Income" is up to R$520, "Middle Income" is R$520.01–R$1,300, and "High Income" is R$1,300.01 and above. Identical ranges are applied to 2002 survey, deflating for inflation using IPCA index. Findings are robust to alternative income specifications.
Source: Author's analysis using data from the 2002 Brazilian Electoral Study (ESEB) and 2007 LAPOP AmericasBarometer survey.

declines monotonically as income rises. Although we must be careful not to assume that all citizens will act as their hypothetical responses suggest, these systematic differences seem to indicate that poor Brazilians are less resistant to delivering vote choices in exchange for material benefits. Unlike the longer-term decline in electoral clientelism documented in Chapter 2, Figure 4.1 does not indicate a decline in the perceived acceptability of clientelist offers between 2002 and 2007. However, more recent hypothetical scenarios in the 2014 Brazilian Electoral Panel Study provide some evidence of a reduction in perceived acceptability, in addition to similar heterogeneity across income.[31]

[31] The 2014 survey includes two hypothetical questions worded identically to the earlier surveys, but an extra answer choice limits comparability. Overall responses for medical/bricks: should

4.2 Income and Clientelism

In order to examine actual behavior, consider nationally representative data from the 2010 Brazilian Electoral Panel Study (Ames et al., 2013). Citizens who reported receiving vote-buying offers during recent elections were asked whether their latest offer increased or decreased their inclination to vote for the politician or party who offered the benefit. Clientelist offers were apparently not very effective: only 18 percent indicated they were more inclined to vote for the politician, whereas 44 percent indicated they were less inclined and 38 percent remained the same. One might suspect that this question evokes social desirability bias, but unless the extent of such bias differs systematically and substantially across income levels, it is nevertheless informative to investigate whether poor citizens responded differently than others. And indeed they did. The poorest Brazilians, whose families earned no more than one minimum salary per month, were nearly twice as likely as other respondents to report an increased inclination to vote for the reward offerer (29 versus 15 percent).[32] By contrast, the poorest respondents were also far less likely than others to report a disinclination to vote for the candidate or party that offered the benefit (31 versus 48 percent). This association between income and reported responsiveness to rewards is statistically significant (at the 5 percent level) when controlling for various political and socioeconomic characteristics and state-level fixed effects.[33] Overall, this nationally representative survey suggests that the poor are indeed more responsive to vote-buying offers in Brazil.

Although such evidence suggests that poor Brazilians are more responsive to vote-buying offers, how do *changes* in their incomes affect this responsiveness? In my joint work with Gustavo Bobonis, Paul Gertler, and Marco Gonzalez-Navarro (2018), we tackle this question by investigating the impact of rainfall shocks on rural citizens' willingness to accept vote-buying offers. Rainfall is frequently used as a source of exogenous variation in income in rural or agricultural settings (e.g., Miguel et al., 2004; Paxson, 1992), including in my prior work on rural Brazil (Hidalgo et al., 2010). In the present analysis, the Rural Clientelism Survey and rainfall data are used to compare responses from citizens in municipalities with above- versus below-median rainfall during

---

accept and vote for the candidate (27.7/22.8 percent); reject and vote for another candidate (41.8/53.6 percent); should accept and vote for another candidate (30.5/23.6 percent).

[32] The inclination question was answered by 374 citizens in the sample who received offers; of these, 90 had household income below one minimum salary, which corresponded to R$510 per month in 2010. A dichotomous scale is used here due to the small sample size of offer recipients. Similar patterns are observed when examining the data more granularly.

[33] Analysis of offer recipients employs an ordered logit regression controlling for income, education, age, gender, rural location, party preference (PT, PMDB, PSDB, and DEM dummy variables), and prior turnout (not shown). Dependent variable coded as 0 if disinclined, 1 if no effect, and 2 if inclined. Coefficient on income (an 11-point scale) is negative with a p-value of 0.035. Results also hold using separate logit analyses, with or without the inclusion of state fixed effects. With the dependent variable coded as 1 if inclined (0 otherwise), income is negative with a p-value of 0.011. With the dependent variable coded as 1 if disinclined (0 otherwise), income is positive with a p-value of 0.095.

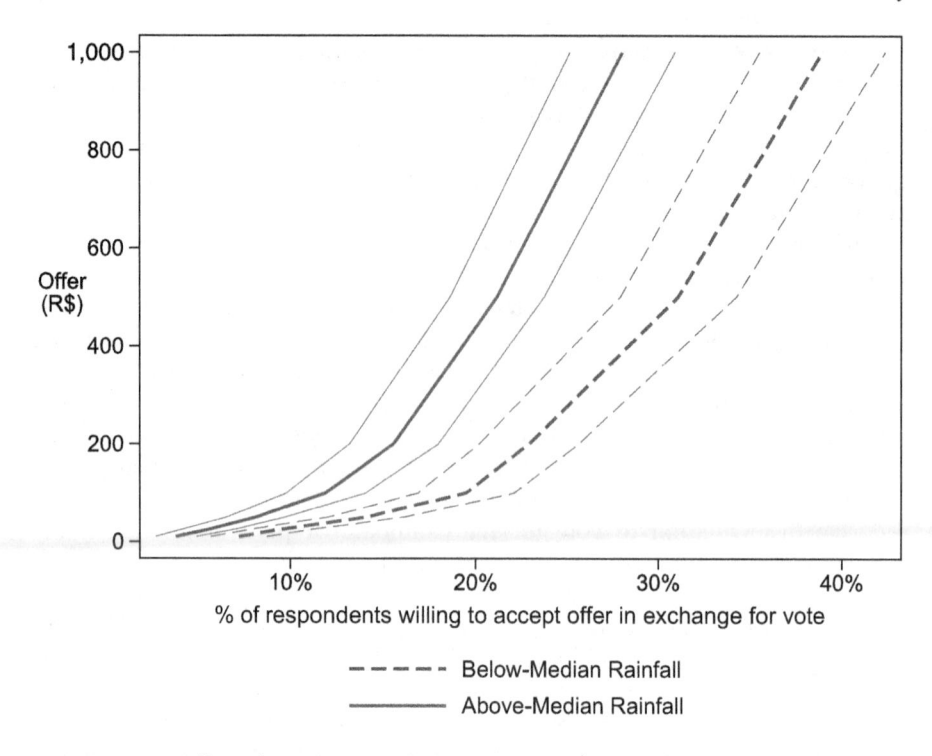

FIGURE 4.2 Effect of rainfall on willingness to accept clientelist offers (2012)
Note: Figure shows percentage of respondents willing to accept hypothetical offers of specific amounts in exchange for their votes, comparing municipalities with below- versus above-median standardized rainfall during the 2012 campaign. Respondents were asked after the 2012 campaign if they would accept offers of increasing amounts until answering affirmatively, or reaching the maximum offer of R$1,000. The center dashed (solid) line shows results for citizens in municipalities with below-median (above-median) standardized rainfall during campaign. The outer dashed (solid) lines represent 95 percent confidence intervals. For each municipality, standardized rainfall for 2012 campaign sums the standardized rainfall for July, August and September 2012. Each month's 2012 rainfall was de-meaned and then divided by the historical standard deviation of rainfall for that month in 1986–2011.
Source: Analysis by Bobonis, Gertler, Gonzalez-Navarro and Nichter (2018). Data from the Rural Clientelism Survey and the Climate Hazards Group Infrared Precipitation with Station (CHIRPS) database.

the 2012 municipal campaign. Given climactic variation in Brazil, it is inappropriate to compare municipalities using raw rainfall levels. Instead, as is common in the literature, comparisons use a standardized measure that adjusts for the average and standard deviation of rainfall in the municipality over the last quarter century (1986–2011).[34] Figure 4.2 shows that citizens in the twenty municipalities experiencing above-median standardized rainfall

[34] Caption for Figure 4.2 provides details about standardization.

4.2 Income and Clientelism

were less willing to accept vote-buying offers than citizens in the twenty municipalities with below-median standardized rainfall (significant at the 1 percent level). These supply curves of citizens willing to accept offers are based on questions in the Rural Clientelism Survey. Respondents were presented numerous hypothetical reward amounts and asked in each instance if they would accept the vote-buying offer from a fictitious candidate. We began with an offer of R$10 and progressively increased the amount up to R$1,000, stopping whenever the citizen indicated acceptance of an offer. Across all respondents, 5.4 percent would accept an offer of R$10, 11.2 percent would accept R$50 or below, 15.7 percent would accept R$100 or below, 26.2 percent would accept R$500 or below, and 33.1 percent would accept R$1,000 or below.[35] In addition, a fifth of respondents indicated there was an unspecified higher amount they would accept, while nearly two-fifths insisted their votes could not be bought for any price.

The differences in citizens' willingness to accept vote-buying offers across rainfall level – shown in Figure 4.2 – are particularly important because they help to corroborate the standard argument in the literature that income growth reduces citizens' propensity towards clientelism. In municipalities with above-median standardized rainfall, only 3.7 percent of citizens would accept the R$10 offer (versus 7.1 percent in below-median municipalities), 11.9 percent would accept R$100 or below (versus 19.5 percent in below-median municipalities), and 21.2 percent would accept R$500 or below (versus 31.1 percent in below-median municipalities).[36] These differences are statistically significant (at the 1 percent level), but a few caveats are in order. First, rainfall shocks involve transitory income, so effects may differ from income growth perceived to be more permanent. Second, there may be a channel other than income by which increased rainfall decreases citizens' willingness to accept vote-buying offers. Third, questions refer to vote buying, so income effects could differ when examining other forms of clientelism. And fourth, these findings only examine citizens' acceptance of *hypothetical* offers, rather than actual experiences with clientelism. But this last point also confers an advantage, because examining actual experiences would make it harder to disentangle the impact of income growth on citizens' acceptance of offers from its impact on politicians' provision of offers.

Stepping back, while the evidence presented thus far is by no means dispositive, it suggests that rising incomes in Brazil are likely to have undermined citizens' willingness to accept payoffs in exchange for their votes. Brazilians with higher incomes are less likely to view clientelist exchanges as acceptable and less frequently vote for candidates who offered them benefits. Moreover,

---

[35] As of January 2014, currency conversions were: R$10 ($4); R$50 ($21); R$100 ($42); R$500 ($212); and R$1,000 ($424). Figure 4.2 also shows data for additional offers of R$25 and R$200.

[36] Differences between municipalities with above- and below-median standardized rainfall are statistically significant at the 1 percent level for these and all other offer amounts.

the rainfall analysis suggests that positive income shocks reduced citizens' willingness to accept vote-buying offers. Taken together, these findings suggest that a familiar argument from the clientelism literature applies to Brazil: rising incomes pose a challenge for clientelism.

4.3 VULNERABILITY

Given these effects of rising incomes – as well as the monumental institutional and legal challenges faced by electoral clientelism in Part I – one might be tempted to conclude that Brazil is an unpropitious environment for all forms of clientelism. But another crucial factor spurs many citizens to undertake purposive actions to help sustain ongoing exchange relationships. Despite rising incomes, many citizens remain highly vulnerable to risks such as unemployment, illness, and drought. Notwithstanding state efforts to improve the nation's inadequate social safety net, many Brazilians experience profound insecurity in their lives. Although self-insurance remains unaffordable to most of the population, evidence in this book suggests that many local politicians have discretionary control over resources that can be used in a contingent manner to help clients cope with adverse shocks. Vulnerability thus provides a key motivation for citizens to undertake actions to help sustain clientelist relationships with politicians through mechanisms elaborated in Chapter 3. To be precise, the present book conceptualizes vulnerability as encompassing *both* poverty and risk, because both low average income and high uncertainty can reduce a citizen's welfare (Ligon and Schechter, 2003).[37] Even though the first component of vulnerability (poverty) has declined markedly in Brazil, this section shows that the second component of vulnerability (risk) continues to afflict much of the nation's population.

To explore vulnerability in Brazil, one of the nation's leading government research institutions – the Institute for Applied Economic Research (Instituto de Pesquisa Econômica Aplicada, or IPEA) – launched an "Index of Social Vulnerability" in 2015.[38] It suggests that vulnerability persists across much of the country, despite improvements since 2000. And vulnerability is "very high" in much of the North and Northeast regions, particularly in the states of Acre, Alagoas, Amapá, Amazonas, Maranhão, Pará, Pernambuco, Rondônia, and parts of Bahia (IPEA, 2015, 24). Brazil's problem of continued vulnerability in spite of poverty reduction is mirrored across much of the world (Birdsall et al.,

---

[37] For a more extensive definition and formal analyses of vulnerability, see Ligon and Schechter (2003). Alternative conceptualizations of vulnerability abound; for example, see Alwang et al. (2001), De León (2006), Miller et al. (2010), and Tesliuc and Lindert (2002).
[38] According to IPEA (2015, 13–16), it is calculated at the municipal level, based on sixteen indicators in three subcategories: urban infrastructure (e.g., water and sanitation), human capital (e.g., mortality and education), and income and work (e.g., insufficient income and unemployment).

4.3 Vulnerability

2014; Ravallion, 2010, 452), leading the *Financial Times* to call 40 percent of world's population "The Fragile Middle."[39] Similarly, the World Bank estimates that 38 percent of Latin Americans are part of the "vulnerable class," earning between $4 and $10 per person a day (Ferreira et al., 2013, xi–3, 37). And although approximately 40 percent of Latin American households advanced in terms of socioeconomic class between 1995 and 2010, most of the poor in Brazil and in the overall region entered the vulnerable class, not the middle class (Ferreira et al., 2013, xi, 5; Vakis et al., 2015, 7).[40]

One key dimension of vulnerability is the probability that a household will reenter poverty in a given time period (e.g., Ferreira et al., 2013, 2; Barrientos, 2013, 13), though the problem encompasses far more than income swings. Even with this restrictive measure, the vulnerability of many Brazilians is striking: Soares et al. (2010c, 12) report that 46 percent of Brazilians who exited poverty reentered it the very next month. This dynamic nature of poverty is a major reason why Bolsa Família fails to reach 20 percent of Brazilians in extreme poverty (Campello and Neri, 2013, 173); many citizens are ineligible during beneficiary selection but fall into poverty before subsequent surveys (Soares et al., 2010c, 11). In addition, citizens already mired in poverty tend to be vulnerable to a wide range of shocks. While poverty rates have fallen in Brazil, they remain stubbornly high in certain pockets of the country. For example, 40 percent of citizens in the Northeast state of Ceará have been poor their entire lives, compared to just 5 percent of citizens in the southern state of Santa Catarina (Vakis et al., 2015, 13). As further evidence of this concentration of poverty, consider that 64.9 percent of all Brazilians in extreme poverty – and 50.7 percent of all Brazilians in moderate poverty – live in small municipalities in the North and Northeast regions, even though just one-fifth of Brazilians live in such municipalities (de Souza and Osorio, 2013, 144).

While the problem of vulnerability is widely recognized in Brazil, efforts to tackle its sources have typically fallen short. Despite impressive efforts by Brazil's government to expand social insurance programs, including those described in the present chapter, many citizens remain exposed to significant uninsured risk. And even when targeted programs alleviate risks borne by the poor, the modestly higher income level of the "vulnerable class" often renders its members ineligible for assistance (Ferreira et al., 2013, 12–13). In Brazil, members of the vulnerable class (i.e., with daily income of $4–$10 per capita) receive less government transfers than their counterparts who are poor or in the middle class (Ferreira et al., 2013, 173).[41] Exacerbating this vulnerability, the majority of Brazilians lack the financial wherewithal to self-insure.

---

[39] "The Fragile Middle: Millions Face Poverty as Emerging Economies Slow," *Financial Times*, April 13, 2014.
[40] Middle class is defined as earning above $10 and up to $50 per person a day (2005 US$ PPP).
[41] Poor is defined as earning below $4 per person a day; middle class as above $10 but no more than $50 per person a day (2005 US$ PPP).

Income and Vulnerability

To shed light on the substantial vulnerability confronting many Brazilians, I now turn to three specific spheres of insecurity: health care, employment, and water. In the Rural Clientelism Survey in Northeast Brazil, these three issues were identified as the most pressing issues; in nationally representative surveys, health care and employment (but not water) are also amongst the top issues mentioned.[42] Evidence suggests that despite considerable efforts to improve Brazil's public services with regards to each issue, many citizens continue to face debilitating risks to their livelihood. Moreover, municipalities have considerable resources and discretion to address each issue, providing local politicians the opportunity to mitigate some citizens' vulnerability through relational clientelism.

4.3.1 Health Care

Over the past few decades, Brazil achieved remarkable progress in expanding access to health care. Until the 1980s, many Brazilians suffered from exclusion because the public health care system focused on a narrow share of the population: formal urban workers making social security contributions (IPEA, 2009, 60). Progressive medical reformers, members of what is known as the "sanitary movement," worked fervently to ensure the 1988 Constitution universalized the public health care system, thereby expanding medical care for broad swathes of the population including informal workers and the rural poor (Weyland, 1996, chap. 7). Wider coverage contributed to marked improvement in various indicators; for example, infant mortality fell sharply from 77.2 to 13.5 deaths per thousand births between 1980 and 2016.[43] Meanwhile, the Brazilian government's expenditure on health care increased markedly, growing roughly fivefold from $107 to $512 per capita between 2000 and 2012.[44]

Notwithstanding this considerable progress, inadequate health care continues to contribute to the vulnerability of many Brazilians. Even after this fivefold increase, public health care expenditures still lagged the world average ($615 per capita) and reached only a fifth of the developed-country average ($2,800 per capita).[45] In a nationally representative survey in 2013, respondents by far mentioned health care the most when asked to choose three pressing problems at the municipal level.[46] Health care was similarly chosen as the top issue

---

[42] In the 2012 wave of the Rural Clientelism Survey, 43 percent identified water, 31 percent health care, and 11 percent employment. In 2013, health care was more important than water. In the nationally representative 2010 Brazil Electoral Panel Study, health care and unemployment were mentioned second- and third-most often as "the most serious problem the country is facing" (behind violence); water was mentioned far less often (Ames et al., 2013).

[43] "World Development Indicators," World Bank, 2017.

[44] "Gasto Público do Brasil com Saúde é Inferior à Média Mundial," *Estado de São Paulo*, May 13, 2015.

[45] "Gasto Público do Brasil com Saúde é Inferior à Média Mundial," *Estado de São Paulo*, May 13, 2015. All figures are for 2012.

[46] Survey of 7,686 individuals in 434 municipalities by Confederação Nacional da Indústria and IBOPE. Respondents chose three from nineteen options. Top responses were health care

4.3 Vulnerability

at the state and federal level, and 87 percent of the survey's respondents rated the quality of health clinics and hospitals as "low" or "very low." Although the 1988 Constitution guarantees comprehensive health care, reality falls quite short of this objective. According to surveys of users of Brazil's public health system (commonly known as SUS for Sistema Único de Saúde, or Unified Health System), crucial areas for improvement include adding doctors, providing specialized consultations more quickly, increasing the types of medicines distributed freely, and ensuring availability of free medicines (SIPS, 2011, 88–93).

Such problems help explain why even with ostensibly universal and comprehensive public health care, 52.5 percent of Brazil's health expenditures are private (i.e., either from private insurers or out of pocket).[47] Underscoring the extent of vulnerability, the poorest quintile of Brazilians is over seven times as likely to experience catastrophic health spending as the richest quintile (Barros et al., 2011, 257). Whereas poor Brazilians spend the majority of their health care expenditures on medicine, wealthier citizens devote most of their health care expenditures to paying for private health plans, which enable them to complement or circumvent the inadequate public system (Garcia et al., 2013, 118–123). A quarter of all Brazilians enroll in private health plans (TCU, 2014, 103), even though the public health system is free. Citizens' use of this mechanism to mitigate vulnerability is geographically uneven: 38 percent of the population in the wealthier Southeast region enrolls in private health plans, versus just 12 percent in the poorer Northeast region (TCU, 2014, 44). Surveys suggest the top reason for using private health plans is the ability to get medical consultations and exams more quickly (SIPS, 2011, 96), and data show that medical staffing is much greater in the private sector (TCU, 2014, 38). A recent study draws a stark contrast between public and private health care in Brazil when evaluating the per capita availability of computerized tomography (CT) and magnetic resonance imaging (MRI) machines in twenty-nine countries. Brazil's private health plans exhibited more availability of this technology than Germany, the United States, and all other countries except Japan and Australia. By contrast, Brazil's public health care system had worse availability than all countries except Mexico.[48]

Some citizens are particularly underserved by public health care in Brazil, heightening their vulnerability to illness. The country exhibits stark regional inequalities in both health care outcomes and services. While some states' health indicators compare favorably to much of the developed world, other

---

(59 percent), public security (43 percent) and education (32 percent). As mentioned, respondents of the 2010 Brazilian Electoral Panel Study chose health care as the second-most important problem facing the *country*.

[47] "Gasto Público do Brasil com Saúde é Inferior à Média Mundial," *Estado de São Paulo*, May 13, 2015.

[48] "Exames de Alta Complexidade são para Poucos no Brasil," *Veja*, November 19, 2010. See also Matijascic (2015, 19).

states' indicators are more comparable to Africa (TCU, 2014, 15). A child born in the relatively poor Northeast states of Bahia or Piauí is nearly twice as likely to perish as one born in the wealthier southern states of Rio Grande do Sul or Santa Catarina.[49] Similar contrasts emerge when considering the number of doctors per capita, which tripled across Brazil between 1970 and 2010, but continues to be about double in wealthier regions than in poorer regions (CFM, 2013, 35–36).[50] Partly as a consequence, whereas the average Brazilian received 4.0 medical consultations in 2010, the average resident of the North and Northeast regions obtained access to only 2.5 and 2.7 consultations, respectively (TCU, 2014, 31).

Gaps in health care, and thus vulnerability to illness, also tend to be worse in the countryside. In 2009, 7.7 percent of Brazilian municipalities lacked even a single doctor in residence providing public health care (Matijascic, 2015, 16). For every thousand citizens, state capitals have on average 4.6 doctors, compared to just 1.1 doctors for all other municipalities (TCU, 2014, 37). The same metric is even more disturbing outside state capitals in several Northeast states: only 0.06 in Piauí, 0.09 in Sergipe, and 0.10 in Alagoas. This dire lack of medical personnel spawned a major government initiative to improve access, Programa Mais Médicos, in 2013. As an example of how these health care gaps affect services, consider that a quarter of Brazilian women at least forty-five years of age have never had a clinical breast exam (not to mention a mammogram); this figure reaches two-thirds in the rural Northeast.[51] And even though Brazil has more dentists than any other country (and one-fifth of the world's dentists), over a quarter of citizens in the rural Northeast – and 12 percent of all Brazilians – have never consulted a dentist in their lives.[52]

Further insights about citizens' vulnerability to illness are provided by the 2011 localization wave of the Rural Clientelism Survey, which reached over 4,000 rural households across nine states in Northeast Brazil. Many respondents diverted a large share of their incomes to pay for medicine and treatments. A quarter of households had spent 10.3 percent of their total expenditures over the past thirty days on health care expenses; this figure reached 19.6 percent for a tenth of households.[53] Even more alarming, health care accounted for 28.2 percent of total expenditures in the past month for 5 percent of households – and it accounted for *over half* of all expenditures

---

[49] In 2011, infant mortality in these states was 20.1, 20.8, 11.1, and 10.8 per 1,000 live births, respectively. Data from SUS Indicadores e Dados Básicos, IDB, 2012.
[50] In this period, Brazil's doctors increased over sixfold (from 58,994 to 388,015) as population doubled. The Southeast, South, and Center-West regions have 2.7, 2.1 and 2.1 doctors per 1,000 citizens. The poorer North and Northeast regions have only 1.0 and 1.2, respectively.
[51] Author's analysis of 2008 Datasus/PNAD data.
[52] Author's analysis of 2008 Datasus/PNAD data.
[53] For the median household, health care expenditures were R$3, comprising less than 1 percent of overall expenditures in the last month. Over a tenth of respondents had spent R$100 or more.

4.3 Vulnerability

for one percent of households. As an example of such health care expenditures, 44.8 percent of respondents in the 2012 wave of the Rural Clientelism Survey reported a previous instance in which they needed medicine unavailable in the public pharmacy. The broader point is that Brazil's public health care system does not protect all citizens from vulnerability to illness.

As shown in the next two chapters, many Brazilians cope with their vulnerability to health shocks through relational clientelism – that is, through ongoing exchange relationships with politicians who provide contingent benefits that extend beyond campaigns. Two features enhance the capability of local politicians to mitigate this source of vulnerability through clientelism: municipalities have considerable health care resources as well as discretion about expenditures. With respect to resources, municipalities' health care coffers increased as public health care expenditures grew and decentralized. Brazil's 1988 Constitution, which declared the right to universal, comprehensive health care, placed duties on all levels of government. As overall public health care expenditures rose, the federal government increasingly transferred funds to municipalities. Such transfers to municipalities now account for the largest share of public health care expenditures: 47.5 percent in 2013 (TCU, 2014). With respect to discretion, many important health services (such as primary care) are implemented at the municipal level (IPEA, 2010a, 73). Brazil's federal audit court reports that municipal officials have substantial levels of autonomy when providing some aspects of healthcare, often with little oversight or guidance at the state level (TCU, 2011).[54] Although municipal health councils involve civil society and therefore could potentially limit such discretion, in practice these councils have limited autonomy – especially in smaller municipalities – and typically rely on municipal governments for operational resources (Moreira and Escorel, 2009, 798, 801–803).

To illustrate this point about health care resources and discretion at the municipal level, consider the case of pharmacy benefits. At least on paper, Brazil provides free access to a wide variety of medicine, such as through Programa Farmácia Popular do Brasil (Brazil's Popular Pharmacy Program). Municipalities receive substantial funds to provide free medicine, and are supposed to base decisions about what types and quantity of drugs to purchase on federal and state guidelines.[55] But according to audits by Brazil's federal accountability office (Tribunal de Contas da União, or TCU), in practice many municipalities stray far from these guidelines. Reasons include mismanagement and political malfeasance, and higher-level officials frequently neglect to monitor municipal actions with regards to pharmaceuticals

---

[54] See especially Sections 252–258 of the TCU report.
[55] For the broader role of municipalities, see the National Medicine Policy (Portaria No. 3.196, October 30, 1998). The most prominent guidelines are the Ministry of Health's Relação Nacional de Medicamentos Essenciais (RENAME).

(TCU, 2011).⁵⁶ Furthermore, the inflow and outflow of drugs from medical facilities is poorly monitored, providing scant control over how publicly procured medicine is distributed (TCU, 2011). Such findings not only suggest considerable local autonomy about some health care expenditures, but also reveal one reason why medicine may be unavailable to citizens who become ill, exacerbating vulnerability to health shocks.⁵⁷ This problem is acute: Bertoldi et al. (2012, 1) cite evidence suggesting that "on average, 40 percent of the medicines prescribed in public primary health care were not available when needed."⁵⁸

More broadly, many Brazilians continue to face substantial vulnerability to health risks, despite major efforts to improve Brazil's social safety net. Local politicians have the opportunity to help clients cope with these risks through ongoing exchange relationships, given municipalities' significant resources and discretion surrounding health care.

4.3.2 Employment

Employment is another arena of vulnerability for many Brazilians. At the outset, it is important to recognize Brazil's advances over the past quarter century in tackling labor market insecurity – in the formal sector – through the provision of unemployment insurance. While the 1946 Constitution had called for unemployment insurance, implementation struggles ensued, and it did not materialize until 1986 (IPEA, 2010a, 79; ILO, 2013, 1). By some measures, the federal unemployment insurance program (Seguro-Desemprego) is now sizable, as its expenditures are 2.5 percent of the total eligible payroll – over triple the level in the United States (Gerard and Gonzaga, 2014, 6). The number of recipients in Brazil expanded rapidly from 734,000 in 1987 to 4.2 million in 2000 and 8.2 million in 2014 (MTE, 2015). This rapid increase is partially explained by sharp growth in the formal labor market, which exhibits high levels of turnover (DIEESE, 2014a, 12). Unemployment insurance compensates registered workers who involuntarily lost their jobs, for three to five months, with the specific duration based on time worked and number of prior requests for benefits. The monthly benefit depends on the salary earned during the last three months of employment, and averaged R$941 in 2014 (MTE, 2015).

---

[56] A 2011 TCU audit in 30 municipalities across 10 states found that many municipalities' health plans ignore or inadequately cover pharmaceuticals, and states often neglect to monitor municipalities (see sections 55 and 57). Although some interviewees blame politicians for the lack of medicine, Barreto and do Carmo Lessa Guimarães (2010, 1212) found in Bahia essential medicine was missing largely because no pharmacist managed programming.

[57] Despite the supposed availability of free medicine, the poorest fifth of Brazilians spend 58 percent of their health care expenditures on medicine (Garcia et al., 2013, 122–123). The issue led Senator Vanessa Grazziotin to call the lack of medicine in the Amazon region "unsustainable" on the floor of the national legislature in 2013.

[58] The authors' analyses show that even in the relatively wealthy South region, public sector medicines are inadequate to meet demand.

4.3 Vulnerability

Even though unemployment insurance has thus expanded substantially in Brazil, most of the country's population remains entirely unprotected from job loss. Social protection is focused primarily on the formal labor market, leaving many Brazilians in a state of vulnerability. For example, unemployment insurance for unregistered salaried employees and temporary workers is "practically inexistent," because such citizens typically cannot afford to obtain optional coverage through independent contributions (IPEA, 2010a, 283).[59] Although the Brazilian workforce has increasingly formalized since 2003 (Campos, 2015, 14), over half of workers are in the informal sector (cf. Gerard and Gonzaga, 2014, 1). Higher informality in rural areas and small municipalities leaves even more workers in a precarious situation. In rural areas, 59.4 percent of all employees are unregistered, a figure that reaches 77.1 percent in the North and Northeast regions (DIEESE, 2014a, 12). And only 28 percent of formal employees live in municipalities with populations of 100,000 and below, even though such municipalities are home to 45 percent of Brazilians (IBGE, 2010; DIESSE, 2011, 76). Particularly distressing is the fact workers who are unprotected by unemployment insurance often face relatively greater risks than those who are covered. Their incomes tend to be lower and less stable, and they are typically uninsured during times of sickness and accidents (IPEA, 2010a, 295).

Among formal sector workers, many are still vulnerable to unemployment. Eligibility requirements became even more stringent in 2015: for example, first-time applicants must now have worked eighteen of the past twenty-four months to receive any benefits at all.[60] High turnover in the labor market makes it challenging for many workers to stay employed for such durations, and more generally results in reduced coverage (IPEA, 2010a, 298–299). For instance, in the formal sector in 2012, the number of separations as a share of total employment was 42.3 percent, and even reached 87.4 percent in construction and 65.9 percent in agriculture (DIEESE, 2014b, 12).[61] Due to such factors – and because much of the unemployed population works informally or has never worked at all – the ILO (2013, 1–2) estimates that only 7 percent of Brazil's unemployed workers actually procure benefits from unemployment insurance. And beneficiaries end up struggling to find another job. An analysis of employees terminated between 1995 and 2009 found that almost all recipients exhausted their unemployment benefits, and half continued to be unemployed twelve months after their layoffs (Gerard and Gonzaga, 2014, 14–15).

This inadequacy of Brazil's social safety net is especially pernicious because so many citizens are vulnerable to the risk of unemployment. Although the

---

[59] However, Brazil expanded unemployment insurance to domestic workers in 2015. See "Empregados Domésticos Passam a ter Direito ao Seguro-Desemprego," *O Globo*, August 28, 2015.

[60] "Nova Regra do Seguro-Desemprego Vale para Demitidos a Partir de Sábado," *Globo*, February 27, 2015.

[61] Separations exclude four types of departures ineligible for unemployment insurance: death, retirement, transfer, and by worker request.

country demonstrated substantial job creation and relatively low unemployment rates in some (though not all) recent years, aggregate figures mask just how challenging it is for many citizens to obtain and stay in work. Unemployment is uneven in Brazil: the Northeast region had nearly double the unemployment rate as the South in early 2015 (9.6 versus 5.1 percent) and ranged from 3.9 percent in Santa Catarina to 11.5 percent in Rio Grande do Norte.[62] The extreme poor in particular have much higher unemployment rates, reaching 25.4 percent in 2011, with only 3.6 percent of this subgroup working in the formal sector (Dedecca, 2015, 21–22). Moreover, unemployment rates capture neither the 39 percent of Brazilians of legal working age who have not actively sought paid work over the past month (IBGE, 2014, 8), nor the many citizens who are underemployed. According to a recent survey, most Brazilians believe that unemployment is the top reason for poverty in Brazil (SIPS, 2011b, 8–9).[63]

As with health care, the next two chapters show how many Brazilians facing vulnerability to unemployment turn to relational clientelism as a risk-coping mechanism. Two features enhance the ability of local politicians to alleviate this source of vulnerability through clientelism: municipalities hire many employees and have considerable discretion in their selection. With respect to employment, the number of citizens working directly for municipalities increased sharply over the last decade, from 3.9 million workers in 2002 to 6 million in 2012.[64] This growth was feasible despite the Fiscal Responsibility Law of 2000, which capped each municipality's personnel expenditures at 60 percent of its net current revenues, because municipal revenues expanded rapidly.[65] Growth in municipal employees was especially rapid in municipalities with 10,000 to 500,000 residents – twice as fast as in larger cities.[66] As one councilor suggests, many citizens in small towns are "dependent" on local politicians "because the primary job creator is the municipal administration."[67] As of 2012, municipal workers constituted 3.2 percent of Brazil's population (IBGE, 2012b, 19), a share that decreases monotonically with municipality size. For example, municipalities employ 6.8 percent of the population in the 1,298 municipalities with up to 5,000 residents, versus just 1.7 percent of the population in the 38 municipalities with over 500,000 residents. And such

---

[62] "Desemprego Ficou em 7.9% no Primeiro Trimestre de 2015, Diz IBGE," *Globo*, May 7, 2015.
[63] Poor Brazilians are nearly four times more likely to provide that explanation than the next most frequently cited reason, low education.
[64] Reflects personnel working in direct municipal administration; data from the 2002 and 2012 Perfil dos Municípios Brasileiros (IBGE).
[65] As municipalities' share of public expenditures increased, their current revenues grew nearly 5 percent from 2000 to 2011, slightly faster than employee growth (IPEA data adjusted for inflation using IGP-DI index).
[66] Data reflect growth in municipal employees from 2005–2012 (IBGE, 2012b, 20).
[67] Author's interview of a councilor in a Bahian municipality with 30,000 citizens, December 3, 2008.

4.3 Vulnerability

employment influences a greater share of the population, as a single stable job may sustain numerous individuals in many poor households. Municipalities have more public employees than state and federal governments combined (4.4 million versus 3.2 million and 0.7 million, respectively, in 2008),[68] and the number of public workers they employ has also grown at a much faster rate than other levels of government (Barone, 2010, 12).

Local politicians also have considerable discretion when hiring this expanding number of municipal workers. To be sure, Brazil has made impressive strides against such discretion with regards to permanent employees: it was the first country in Latin America to institute a formal civil service (Grindle, 2012, 16) and continually strengthened this bureaucracy through important measures including competitive exams for permanent positions (*concursos públicos*). But while mayors and councilors are relatively constrained from offering permanent positions for clientelist purposes, they can skirt many regulations through temporary employment. Unlike permanent positions, temporary jobs do not require competitive exams and allow considerably more discretion while hiring.[69] Across Brazil, 17.1 percent of direct municipal employees are in temporary positions (IBGE, 2012b, 194). And moreover, this figure is even higher in the poorer North and Northeast regions (26.6 and 23.3 percent, respectively), even reaching 41.1 percent in Roraima state (IBGE, 2012b, 195). Temporary positions are also subject to restrictions; for instance, they are included in the cap on total personnel expenditures imposed by the Fiscal Responsibility Law of 2000, and they can only be filled for limited durations if there exists an "exceptional public interest."[70] However, local politicians have various ways to circumvent these restrictions. One technique is indirect hiring through civil society organizations that conduct work for the municipality – they can be pressured to misclassify expenditures in order to contract more employees than is officially reported.[71] Hiring contracted workers in education is no longer as easy as it once was given legal restrictions, while public works and sanitation are considered "easier" places for such activity. But even in education, a quarter of all public teachers in Brazil – and as many as two-thirds in some contexts – are temporary workers, providing ample opportunity for political appointments.[72]

Overall, vulnerability to unemployment remains a major problem for many Brazilians, given that unemployment insurance still covers just a minority of the

---

[68] IPEA, 2010b, 15.
[69] For a case study of the use of temporary employment in Maranhão, see Sousa (2014).
[70] For example, see TCE-MT (2013).
[71] Author's interview of a councilor in a Bahian municipality with 10,000 citizens, November 24, 2008.
[72] For overall statistics, see "Brasil Gasta Demais com Funcionários Públicos," *Época*, October 2, 2014. In addition, the share of secondary-school teachers in temporary contracts is 66.6 percent in Espírito Santo, 64.8 percent in Mato Grosso, and 59.9 percent in Ceará (TCU, 2014, 27).

population. Local politicians have the capacity to help their clients cope with such shocks through ongoing exchange relationships, as municipal employment is growing and considerable discretion exists when hiring temporary workers.

4.3.3 Water

Water shortages are yet another source of vulnerability for many Brazilians, especially in rural areas and in the Northeast region. Before documenting this vulnerability, Brazil's considerable efforts to improve drinking water access deserve mention. Whereas the country's 1877 drought killed as many as 500,000 people (Coelho, 1985, 27), and frequent droughts continued to kill many citizens until the mid-twentieth century, fatalities are now relatively uncommon due largely to government actions (Nelson and Finan, 2009). Infrastructure investments play a key role, as the share of households with water piped from the public system rose from 32.8 to 83.0 percent between 1970 and 2010.[73] Moreover, Brazil launched the Água para Todos (Water for All) program in 2011, which installed over 911,000 cisterns for storing and collecting water through January 2016.[74] Emergency responses to droughts have also been highly beneficial. Most prominently, Operação Carro-Pipa (Operation Water Truck) contracts trucks to deliver water directly to citizens in municipalities facing a "state of emergency." During a drought in May 2015, for example, the program dispatched 6,754 water trucks to help 3.8 million citizens in 793 municipalities across the Northeast region.[75]

Notwithstanding such government efforts, water shortages continue to pose a threat. Although Brazil has over 13 percent of the world's available fresh water (ANA, 2014), drought frequently afflicts much of the country. Only a fifth of this water is located outside the sparsely populated Amazon, leaving much of the country parched for long periods. The Northeast region – which has just 3 percent of Brazil's water – faced its worst drought in fifty years in 2013, and large portions of Brazil (especially São Paulo) remained in severe drought in 2014 (WMO, 2014, 2015). Particularly susceptible to drought is the semi-arid zone of the Northeast region, which has twenty-eight million residents and as much land area as France and Germany combined.[76] The area is often parched because its rainfall is temporally concentrated and evaporates quickly, given high winds and excessive temperatures (Febreban, 2007, 2008).

Droughts exacerbate the vulnerability of many Brazilians. In the words of a fifty-three-year old woman in Ceará: "If it wasn't for the [water] truck, we would die of thirst" (Instituto Agropolos de Ceará, 2012, 20). Vulnerability is

---

[73] Data from IBGE (1977) and IBGE (2010).
[74] "Água para Todos Entregou 159 Mil Tecnologias Sociais de Apoio á Produção desde 2011," *Portal Brasil*, February 18, 2016.
[75] Comando de Operações Terrestres do Exército Brasileiro, May 2015.
[76] Part of Minas Gerais state is also in the semi-arid region.

4.3 Vulnerability

high in many rural areas of the country, where 30.7 percent of citizens lacked access to piped water in 2010, and an additional 42 percent relied on sources of piped water unconnected to the public system (primarily using wells and springs, which can be less reliable).[77] Many citizens throughout Northeast Brazil are especially vulnerable. In 2013, an elite survey of municipalities in that region estimated that over 55,000 citizens seek out water each day from officials (CNM, 2013, 14). And in the 2012 wave of the Rural Clientelism Survey conducted across Northeast Brazil, 40.9 percent of respondents indicated that they had at some point faced an emergency in which they lacked water. Droughts threaten not only citizens' ability to procure drinking water, but also their economic livelihood through effects on animal husbandry and crop production. In 2012, Northeast Brazil lost four million animals, largely due to drought. Approximately 1.3 million head of cattle perished, including a quarter of all cattle in Paraíba and Pernambuco.[78] In states such as Ceará, many municipalities faced catastrophic crop losses, with as much as 90 percent of harvests decimated (Gutiérrez et al., 2014). In short, droughts are a source of vulnerability for many Brazilians.

As with employment and health care, the next two chapters explore how many Brazilians facing vulnerability to droughts turn to relational clientelism as a risk-coping mechanism. Clientelist water provision most frequently involves deliveries by water truck.[79] Two conditions facilitate local politicians' clientelist use of water trucks to address vulnerability: municipalities have resources to provide water-truck deliveries and discretion to select recipients. Trucks typically draw water from existing public sources (such as reservoirs, ponds, rivers, or groundwater), so the additional resources needed are trucks and funds for operating them. Water trucks are often available at the local level: some municipalities possess one or more trucks, and some mayors and councilors own personal water trucks or have close ties to local truck owners.[80] In addition, funds for fuel and other operating costs can be budgeted as a municipal water program, diverted from other programs, or paid for from politicians' salaries or illicit sources. Resources for water deliveries multiply when drought strikes. Municipalities can obtain substantially more water-truck deliveries through the aforementioned Operação Carro-Pipa (Operation Water Truck) by declaring a "state of emergency," a formal process requiring federal approval. The program, which is a partnership between the Ministry of National Integration, the National Guard and the Army, involves multiple levels of government. Through this program in 2014, the federal government dispatched 6,541 water trucks to 785 municipalities, while

---

[77] IBGE (2012a). By contrast, figures for urban residents were 6.8 and 11.9 percent, respectively.
[78] "Seca Fez Nordeste Perder 4 Milhões de Animais em 2012, Diz IBGE," *UOL*, October 15, 2013.
[79] Other less common modalities for clientelism include boring wells and building cisterns.
[80] See Eiró and Lindoso (2015, 68) and "Parlamentar Denuncia Indústria da Seca no CE," *Diário do Nordeste*, August 18, 2015.

state governments dispatched 1,453 water trucks to 307 municipalities.[81] All in all, resources are available at the local level to provide water-truck deliveries.

Moreover, local politicians often have discretion when selecting recipients of these deliveries. Politicians with access to private water trucks have substantial latitude about how to dispatch them. For instance, a federal deputy complained about how mayors with their own private water trucks engage in clientelism in the interior of his state (Ceará) by exchanging votes "for a guaranteed supply of water."[82] Local politicians can also often influence who receives deliveries from municipal water trucks. As Santana et al. (2011, 7, 9) argue, water truck deliveries typically involve clientelist relationships between citizens and politicians rather than institutionalized channels. In a recent news article, residents of a small municipality in Piauí complained that its water trucks deliver only "to those houses that the mayor wants," while community agents elsewhere in the state reported that only the mayor's supporters receive water from a water truck contracted by the municipality.[83] Local politicians have relatively less discretion with trucks from Operação Carro-Pipa because of direct Army involvement. In order to receive payment from the Army, truck drivers must submit official vouchers that they receive from beneficiaries at the time of water deliveries. As then-President Dilma Rousseff explained in 2013: "This water-truck operation is seen as a traditional operation in the Northeast. Only this time, the federal government placed 5,700 water trucks and employed the Brazilian Army to coordinate the operation to prevent any use of the operation for actions in the past called clientelist."[84] As explored in Chapter 5, although the program strives to reduce discretion, it is by no means foolproof, so opportunities for clientelism exist. First, the municipality is involved in preparing the water distribution plan that identifies specific locations to which trucks are dispatched. More specifically, municipal employees have a substantial role in the National Guard coordinating committee (COMDEC) in each municipality that is tasked with writing the plan (Calheiros et al., 2007, 6), and are directly responsible for the plan when such a committee does not yet exist in the municipality (CGU, 2014, 7-9).[85] In addition, an audit of Operação Carro-Pipa found "high variability" of internal monitoring across Army subunits and incomplete compliance with required documentation about contracts, receipts and plans (CGU, 2014, 1, 60–63), and media outlets have reported on potential corruption in some

---

[81] "Informativo sobre a Estiagem no Nordeste, No. 77," Ministério da Agricultura, Pecuária e Abastecimento, February 15, 2015.
[82] "Parlamentar Denuncia Indústria da Seca no CE," *Diário do Nordeste*, August 18, 2015.
[83] "Água em troca de votos," *Correio Braziliense*, July 1, 2012.
[84] "Discurso da Presidenta da República, Dilma Rousseff, durante Cerimônia de Assinatura de Termos de Compromisso do Programa Água para Todos com Municípios do Semiárido Brasileiro," Brasília, Palácio do Planalto, September 10, 2013.
[85] Locations typically include clusters of homes, not individual homes, but can be granular.

aspects of the water-truck program.[86] More broadly, local politicians often have discretion with regards to water deliveries, though their ease of influencing beneficiary selection may depend on who owns or funds the trucks involved.

The upshot of this discussion of water shortages closely parallels that of health care and unemployment. Once again, many Brazilians continue to face substantial vulnerability, despite major efforts by the state to improve the social safety net. And similar to the other two domains, local politicians are often able to reduce citizens' exposure to risk in a clientelist manner, due to their considerable access to water trucks and discretion in selecting recipients.

4.4 SUMMARY

This chapter has examined why vulnerability provides a pressing motivation for many Brazilians to help sustain long-term clientelist relationships. While most studies emphasize the role of poverty in clientelism, it is also crucial to consider vulnerability – a broader concept that encompasses both poverty and risk – because both low average income and uncertainty are detrimental to a citizen's welfare (Ligon and Schechter, 2003). Vulnerability continues to afflict much of the world's population, even as the incomes of the poor have risen across the globe (Birdsall et al., 2014; Ravallion 2010, 452). With respect to Brazil, this chapter has shown that although one component of vulnerability has declined markedly (poverty), another component of vulnerability continues to threaten the lives of many Brazilians (risk).

On the one hand, rising incomes present a challenge for all forms of clientelism in Brazil. Notwithstanding a recent economic downturn, the nation has experienced substantial income growth over much of the last quarter century. This growth has been especially pronounced for poor Brazilians, with considerable gains fueled by labor income, pensions, and conditional cash transfers. Evidence from Brazil corroborates the conventional wisdom that higher incomes blunt the appeal of clientelist rewards. Surveys show that higher-income Brazilians tend to view clientelist exchanges as less acceptable – and are less likely to vote for candidates who offered them benefits – than their poorer counterparts. In addition, positive rainfall shocks during the 2012 municipal campaign reduced rural citizens' willingness to accept hypothetical vote-buying offers. More broadly, income growth compounds the numerous threats to electoral clientelism described in Part I, and also strains ongoing patterns of relational clientelism.

Despite rising incomes, many Brazilians continue to face substantial vulnerability, which often spurs citizens to fortify long-term clientelist relationships as a risk-coping mechanism. State efforts to expand Brazil's social safety net

---

[86] For example, the first page of this CGU audit explains it was prodded by corruption allegations on *Rede Globo's* prominent television show Fantástico. See also "Fantástico Aponta Irregularidades no Programa de Combate a Seca em AL," *Gazetaweb.com*, December 1, 2013.

have failed to shield much of the population from a wide range of risks. In particular, this chapter demonstrated that many citizens remain highly vulnerable to illness, unemployment, and drought. Most Brazilians cannot afford private health insurance, and inadequacies in the public health care system often contribute to catastrophic out-of-pocket expenditures. Less than a tenth of Brazilians who lose their jobs receive unemployment insurance, which is focused on formal employees and imposes stringent requirements. And recurring droughts create severe water shortages, leaving over 40 percent of survey respondents in rural Northeast Brazil in an emergency situation at some point in their lives. This chapter also demonstrated why local politicians are often able to assist clients in exchange for political support: at the municipal level, there are considerable resources and discretion in the spheres of health care, employment, and water. As shown in the remainder of Part II, many politicians do indeed provide clients with favored assistance in such domains. Overall, vulnerability provides many citizens a powerful motivation to buttress the stability of their ongoing exchange relationships. Given this motivation, how can citizens enhance the survival of these relationships? Building on the theoretical logic elaborated in Chapter 3, the next two chapters investigate two key mechanisms that citizens often employ to reinforce relational clientelism – declared support and requesting benefits.

5

Declared Support

Given their vulnerability to shocks such as illness, unemployment, and drought, many citizens across the world are motivated to fortify their ongoing exchange relationships with politicians who mitigate such risks. This book argues that the purposive actions of citizens are often instrumental to the survival of relational clientelism. As discussed extensively in Chapter 3, ongoing exchange relationships are relatively resilient to challenges faced by electoral clientelism in Part I, but also involve a dual credibility problem that citizens' actions alleviate.

Unlike vote buying and other forms of electoral clientelism, relational clientelism involves contingent benefits that extend beyond election campaigns. Because all promised benefits are not delivered by Election Day, relational clientelism raises especially complex issues regarding the trustworthiness of promises. First, politicians are uncertain whether citizens will follow through on their promises to provide political support – a concern that arises with all forms of clientelism. And second, citizens are uncertain whether politicians will follow through on their promises of assistance after they cast their votes – a concern that arises with relational but not electoral clientelism. Both sides of this dual credibility problem threaten the viability of relational clientelism. The theoretical logic elaborated in Chapter 3 suggests that voter choices can mitigate both credibility issues and thereby help to sustain ongoing exchange relationships, a key point now investigated in the Brazilian context. The present chapter examines how citizens declare support to signal their own credibility, and Chapter 6 investigates how they request benefits to screen politician credibility. Both mechanisms enable citizens to reinforce relational clientelism, and as shown in Part III are observed well beyond Brazil.

In part due to rigorous ballot secrecy, Brazilian politicians are often uncertain about whether to believe citizens' vote promises. During interviews, various candidates expressed concern that such promises are in many cases nothing more than cheap talk. As one councilor explained, "I had more than 5,000 promises to vote for me. But only 10 percent of those promises" actually translate into votes.[1] Some citizens even admit to pledging their votes deceptively behind closed doors to multiple candidates, in an effort to obtain more handouts. The signaling model elaborated in Chapter 3 suggests how citizens in ongoing clientelist relationships can distinguish themselves from these insincere promisers: they can signal the credibility of their vote promises by displaying political paraphernalia on their bodies, on their homes, and at rallies. Such declared support transmits information to politicians and can thus serve clientelist purposes, in addition to providing a means of expressing preferences or advertising on behalf of a favored candidate.

As investigated in this chapter, empirical materials from Brazil are consistent with this theoretical logic. First, public declarations of political support are a widely observed phenomenon, suggesting that many citizens do indeed undertake this action. Second, declared support increases during droughts, which is indicative of how vulnerability motivates citizens to engage in this action. Third, citizens' public declarations of political support are linked to relational clientelism. Two original surveys, as well as interviews with citizens and elites, reveal the widely shared perception that declaring during a campaign often influences benefits received beyond election campaigns. Moreover, regression analyses suggest that citizens who declare support for victorious candidates are indeed more likely to receive benefits during both election and non-election years. And fourth, declarations transmit meaningful information to politicians. Both qualitative and quantitative evidence suggest that citizens overwhelmingly vote and hold perceptions in accordance with their declarations.

Overall, evidence from Brazil is consistent with the argument that declared support is an important mechanism by which voters help to sustain relational clientelism. Through public displays of political paraphernalia, citizens in ongoing exchange relationships alleviate politicians' concerns about whether their vote promises are trustworthy.

5.1 PREVALENCE OF DECLARED SUPPORT

As with legions of citizens around the world, many Brazilians publicly express support for politicians. Especially before local elections, vast numbers of homes are checkered with vibrantly colored political flags. Citizens often wear candidates' stickers or place banners on their homes, reinforcing slogans blaring through loudspeakers on campaign vehicles and bicycles. In many cases, such actions are orthogonal to clientelism; for example, they may exclusively serve to express political preferences or provide free advertising for preferred candidates. But in contexts where citizens are vulnerable to adverse shocks, the need to sustain ongoing exchange relationships with politicians is another important

---

[1] Author's interview, municipality in Bahia with 100,000 citizens (December 18, 2008).

5.1 Prevalence of Declared Support

motivation. The present chapter examines this commonly overlooked reason why many citizens publicly declare their political support.

Before examining the link between declarations and relational clientelism, it is important to establish that many Brazilians do indeed engage in this action. Nationally representative surveys provide insight. The 2002 Brazilian Electoral Study (ESEB) included a single question asking whether respondents had displayed a candidate's banner or poster at home or work, or placed a candidate's sticker on their cars. During the campaign for that year's federal and state elections, 24.1 percent of respondents declared support in this manner. Declaration varied substantially across regions. In the relatively poor Northeast and North regions, 31.4 and 42.2 percent of respondents declared support, respectively. By contrast, in the wealthier Southeast and South regions, only 18.7 and 23.7 percent declared support, respectively.[2] Similar findings emerged in the 2007 LAPOP AmericasBarometer survey, which fielded the identical question. During the 2006 campaign for federal and state offices, 22.1 percent of respondents indicated they had declared support. And whereas 28.4 and 35.9 percent of respondents declared support in the Northeast and North regions, just 18.5 and 11.7 percent did so in the Southeast and South regions, respectively.[3] While these two surveys shed light on declaration patterns across Brazil, I do not analyze them further because they lack questions about respondents' experiences with clientelism.[4]

The Rural Clientelism Survey, which does not suffer from this limitation, provides more nuanced insights about declared support in the countryside of Northeast Brazil. During the 2012 municipal campaign, 37.5 percent of respondents reported placing a political flag or banner on their homes.[5] Given strict regulations, only 1.3 percent of respondents had household walls painted with political propaganda.[6] Declared support also extends beyond the household. For instance, 18.7 percent of respondents wore campaign stickers or even political T-shirts, which can no longer be distributed by candidates (see Chapter 2). A quarter of these wearers donned their stickers or shirts on Election Day, often to the polls. Rallies provide another conduit for declaring support through displays of political paraphernalia. Over 22.3 percent of respondents used political flags, banners, or T-shirts to show support while attending a political rally during the 2012 campaign.[7] The level of effort

---

[2] This question had 2,509 respondents. In the Center-West region, 32.5 percent declared support.
[3] This question had 1,180 respondents. In the Center-West region, 31.5 percent declared support.
[4] To the best of my knowledge, no national survey in Brazil inquires about both declared support and clientelism. For instance, ESEB and LAPOP studies do not inquire about both topics in the same surveys. As discussed later, to gather such national data, I fielded an online survey across Brazil in collaboration with Salvatore Nunnari.
[5] For figures in this paragraph, the number of observations ranges from 3,643 to 3,674.
[6] In 2012, various municipalities forbade campaigns from painting walls for citizens; national law permitted a 4m^2 painting. In 2015, Law 13165 prohibited all campaigns from using paint.
[7] Approximately 41.3 percent of respondents attended a rally; however, mere rally attendance is not considered a form of declared support.

involved in each form of declaration varies across citizens. For instance, while some interviewees in Bahia report expending time and resources to travel to a campaign office for political paraphernalia, others report home deliveries of flags and banners.[8] Analyses later examine the link between such declaration actions and relational clientelism. Although this chapter focuses primarily on favored access to benefits during non-election years – which by definition cannot involve electoral clientelism – interviewees also did not report direct payments for declared support during campaigns.[9]

If citizens declare support in part to buttress exchange relationships that help them cope with risk, one might expect more declarations when citizens face adverse shocks. This pattern is indeed observed in rural Northeast Brazil. Building on the methodology described in Chapter 4, my joint work with Gustavo Bobonis, Paul Gertler, and Marco Gonzalez-Navarro (2018) examines the effect of exogeneous rainfall shocks on declarations. More specifically, we assess whether citizens are more likely to declare support in municipalities experiencing droughts, using standardized precipitation data.[10] As expected, droughts increased declared support: a one standard deviation decrease in rainfall increased the overall prevalence of declarations by 7.1 percentage points (significant at the 1 percent level). More specifically, declaration on citizens' bodies increased 2.3 percentage points, at rallies increased 3.9 percentage points, and on homes increased 6.3 percentage points (significant at the 1–5 percent level). In addition, droughts increased citizens' intensity of declared support, in that many citizens engaged in multiple forms of declaration. One might be concerned that heavy rain influenced these results by making it logistically challenging to declare. Alleviating that concern, we find that rainfall earlier in the year also significantly reduced declarations during the municipal campaign, even when controlling for the amount of rainfall experienced during the campaign period. Thus, droughts motivate Brazilians to declare support, consistent with the argument that citizens facing adverse shocks undertake actions that help sustain relational clientelism.

Beyond rainfall shocks, numerous other contextual characteristics influence the prevalence of declared support in a particular locality. In addition to the regional variation in national surveys described earlier, declaration also varies across neighborhoods and municipalities in the Rural Clientelism Survey. While

---

[8] Similarly, some citizens who display support incur costs of traveling to rallies of varying distances, while others receive free bus transport to rallies.
[9] Even if such payments existed, the link between declarations and post-election benefits demonstrated in Section 5.3.1 points to relational clientelism. Any direct payments would violate Law 9840, with penalties described in Chapter 2. Although no evidence suggests direct payments, Section 5.3.2 shows that declarers disproportionately receive campaign handouts (a finding consistent with both relational and electoral clientelism).
[10] As discussed in Chapter 4, we employ the CHIRPS satellite database, standardizing municipal rainfall with data from the past quarter century (as municipalities have different climactic conditions).

recognizing such heterogeneity, the present chapter focuses primarily on how – within a given context – citizens' declaration choices are associated with the benefits they later receive. As such, empirical analyses later undertake measures to help control for contextual variation, such as including municipality fixed effects.[11] Section 5.5 returns to the question of how various contextual factors also affect the voter calculus of declared support.

Evidence discussed thus far suggests that declaration is prevalent across Brazil, and increases substantially in the rural Northeast amidst droughts. I now examine the link between declaration and relational clientelism.

5.2 DECLARED SUPPORT AND RELATIONAL CLIENTELISM

The theoretical logic elaborated in Chapter 3 suggests that citizens can help to sustain relational clientelism through declared support, as it signals the credibility of their vote promises. An important first step in testing this logic is to ascertain whether any link between declarations and relational clientelism actually exists. After all, public expressions of political support are common even in countries where contingent exchanges are rare, and many Brazilians undertake such actions without considering any potential contingent benefits. When investigating this link, I consider three alternative hypotheses. First, one might hypothesize that citizens who declare support for a victorious candidate are in fact no more likely to receive benefits than non-declarers. Second, declared supporters might disproportionately receive benefits, but only during electoral campaigns. Such a pattern might just indicate spot-market payments for declaration – with relational clientelism, one would also expect favoritism towards declared supporters involving post-election benefits. And third, one might hypothesize that declared supporters are more likely to receive benefits, but only because declaration is correlated with characteristics associated with the receipt of benefits (e.g., partisanship). As explored, evidence belies these alternative explanations and suggests a robust link between declared support and relational clientelism.

To motivate a deeper analysis of this link, consider a simple comparison of means from the Rural Clientelism Survey. Approximately 11.8 percent of citizens who declared support for a victorious mayoral or councilor candidate during the 2012 municipal campaign received private benefits from elected politicians the following year. By contrast, only 3.9 percent of undeclared citizens received such benefits in 2013. This difference, which is statistically significant (at the 1 percent level), points against the first two alternative hypotheses just outlined – there *is* a link between declarations and handouts, and this link *is* observed with post-election benefits. However, it does not counter the third alternative explanation that this link may be spurious. Alleviating this concern, regressions in Section 5.3 suggest that the link between

---

[11] In addition, all findings are robust to controlling for declarations by neighbors.

declared support and post-election benefits persists even when controlling for various factors. Furthermore, they reveal similar patterns for post-election job assistance, municipal benefits, and even emergency water deliveries during a severe drought. Before turning to regressions, I examine qualitative and survey evidence about how citizens perceive declaration to affect benefits received from politicians. In order to illustrate a broader link between declared support and relational clientelism, the discussion focuses on the three areas of vulnerability investigated in Chapter 4: health care, employment, and water.

5.2.1 Health Care

With respect to health care, many Brazilians perceive that declaring support publicly for a candidate during a municipal campaign affects one's access to post-election benefits. While such perceptions need not necessarily reflect reality, they provide useful insights for at least two reasons. First, beliefs and perceptions are important because they can influence citizens' decisions involving clientelism (Weitz-Shapiro, 2014, 43–44). And second, perceptions about favoritism towards declared supporters corroborate observed patterns revealed in regression analyses, thereby providing confirmatory evidence. In addition to such favoritism, many Brazilians perceive that elected officials discriminate against citizens who declared support for defeated candidates; however, regressions provide mixed evidence about discrimination. At the outset, it should be underscored that the signaling logic of declared support (elaborated in Chapter 3) does not require any such discrimination.

To explore perceptions about the link between declaration and health care, the Rural Clientelism Survey included hypothetical questions involving fictitious candidates. Our team sequentially showed respondents drawings of three homes – one without a campaign flag, one with a flag for a victorious mayoral candidate, and one with a flag for a defeated mayoral candidate – and asked how easy or difficult it would be for the resident in each home to receive a medical treatment. Respondents overwhelmingly believed that the elected mayor's declared supporter would receive preferential access. Of 3,668 respondents, 78.8 percent believed that receiving a medical treatment would be easier for a citizen who had declared support for the victorious candidate, compared to a citizen who had remained undeclared.[12] Moreover, respondents expected discrimination against the citizen who had declared for a defeated mayoral candidate. Indeed, 78.2 percent of respondents believed it would be tougher for her to obtain a medical treatment than it would be for an undeclared citizen.[13]

---

[12] Almost 7.8 percent responded there would be no difference, 10.8 percent responded it would be tougher, and 2.6 percent did not know.

[13] Almost 9.7 percent responded there would be no difference, 9.4 percent responded it would be easier, and 2.8 percent did not know.

5.2 Declared Support and Relational Clientelism

To examine whether such perceptions extend beyond rural Northeast Brazil, I also conducted an online survey experiment with Salvatore Nunnari in 2016.[14] Over 1,900 subjects in 1,096 municipalities across Brazil were randomly exposed to one of three vignettes, depicting either a declared supporter, declared opposer, or undeclared citizen.[15] Over 43.3 percent of respondents viewing the declared-supporter vignette thought it would be "easy" or "very easy" for the citizen to receive a medical treatment, versus just 35.3 percent of those viewing the undeclared-citizen vignette. This difference is statistically significant (at the 1 percent level) and suggests perceived favoritism. Whereas this finding is consistent with the Rural Clientelism Survey, the online survey experiment differs in that respondents did not perceive discrimination of declared opposers: 34.9 percent of subjects exposed to that vignette thought that receiving a medical treatment would be "easy" or "very easy." While this figure is significantly less than the declared-supporter vignette, it is statistically indistinguishable from the undeclared-citizen vignette.

The perceptions of favoritism in both surveys were also observed in many of the interviews I conducted in both rural and urban areas of seven municipalities across Bahia state in Northeast Brazil.[16] Numerous citizens indicated that declared supporters of local politicians receive preferential access to medicines and medical treatments that extends beyond campaigns. Some interviewees even provided specific examples of health-related assistance that they had received, attributing them to their own declarations of political support. Examples include medicine, help from politicians to obtain consultations and surgeries in the state capital of Salvador, rides or bus fare to reach those distant medical appointments, and access to ambulances during emergencies. Consistent with the argument that declared support plays a role in risk-mitigating exchange relationships, some citizens discussed prospectively how their declarations would help them cope with illness. For instance, a mason explained that if he needed a costly medical procedure, he would turn to "the politicians he voted for," who would help him "because he declares his vote before voting."[17] Interviews with politicians provide additional evidence; for instance, a councilor paraphrased a famous quote when explaining why declared support sometimes affects health care: "For friends of the king, everything," and for others, "nothing. ... Not everyone thinks so, but this,

---

[14] The survey recruited participants through Facebook advertisements in all Brazilian municipalities with populations up to 250,000 citizens. Municipalities of this size comprise 98.2 percent of Brazil's municipalities and 59.7 percent of the nation's population. See Appendix B for more details.

[15] N = 1,935. Vignettes employed both text and images. Respondents were asked about the depicted citizen's ease of obtaining medical treatments, employment and water cisterns (discussed later) on a four-point scale: "Very Easy," "Easy," "Hard," and "Very Hard."

[16] See Appendix A for a description of the overall qualitative work, which included 132 formal interviews of both citizens and elites. Interviews in Pernambuco did not focus on declared support (N = 22).

[17] Author's interview, municipality in Bahia with 80,000 citizens (November 21, 2008).

practically, is customary."[18] While relational clientelism frequently involves preferential access to the public health care system, numerous interviewees indicated that some politicians also procure private medical assistance for their supporters. For instance, when medicines are unavailable at the public pharmacy, politicians frequently purchase them for their declared supporters at private pharmacies, using their own salaries (especially councilors) or public funds (especially mayors).

A considerable share of interviewees also perceived health care discrimination, a finding consistent with one of the surveys discussed earlier. Among the Bahian citizens whom I asked directly, about half indicated that someone who had declared support for a defeated candidate would be less likely to obtain a medical treatment in the state capital.[19] Interviewees often voiced the word *marcação* ("labeling" or "marking") to describe how politicians identify and disfavor citizens who declared against them. As one example, a councilor explained that politicians can learn how citizens vote through their public declarations of support and then discriminate when providing health care benefits. If a medicine is available at a private pharmacy but not the hospital, he asserted, "and you didn't vote for the mayor, don't even go there, because he won't give it to you."[20] Numerous citizens concurred, even revealing disturbing details about their own or family members' untreated ailments. A voter explained that declared opposers experience the "business of mistreatment, of spite," illustrating with the example of a politician who refused to help his mother obtain a medicine unavailable in the public pharmacy.[21] Some interviewees carped about the "persecution" of declared opposers, who reportedly face greater challenges when trying to obtain specialized appointments and surgeries that could only be performed outside the municipality, or transportation to such health care needs in distant cities. For instance, a teacher complained, using the nickname *jacu* (a bird species) that voters call declared opposers in various parts of Bahia: "He is persecuted by the candidate, secretary, councilor. The *jacu* is persecuted, and therefore is unable to obtain a medical treatment in Salvador."[22] A maid explained that she was unable to get an ultrasound at the local hospital, and when she went to a councilor to ask for help, he responded, "No, you didn't vote for me, you voted for João, so I'm not going to help you, go ask João."[23] Others reported political discrimination in dentistry, usually

---

[18] Author's interview, municipality in Bahia with 60,000 citizens (November 4, 2008).
[19] Of forty-three citizens asked this question, twenty-one said less likely, eighteen said no difference, zero said more likely, and four did not know. Unlike the aforementioned survey question, interviews did not employ drawings and indicated the treatment was in Salvador. The interview protocol did not include a comparable question about a declared supporter of a victorious candidate, though the topic was often mentioned by participants.
[20] Author's interview, municipality in Bahia with 15,000 citizens (January 13, 2009).
[21] Author's interview, municipality in Bahia with 10,000 citizens (October 2, 2008).
[22] Author's interview, municipality in Bahia with 60,000 citizens (November 3, 2008).
[23] Author's interview, municipality in Bahia with 10,000 citizens (October 14, 2008). The interviewee reported paying out of pocket to receive the ultrasound at a private clinic in another municipality.

5.2 Declared Support and Relational Clientelism

regarding the inability to obtain appointments, but with one informant making a more shocking claim: whereas a declared supporter might get a root canal from a public dentist, a declared opponent in the same condition would have his tooth pulled.[24]

While such perceptions were by no means universal, some interviewees in Bahia pointed to potential consequences when indicating that it was better to remain undeclared. With respect to health care, these citizens tended to focus on the perceived risk of losing health care benefits, rather than on potential opportunities for preferential access. For example, a snack shop worker explained that she did not declare support "because then you end up well-known." Declaring for a politician involves risk, she explained, because a citizen "doesn't know who's going to win," and "if he falls sick," the elected politician will refuse help and say, "You didn't vote for me."[25] A vice-mayor provided a harrowing explanation of why political discrimination in emergency situations prevents some citizens from declaring support or even talking about their political preferences:

"Many 'undecided' people are afraid of saying who they're going to support or vote for, because if you say you're going to vote for someone who loses, the other labels. ... I'm going to give another example that is disgraceful, that's even vulgar, that's inhumane, but is true. You voted for me, he voted against me. A car happens to flip and there's one of your relatives and one of his relatives. And the two need to go urgently to Salvador [distant state capital], and the ambulance only transports one. His doesn't go, yours goes first, you understand?"[26]

This account is gravely disturbing, but care must be taken when drawing broader inferences about the severity or prevalence of discrimination against declared opposers. Given that declared support is often observed in Brazil, many citizens clearly perceive the benefits from this action as outweighing the costs, or are motivated to declare in spite of such costs due to non-clientelist considerations (e.g., expressive utility). In addition, nearly half of interviewees denied any modicum of discrimination in health care, such as a farmer who explained that a declared opposer in need of a medical treatment "is attended to the same."[27] Others emphasized limits to its scope. For instance, a councilor insisted that no discrimination exists in emergency situations, but claimed that otherwise it is possible to "push with the belly" (*empurrar com a barriga*) – i.e., postponing or failing to provide an appropriate remedy.[28]

In sum, evidence suggests a perceived link between declared support and relational clientelism in the sphere of health care. More specifically, the Rural Clientelism Survey and many interviews reveal perceptions that declaration

---

[24] Author's interview, municipality in Bahia with 10,000 citizens (September 20, 2008).
[25] Author's interview, municipality in Bahia with 10,000 citizens (October 16, 2008).
[26] Author's interview, municipality in Bahia with 60,000 citizens (November 5, 2008).
[27] Author's interview, municipality in Bahia with 15,000 citizens (January 15, 2009).
[28] Author's interview, municipality in Bahia with 30,000 citizens (December 2, 2008). Explanation of phrase based on Peterson (1998).

actions lead to favoritism and discrimination in the provision of post-election health care benefits, and the online survey experiment across Brazil points to perceived favoritism but not discrimination. Such perceptions motivate some citizens to remain undeclared.

5.2.2 Employment

Just as with health care, many Brazilians also perceive a link between declared support and post-election employment opportunities. First, consider another hypothetical scenario included in the Rural Clientelism Survey. As described earlier, respondents were shown drawings of three fictitious homes: (a) one without a campaign flag, (b) one with a flag for a victorious mayoral candidate, and (c) one with a flag for a defeated mayoral candidate. When asked about the ease of obtaining a job, the preponderance of respondents believed that the declared supporter would receive preferential treatment and that the declared opposer would face discrimination. Of 3,670 respondents, 78.5 percent reported that obtaining employment would be easier for a citizen who had declared support for the victorious candidate, compared to the undeclared citizen.[29] In addition, 87.9 percent of respondents believed it would be tougher for the citizen who declared for the defeated mayoral candidate to obtain a job than it would be for an undeclared citizen.[30]

To explore whether these perceptions were limited to Northeast Brazil, the vignettes were again explored in the online survey experiment conducted across Brazil.[31] Nearly 39.2 percent of respondents randomly assigned to view the declared-supporter vignette thought it would be "easy" or "very easy" for the citizen to obtain employment, versus just 18.2 percent of those viewing the undeclared-citizen vignette. This difference, which is statistically significant at the 1 percent level, again suggests perceived favoritism. But as with health care, participants in the online survey experiment did not perceive that declared opposers are singled out for discrimination in the sphere of employment (unlike in the Rural Clientelism Survey). Among citizens exposed to the declared-opposer vignette, 20.8 percent thought that obtaining a job would be "easy" or "very easy," which is significantly less than the declared-supporter vignette, but statistically indistinguishable from the undeclared-citizen vignette.

Turning to qualitative evidence, many interviewees in Bahia shared the perception that declared supporters are favored with respect to employment. Of those I asked, nearly three-fourths responded that obtaining a public sector job would be easier for someone who had declared support for a victorious

---

[29] In addition, 5.9 percent responded there would be no difference, and 13 percent responded it would be tougher (98 citizens did not know and 1 did not answer this question).
[30] In addition, 5 percent responded there would be no difference, and 4.7 percent responded it would be easier (86 citizens did not know and 3 did not answer this question).
[31] $N = 1,935$.

5.2 Declared Support and Relational Clientelism

candidate, compared to an undeclared citizen.[32] A teacher responded that "it would be easier, definitely," and a hairdresser explained that "of course [a politician] will first help those people who were there with him all the time he needed it, backing his victory."[33] A retired butcher concurred and underscored that declaration boosts a politician's confidence in one's vote choice. A declared supporter would have an easier time receiving municipal employment, he posited, "because if the candidate is certain that I voted for him, he will give me work."[34] Some citizens suggested that politicians would "recognize" the ongoing support provided by declarers when allocating job opportunities. In the words of a homemaker, it is "easier for someone who declared" because a politician says, "You were on my side. I am going to give you work."[35] In a point explored further in Chapter 6, self-selection also plays a role in the link between declared support and employment. Declaration increases some interviewees' comfort with asking for a job, even conferring "the right to demand" employment.[36]

In addition, the majority of interviewees in Bahia perceived that declared opposers face post-election discrimination with respect to employment. Of those I asked, over two-thirds indicated that obtaining a public sector job would be more difficult for someone who had declared support for a defeated candidate than it would be for an undeclared citizen.[37] For example, a mason responded it is "definitely" more difficult for a declared opposer, adding: "Because he declared his vote. ... It's hard. Not even I would give work to him."[38] Yet some interviewees drew a clear distinction between temporary contracts and civil service positions. For instance, an athletics instructor argued that obtaining a contract position is "very difficult" for a declared opposer, and even role-played how a politician's staff "persecutes": "I'm not going to give him a job, I'm going to humiliate him, I'll step on him a lot." On the other hand, he emphasized that such discrimination does not exist for permanent positions with competitive exams (*concursos*), as well as for any citizen who remains undeclared because the politician "will not know who he voted for."[39] Some politicians likewise indicated that declared opposers would be cut off from contract work; in the words of one vice-mayor, "If you have a job, you're not going to give it to that person who wasn't with you. Then you have a way

---

[32] Of thirty-three interviewees asked this question, twenty-four said easier, six said no difference, zero said more difficult, and three did not know.
[33] Author's interviews, municipalities in Bahia with 60,000 and 15,000 citizens (November 3, 2008, and January 12, 2009), respectively.
[34] Author's interview, municipality in Bahia with 60,000 citizens (November 4, 2008).
[35] Author's interview, municipality in Bahia with 10,000 citizens (October 22, 2008).
[36] Author's interview, municipality in Bahia with 10,000 citizens (October 15, 2008).
[37] Of forty-seven interviewees asked this question, thirty-two said more difficult, ten said no difference, one said easier, and four did not know.
[38] Author's interview, municipality in Bahia with 80,000 citizens (November 18, 2008).
[39] Author's interview, municipality in Bahia with 60,000 citizens (November 3, 2008).

to retaliate."[40] Citizens who are already employed in the public sector may also risk reprisals if they declare for a candidate who loses: many interviewees thought contract workers would be fired, and a few also considered civil service employees to be at risk. A mayor explained that public employees frequently opt to remain undeclared and silent about their preferences "because they have fear exactly of retaliation going forward."[41] Election winners can punish teachers in permanent positions, explained a party leader, by shuffling them away from their schools, moving them to more distant and less accessible locations, and halving their work schedule and pay from forty to twenty hours a week – and "all of this is political persecution."[42]

Though most interviewees expressed perceptions of such employment discrimination, their views were not uniform. About a fifth of citizens interviewed believed that declared opposers face no such employment discrimination. Furthermore, at least one interviewee indicated that a benefit as valuable as employment would instead be used for persuasion. More specifically, a janitor explained that a declared opposer would have a "greater opportunity to get a job" because politicians follow the logic: "That's already mine, I have to win what I lost."[43]

Despite such heterogeneity, the evidence suggests that citizens tend to perceive both potential benefits and costs of declaring support: the chance of obtaining a job increases if one's candidate is victorious, but declines otherwise. As mentioned earlier, the prevalence of declared support in Brazil indicates that the overall benefits of declaring outweigh the costs for many citizens. But as with health care, some citizens are wary of declaring support for fear of risking job opportunities. For example, a saleswoman explained, "If I don't declare my vote, I think it is easier to obtain work because nobody will know who I voted for," and also noted that many fellow citizens "prefer to keep quiet so that we don't harm ourselves in the future."[44] A homemaker revealed that she didn't declare support because there is a "lot of *marcação*" ("labeling" or "marking").[45] Similarly, a computer technician indicated he wouldn't declare through stickers or other means because "you will burn yourself." To illustrate, he shared how a councilor denied his own request for job assistance during a bout of unemployment: "Gosh, you have to find your candidate ... weren't you with him?"[46]

Overall, these findings for employment are broadly similar to the case of health care, in that they both suggest a perceived link between declared support and relational clientelism. As before, many interviewees and the Rural

---

[40] Author's interview, municipality in Bahia with 80,000 citizens (November 20, 2008).
[41] Author's interview, municipality in Bahia with 60,000 citizens (November 7, 2008).
[42] Author's interview, municipality in Bahia with 50,000 citizens (November 12, 2008).
[43] Author's interview, municipality in Bahia with 10,000 citizens (October 3, 2008).
[44] Author's interview, municipality in Bahia with 80,000 citizens (November 21, 2008).
[45] Author's interview, municipality in Bahia with 15,000 citizens (January 13, 2009).
[46] Author's interview, municipality in Bahia with 80,000 citizens (November 18, 2008).

5.2 Declared Support and Relational Clientelism

Clientelism Survey reveal perceptions of both favoritism and discrimination based on declarations, whereas the online survey experiment across Brazil suggests perceived favoritism but not discrimination.

5.2.3 Water

Consistent with findings for health care and employment, many Brazilians also perceive a link between declared support and post-election water provision. To explore this issue, consider another hypothetical scenario in the Rural Clientelism Survey that involves water cisterns, which are large tanks used by many Brazilians to collect and store rainwater. As described earlier, respondents viewed drawings of three fictitious homes corresponding to a declared supporter, a declared opposer, and an undeclared citizen. When asked about the ease of obtaining a water cistern, most respondents believed the declared supporter would be favored and the declared opposer would be disfavored. Of 3,667 respondents, 77.1 percent reported that obtaining a cistern would be easier for a citizen who had declared support for the victorious mayoral candidate, compared to a citizen who had remained undeclared.[47] In addition, 81.6 percent of respondents believed it would be tougher for the citizen who declared for the defeated mayoral candidate to obtain a cistern than it would be for an undeclared citizen.[48]

As before, the breadth of such perceptions was examined in the online survey experiment with over 1,900 participants in 1,096 municipalities across Brazil. Nearly 39.5 percent of respondents viewing the declared-supporter vignette thought it would be "easy" or "very easy" for the citizen to obtain a water cistern, versus just 28.4 percent of those viewing the undeclared-citizen vignette. This difference, which is statistically significant at the 1 percent level, again suggests perceived favoritism. Similar to the Rural Clientelism Survey, online participants across Brazil perceived that declared opposers would be singled out for discrimination when obtaining a cistern: only 22.9 percent of subjects exposed to this vignette thought that obtaining one would be "easy" or "very easy." This percentage is significantly less than those in both the declared-supporter and undeclared-citizen vignettes.

Qualitative evidence about the link between declared support and water is relatively limited; my interviews in Bahia asked about health care and employment but not water. However, an ex-mayor I later interviewed in Pernambuco provided relevant insights.[49] He emphasized that cisterns and water trucks are channeled to supporters, and pointed to rallies – which involve

---

[47] In addition, 10 percent responded there would be no difference, while 10.1 percent responded it would be tougher (104 citizens did not know and 4 did not answer this question).
[48] In addition, 8.5 percent responded there would be no difference, while 7.3 percent responded it would be easier (ninety-six citizens did not know and six did not answer this question).
[49] Interview by Gustavo Bobonis, Marco Gonzalez-Navarro and Simeon Nichter; municipality in Pernambuco with 15,000 citizens (July 26, 2012).

declarations when citizens display political paraphernalia – when explaining why "you know who the people are who back you, who follow you, who vote for you." His further comments about water cisterns suggest why such knowledge can influence whether citizens receive benefits:

"Normally, a politician will seek to benefit more the people on his side. If I am going to make 100 cisterns, I will make 100 cisterns for people who vote for me. ... You will always seek to favor the one who is your partisan, who is your voter, who is on your side. It shouldn't be that way, but this is the culture in any municipality in Pernambuco."

Furthermore, consistent with reports from the states of Ceará and Piauí discussed in Chapter 4, the ex-mayor explained that a mayor's water truck would "only supply the people on his side."[50] While this single account cannot be deemed definitive, it sheds light on the ways in which declared support can potentially affect water benefits.

Media reports elsewhere in Northeast Brazil provide additional evidence. An alleged link between declared support and clientelist water delivery surfaced on national television in 2015 as the focus of a prominent, hour-long investigative show.[51] The show claimed that in a small municipality in Paraíba state, the mayor and his staff dispatched water trucks exclusively to supporters on an ongoing basis after the election. The ex-manager of water delivery for the municipality "confirmed the existence of a 'drought list' – with the names of residents who voted for the mayor and have water guaranteed during the dry period." The reporter also interviewed several citizens who claimed they were excluded from water deliveries because they had "declared" their votes – a word used repeatedly in the show. One mechanic complained that he no longer received water deliveries because he had voted against the mayor, explaining his vote choice was known "because every election I put a sticker on my house." Separately, a news magazine in Bahia reported on similar allegations, without describing how citizens expressed support. For instance, it quotes a farmer bemoaning that: "Since the day of the election, water never again arrived at my land. ... For over a month, I asked for the municipality's water truck to come, and nothing. They refuse to give water because I supported the opposition candidate."[52] While these allegations are unsubstantiated, they again point to perceived favoritism and discrimination.

With respect to water, this survey and qualitative evidence reveals perceptions that declarations of political support can influence benefits beyond electoral campaigns. More broadly, this section demonstrates that many Brazilians

---

[50] He contrasted such patterns to Army-controlled water trucks, which he described as not involving clientelism (see discussion of Operação Carro-Pipa later in this chapter and in Chapter 4).
[51] The show, *Repórter Record Investigação*, aired on January 26, 2015, and can be viewed at www.youtube.com/watch?v=pkoXRoFMazI. The Rural Clientelism Survey preceded this TV show.
[52] "Nem Mandacaru Suporta," *Carta Capital*, April 26, 2013.

5.3 Quantitative Analysis of Declared Support

perceive a link between declared support and relational clientelism in these three arenas of vulnerability, which serve as examples of a broader range of uninsured risks. Across interviews and both surveys, citizens who declared support for victorious candidates are widely viewed as experiencing favoritism with health care, employment, and water. Perceptions of discrimination are more mixed: while the Rural Clientelism Survey and many interviewees suggest that declared opposers are disfavored relative to non-declarers in all three issue areas, the online experiment finds such patterns only for water.[53] Across all issue areas, however, both surveys find that declared opposers are perceived as being significantly less likely to receive benefits than declared supporters. Another important finding is that although declaration is frequently observed in Brazil, some citizens who perceive risks are motivated to remain undeclared. Given such perceptions, I now further scrutinize the link between declared support and relational clientelism through regression analyses.

5.3 QUANTITATIVE ANALYSIS OF DECLARED SUPPORT

Evidence presented thus far suggests that many Brazilians publicly declare support for political candidates, and this phenomenon is widely believed to influence whether citizens receive material benefits from elected politicians. Before testing if declarations transmit meaningful information to politicians, I investigate whether the perceived link between declared support and relational clientelism is observed when analyzing the experiences of survey respondents. Regressions in this section demonstrate this link, but it deserves emphasis that analyses do not establish causality. Efforts are taken to ameliorate concerns about omitted variables bias and reverse causality, but such threats cannot be ruled out. Notwithstanding this limitation, results are consistent with relational clientelism.

5.3.1 Post-Election Benefits

Favoritism during non-campaign periods is a hallmark of relational clientelism, so I first examine whether declared supporters disproportionately receive post-election benefits. Recall from Section 5.2 that respondents in the Rural Clientelism Survey who declared support for a victorious candidate in 2012 were three times more likely than non-declarers to receive private benefits directly from a politician the following year (11.8 versus 3.9 percent). Extending this analysis, the first row in Figure 5.1 summarizes results from a regression, in which the outcome variable is whether a respondent received a private benefit

---

[53] One conjecture is that the online experiment across Brazil only detects this pattern of discrimination for water because of its particular scarcity during survey implementation. In 2016, Northeast Brazil was experiencing its most severe drought in a century, as highly publicized nationwide. See: "Nordeste Enfrenta Maior Seca em 100 Anos," *Estadão*, January 9, 2017.

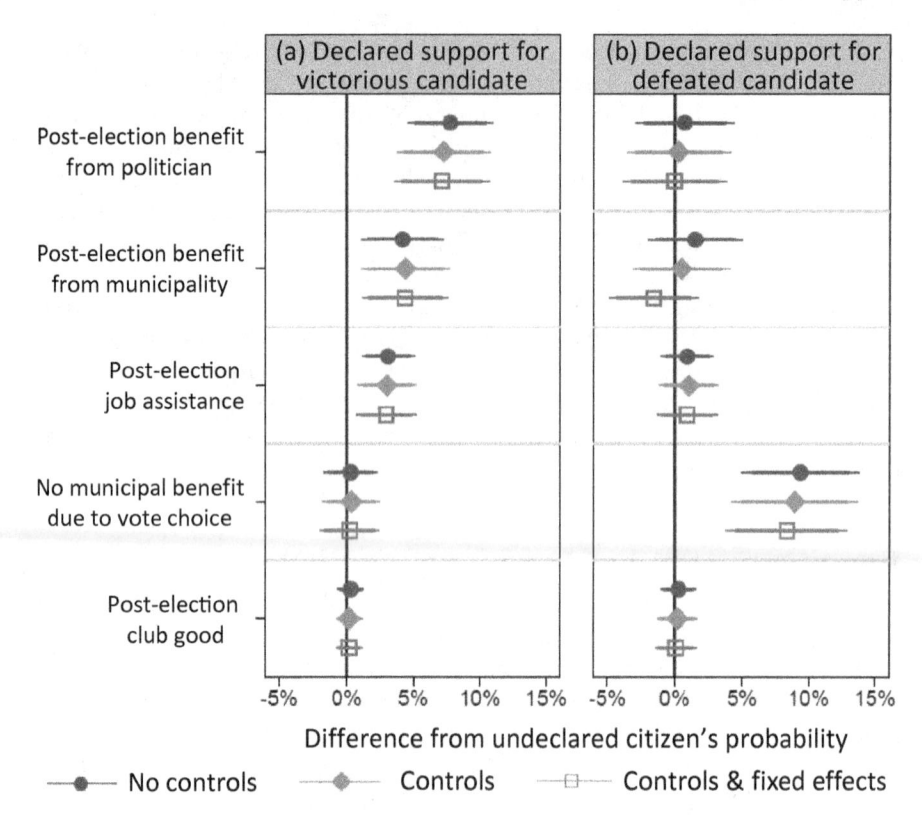

FIGURE 5.1 Declared support and benefits, rural Northeast Brazil (2013)
Note: Markers correspond to regression coefficients for the two explanatory variables on horizontal axis. These variables are coded 1 if respondent declared support for a victorious (defeated) candidate for mayor or councilor during the 2012 campaign; 0 otherwise. Outcome variables on the vertical axis are coded 1 if citizen experienced the outcome in 2013; 0 otherwise. Circles are shown for regressions with only these two explanatory variables, diamonds include controls, and squares include controls and municipal fixed effects. Thin (thick) whiskers denote 95 (90) percent confidence intervals, based on standard errors clustered at neighborhood level. Linear probability models are employed; results are robust using logit specifications. Appendix D reports full regression tables. Appendix B describes controls, which are: age, education, gender, household wealth, turnout, mayoral vote choice, political preferences (dummies for PT, PMDB, PSDB, and DEM parties), frequency of conversations with politicians, association membership, collaborative efforts with neighbors, has piped water, has own cistern, has access to shared cistern, reciprocity, risk aversion, time preference, and public goods contribution. Number of observations for the most inclusive specification is 3,218 (Row 1), 3,247 (Row 2), 3,243 (Row 3), 3,158 (Row 4), and 3,218 (Row 5).
Source: Author's analysis of the Rural Clientelism Survey. Data collected by Gustavo Bobonis, Paul Gertler, Marco Gonzalez-Navarro, and Simeon Nichter.

5.3 Quantitative Analysis of Declared Support

directly from a politician in 2013, and the explanatory variables are whether a respondent had declared for a victorious (defeated) candidate during the 2012 campaign.[54] In the left panel (a), the "No Controls" specification denoted by a filled circle suggests that declared supporters were 7.7 percentage points more likely than non-declarers to receive such help, a finding significant at the 1 percent level.

One might be concerned about bias because the preceding estimate ignores important characteristics correlated with both declarations and benefits. To mitigate this concern, the adjacent "Controls" specification in Figure 5.1a shows robustness when including a broad range of covariates: the point estimate decreases to 7.3 percentage points but remains significant. All regression tables are included in Appendix D, and a detailed description of control variables is provided in Appendix B. These controls include respondents' socioeconomic factors (age, education, gender, and household wealth), political characteristics (turnout, mayoral vote choice, preferences for the PT, PMDB, PSDB, and DEM parties, and frequency of conversations with politicians), horizontal linkages (association membership and collaborative efforts with neighbors), water availability (piped water, own cistern, and access to shared cistern), and behavioral attributes measured by experimental games (reciprocity, risk aversion, time preference, and public goods contribution). Directly below the "No Controls" and "Controls" estimates is another specification that also includes municipal fixed effects ("Controls & Fixed Effects"), addressing any omitted variables that are invariant across respondents in a given municipality. With this most inclusive specification, citizens who declared support for a candidate who won in 2012 were 7.1 percentage points more likely than non-declarers to receive a benefit directly from a politician in 2013 (significant at the 1 percent level).

Consistent with relational clientelism, the Rural Clientelism Survey also reveals favoritism in the sphere of employment. Finding work is especially challenging in rural Brazil, where a single job often helps to sustain an extended family. Although only 0.7 percent of non-declarers reported that a politician helped them obtain work in 2013, the figure was sixfold (4 percent) for citizens who had declared support for a victorious candidate during the prior year's campaign. As shown in Figure 5.1a, the difference is 3.0–3.1 percentage points and significant across all specifications (at the 1 or 5 percent level). Assistance from the municipal government is also important to consider, as politicians may

[54] Analyses in Figure 5.1 employ 2013 questions about whether and for whom respondents declared in 2012. The 2012 wave also inquired whether respondents declared, but not for whom. A more restrictive approach codes respondents as declaring for a victorious (defeated) candidate only if they: (a) indicated that response in the 2013 wave *and* (b) indicated they declared in the 2012 wave. All findings in Figure 5.1 are robust to this coding except Row 2, which becomes significant only in the most inclusive specification at the 10 percent level.

help clients to obtain benefits from municipal offices rather than using their own funds. Again consistent with relational clientelism, declared supporters were over twice as likely as non-declarers to receive benefits from municipal offices in 2013 (8.4 versus 3.9 percent). This difference is 4.2–4.4 percentage points (significant at the 1 percent level), even when including controls and/or municipal fixed effects.

Given that Northeast Brazil had its worst drought in fifty years in 2013 (WMO, 2014), is such favoritism also observed in rural water delivery? Evidence suggests that during this period of heightened vulnerability, declared supporters were more likely to receive water from Operação Carro-Pipa (Operation Water Truck) – by far the principal source of water deliveries in the Rural Clientelism Survey.[55] As discussed in Chapter 4, municipal politicians can influence the implementation of this program, and federal audits reveal imperfect compliance with its regulations (CGU, 2014). For each month, the survey asked respondents about water truck deliveries to their homes. Citizens who had declared for a victorious candidate received Operação Carro-Pipa water deliveries during an average of 1.5 months in 2013, compared to 0.9 months for non-declarers. Furthermore, declared supporters received an average of 11,000 total liters of water through the program in 2013, versus just 6,978 liters for non-declarers.[56] Both differences are significant at the 1 percent level, and regressions in Appendix D show robustness to the inclusion of controls and municipal fixed effects.[57] In the most inclusive specifications, declared supporters received 0.44 additional months of water-truck deliveries – and 2,590 more liters of overall water – than non-declarers (with p values of 0.02 and 0.08, respectively).[58] These analyses again point towards relational clientelism by revealing post-electoral favoritism towards declared supporters.

While the Rural Clientelism Survey thus provides strong evidence of favoritism, it offers only mixed evidence of discrimination. In the same specifications just analyzed, Figure 5.1b and Appendix D show that citizens who declared for a defeated candidate were no less likely than non-declarers to receive each form of post-electoral assistance. Nevertheless, they were significantly less likely to be recipients than declared supporters. Whereas analyses throughout this chapter identify declared opposers as respondents

---

[55] It provided over three times as many deliveries, and four times as many total liters of water, as municipal governments and local politicians combined in 2013.

[56] As context, the average daily water consumption across *all* Brazilians in 2013 was 166.3 liters per person (SNIS, 2014).

[57] Analyses include all controls used in Figure 5.1, as well as standardized municipal rainfall. Such patterns are not detected with other less common sources of emergency water or in 2012.

[58] When employing the more restrictive coding described in note 54, all specifications regarding deliveries are significant (at the 5–10 percent level), but specifications regarding liters are only significant (at the 10 percent level) without controls and fixed effects. Point estimates are comparable, but precision is reduced as observations fall. The primary reason is that not all household members who took the survey in 2013 were present in 2012.

5.3 Quantitative Analysis of Declared Support

who declared for *any* defeated candidate in the 2012 election, evidence of discrimination is observed when honing in on a much smaller subset – those who declared for *both* a defeated mayoral candidate and a defeated councilor candidate. These declared opposers were less likely than non-declarers to receive job assistance from politicians, municipal benefits and club goods (not shown).[59] Even without focusing on this subset, the survey also reveals perceptions of discrimination. When asked if they had been denied a municipal benefit in 2013 due to their vote choice, declarers for any defeated candidate were four times more likely to answer affirmatively than non-declarers (12.1 vs 2.6 percent). As shown in the fourth row of Figure 5.1b, the difference between declared opposers and non-declarers is 8.3–9.4 percentage points – and significant at the 1 percent level – across all specifications. Given such mixed evidence, it again deserves emphasis that declared support does not require any discrimination to transmit meaningful information about the credibility of vote promises.[60] This point is clarified by the formal model elaborated in Chapter 3, which shows that under reasonable conditions, favoritism is sufficient for declared support to serve as an effective signaling mechanism.

As with most of the literature on clientelism, analyses discussed thus far focus on private benefits. Club goods also warrant investigation, given that collective benefits in some contexts are also distributed in contingent exchange for political support (e.g., Diaz-Cayeros et al., 2016; Kitschelt and Wilkinson, 2007).[61] In the Rural Clientelism Survey, less than one percent of respondents reported receiving a club good from a politician in 2013. Over three-fourths of these benefits involved the provision of community water (e.g., filling neighborhood ponds), while the remainder involved roads, education and health. As shown in the bottom row of Figure 5.1, declared support is not associated with receiving club goods from a politician; point estimates are virtually zero across all specifications. Other analyses suggest that declared supporters were slightly more likely than non-declarers to receive club goods from municipal offices in 2013, but that finding is not robust and only significant at the 10 percent level (not shown).[62] Unlike for private benefits, such evidence does not strongly point to favoritism (or discrimination) with club goods, though further analysis is warranted.

---

[59] This subset accounts for about a tenth of all declared opposers. No discrimination is observed with private benefits from politicians or water.
[60] In some contexts, discrimination may be inhibited by limited information. Even when politicians observe declarations of their supporters in ongoing exchange relationships, they may lack the capacity to observe if other citizens declare for competitors or remain undeclared.
[61] Kitschelt and Wilkinson (2007, 11–12) explain that discretion affects whether club goods – which are enjoyed by all citizens in a group or boundary – are programmatic or clientelist.
[62] The survey does not facilitate analyses of club goods using other outcome variables just examined. Other analyses suggest that club goods are not more likely to be distributed to respondents in neighborhoods where more citizens declared for the victorious candidate (not shown).

Are patterns of declared support limited to rural Northeast Brazil? The online survey that I conducted with Salvatore Nunnari across one-fifth of Brazil's municipalities suggests otherwise. We asked respondents if they had publicly declared support for a candidate during the 2012 municipal campaign, and about post-election benefits received between January 2013 and June 2016.[63] At the outset, it should be noted that unlike the Rural Clientelism Survey, participants in the online survey were not randomly selected from a sampling frame (see Appendix B), though their characteristics are fairly representative of Brazil with respect to gender, age, and geographic region. Respondents were asked far fewer questions; for example, the survey did not inquire about employment assistance, water deliveries, or club goods. And because the online survey asks about declaration actions undertaken several years earlier, results are more subject to recall issues.[64] These points notwithstanding, the online survey also offers some advantages. Beyond its national scope, the survey also asks about post-election benefits distributed over a longer time frame than the Rural Clientelism Survey (3.5 years versus 1 year). It is thus able to detect relational clientelism during nearly a full term in office, which likely amplifies the magnitude of effects. Most important, the online survey helps to triangulate results: the broad consistency of findings across the two surveys and qualitative evidence suggests a robust link between declared support and relational clientelism in Brazil.

Similar to the Rural Clientelism Survey, declared supporters in the online survey were significantly more likely to report receiving post-election benefits from politicians. Over 27.2 percent of respondents who declared for a victorious candidate in 2012 reported receiving benefits from politicians in 2013–2016, versus just 11.2 percent of non-declarers. The first row of Figure 5.2a summarizes regression analyses, which show a difference of 15.8 to 18.1 percentage points – and significance at the 1 percent level even with the inclusion of various covariates and/or state fixed effects.[65] All regression tables are shown in Appendix D, and Appendix B provides a description of control variables in the online survey, which include: respondents' socioeconomic factors (age, education, gender, and income), political characteristics (turnout, mayoral vote choice, preferences for the PT, PMDB, PSDB, or DEM parties), risk aversion, and screeners for attentiveness.[66] In line with the Rural Clientelism Survey,

---

[63] This timing spans mayors' inauguration until the start of the following mayoral campaign; hence, benefits are post-electoral with respect to declarations in the 2012 municipal election. Unlike analyses of the Rural Clientelism Survey, the post-electoral period in the online survey overlaps with federal and state elections in October 2014.

[64] This survey was fielded around the 2016 municipal election, so the present analysis of post-election benefits examines declarations during the 2012 municipal campaign. The next section about campaign handouts examines declarations in the 2012 and 2016 campaigns.

[65] State fixed effects are used as most municipalities in the online survey have one observation.

[66] Two screeners were included to control for the effects of participants' attentiveness in the online survey (following Berinsky et al., 2014).

5.3 Quantitative Analysis of Declared Support

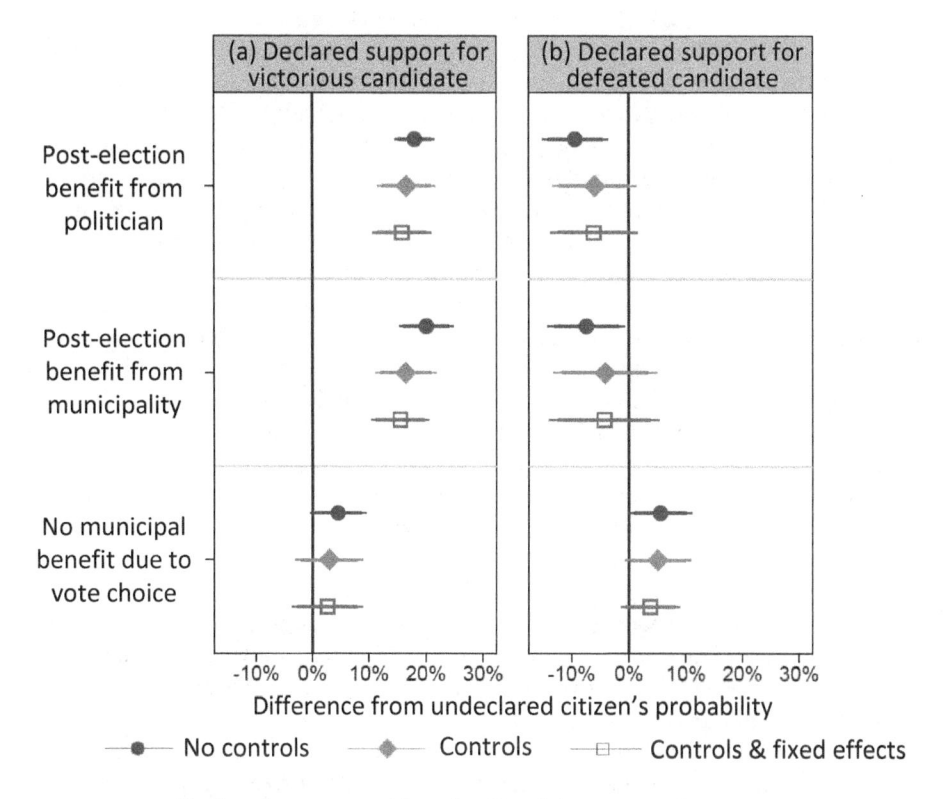

FIGURE 5.2 Declared support and benefits, Brazil (2012–2016)
Note: Markers correspond to regression coefficients for the two explanatory variables on horizontal axis. These variables are coded 1 if respondent declared support for a victorious (defeated) candidate for mayor or councilor during the 2012 campaign; 0 otherwise. Outcome variables listed on vertical axis are coded 1 if a citizen experienced outcome between January 2013 and June 2016, 0 otherwise. Circles shown for regressions with only these two explanatory variables: diamonds include controls, and squares include controls and state fixed effects. Thin (thick) whiskers denote 95 (90) percent confidence intervals, based on standard errors clustered at state level. Linear probability models are employed; results are robust using logit specifications. Appendix D reports full regression results. Appendix B describes controls, which are: age, education, gender, income, turnout, mayoral vote choice, political preferences (dummies for PT, PMDB, PSDB, and DEM parties), risk aversion, and screeners for attentiveness. Number of observations for the most inclusive specification is 1,466 (Row 1), 1,470 (Row 2), and 1,493 (Row 3).
Source: Author's analysis of the Online Clientelism Survey. Data collected by Simeon Nichter and Salvatore Nunnari.

declared supporters were also over twice as likely as non-declarers to receive post-election benefits from municipal offices (34.3 versus 15.4 percent). The second row of Figure 5.2a reports that citizens who declared for a victorious candidate during the 2012 municipal election were 15.5–20.1 percentage points more likely than non-declarers to receive such benefits in 2013–2016. This association remains significant at the 1 percent level across all specifications.

As with the Rural Clientelism Survey, the online survey thus reveals substantial favoritism, but provides only mixed evidence of discrimination. The first two rows of Figure 5.2b show that in "No Controls" specifications, citizens who declared for a defeated candidate were 9.3 (7.4) percentage points less likely than non-declarers to receive post-election benefits from politicians (municipal offices). However, these findings of discrimination are not robust: point estimates fall and are statistically indistinguishable from zero with the inclusion of controls and/or fixed effects. Some specifications point towards perceptions of discrimination, a finding again comparable to the Rural Clientelism Survey. As shown in the third row of Figure 5.2b, citizens who declared for a defeated candidate in 2012 were 3.8–5.5 percentage points more likely than non-declarers to report that they had been denied a post-election benefit due to their vote choice. This association is significant at the 10 percent level when including controls but not fixed effects.[67]

In sum, quantitative analyses using both original surveys suggest a robust link between declared support and relational clientelism, thereby corroborating many perceptions in Section 5.2. Citizens who publicly pledged allegiance to a victorious candidate during a municipal campaign were more likely than non-declarers to receive several forms of post-election benefits. Findings thus point substantially towards favoritism, though evidence of discrimination is mixed. The next section, which analyzes handouts distributed during campaigns, provides additional evidence consistent with a link between declared support and relational clientelism.

5.3.2 Campaign Handouts

Are declarers favored with material benefits during electoral campaigns? This pattern would be expected if declaration plays a role in relational clientelism, because ongoing exchange relationships persist during both election and non-election periods. Analyses in the present section suggest that citizens who publicly declare their political allegiance are indeed more likely to receive campaign handouts from politicians. Observe that campaign handouts precede the 2012 election; thus, no distinction is made between declared supporters and declared opposers, and analyses do not examine discrimination.[68] Findings

---

[67] The p values are 0.053, 0.082, and 0.143 in the "No Controls," "Controls," and "Controls and Fixed Effects" specifications, respectively. Citizens who declared for a victorious candidate were no more or less likely than non-declarers to report discrimination; "No Controls" is significant at the 10 percent level, but more inclusive specifications are insignificant (coefficients are positive).

[68] This section does not discuss club goods, as only three respondents reported their receipt as campaign handouts. The 2012 wave did not include a comparable question about benefits from the municipality. Water deliveries are not associated with declarations, during the campaign.

5.3 Quantitative Analysis of Declared Support

in this section corroborate the argument that declared support and relational clientelism are linked, but it should be emphasized that they provide only collateral evidence. Whereas the preceding section focused on post-election benefits – which by definition do not involve electoral clientelism – the present focus on campaign handouts could plausibly involve electoral and/or relational clientelism. As emphasized in Chapter 1, a campaign handout may comprise electoral or relational clientelism, depending on whether a citizen's receipt of contingent benefits extends beyond campaigns. For example, although interviews did not reveal evidence of spot-market payments to citizens for placing campaign posters on their own homes, quantitative analyses presented here cannot rule out this possibility. As before, these analyses also cannot entirely rule out omitted variables bias or reverse causality, though they do show robustness to a wide range of control variables and fixed effects.

Notwithstanding such limitations, the Rural Clientelism Survey provides considerable evidence that declarers are favored with campaign handouts. In the overall sample, 6.2 percent of respondents received benefits from politicians during the 2012 campaign. This aggregate figure masks considerable variation: under 4.7 percent of non-declarers received handouts, compared to over 7.8 percent of citizens who declared support for any candidate during that campaign. As shown in the first row of Figure 5.3 – in the "No Controls" specification – this unadjusted difference of 3.2 percentage points (with rounding) is significant at the 1 percent level.[69] This association continues to be significant when including control variables described in Appendix B, as well as municipal fixed effects.[70] The point estimate falls to 3.0 and 2.5 percentage points in the "Controls" and "Controls & Fixed Effects" specifications, respectively (see Appendix D). Similar patterns are observed when examining the value of campaign handouts, as estimated by recipients in the 2012 wave (not shown). On average, declarers received 23.4 percent more reais of campaign handouts than non-declarers (significant at the 5 percent level).[71]

The survey also suggests that citizens who engage in multiple forms of declared support are more likely to receive campaign handouts. Such effort provides an especially meaningful signal of whether vote promises are credible. Recall from Chapter 3 that declarations provide a more informative signal when the cost of declaring increases. Citizens who employ a single type of declaration may choose their cheapest method, which often varies across individuals.[72] But employing multiple ways increases declaration costs. To explore

---

[69] Given this section analyzes only one outcome variable, the vertical axis in Figure 5.3 provides alternative specifications of the independent variable.
[70] Not all questions were repeated across survey rounds, so analyses of the 2012 wave include most but not all of the control variables as analyses of the 2013 wave.
[71] Specification includes controls and fixed effects as in Figure 5.3. Values are logged and winsorized at 95 percent (given outliers). When regression includes only recipients, the estimate is similar but imprecisely estimated.
[72] For example, costs depend on how far a citizen must travel to campaign offices or rallies, opportunity costs, transportation options, and if candidates deliver or affix declarations.

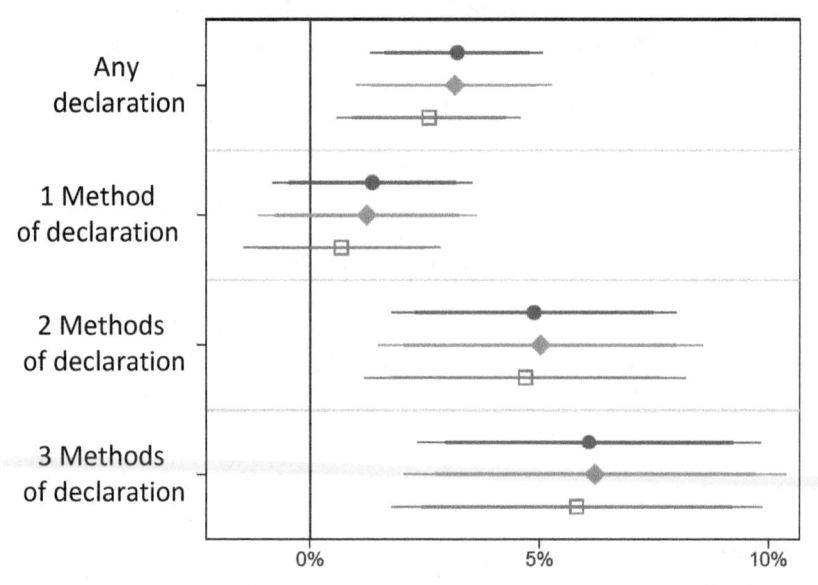

Campaign handout

- Any declaration
- 1 Method of declaration
- 2 Methods of declaration
- 3 Methods of declaration

Difference from undeclared citizen's probability

— ● — No controls   — ◆ — Controls   — □ — Controls & fixed effects

FIGURE 5.3 Declared support and campaign handouts, rural Northeast Brazil (2012)
Note: Markers correspond to regression coefficients for explanatory variables on the vertical axis. In the top row, "Any Declaration" is coded 1 if the respondent declared support for any candidate during the 2012 campaign; 0 otherwise. Variables in the bottom three rows are included together in another specification; they are coded 1 if the respondent declared support using the number of methods listed; 0 otherwise. The three methods are displaying political paraphernalia on one's body, on one's house, or at a rally. The outcome variable is coded 1 if respondent reported receiving a private benefit from a politician during the 2012 campaign; 0 otherwise. Circles shown for bivariate regressions, diamonds include controls, and squares include controls and municipal fixed effects. Thin (thick) whiskers denote 95 (90) percent confidence intervals, based on standard errors clustered at neighborhood level. Linear probability models are employed; results are robust using logit specifications. Appendix D reports full regression tables. Appendix B describes controls, which are: age, education, gender, household wealth, turnout, mayoral vote choice, political preferences (dummies for PT, PMDB, PSDB, and DEM parties), frequency of conversations with politicians, association membership, has piped water, has own cistern, has access to shared cistern, reciprocity, risk aversion, and time preference. Number of observations for the most inclusive specifications in all rows is 2,725.
Source: Author's analysis of the Rural Clientelism Survey. Data collected by Gustavo Bobonis, Paul Gertler, Marco Gonzalez-Navarro, and Simeon Nichter.

5.3 Quantitative Analysis of Declared Support

the effects of more extensive declaration, the 2012 wave included separate questions about whether respondents had displayed political paraphernalia on their bodies, on their homes, or at rallies during that year's campaign.[73] As demonstrated by the most inclusive specifications in Figure 5.3, citizens undertaking two of these declaration methods were 4.7 percentage points more likely – and those undertaking three declaration methods were 5.7 percentage points more likely – to be recipients than non-declarers. Both findings are statistically significant at the 1 percent level.[74] By contrast, citizens using just one declaration method were no more likely than non-declarers to receive a campaign handout.[75] Similar patterns are observed when examining the value of campaign handouts (not shown). Citizens undertaking two declaration methods received 44.8 percent more – and those undertaking three declaration methods received 66.2 percent more – reais of benefits than non-declarers (significant at the 5 and 1 percent level, respectively). In contrast, the effect of 5.4 percent for one declaration method is statistically insignificant.[76] Beyond revealing insights about effects on the extensive margin, the granular questions also confirm the robustness of the broader link between declared support and handouts: all specifications in the first row of Figure 5.3 remain statistically significant when using any of the three declaration methods in lieu of the "Any Declaration" variable (not shown).[77] The granular questions also demonstrate that the link is not merely due to any distribution of benefits at rallies; furthermore, the relationship between declared support and campaign handouts is virtually unchanged if rallies are excluded altogether as a form of declaration.[78]

---

[73] These granular questions were not repeated in the 2013 wave. Post-electoral analyses in the preceding section did not analyze these granular questions, as they do not differentiate between declarations for winners and losers. The questions asked about respondents' displays on their bodies (with campaign stickers or T-shirts), on their homes (with flags, banners or painted walls), and at rallies (with flags, banners or T-shirts).

[74] For all analyses in this paragraph, coefficients for two and three methods are statistically indistinguishable from each other, but are each significantly different than estimates for one method.

[75] About 4.7 percent of non-declarers received handouts, which is statistically indistinguishable from the corresponding percentage for those declaring in just one manner (5.1, 5.3, and 6.3 percent for citizens who declared exclusively on bodies, at rallies and on homes, respectively).

[76] When regressions include only recipients, extensive declaration is also linked to higher valued benefits.

[77] When including only one declaration method in a specification with controls and fixed effects, the effect is 2.5, 3.4, and 4.5 percentage points for declarations on homes, on bodies, and at rallies, respectively. These coefficients do not isolate effects of each declaration type, as citizens often declare with multiple types. Mere rally attendance without displays is *not* considered declaration, and has no effect on handouts.

[78] When excluding rallies from the "Any Declaration" dummy, the point estimate in the first row is nearly identical and remains significant at the 1 percent level. Analyses also show that citizens who attend but do not display paraphrenalia at rallies are no more likely than non-declarers to receive campaign handouts (not shown).

Any declared support

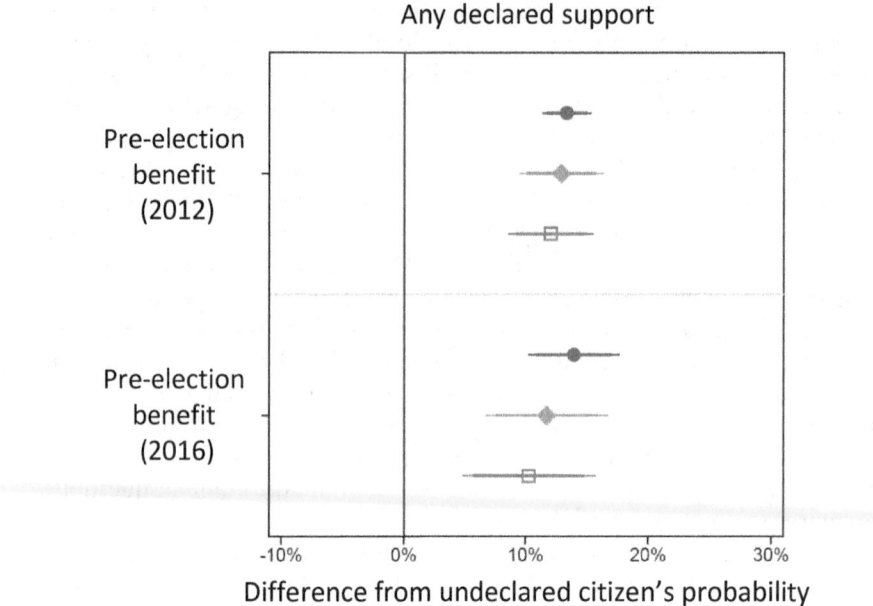

[Forest plot showing regression coefficients for "Pre-election benefit (2012)" and "Pre-election benefit (2016)" on the vertical axis, with "Difference from undeclared citizen's probability" ranging from -10% to 30% on the horizontal axis. Three specifications shown: No controls (circles), Controls (diamonds), Controls & fixed effects (squares).]

FIGURE 5.4 Declared support and campaign handouts, Brazil (2012 and 2016)
Note: Outcome variables listed on vertical axis; coded 1 if citizen received a private benefit during the 2012 (2016) municipal campaign. Markers correspond to regression coefficients for the explanatory variable, coded 1 if the respondent reported declaring support for any candidate during the contemporaneous campaign, 0 otherwise. Explanatory variable for the top (bottom) row is whether the respondent declared in 2012 (2016). Circles are shown for bivariate regressions; diamonds include controls, and squares include controls and state fixed effects. Thin (thick) whiskers denote 95 (90) percent confidence intervals, based on standard errors clustered at state level. Linear probability models are employed; results are robust using logit specifications. Appendix D reports full regression tables. Appendix B describes controls, which are: age, education, gender, income, turnout, mayoral vote choice, political preferences (dummies for PT, PMDB, PSDB, and DEM parties), risk aversion, and screeners for attentiveness. Number of observations for the most inclusive specification is 1,451 (Row 1) and 1,447 (Row 2).
Source: Author's analysis of the Online Clientelism Survey. Data collected by Simeon Nichter and Salvatore Nunnari.

Just as with the Rural Clientelism Survey, the online survey across Brazil also suggests that campaign handouts disproportionately flow to declarers. The first row of Figure 5.4 examines both declarations and pre-election benefits from politicians during the 2012 municipal campaign (regression tables are in Appendix D). Citizens who declared support for any candidate were 13.3 percentage points more likely than non-declarers to receive a campaign handout (significant at the 1 percent level). Indeed, over 21 percent of declarers reported

5.4 Declared Support and Signaling

receiving campaign handouts, compared to just 7.7 percent of non-declarers. This association continues to be significant when including all control variables described in the prior section, as well as state fixed effects.[79] Point estimates are 12.9 and 12.0 percentage points in the "Controls" and "Controls & Fixed Effects" specifications, respectively. The second row of Figure 5.4 examines declarations and pre-election benefits that occurred during the next municipal campaign, in 2016. Similarly, declarers were over 13.9 percentage points more likely than non-declarers to receive a campaign handout (21.2 versus 7.2 percent). Again, this association remains comparable in magnitude and significant at the 1 percent level in more inclusive specifications. Point estimates are 11.7 and 10.3 percentage points in the "Controls" and "Controls & Fixed Effects" specifications, respectively. The online survey did not include granular questions about specific forms of declaration or the value of handouts.

In sum, both the face-to-face survey in rural Northeast Brazil and the online survey across Brazil suggest that declarers disproportionately receive campaign handouts. These findings dovetail with the preceding section's key result – declared supporters experience favoritism with *post-election* benefits – which offered a more specific test of relational clientelism. When considered holistically, quantitative analyses thus suggest a robust link between declared support and relational clientelism, broadly consistent with interviews in Section 5.2. Notwithstanding this substantial evidence, it is important to emphasize that the regressions do not establish causality. As discussed in Chapter 1, some endogeneity is expected with relational clientelism because it involves a mutually reinforcing cycle: declared support reinforces established exchange relationships (which may originate from various sources).[80]

So far, this chapter has shown a strong empirical link between declared support and relational clientelism. Chapter 3 provided theoretical underpinnings to explain this link, based on a signaling model in Appendix C. To what extent is evidence consistent with this mechanism? The next section explores whether declarations indeed transmit meaningful information about the trustworthiness of citizens' vote promises.

5.4 DECLARED SUPPORT AND SIGNALING

Especially given the degree of ballot secrecy in Brazil documented in Chapter 2, it is important to investigate whether declarations convey meaningful information. Consistent with the theoretical logic elaborated in Chapter 3, evidence

---

[79] Control variables are fully described in Appendix B. Analysis employs state fixed effects as most municipalities in the sample have only one observation.

[80] In turn, citizens who continue to receive benefits extending beyond campaigns are more likely to declare support in future elections. For example, consider respondents in the online survey who indicated they declared support during the 2016 municipal campaign. In this subset, 24.2 percent said they had received a benefit from a politician during the preceding four years, versus just 9.1 percent of non-declarers (significant at the 1 percent level).

suggests that declared support enables many Brazilians to signal the credibility of their vote promises. Local politicians expressed confidence that declared support is informative, and both qualitative and quantitative evidence suggests that citizens overwhelmingly vote and hold preferences in accordance with their declarations.

Various politicians discussed how declared support provides information about how citizens vote. A councilor in Bahia argued that "the vote is only secret" when ballots are cast, "but nothing in this country works secretly." He then explained why many citizens' vote choices are known by politicians: "They put on a t-shirt, they put propaganda on their homes, they go out with a flag, they really declare. A good share."[81] Another politician remarked that when a voter publicly declares, a candidate "rests assured" about his or her support.[82] In Pernambuco, a councilor explained that when a person declares support with a flag or sticker on his home, he is 95 percent certain that he will vote for him.[83] Another councilor similarly indicated that observing such a declaration would provide "much more certainty" that someone will vote for him: "only 10 percent, or perhaps less" will not do so.[84] A few politicians, however, suggested some forms of declaration are less informative than others. For instance, one noted that political stickers are easily removed and can be swapped when visiting different places.[85]

Numerous citizens also expressed the belief that declared support would convey information about vote choices to politicians. An interviewee explained that the local politician he would turn to for medical assistance "knows that he voted for him ... because he declares his vote before voting."[86] Likewise, a carpenter indicated that his vote choice was known because his son had put a candidate's poster on the front door. He noted that a candidate observes such posters when passing by, and thus "sees who will vote for her and who won't. Whoever isn't going to vote for her, won't put up a poster on the door."[87] In another municipality, a citizen explained that "during the campaign, there are people monitoring all the streets," which enables politicians to "know who you vote for, who you don't vote for, if you have a sticker, if you don't."[88] In the words of a housekeeper, a politician "has confidence the person using his sticker will vote for him."[89]

---

[81] Author's interview, municipality in Bahia with 30,000 citizens (December 1, 2008).
[82] Author's interview, municipality in Bahia with 30,000 citizens (December 3, 2008).
[83] Interview by Gustavo Bobonis, Marco Gonzalez-Navarro, and Simeon Nichter; municipality in Pernambuco with 20,000 citizens (July 12, 2012).
[84] Interview by Gustavo Bobonis, Marco Gonzalez-Navarro, and Simeon Nichter; municipality in Pernambuco with 15,000 citizens (July 25, 2012).
[85] Author's interview, municipality in Bahia with 30,000 citizens (December 1, 2008, Interview 2).
[86] Author's interview, municipality in Bahia with 80,000 citizens (November 21, 2008).
[87] Author's interview, municipality in Bahia with 80,000 citizens (November 17, 2008).
[88] Author's interview, municipality in Bahia with 10,000 citizens (October 2, 2008).
[89] Author's interview, municipality in Bahia with 10,000 citizens (October 14, 2008).

5.4 Declared Support and Signaling

Survey evidence also suggests that declared support conveys meaningful information about whether citizens will vote for a given candidate. Both surveys discussed earlier asked respondents if they had publicly expressed support for any candidate, and then directly asked if they had voted for that candidate. In the Rural Clientelism Survey in Northeast Brazil, 92.6 percent of declarers indicated that they voted as they had declared. Furthermore, the quality of the signal appears to improve as declaration intensifies. While 90.0 percent of respondents declaring with a single method reported voting as they had declared, comparable figures were 93.8 percent and 95.7 percent for those declaring with two and three methods, respectively.[90] In the online survey across Brazil, 88.4 percent of respondents who had declared for a candidate reported that they had also voted for that same candidate.[91] The remainder of this section focuses on the Rural Clientelism Survey, which provides richer evidence about declarations and citizen credibility.

One might be concerned that this consistency is merely an artifact of self-reporting. For instance, citizens who report declarations might be inclined to say they voted for that candidate to avoid cognitive dissonance or due to clientelism. While such concerns cannot be entirely eliminated, a second approach is to compare for whom respondents say they voted – and for whom respondents say they declared support during that campaign – in different survey waves. Figure 5.5 employs this approach by using vote choices reported in the 2012 wave and declaration reported in the 2013 wave. As shown, the vast majority of citizens who publicly expressed support for a mayoral candidate (through displays of political paraphernalia on their bodies, on their homes or at rallies) also reported voting for the same candidate. Of citizens who had declared support for the victorious mayoral candidate, 92.5 percent also voted him or her. And of citizens who had declared support for a defeated candidate, 89.3 percent also voted for that candidate.

A third approach that does not involve self-reported declaration also finds similar patterns. When visiting respondents' homes after the 2012 election, enumerators noted whether they observed any declarations of support for political candidates. Overall, 16.5 percent of respondents' homes had at least one form of declaration: 9.0 percent had flags, 8.3 percent had stickers, 5.4 percent had signs, and 0.7 percent had painted declarations. Among homes with declarations observed for the elected mayor, 89.7 percent of respondents reported that they voted for him or her. And among homes with declarations observed for a defeated candidate, 80 percent of respondents reported they voted for that candidate. It should be noted that this alternative measure has some important drawbacks; for example, declaration may reflect the actions

---

[90] This calculation includes the following activities: (1) wearing campaign stickers or T-shirts, (2) placing political flags or banners on one's home, (3) painting one's home with a candidate's name, and (4) waving flags or wearing campaign T-shirts at a rally.

[91] $N = 836$. Of these declarers, 7.2 percent said they had not voted for that candidate, and 4.2 percent said they did not know.

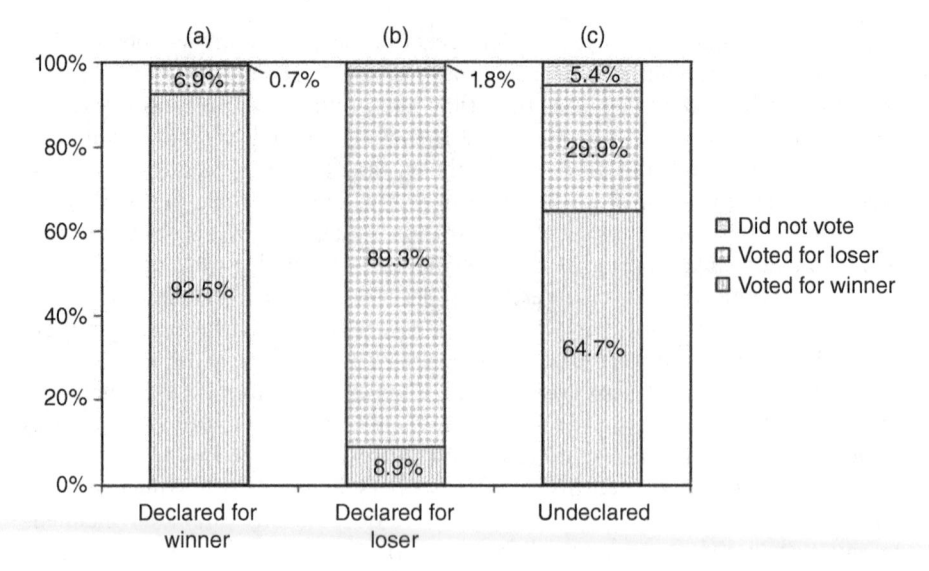

FIGURE 5.5 Declared support and voting for mayor, rural Northeast Brazil (2012)
Note: Respondents are divided into three subgroups (each represented by a bar): (a) respondents who declared during the 2012 campaign for the victorious mayoral candidate, (b) respondents who declared for a defeated mayoral candidate, and (c) respondents who did not declare for a mayoral candidate. The breakdown of each bar shows the share of each subgroup that: reported voting for the victorious candidate, voting for a defeated candidate, or not voting in the 2012 mayoral election. Vote choices from 2012 survey; declaration from 2013 survey. Excludes null and blank votes, which represent less than one percent of votes for all subgroups.
Source: Author's analysis of the Rural Clientelism Survey. Data collected by Gustavo Bobonis, Paul Gertler, Marco Gonzalez-Navarro, and Simeon Nichter.

and preferences of household members other than the respondent, and enumerators visited homes weeks after the 2012 election when many declarations had already been removed. Notwithstanding limitations of each approach, evidence suggests that the vast majority of survey respondents reported voting in accordance with their declaration actions.

Given that the theoretical discussion in Chapter 3 focuses specifically on citizens who promise to vote for a clientelist politician, it deserves emphasis that findings are similar when honing in on such respondents. Over a quarter of respondents said they had communicated their intended vote choices to politicians or their representatives during campaign visits to their homes. When asked directly, nearly 96.5 percent of declarers in this subset reported that they had voted for their declared mayoral candidate, a figure that climbs to 99.1 percent among those undertaking at least three declaration methods. Applying the second approach to this subset, 92.5 (97.7) percent of citizens who reported declaring support for the victorious (defeated) candidate also reported in a different wave that they had voted for him or her. And following the

5.4 Declared Support and Signaling

third approach, 95.1 (77.2) percent of respondents with enumerator-observed declarations for the victorious (defeated) candidate on their homes reported voting for him or her. Results are thus broadly consistent with this subset of respondents who had conveyed their vote choices to politicians.

Such patterns are also observed when using measures other than reported voting behavior. Just after the 2012 election, the Rural Clientelism Survey asked respondents to assess four characteristics of the mayor-elect, and subsequently those of the runner-up, as "very good," "good," "bad," or "very bad." These perceptions were strongly associated with declared support, even as reported in a different wave.[92] Only a small minority of declarers suggested the candidate they had publicly supported was weaker than the competitor on any measure. More specifically, the share ranking their declared candidate lower was 5.4 percent for competence, 5.9 percent for honesty, 12.3 percent for experience, and 14.6 percent for accessibility.[93] Regression analyses also reveal a strong association between declared support and perceived attributes of candidates. In comparison to non-declarers, Figure 5.6 shows that declarers for the mayor-elect ranked him or her higher across all attributes – and ranked the defeated candidate lower on all attributes. Moreover, declarers for the defeated candidate ranked him or her higher across all attributes – and ranked the mayor-elect lower on all attributes – than did non-declarers. All findings in Figure 5.6 are significant at the 1 percent level of significance, even when including controls and municipal fixed effects (regression tables are in Appendix D). For example, consider the four-point composite measure for each candidate, which averages a respondent's ratings for competence, honesty, experience, and accessibility. In the most inclusive specification, declarers for the mayor-elect ranked that candidate 0.24 points higher – and ranked the defeated candidate 0.31 points lower – than did non-declarers. Moreover, declarers for the defeated candidate ranked that candidate 0.45 points higher – and ranked the mayor-elect 0.50 points lower – than did non-declarers. All findings in Figure 5.6 are also significant (at the 1 percent level) when using declaration observed by enumerators instead of self-reported declaration.

As with voting, findings are robust when honing in on citizens who communicated their intended vote choices to politicians and their representatives during home visits. Among this subset, few declarers suggested that the candidate they publicly supported was weaker on any attribute than the competitor – only 3.5 percent for competence, 8 percent for honesty, 8.2 percent for experience, and 14.5 percent for accessibility.[94] And when conducting

---

[92] As discussed, only the 2013 wave asked respondents whether they had declared for victorious or defeated candidates.

[93] Analysis includes municipalities with two candidates. Declarers most often rated their own candidates most favorably (56.4, 48.5, 54.8, and 55.1 percent, respectively), but many rated the candidates equivalently (38.3, 45.6, 32.9, and 30.4 percent, respectively).

[94] Most often, respondents ranked their own candidate the highest, but 27.4–40 percent ranked both candidates equally (depending on the attribute).

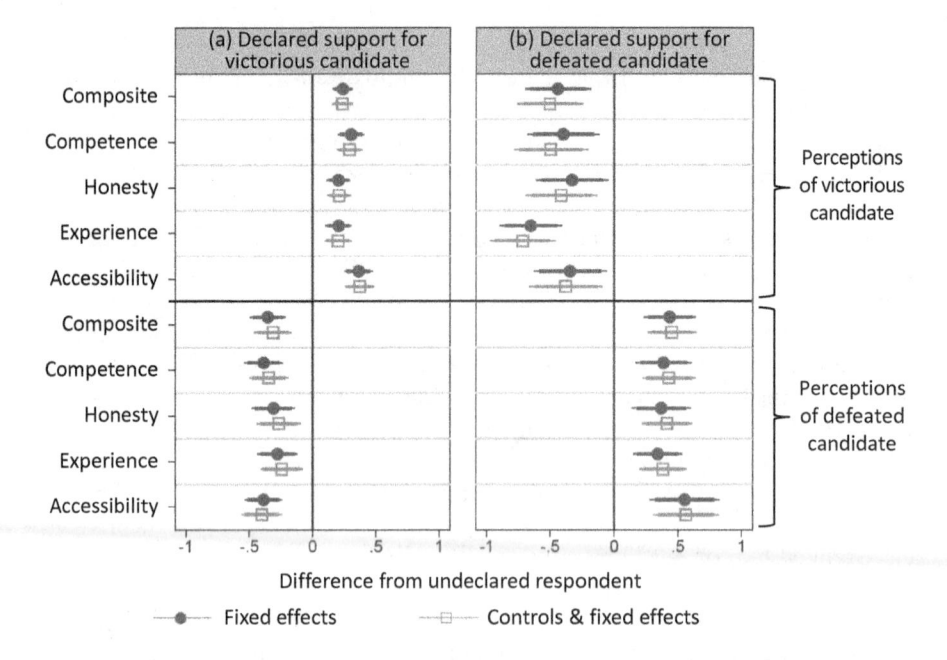

FIGURE 5.6 Declared support and perceptions of mayoral candidates, rural Northeast Brazil, 2012–2013
Note: Markers correspond to OLS regression coefficients for explanatory variables on horizontal axis; coded 1 if the citizen declared for victorious (defeated) mayoral candidates in 2012; 0 if undeclared. Outcome variables on the left axis are four perceived characteristics of the mayor-elect, and of the runner-up candidate, scored by respondents in 2012 on a four-point scale: "very good," "good," "bad," or "very bad" (greater values are better assessments). "Composite" averages these scores. Circles are regressions with municipal fixed effects; squares are those with controls and municipal fixed effects. All regressions include municipal fixed effects to compare across identical politicians. Perceptions from 2012 wave; declarations from 2013 wave. Thin (thick) whiskers denote 95 (90) percent confidence intervals, based on standard errors clustered at neighborhood level. Appendix D reports full regression tables. Appendix B describes controls, which are: age, education, gender, household wealth, turnout, mayoral satisfaction (from 2011 baseline), political preferences (dummies for PT, PMDB, PSDB, and DEM parties), frequency of conversations with politicians, association membership, collaborative efforts with neighbors, has piped water, has own cistern, has access to shared cistern, reciprocity, risk aversion, time preference, and public goods contribution. Number of observations for the most inclusive specification in rows 1–10 (respectively) is: 1,066; 1,375; 1,255; 1,397; 1,459; 1,067; 1,362; 1,191; 1,367; and 1,438.
Source: Author's analysis of the Rural Clientelism Survey. Data collected by Gustavo Bobonis, Paul Gertler, Marco Gonzalez-Navarro, and Simeon Nichter.

analyses in Figure 5.6 using only data from respondents who communicated their intended vote choices, findings are comparable, with 18 of the 20 most inclusive specifications significant at the 5 percent level or higher.[95] Employing

[95] Of 20 specifications, $p < 0.01$ for thirteen specifications, $p < 0.05$ for five specifications, and $p < 0.10$ for one specification.

the composite measure, citizens who reported declaring for the mayor-elect ranked him or her 0.22 points higher (on a four-point scale) – and ranked the defeated candidate 0.37 points lower – than did non-declarers. Moreover, declarers for the runner-up ranked that candidate 0.43 points higher – and ranked the mayor-elect 0.65 points lower – than did undeclared citizens. Furthermore, all results in Figure 5.6 are significant (at the 1 percent level) among this subset when using enumerator-observed instead of self-reported declaration.

Altogether, these findings about voting and perceptions are broadly consistent with the theoretical logic of declared support. Despite rigorous ballot secrecy in Brazil, this mechanism provides a highly informative signal about whether citizens will provide political support. After all, citizens overwhelmingly vote and hold perceptions in accordance with their declarations.

5.5 VOTER CALCULUS OF DECLARED SUPPORT

As explored thus far, evidence from Brazil corroborates the signaling logic of declared support, which provides an important mechanism by which citizens help to sustain relational clientelism. Recall that in addition to elaborating a signaling model, Chapter 3 briefly discussed a complementary model by Nichter and Nunnari (2017) that examines how numerous factors influence citizens' declaration choices. Given that the latter model provides further predictions about the voter calculus of declared support, it warrants investigation whether it offers additional insights into the behavior of Brazilians. For example, the complementary model suggests how and why various factors, such as politicians' monitoring ability and likelihood of electoral victory, can influence citizens' propensity to declare for a clientelist candidate. Furthermore, it examines how citizens weigh this decision vis-á-vis two alternative options: remaining undeclared and declaring for a programmatic candidate who does not provide contingent benefits. In Nichter and Nunnari (2017), we test the model's predictions experimentally in Brazil, so as to isolate the effects of particular contextual characteristics while holding all others constant.

The experiment, which was conducted as part of the Online Clientelism Survey, included 1,259 participants from 1,061 municipalities across Brazil.[96] It examined subjects' willingness to declare support for two fictitious mayoral candidates (A and B), using lottery tickets as clientelist rewards and to induce preferences about candidates. Participants increased their chance of winning an iPhone by earning more lottery tickets, based on their declaration actions and the election outcome. As clientelist inducements, citizens received additional lottery tickets if they declared for clientelist candidate A who subsequently won the election; the case of competitive clientelism was also examined. Subjects were randomly assigned to have different preferences about the

---

[96] See Appendix B for details about the broader Online Clientelism Survey, which also included additional participants in more municipalities.

candidates, induced through the number of iPhone lottery tickets received from each candidate's victory (regardless of declaration decisions). Participants made declaration choices in a set of randomly ordered elections, which each correspond to different treatments with distinct contextual characteristics. Before making a choice in a given election, the subject viewed a vignette with information including clientelist inducements, declaration costs, the probability of each candidate's victory, and the probability declarations are observed. After choosing whether – and for whom – to declare in an election, the subject was informed about which candidate won and any clientelist rewards earned; the computer selected the election winner based on odds resulting from the subject's declaration choice.[97] As a benchmark, one of the treatments was a baseline scenario involving clientelism. Each of the other treatments changed only one aspect of this baseline; thus, causal effects are identified by comparing differences in declarations between a given treatment and the baseline.

Experimental results corroborated most predictions in Nichter and Nunnari (2017), suggesting that the model provides meaningful insights into the voter calculus of declared support. The first treatment examined how participants' declarations changed in response to post-election contingent benefits. As predicted, fewer participants declared for the clientelist candidate when she eliminated benefits, whereas more participants chose to remain undeclared and to declare for the non-clientelist candidate. The second treatment investigated electoral competition, a contextual factor that is commonly understood to influence clientelist exchanges (e.g., Corstrange, 2018; Kitschelt and Wilkinson, 2007). In accordance with predictions, a greater share of participants declared for the clientelist candidate when she was highly likely to win the election, while fewer opted to remain undeclared and to declare for the non-clientelist candidate. The third treatment explored social costs, given that declarations for a particular candidate may be discouraged (or encouraged) in a given neighborhood (Huckfeldt, 1979; Huckfeldt and Sprague, 1992). As expected, when declaring for the clientelist candidate involved social costs, fewer subjects choose to declare for her, and more subjects chose to declare for the non-clientelist candidate. However, a predicted increase in non-declarations was not observed in the experiment. The fourth treatment examined the ability of the clientelist candidate to monitor citizens' actions, which often requires substantial resources and organizational infrastructure (Kitschelt and Wilkinson, 2007; Stokes, 2005). In line with the model, fewer participants declared for the clientelist candidate when her ability to monitor declarations decreased. But an expected increase in non-declarations and declarations for the non-clientelist candidate was not observed experimentally (though signs conformed with this prediction). Given that elites in various contexts employ negative inducements

---

[97] Candidates had equal odds of victory if the participant remained undeclared. If the participant declared for a given candidate, that candidate's probability of victory increased by an indicated amount. Formal predictions are identical if declarations have no election influence.

(Mares and Young, 2016, 2018), a fifth treatment investigated the effect of using punishments instead of rewards. As predicted, when the clientelist candidate punished citizens who declared for her competitor, more participants declared for the clientelist candidate, and fewer declared for the other candidate. However, non-declarations did not increase as anticipated.[98] In the sixth treatment, the clientelist candidate combined the use of positive and negative inducements. As predicted, more subjects declared for her, and fewer opted to remain undeclared; but contrary to expectations, declarations for the non-clientelist candidate did not decrease.[99] Since clientelism is often a competitive rather than monopolistic phenomenon (Corstange, 2016; Kitschelt, 2013), the seventh treatment examined the impact on citizens' declarations when not only candidate A, but also candidate B, distributed post-election benefits to her own declared supporters. All three findings comport with theoretical predictions: non-declarations and declarations for A decreased, while declarations for B increased. Summing up, experimental results were consistent with sixteen of the complementary model's twenty-one unconditional predictions.[100]

Overall, these results suggest that beyond vulnerability, various characteristics of the political environment shape citizens' propensity to declare support. As argued in this book, such declarations alleviate concerns about citizens' trustworthiness in the context of long-term exchange relationships, and thereby help to ensure the survival of relational clientelism.

5.6 SUMMARY

Substantial vulnerability spurs many citizens to buttress the stability of their ongoing exchange relationships with politicians. This chapter examined how declared support enables many Brazilians to mitigate a key challenge facing relational clientelism. Electronic voting and other factors discussed in Chapter 2 inhibit politicians from monitoring vote choices, exacerbating their concerns about whether clients will follow through on promises to provide political support. Through the mechanism of declared support, citizens are able to allay politicians' concerns about opportunistic defection by displaying political paraphernalia on their bodies, on their homes, and at rallies. The signaling model in Chapter 3 suggests that by declaring support, citizens can transmit meaningful information about whether their vote promises are credible. Both qualitative and quantitative evidence in the present chapter corroborates this theoretical logic.

[98] In order to isolate the effect of introducing punishments, analyses compare these results from those in the first treatment, in which A distributes no rewards.
[99] Analyses compare these results to the prior treatment, in which A only employs punishments.
[100] Nichter and Nunnari (2017) also examine two other factors, expressive utility and election influence, with predictions conditional on which candidate the subject is assigned to prefer. For those factors, results have the predicted signs but are only significant in some instances; statistical precision is lost when splitting the sample by preferences.

Many Brazilians publicly declare their political support through displays of campaign paraphernalia. These declarations are not only prevalent, but also increase during droughts, consistent with the argument that vulnerability motivates citizens to undertake actions that reinforce relational clientelism. Although citizens have multifaceted reasons for declaring support, substantial evidence points to a robust link between this phenomenon and relational clientelism. Two original surveys and many interviews with citizens and elites reveal widespread perceptions that declaring for a victorious candidate can increase citizens' receipt of post-election benefits. In concordance with these perceptions, regression analyses suggest that declared supporters of elected politicians are indeed more likely to receive benefits that extend beyond campaigns. In line with the signaling model, declared support transmits a highly informative signal of whether citizens in ongoing exchange relationships will follow through on their vote promises. Evidence suggests that citizens overwhelmingly vote and hold perceptions in accordance with their declarations.

Thus, declared support is an important mechanism by which citizens in ongoing exchange relationships can alleviate politicians' concerns about their trustworthiness. But another credibility problem also threatens the viability of relational clientelism. How can citizens assess whether an entrusted politician will actually follow through on promises of assistance during adverse shocks? The next chapter investigates another mechanism – requesting benefits – by which citizens glean information about politicians' trustworthiness and thereby further enhance the survival of relational clientelism.

6

Requesting Benefits

As explored thus far, the vulnerability of many citizens to adverse shocks motivates their purposive actions to sustain relational clientelism, which by definition provides contingent benefits that extend beyond election campaigns. Although incomes in many countries have risen substantially in recent decades, much of the world's population continues to be threatened by illness, unemployment, drought, and other shocks. In contexts where the state provides an incomplete safety net, many citizens depend on ongoing exchange relationships with politicians to cope with various risks. Yet the stability of such relational clientelism rests on the credibility of promises between politicians and citizens. The preceding chapter, which tested the logic of declared support in the Brazilian context, examined only one direction of the dual credibility problem inherent in relational clientelism. Citizens' declarations mitigate politicians' concerns about whether they will actually follow through with vote promises, but do not address citizens' concerns about *politician* credibility. How can a voter know whether to trust a politician who vows to help when severe drought or illness strikes? Such concerns are often justified. Many politicians make a broad range of promises about help they will supposedly provide to individuals, only to renege once elected. Building on the theoretical logic in Chapter 3, the present chapter investigates how many Brazilians undertake an important action – requesting benefits – that reveals information about politician credibility and thus helps to sustain relational clientelism.

If citizen requests are a rare phenomenon, then their potential role in relational clientelism would be rather limited. But a vast number of people across the globe ask politicians for benefits, a point emphasized in Chapter 7. Although few researchers would deny that many citizens initiate requests, the logic and implications of these demands are largely unexplored in the literature on clientelism. Most studies focus squarely on the supply side of clientelism, examining how and why politicians target citizens when offering handouts.

By contrast, this chapter focuses on citizen demands and how they can enhance the survival of relational clientelism. As Chapter 3 elaborated, citizens in ongoing exchange relationships not only elicit assistance through their requests, but also glean valuable information about whether their politicians' promises are trustworthy. By observing whether entrusted politicians fulfill their own requests over time, citizens can draw inferences about and screen against candidates whose promises of assistance are not credible.

As explored in this chapter, qualitative and quantitative evidence from Brazil favors this theoretical argument. First, many Brazilians request private benefits from politicians. Even in rural Northeast Brazil – a region often depicted as having a paucity of autonomous voters – citizens are not merely passive recipients of handouts. Second, vulnerability often motivates citizens to demand benefits: most requests pertain to life necessities, and they are more prevalent when adversity strikes. Moreover, in a collaborative field experiment in which our team randomized the construction of water cisterns, we found that reducing citizens' vulnerability to droughts reduces a broad array of demands from politicians. Third, politicians are responsive to many citizen demands in a manner consistent with relational clientelism. Requesters are more likely than non-requesters to receive benefits during both election and non-election periods – countering the possibility that politicians are either entirely unresponsive to citizen demands or are only responsive during campaigns. Furthermore, citizens who declared support for victorious candidates disproportionately receive benefits through requests – belying the possibility that this phenomenon merely reflects constituency service. And fourth, citizens often draw inferences about and screen against politicians, based on whether those politicians fulfill their requests. Analyses of hypothetical trust games and direct survey questions, as well as interviews, reveal a robust link between politicians' responsiveness and citizens' beliefs and behavior. Citizens with unfulfilled requests have worse perceptions of their politicians and are more likely to switch their votes away from candidates they have supported in the past.

Overall, evidence from Brazil corroborates the argument that requesting benefits is an important mechanism by which citizens fortify relational clientelism. Within the context of ongoing exchange relationships, voters screen against politicians with poor track records of fulfilling requests, and thereby alleviate their own concerns about opportunistic defection.

6.1 PREVALENCE OF CITIZEN REQUESTS

Across the world, many citizens make requests to politicians. This section establishes the prevalence of citizen requests; later sections demonstrate that many of these requests are fundamentally clientelistic in nature. A 2012 survey by the Latin American Public Opinion Project (LAPOP) suggests that over 13.9 percent of approximately 28,000 citizens in the Americas requested assistance

6.1 Prevalence of Citizen Requests

TABLE 6.1 *Share of Brazilians requesting help from politicians (1988–2014)*

	1988 PNAD	1996 PME	2007 LAPOP	2008 LAPOP	2010 LAPOP	2012 LAPOP	2014 LAPOP
Capital cities	3.5% (69,190)	3.8% (110,496)	10.2% (334)	11.9% (378)	6.3% (938)	9.9% (463)	2.9% (35)
Large cities	–	–	13.8% (167)	15.3% (281)	15.7% (515)	8.4% (83)	9.8% (479)
Medium cities	–	–	14.5% (207)	17.2% (233)	12.2% (263)	9.0% (424)	14.3% (468)
Small towns	–	–	10.7% (253)	22.0% (304)	13.4% (388)	14.6% (323)	18.0% (312)
Rural areas	5.0% (35,343)	–	13.9% (202)	19.4% (279)	15.7% (343)	14.7% (204)	18.6% (204)
Overall survey	4.3% (171,289)	3.8% (110,496)	12.2% (1,163)	16.9% (1,475)	11.4% (2,447)	11.2% (1,497)	14.0% (1,498)

Note: Table shows percentage of respondents requesting help from politicians, with number of observations in parentheses. Surveys in 1988 and 1996 asked if respondents made a personal request of any politician "by letter or telephone" in the last year. Surveys in 2007–2014 asked if respondents had "sought assistance from or presented a request to any office, official or councilperson of the municipality within the past 12 months." Overall survey total for 1988 PNAD includes 66,756 respondents in urban areas outside of capitals (population unspecified).
Source: PNAD 1988 (IBGE national household surveys); PME April 1996 (IBGE monthly employment survey in six state capitals); Latin American Public Opinion Project (2007–2014).

of local officials in the past year, with figures exceeding 22 percent in El Salvador and Guatemala.[1] In Brazil, five LAPOP surveys conducted between 2007 and 2014 indicate that between 11.2 and 16.9 percent of respondents had requested such assistance. Table 6.1 shows that citizen requests in Brazil tend to be most prevalent in small towns and rural areas, but are also substantial in metropolitan areas. Historical data on requests, while limited, demonstrate that citizen requests are not a new phenomenon. The census bureau's 1988 household surveys asked over 171,000 citizens across Brazil whether they made a personal request of any politician "by letter or telephone" in the last year. About 4.3 percent of respondents had made such requests, with a somewhat greater prevalence in rural areas than in capital cities (5.0 versus 3.5 percent). Eight years later, the census bureau repeated the question in the April 1996 Monthly Employment Survey of over 110,000 citizens in six state capitals, and found that 3.8 percent of respondents had made such requests of politicians. While this historical prevalence of requests is lower than figures in the more recent LAPOP surveys, they are not directly comparable as the earlier data only include requests by "letter and telephone."

[1] See question wording in caption of Table 6.1.

The Rural Clientelism Survey in Northeast Brazil provides deeper insights about citizen requests and is the primary data source employed in this chapter.[2] In 2013, a non-election year, over 7.7 percent of respondents requested private help from a mayor or councilor.[3] Given that an individual may request assistance on behalf of his or her family, it is also revealing to consider whether *any* respondent in each surveyed household had made a request.[4] Using this measure, 12.9 percent of surveyed households had requested help from local politicians in 2013. Citizens are more likely to request benefits from councilors, who are relatively more numerous and accessible than the mayor. Of respondents who requested help, 70.7 percent asked a councilor, 19.2 percent asked the mayor, and 10.1 percent asked both. Because the majority of councilors typically serve as part of the mayor's coalition, councilors also play an intermediary role in helping citizens to obtain benefits from the mayor.

Although requesting assistance from politicians does not inherently constitute clientelism, the fact that citizen requests swell during election years suggests that many Brazilians perceive a link between such requests and the provision of political support. Politicians overwhelmingly point to a surge in requests, such as a councilor who explained: "Right now it's election time ... it's the time that voters ask the most."[5] According to the Rural Clientelism Survey, 21.5 percent of respondents requested private benefits from a mayoral or councilor candidate during the 2012 municipal election year.[6] Again, the number of requests is even more striking when aggregating at the household level: in 37.5 percent of households in our sample, at least one surveyed individual had made a request of a candidate. Over three-fourths of requests in 2012 were directed at incumbents and challengers vying for the position of councilor rather than those vying for mayor.

The composition of handouts in Northeast Brazil draws attention to the role of citizen demands, as it is rather implausible that a politician would otherwise choose such a varied assortment of goods and services, especially if distributing a narrower list would yield economies of scale. Most requests fall in three broad categories: health care, water, and construction. In the 2012 and 2013 waves of the Rural Clientelism Survey, approximately one-third of private requests of politicians involved health care. When citizens ask the mayor or a councilor for such assistance, about half of requests involve medicine and half involve

---

[2] Appendix B provides details about this panel survey collected by Gustavo Bobonis, Paul Gertler, Marco Gonzalez-Navarro, and Simeon Nichter.

[3] Section 6.3 also includes a discussion of collective benefits; in 2013, 1.3 percent of respondents requested such benefits. Of course, some collective benefits may be distributed in contingent exchange for political support, and not all particularistic benefits involve clientelism (e.g., Kitschelt and Wilkinson, 2007).

[4] The 2012 wave of the Rural Clientelism Survey had 3,685 respondents. The 2013 wave had 3,761 respondents.

[5] Author's interview, municipality in Bahia with 10,000 citizens (November 26, 2008).

[6] In 2012, 3.1 percent of respondents requested community benefits. The 2012 wave asked about requests to candidates, and followed up to inquire whether the candidate was an incumbent. Of requests to councilor (mayoral) candidates, 58.6 (53.5) percent were of an incumbent.

6.2 Requests and Vulnerability

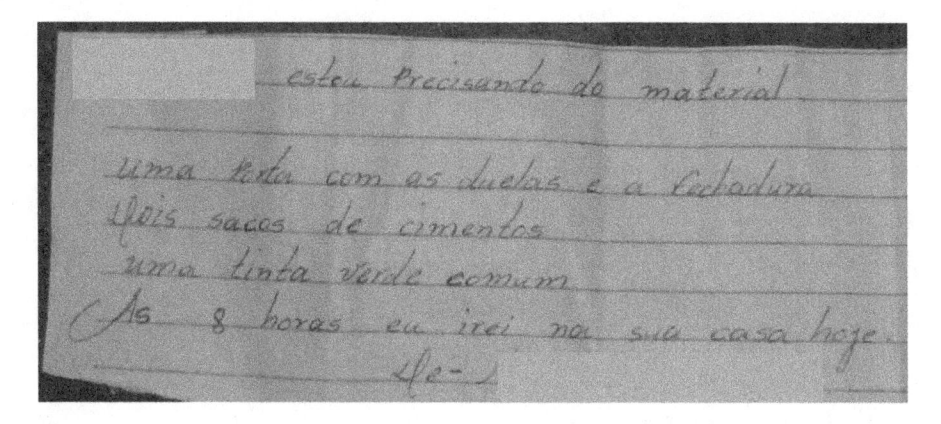

FIGURE 6.1 Example of citizen's request to councilor
Note: This note was shown by an interviewed councilor as he complained about the number of requests received during his 2008 reelection campaign. Without prompting, the councilor's supporter had slipped the note under his home's front door. It reads: "I need material. One door with hinges and a lock. Two sacks of cement. Plain green paint. At 8 o'clock I will go to your house today."
Source: Author's interview, municipality in Bahia with 10,000 citizens (September 26, 2008).

medical services. According to survey respondents, these services span various needs, such as eyeglasses, dentures, tooth extraction, ultrasounds, pediatric visits, female sterilization, MRIs, electrocardiograms, knee and gallbladder surgeries, and transportation to distant medical appointments. Another quarter of private requests directed towards politicians involve water. Examples include delivering water, constructing a cistern, digging a well, or installing household water pipes. Furthermore, a quarter of private requests of politicians involve other construction, such as asking for cement, bricks, tiles, bathroom construction, or tractor usage. While health care, water, and construction account for over three-fourths of all private requests, citizens also asked for a wide gamut of other benefits. As one councilor remarked, "there are requests for tires, requests for medicine, requests for food baskets. There are requests for everything."[7] Examples of other requests from survey responses include help with official documents, funeral assistance, food, gas (for cooking and driving), bicycle and motorcycle tires, automotive repairs, refrigerator repairs, beds, and soccer cleats. Overall, both the prevalence and varied composition of citizen requests suggest that this phenomenon warrants further investigation.

6.2 REQUESTS AND VULNERABILITY

The broader argument of this book is that vulnerability motivates many citizens to undertake purposive actions – such as requesting benefits and declaring

---

[7] Author's interview, municipality in Bahia with 10,000 citizens (November 24, 2008).

support – that help to sustain relational clientelism. Before examining the link between requests and clientelism, it is important to confirm the premise that vulnerability motivates citizens to ask for help.

Evidence suggests that the substantial vulnerability to life risks documented in Chapter 4 underlies many citizen requests in Brazil. One indication is the composition of benefits demanded: as just described, over half of requests involved health care and water, and many construction requests involved improving dilapidated homes. Numerous elites in Bahia explained that a lack of basic public services drives many citizens to ask politicians for such help. As a vice-mayor explained, "Since the state doesn't give you what you deserve, what you need, and there is no other way, what's the way you're going to seek it? It's the politician."[8] With respect to health care, a councilor elsewhere in Bahia argued that the "failure of the state" contributes to "the habit of requesting." This "habit" is so ingrained, he contended, that sometimes a citizen who obtains a doctor's prescription doesn't "even want to have the work of going to check if the medicine is available. He already knows there is a politician he can seek out, and the politician will try to resolve his problem, and he prefers to go to the politician."[9] A mayor further clarified why citizens often depend on politicians to supplement the public health system: "There are medicines we don't have in the public pharmacy. So they don't take the medicine, they don't resolve the problem for which they had a consultation. So they turn to us."[10] Raising an issue considered extensively in the present chapter, the mayor added that citizens often emphasize their political support when asking for medicine – they frequently insist: "Oh mayor, I voted for you, you have to give it to me." Such qualitative evidence, when considered in conjunction with the fact that most citizen demands involve necessities, suggests that the incomplete provision of public services contributes to many citizen requests directed towards politicians.

Hypothetical scenarios provide further evidence that citizens turn to politicians when facing adversity. Given that not all citizens experience shocks such as serious illness and drought in a particular year, the Rural Clientelism Survey included questions about whom respondents would turn to in three adverse situations. During the 2012 election year, about a quarter of respondents indicated they would ask a local politician for help before turning to any other source (including family, friends, and official channels): more specifically, 23.4 percent when out of water, 28.3 percent when in need of a medical treatment provided in the distant state capital, and 23.5 percent when in need of a medicine unavailable in the subsidized public pharmacy and public health clinic. The share that would first turn to a politician declined in 2013 but remained significant: 10.0 percent for the water scenario, 18.0 percent for

---

[8] Author's interview, municipality in Bahia with 80,000 citizens (November 19, 2008).
[9] Author's interview, municipality in Bahia with 80,000 citizens (November 21, 2008).
[10] Author's interview, municipality in Bahia with 30,000 citizens (December 1, 2008).

6.2 Requests and Vulnerability

the medical treatment scenario, and 11.0 percent for the medicine scenario.[11] These hypothetical scenarios – which had been experienced by a substantial share of respondents[12] – suggest that a large number of rural Brazilians turn to politicians as their first source of help when adversity strikes. The greater reliance on politicians during an election year points to an important issue explored later. For electoral purposes, many politicians fulfill requests during campaigns and also promise to provide future assistance. However, only a subset of these politicians actually help citizens after Election Day. Given that campaigns only represent a small share of the time that citizens are vulnerable to shocks, many Brazilians in ongoing exchange relationships are keen to ensure that such promises from their entrusted politicians are credible.

More rigorous evidence suggests that adverse shocks, in particular droughts, render citizens especially likely to turn to politicians for help. To explore this relationship, the Rural Clientelism Survey annexed satellite data on municipal precipitation to investigate whether survey respondents had recently experienced negative rainfall shocks. As described in Chapter 4, rainfall data were standardized to account for municipalities' rainfall patterns over the past quarter century. According to analyses conducted jointly with Gustavo Bobonis, Paul Gertler, and Marco Gonzalez-Navarro (2018), a one standard deviation decrease in rainfall between January and September of 2012 – before that year's municipal elections in October – resulted in a 3.9 percentage point increase in citizen requests of politicians over the course of 2012 (significant at the 1 percent level). Excluding requests for water, the negative rainfall shock increased requests by 2.0 percentage points (significant at the 5 percent level). Likewise, a one standard deviation decrease in rainfall during the municipal campaign led to an increase in overall citizen requests, a finding significant at the 1 percent level.[13] Overall, this evidence points to a link between adverse shocks and citizen requests.

In addition, our collaborative study shows that reducing citizens' vulnerability to adverse shocks reduces their demands of politicians (Bobonis et al., 2018). As discussed more extensively in Chapter 8, we randomized the construction of water cisterns, which reduce households' exposure to droughts by collecting and storing rainwater. More specifically, our team randomly selected households in our sample to receive 16,000 liter concrete water

---

[11] In 2012, the modal response in the medical treatment / medicine / water scenarios was turning first to a politician / family member / friend or neighbor. In 2013, the modal response in all scenarios was turning first to a family member. In all scenarios, under 1 percent indicated they would first ask associations, community leaders, or churches.
[12] The following percentages of respondents had previously experienced the scenarios: water (40.9 percent), medical treatment (24.1 percent), and medicine (44.8 percent).
[13] However, unlike the earlier period, the effect of drought on non-water requests during the campaign, while positive, was not statistically significant. Based on monthly rainfall data from July, August, and September 2012.

cisterns (valued at about $1,000 each); with respect to baseline characteristics, members of these households were statistically indistinguishable from control households. Receiving a cistern led to a significant overall decline in various requests of politicians in both the 2012 election year and the 2013 non-election year. When examining heterogeneity, this effect was only significant among citizens with established relationships with politicians, as defined by those who conversed at least monthly with them before the 2012 election campaign began. As explained in Chapter 8, these experimental findings are consistent with the logic that requesting benefits – an important mechanism of relational clientelism – is undercut when citizens' vulnerability declines.

Evidence thus far reveals that citizens frequently ask for help from politicians in Brazil, and these demands are often motivated by citizens' vulnerability to adverse shocks. The theoretical mechanism elaborated in Chapter 3 suggests that citizen requests help to sustain relational clientelism by revealing information about politician credibility. By definition, relational clientelism involves promises of post-election benefits, raising the threat of opportunistic defection by politicians. When a citizen asks a politician for help, she not only potentially receives a material benefit but also elicits information about the trustworthiness of that politician's promises to provide help reliably during times of need. Citizens screen politicians based on their track record of fulfilling requests, thereby alleviating the problem of politician credibility that threatens relational clientelism. The remainder of this chapter examines whether data from the Rural Clientelism Survey are consistent with the theoretical mechanism in Chapter 3. First, it examines whether an empirical link actually exists between citizen requests and relational clientelism. Then, it investigates whether citizens screen against politicians who deny their requests.

6.3 REQUESTS AND RELATIONAL CLIENTELISM

The theoretical mechanism elaborated in Chapter 3 would be inapplicable if Brazilian politicians simply ignored all of their constituents' requests. But the present section shows that is decidedly not the case. Moreover, this section suggests that obtaining benefits through requests is inherently political: for example, declared supporters are more likely to be recipients. And of fundamental importance, this section demonstrates that politicians' responsiveness to requests extends beyond election campaigns, indicating that many requests are part of ongoing clientelistic relationships rather than just electoral clientelism.

Qualitative evidence is explored extensively later, but it should be emphasized at the outset that many interviewees in Bahia conveyed a strong connection between citizen demands and handouts. For example, a mayor explained that "who requests is the voter. It's not the candidate who offers."[14]

[14] Author's interview, municipality in Bahia with 50,000 citizens (January 14, 2009).

6.3 Requests and Relational Clientelism

He attributed this pattern to how years of clientelist exchanges have shaped citizens' expectations, referring to a local idiom: "The habit of smoking a pipe leaves the mouth contorted." In another municipality, a councilor admitted to fulfilling requests – even during campaigns when doing so is illegal – but insisted that he never *offered* any benefits. Raising an issue investigated in the present chapter, he emphasized the pressure faced when supporters demand help: "You're between a rock and a hard place: Will I have to give? If I don't give, I won't get the vote."[15] Many citizens also noted a connection between requests and handouts. As a housekeeper remarked, "they aren't going to offer help to anyone. ... Really, if you want help, go to the local campaign office (*comitê*) and ask for help."[16]

The Rural Clientelism Survey provides evidence of politicians' responsiveness to many – though by no means all – requests during both election and non-election years. Overall, 59.4 percent of requests were fulfilled in 2012, as were 59.9 percent of requests in 2013. Another observation is that in both years, requests for fundamental necessities were far more likely to be fulfilled than other demands. For example, roughly two-thirds of requests for medicine, medical treatments and water were granted, versus just one-fifth of requests for building materials. As explored later, these figures alone do not provide a complete picture of politicians' responsiveness, in part due to self-selection with respect to who requests benefits. Nevertheless, they counter the notion that politicians might simply ignore all requests. The figures not only reveal politicians' responsiveness to many requests, but also point to considerable unmet demands. Unfulfilled requests often involve politicians' overt refusals to help, such as those described in the preceding chapter. In addition, numerous interviewees described an indirect approach by which politicians turn down requests: giving the runaround. For instance, one citizen complained that politicians "say they will help – 'come tomorow, come later' ... and one day passes, and another day passes, and you never obtain it."[17]

If politicians are responsive to many citizen demands, then one would also expect requesters to be more likely to receive help than non-requesters (*ceteris paribus*). The Rural Clientelism Survey reveals this pattern. In 2013, 41.6 percent of requesters received help, compared to just 1.8 percent of non-requesters. And during the 2012 municipal election year, 19.5 percent of requesters received help, compared to just 2.4 percent of non-requesters.[18] Moreover, politicians' fulfillment of requests represented a disproportionate share of handouts distributed. In 2013, requesters comprised nearly two-thirds of all recipients of particularistic benefits – even though just 7.7 percent of

---

[15] Author's interview, municipality in Bahia with 30,000 citizens (December 3, 2008).
[16] Author's interview, municipality in Bahia with 60,000 citizens (November 5, 2008).
[17] Author's interview, municipality in Bahia with 10,000 citizens (October 2, 2008). The survey did not ask whether requests were overtly denied, or how long requests took to be fulfilled.
[18] Unlike questions about whether requests were fulfilled, these separate questions ask if respondents received benefits from any politicians (see Figures 5.1 and 5.3).

citizens requested help. And in 2012, requesters comprised over two-thirds of recipients – even though just 21.5 percent of citizens requested help. While these findings are suggestive of politicians' responsiveness to citizen requests, an important concern is that they do not control for various factors that could affect results if associated with both requests and the receipt of benefits.

Regression analyses tackle this concern and suggest that the link between requests and benefits holds up to closer scrutiny, thereby providing additional evidence of politicians' responsiveness to citizen demands. Given that the provision of assistance beyond electoral campaigns is a defining attribute of relational clientelism, this section first considers requests and benefits in 2013, a non-election year. Figure 6.2 shows results for five outcome variables, each indicating whether a respondent received the specified benefit. Coefficients and confidence intervals are reported for a key explanatory variable: whether a respondent requested private assistance of a local politician at any point during the year. Appendix E provides full results for these specifications. The top row of Figure 6.2 indicates that a citizen who requested assistance from the mayor or councilor in 2013 had a 39.8 percentage point greater probability of receiving a benefit from a politician that year when compared to a non-requester.[19] This finding remains significant at the 1 percent level, with the point estimate falling slightly to 38.4 percentage points, when controlling for the over twenty variables included in analyses in Chapter 5. Recall that these variables are described in Appendix B and include respondents' socioeconomic factors (age, education, gender and household wealth), political characteristics (turnout, mayoral vote choice, preferences for the PT, PMDB, PSDB or DEM parties, and frequency of conversations with politicians), horizontal linkages (association membership and collaborative efforts with neighbors), water availability (piped water, own cistern, and access to shared cistern), and behavioral attributes measured by experimental games (reciprocity, risk aversion, time preference, and public goods contribution). In addition, controls are included for whether the respondent declared support for a victorious or defeated candidate in 2012. The finding in the top row of Figure 6.2 is also robust to the inclusion of municipal fixed effects, which control for unobserved differences across municipalities that do not vary among citizens in a given municipality. With both controls and municipal fixed effects, requesters had a 37.7 percentage point greater probability of receiving a post-election benefit than a non-requester (significant at the 1 percent level).

Similar patterns of politician responsiveness to citizen demands are observed with other post-election outcome variables. The second row of Figure 6.2 examines help from the municipal government, which is important because politicians may respond to demands by helping requesters to acquire a benefit

---

[19] This bivariate coefficient corresponds to the difference in probabilities mentioned in the previous paragraph.

6.3 *Requests and Relational Clientelism* 159

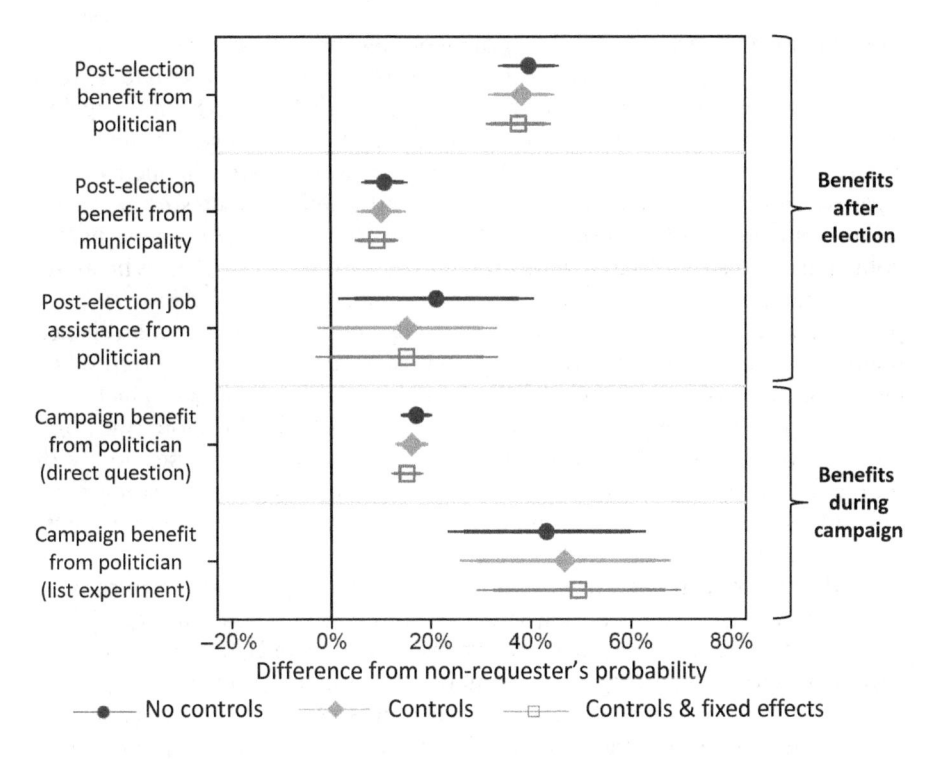

FIGURE 6.2 Citizen requests and private benefits, rural Northeast Brazil (2012–2013)

Note: Figure summarizes regressions in which each outcome variable is listed on the left axis, and the explanatory variable is whether the respondent requested a private benefit from a politician. Outcome variables coded 1 if the respondent received the specified benefit; 0 otherwise. Markers correspond to regression coefficients for the explanatory variable coded 1 if citizen requested a private benefit from a politician in 2013 (Rows 1–3) or 2012 (Rows 4–5). Circles shown for bivariate regressions, diamonds with controls, and squares with controls and municipal fixed effects. Thin whiskers on confidence intervals indicate 95 percent level; thicker lines indicate 90 percent level. Confidence intervals based on standard errors clustered at neighborhood level. Appendix E reports regression tables. Linear probability models are employed for the first four outcome variables; results are robust using logit specifications. Appendix Table E.4 describes analysis of the list experiment. Appendix B describes controls, which are: declared support for winner (loser), age, education, gender, household wealth, turnout, mayoral vote choice, political preferences (dummies for PT, PMDB, PSDB, and DEM parties), frequency of conversations with politicians, association membership, collaborative efforts with neighbors, has piped water, has own cistern, has access to shared cistern, reciprocity, risk aversion, time preference, and public goods contribution. Number of observations for the most inclusive specifications are 3,195 (Row 1), 3,223 (Row 2), 3,220 (Row 3), 2,720 (Row 4), and 3,085 (Row 5).
Source: Author's analysis of the Rural Clientelism Survey. Data collected by Gustavo Bobonis, Paul Gertler, Marco Gonzalez-Navarro, and Simeon Nichter.

from a municipal office rather than doling out resources themselves. As shown, a citizen who requests assistance from the mayor or councilor had a 10.9 percentage point greater probability of receiving a benefit from the municipality in 2013, compared to a non-requester. This finding remains significant at the 1 percent level with the inclusion of controls, as well as with the inclusion of both controls and municipal fixed effects (with point estimates of 10.2 and 9.2 percentage points, respectively). The third row of Figure 6.2 investigates politician responsiveness to requests for employment assistance. In the bivariate specification, a citizen who asked the mayor or a councilor for a job was 21.2 percentage points more likely to report employment assistance from an elected politician in 2013 than a non-requester (significant at the 5 percent level). When including controls, significance falls to the 10 percent level, and when including controls and municipal fixed effects, it falls just shy of that threshold (the point estimate for both specifications is 15.2 percentage points). The sensitivity of results for this indicator is not completely surprising, given that asking for a job and receiving post-election job assistance are both low-probability events in the sample.

Evidence about the first three outcome variables suggests politician responsiveness to citizen requests during a non-election year, as one would expect with relational clientelism. If responsiveness reflects ongoing exchange relationships, requesters should also disproportionately receive benefits during campaigns. The fourth row of Figure 6.2 reports that requesters also disproportionately received benefits during the 2012 municipal campaign. In the bivariate specification, a citizen who requested assistance from a mayoral or councilor candidate was 17.1 percentage points more likely to receive a campaign handout than a non-requester. This finding continues to be significant at the 1 percent level when including controls, as well as when including both controls and municipal fixed effects (point estimates are 16.2 and 15.3 percentage points, respectively). Results for this fourth outcome variable are consistent with relational clientelism, but provide only collateral evidence: unlike politicians fulfilling requests during non-election years, responsiveness during campaigns may reflect electoral clientelism (see Nichter and Peress, 2016). As underscored in Chapter 1, a campaign handout may comprise electoral or relational clientelism, depending on whether a citizen's receipt of contingent benefits extends beyond campaigns.

Given the illegality of campaign handouts in Brazil (see Chapter 2), sensitivity bias is a heightened concern with the fourth outcome variable just discussed. Citizens may not want to admit their involvement in an exchange that is prohibited during campaigns, and systematic bias may influence results (Gonzalez-Ocantos et al., 2012). Allaying this concern, similar patterns are observed even when using a less obtrusive measure designed to address sensitivity bias. Requesters were still far more likely to receive help in 2012 as measured by a list experiment, which involves an indirect approach comparing the responses of respondents randomly assigned to treatment and control groups. The control

6.3 Requests and Relational Clientelism

group was asked how many of four innocuous statements were true, such as whether politicians had radio advertisements or distributed stickers during the campaign. The treatment group was asked how many of five statements were true – the same four innocuous statements, as well as the additional statement that they had received help from a politician during the campaign. As shown in the bottom row of Figure 6.2, the list experiment estimated that requesters were approximately 43.2 percentage points more likely than non-requesters to have received a campaign benefit. This difference between requesters and non-requesters is 46.9 percentage points when including controls, and 49.6 percentage points when including controls and municipal fixed effects (both significant at the 1 percent level).[20] These results suggest that the relationship between requests and campaign handouts – which is indicative of politician responsiveness to requests – is not merely an artifact of sensitivity bias.[21]

Findings thus far belie the possibility that Brazilian politicians simply ignore all of their constituents' requests. Much to the contrary, local politicians are responsive to citizen demands during both non-election and election years. This pattern is consistent with relational clientelism, but it remains important to ascertain whether such responsiveness stems exclusively from constituency service, in which benefits are distributed without favoritism to specific citizens. For example, analyses in Appendix E suggest that politicians were also responsive to some citizen requests for club goods, which may or may not involve clientelism (as discussed in Chapter 5).[22] However, evidence suggests that in many instances, obtaining benefits through requests is inherently political. For example, when considering control variables in Figure 6.2, declared supporters are significantly more likely to be recipients of private benefits. Recall from Chapter 3 and 5 that declared support is an important mechanism of relational clientelism, in which citizens signal the credibility of their vote promises. In all specifications in the first three rows, citizens who had declared support for a victorious candidate during the 2012 campaign were significantly more likely (at the 1 or 5 percent level) – in the year after the election – to receive private benefits from a politician, private benefits from the municipality, and job assistance from a politician.[23] In addition, citizens who declared support for any candidate were significantly more likely (at the 5 percent level) to

---

[20] Analysis of the list experiment follows the method applied by Gonzalez-Ocantos et al. (2012), which employs OLS regressions and reports coefficients interacted with the treatment variable. Results are robust when following the methodology of Blair and Imai (2012).

[21] The Rural Clientelism Survey did not employ list experiments to examine benefits distributed in 2013. Sensitivity bias is arguably less of a concern with assistance given during non-election years, as it is not generally prohibited in Brazil.

[22] As shown in the most inclusive specifications, citizens who asked politicians for club goods were 22.1 percentage points more likely to receive them (significant at the 1 percent level).

[23] As reported in Appendix E, point estimates for the most inclusive specifications are 4.2, 3.5 and 2.8 percentage points, respectively. These specifications are similar to the declared support results presented in Chapter 5, but also include an explanatory variable about requests.

receive a campaign handout before the 2012 election;[24] however, this finding does not hold when using the list experiment. Moreover, in the hypothetical scenarios described in Section 6.1, declared supporters were significantly more likely to indicate that they would first turn to politicians when in need of help (not shown). The finding that declared supporters are more likely to receive benefits during both election and non-election periods points towards relational clientelism and suggests that constituency service cannot fully account for politicians' responsiveness to requests.

This pattern is also observed when the outcome variable is narrowed to benefits received by request. This alternative approach hones in on benefits involving citizens' demands, unlike the aforementioned outcome variables in Figure 6.2, which included both solicited and unsolicited benefits. Respondents are coded as receiving a benefit by request if they reported asking for help from a politician, and in an immediate follow-up question, reported receiving that help.[25] Consistent with relational clientelism, Figure 6.3 suggests that citizens who declared support were significantly more likely to receive benefits in this manner (regression tables are included in Appendix E). The left side of Row 1 reports that citizens who had declared support for a victorious mayoral or councilor candidate in the 2012 election were 4.6 percentage points more likely than non-declarers to receive a benefit by request in 2013 (significant at the 1 percent level). This estimate, which includes controls and municipal fixed effects, is substantial given that only 4.6 percent of all citizens received a benefit by request in 2013.[26] By contrast, citizens who had declared support for a defeated candidate in 2012 were not significantly more (or less) likely than non-declarers to receive a benefit by request.[27] Another indicator – whether a respondent frequently talks to a politician – provides further evidence of a link between responsiveness and ongoing relationships.[28] The right side of Row 1 estimates that in 2013, citizens who talked to a politician at least monthly were 11.9 percentage points more likely to receive a benefit by request than citizens who did not have such conversations; this finding is significant at the 1 percent level and includes controls and municipal fixed effects. Effects are similar but smaller in magnitude when examining handouts distributed during the 2012 election year (Row 3). Citizens who had declared support for any candidate were 3.5 percentage points more likely than non-declarers to receive a benefit

---

[24] The point estimate is 2 percentage points (see Appendix E). Specifications for 2012 examine declaration for *any* candidate because benefits were delivered before a winner was elected.

[25] By contrast, specifications earlier in this chapter examined the association between: (a) this first question about requests, and (b) questions in different part of the survey about whether respondents had received any benefits from politicians.

[26] Recall that 7.7 percent of all respondents requested benefits in 2013, and 59.9 percent of these requests were fulfilled.

[27] Result shown in Appendix E.

[28] This variable is included in all specifications with controls reported in Chapters 5 and 6.

6.3 Requests and Relational Clientelism

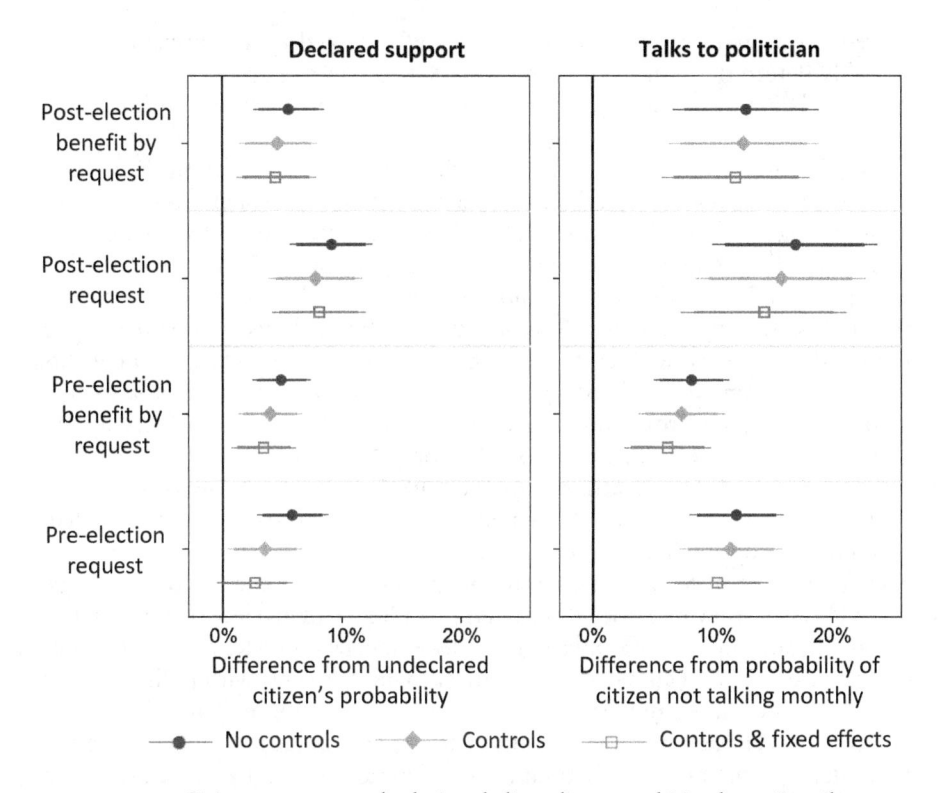

FIGURE 6.3 Citizen requests and relational clientelism, rural Northeast Brazil (2012–2013)

Note: Figure summarizes regression specifications in which outcome variables are listed on the left axis, and explanatory variables are listed on the top axis. With respect to outcome variables, "Post- (pre-) election benefit by request" coded 1 if the respondent reported asking for help from a politician in 2013 (2012), and in an immediate follow-up question, reported receiving that help; 0 otherwise. "Post- (pre-) election request" coded 1 if the respondent reported asking for help from a politician in 2013 (2012); 0 otherwise. With respect to explanatory variables, for Rows 1 and 2, "Declared support" coded 1 if declared for any victorious candidate during the 2012 campaign, and "Talks to politician" coded 1 if conversed with politician at least monthly in 2013; 0 otherwise. For Rows 3 and 4, "Declared support" coded 1 if declared for any candidate during the 2012 campaign, and "Talks to politician" coded 1 if conversed with politician at least monthly in pre-campaign period (January–June 2012). Markers correspond to regression coefficients for each listed explanatory variable. Circles shown for bivariate regressions, diamonds with controls, and squares with controls and municipal fixed effects. Thin whiskers on confidence intervals indicate 95 percent level; thicker lines indicate 90 percent level. Confidence intervals based on standard errors clustered at neighborhood level. Linear probability models are employed; results are robust using logit specifications. Appendix E reports regression tables. See Figure 6.2 for a list of included control variables. Number of observations for the most inclusive specifications are 3,225 (Row 1), 3,224 (Row 2), 3,111 (Row 3), and 3,111 (Row 4).
Source: Author's analysis of the Rural Clientelism Survey. Data collected by Gustavo Bobonis, Paul Gertler, Marco Gonzalez-Navarro, and Simeon Nichter.

by request in 2012.[29] In addition, citizens who talked to a politician at least monthly before the campaign began were 6.2 percentage points more likely to receive a benefit by request in 2012, when compared to citizens without such conversations. These estimates include controls and municipal fixed effects, and are significant at the 5 and 1 percent level, respectively. Overall, these findings are again consistent with relational clientelism. Even though some citizens without ongoing exchange relationships have requests fulfilled by politicians – suggesting the coexistence of some constituency service – the key point is that citizens in such relationships are substantially more likely to receive a benefit through bottom-up demands. Among citizens who both declared support *and* frequently conversed with politicians, the probability of receiving such benefits was 19.8 percent during both years. By contrast, among citizens who met neither criteria, this probability was only 10.5 percent in the 2012 election year, and just 3.3 percent in the 2013 non-election year.[30]

A key reason why such citizens are more likely to receive benefits by request is that they are more likely to demand assistance from politicians. Indeed, qualitative evidence discussed later reveals why some interviewees refrain from asking the mayor or a councilor for help: they expect their requests to be denied because they had not supported the candidacy of an election winner. The Rural Clientelism Survey similarly provides evidence consistent with such self-selection, as declared supporters and citizens who converse with politicians are more likely to initiate requests. Row 2 in Figure 6.3 suggests that citizens who had declared support for a victorious candidate in the 2012 election were 8.1 percentage points more likely than non-declarers to request private assistance from a politician in 2013 (significant at the 1 percent level). This estimate, which includes controls and municipal fixed effects, is substantial given that only 7.7 percent of all citizens made such a request in 2013. Turning to another variable in the same specification, Row 2 also shows that citizens who talked to a politician at least monthly were 14.3 percentage points more likely to request help in 2013, when compared to citizens without such conversations (significant at the 1 percent level). Similar patterns are observed during the 2012 election year. Citizens who had declared support for any candidate were 5.9 percentage points more likely than non-declarers to request help in 2012 (significant at the 1 percent level). Row 4 reports that the significance of this relationship falls to the 5 percent level when adjusting for control variables and to the 10 percent level when also including municipal fixed effects (with point estimates of 3.6 and 2.7 percentage points, respectively). In this most inclusive specification, citizens who talked to a politician at least monthly before the campaign began were 10.4 percentage points more likely to receive a benefit

---

[29] The substantive effect is smaller, as 12.8 percent of all citizens received a benefit by request in 2012. The 2012 analysis examines benefits distributed before the election, so declaration for any candidate is included.

[30] Predicted probabilities employ the most inclusive specifications in Rows 1 and 3 of Figure 6.3. The 2012 (2013) specification refers to declaration for any (victorious) candidates.

6.3 Requests and Relational Clientelism

by request in 2012, when compared to citizens without such conversations (significant at the 1 percent level). These findings are consistent with self-selection and provide an important reason why citizens who declare support or converse frequently with politicians disproportionately receive benefits through requests.

Interviews provide further insight about why self-selection affects citizen requests in a context with relational clientelism. Numerous Bahians attributed their aversion to requesting help to the belief that elite responsiveness is conditional on political support. For example, a homemaker complained that citizens who declared against politicians in the prior campaign are especially discriminated against. Such citizens "can't ask," she explained, because politicians will retort: "Oh you didn't vote for me, so go ask your candidate that you voted for, didn't he lose? They sneer in your face."[31] In another interview described in Chapter 5, a maid relayed a vivid example of her own traumatic experience. She had fallen while pregnant and visited the public hospital in pain. She was told no ultrasound machine was available, so checking her injury would involve traveling to a nearby larger town and paying out of pocket for an ultrasound at a private clinic. Then, she recounted: "I went to the councilor and asked for help, and he said that he couldn't help me because I hadn't voted for him." By working, she earned money to pay for the ultrasound on her own.[32] Overall, various citizens insisted there was no point of asking a politician for help unless one had clearly supported his or her candidacy. "Get this in your head," one interviewee carped, "if I didn't vote for the other side – what do I have to ask something from the other side? ... I'm not going to! I'm not going to!"[33] Despite such interview evidence, however, it is important to emphasize that analyses of the Rural Clientelism Survey find no bias with respect to politicians' fulfillment of the requests they receive. For example, declared supporters are no more (or less) likely to have their requests fulfilled than undeclared citizens or declared opposers. Instead, the reason declared supporters are more likely to receive benefits through bottom-up demands is that they are far more likely to ask politicians for help. Self-selection provides an explanation for this result: citizens who expect to face discrimination do not initiate requests of politicians, so the bias is not explicitly observed.[34]

Another pattern involving citizen requests also points toward relational clientelism, thereby countering the possibility that politicians' responsiveness exclusively reflects constituency service. The vast majority of citizens with requests fulfilled by politicians report a history of supporting those politicians. More specifically, citizens who reported a fulfilled request in 2013 were asked if

---

[31] Author's interview, municipality in Bahia with 15,000 citizens (January 13, 2009).
[32] Author's interview, municipality in Bahia with 10,000 citizens (October 14, 2008).
[33] Author's interview, municipality in Bahia with 10,000 citizens (October 2, 2008).
[34] Analogously, Mares and Young (2016) discuss how negative inducements can be effective without observing punishments if citizens vote for a politician because they believe they will be punished otherwise.

they had previously voted – in the prior municipal elections of 2008 and 2012 – for the politician who recently fulfilled their request.[35] Nearly 84.5 percent of citizens with requests fulfilled by their mayor in 2013 indicated they had voted for that politician in 2012, and 82.1 percent reported voting for him or her in 2008 (if the politician had run).[36] Moreover, 80.3 percent of citizens with requests fulfilled by councilors in 2013 indicated they had voted for them in 2012, and 79.7 percent reported voting for those councilors in 2008 (if they had run).[37] These figures should be interpreted cautiously: vote choices may be hard to recall, the number of observations is relatively small, and responses may be influenced by benefits received. Notwithstanding these concerns, such findings are again consistent with relational clientelism.

In sum, requesters are significantly more likely to receive benefits during both election and non-election years – countering the possibility that politicians are either entirely unresponsive to citizen demands or are only responsive during campaigns. Furthermore, citizens who declared support for victorious candidates, or who frequently converse with politicians, disproportionately receive benefits through requests – belying the possibility that this phenomenon merely reflects constituency service. Although not explored in this chapter, additional survey evidence also points to such patterns more broadly across Brazil.[38] Despite a preponderance of qualitative and quantitative evidence that is suggestive of relational clientelism, it warrants emphasis that these regressions do not establish causality. While they control for various factors and municipal fixed effects, omitted variables bias and reverse causality cannot be ruled out. In fact, some degree of endogeneity is expected with relational clientelism because it involves a mutually reinforcing cycle: the ongoing fulfillment of citizen requests reinforces established relationships (which may originate from various sources).

This overall evidence indicates a strong empirical link between citizen requests and relational clientelism, consistent with the theoretical mechanism of screening elaborated in Chapter 3. To test the underlying logic of that mechanism, I now investigate whether citizens screen against politicians who deny their requests.

6.4 REQUESTS AND SCREENING

Both qualitative and quantitative evidence comports with the theoretical mechanism presented in Chapter 3, in which requesting benefits enables citizens

---

[35] Only the 2013 wave asked this question.
[36] Number of observations is 58 and 28, respectively.
[37] Number of observations is 127 and 69, respectively.
[38] Using LAPOP data, Figure 7.2 shows that Brazilians who request help are more likely to experience clientelism during campaigns. Moreover, analyses of the Online Clientelism Survey suggest requesters are more likely to receive assistance from politicians during both election and non-election years, with declared supporters as more likely recipients (not shown).

6.4.1 Qualitative Evidence of Screening

Interviews in Bahia provide insight about how a politician's reputation for fulfilling requests often serves as a screening device. As now explored, many local politicians promise to provide assistance during future times of need, but citizens encounter both trustworthy and untrustworthy types of politicians. Given uncertainty about politicians' trustworthiness, citizens frequently screen them by refusing to vote for those who have denied their requests. This screening mechanism in turn motivates politicians to fulfill clients' requests, so as not to tarnish their reputations and lose political support.

Interviewees often provided two dramatically different characterizations of politicians, which I refer to as "trustworthy" and "untrustworthy" types. Turning first to the untrustworthy type, many citizens described skepticism toward politicians because so many make empty promises to provide help reliably during bouts of adversity. For example, one farmer claimed that "everything they promise is a lie," while another explained that "[m]any in politics promise heaven and earth and do nothing!"[39] Such distrust is consistent with a national study mentioned in Chapter 1, in which 82 percent of Brazilians reported that most candidates do not fulfill promises they make during campaigns.[40] When evaluating whether politicians will reliably fulfill requests during future times of need, leery citizens strive to avoid such untrustworthy types who "promise, promise and never fulfill."[41]

Despite expressing vitriol toward such politicians, many citizens also described trustworthy types: those who follow through on promises to fulfill requests during times of need.[42] When describing such politicians, citizens overwhelmingly focused on long-standing relationships with politicians who developed reputations for reliably helping them whenever they sought assistance. For instance, a homemaker emphasized the importance of a candidate helping for a long time and explained: "I'll always be able to count on him ... I can trust in him and I am certain that he will help me."[43] She described

---

[39] Author's interviews, municipality in Bahia with 50,000 citizens (November 11, 2008, and November 14, 2008).
[40] National survey of 1,502 Brazilians conducted in July 2008 by research firm Vox Populi on behalf of the Associação dos Magistrados Brasileiros.
[41] Author's interview, municipality in Bahia with 10,000 citizens (October 2, 2008).
[42] While many interviewees described both types of politicians, some described only untrustworthy types. To provide a breadth of perspectives, each quote describing types is from a distinct respondent.
[43] Author's interview, municipality in Bahia with 15,000 citizens (January 13, 2009).

the "loyal" councilor for whom she voted as follows: "When you need him, you go there, speak with him, and he's there ready to help you. Like if your son is sick, and you're unable to buy the medicine ... 'Here's my prescription, I'd like you to help me with the medicine, can you?' And he gave you the medicine." Politicians also recognized the link between a reputation for fulfilling a citizen's requests and trust, though they tended to focus on citizens' trust in them rather than on their own trustworthiness. For example, a mayor explained that a pattern of fulfilled requests, such as transporting one's child to the doctor or providing a coffin for a funeral, creates a "bond of trust." In turn, a citizen "stays loyal" to a politician who repeatedly fulfilled requests because "when you create a real relationship of trust with a certain candidate – a councilor or mayor – you think that he resolves all of your problems."[44]

Developing a reputation for fulfilling a citizen's requests, or more broadly for helping a citizen, typically requires ongoing interactions extending beyond an electoral campaign. Citizens tend to prefer politicians who have helped them for longer durations, often attributing this preference to a greater expectation that such politicians will help them in the future. To investigate this pattern observed during my interviews, the Rural Clientelism Survey asked citizens to choose between two hypothetical mayoral candidates who had given them the same overall amount of particularistic help but over different time spans: (1) João had provided a large amount of help to the citizen during the political campaign, and (2) Francisco had provided small amounts of help repeatedly for more time. Enumerators presented a graphic when asking this question, illustrating that both hypothetical candidates had provided the same amount of cumulative help. Respondents overwhelmingly preferred the candidate with the longer track record of more modest help: 80.2 percent chose Francisco, 17.8 percent chose João, and 2 percent indicated they would choose neither candidate. Using the same question during qualitative research, interviewees in Bahia often explained they preferred Francisco (who provided assistance for a longer duration) because he was deemed more likely to help them in the future. In a typical response, a maid explained that Francisco "is a person who I'll be certain that I can count on at any time, independent of being a campaign or not."[45] A bartender explained that Francisco "has always and he will always help you, because he has. And [João], tomorrow ... he won't help you."[46] Furthermore, many citizens expressed incredulity about the promises of candidates like João who only provide help during the campaign, even if that help is substantial. For example, a fireman explained that João "forgets you" and treats you "like a dog" once elected.[47] Aside from this hypothetical vignette, other comments during various interviews similarly expressed skepticism about promises from

---

[44] Author's interview, municipality in Bahia with 30,000 citizens (December 1, 2008).
[45] Author's interview, municipality in Bahia with 100,000 citizens (December 22, 2008).
[46] Author's interview, municipality in Bahia with 10,000 citizens (October 1, 2008).
[47] Author's interview, municipality in Bahia with 10,000 citizens (October 4, 2008).

6.4 Requests and Screening

politicians who only start to help during a campaign. In the words of a housekeeper: "Why only during the campaign? I think that if somebody is concerned, has the goal of helping us, I think help before, not just now. ... I will never trust these people. Never! My vote? I don't give it!"[48] The same interviewee explained that she chooses her mayoral candidate on the basis of being helpful for years, conveying the example of how her candidate fulfilled a transportation request when her son fractured his arm.

Interviews reveal not only how reputations are developed, but also how reputations are employed as a screening device. Citizens frequently screen politicians by refusing to vote for those who have denied their requests. For example, the bartender just mentioned explained how he would cut off support if his politician were to deny a request: "If he says no, I will already jump to the other side – 'I won't vote for you any more, I'm going to campaign for you to lose because you didn't fulfill your promise ... you're a liar.'"[49] Politicians were even more direct about how citizens sever their support for politicians who fail to fulfill requests. As one councilor explained:

"If you had 200 votes, then your family becomes 200 people. You have an obligation to serve those people, because the day that you stop serving one of those people, you've lost that vote. ... If he asks for medicine, you have to give it. If he asks for food, you have to give it. If you don't give it, then you've lost that voter."[50]

Consistent with the screening logic, interviewees suggest that citizens with denied requests even turn against politicians who had helped them for years. A mayor illustrated this point by discussing a candidate who had previously given a supporter a new bicycle. Just two weeks before the election, the candidate refused to replace its flat tire. The supporter became disgruntled and then voted for a competitor who had fulfilled the tire request. More broadly, he warned that "if you make a visit, and you say to a voter that you aren't able to give, he no longer votes for you."[51] Given that politicians understand the role of citizen requests as a screening mechanism, this threat of losing support is often implicit. However, some politicians also provided examples of requesters overtly threatening to withhold support if denied. For instance, a councilor reported that "I had various voters who pressured me – 'If you don't give me, then I won't vote for you.'"[52]

Given that many citizens screen politicians based on their responsiveness to past requests, politicians often have an incentive to help those who turn to them for assistance. As discussed, developing a favorable reputation in the eyes of a voter often requires a long-term investment in which a politician helps the citizen over an extended period. By fulfilling a citizen's request, a politician

---

[48] Author's interview, municipality in Bahia with 10,000 citizens (September 25, 2008).
[49] Author's interview, municipality in Bahia with 10,000 citizens (October 1, 2008).
[50] Author's interview, municipality in Bahia with 10,000 citizens (November 24, 2008).
[51] Author's interview, municipality in Bahia with 15,000 citizens (January 14, 2009).
[52] Author's interview, municipality in Bahia with 50,000 citizens (November 11, 2008).

protects this reputation and prevents losses in political support. A councilor explained how the risk of losing a loyal supporter contributed to his decision to fulfill a medicine request:

"If a sick person arrived ... and I know this person always helped me, how could I not help? I'd say, 'Look, I'll give you the medicine, here is the money, don't tell that I gave it to you, because this is prohibited by the Electoral Court. ... I knew that if I didn't give I would lose the family's vote. I had to give something."[53]

Politicians warn that even declared supporters may turn against them if their requests are denied. For example, another councilor explained that a politician can be confident she will receive votes from "quiet" declared supporters who do not request help. But if a hypothetical declared supporter named Marcelo "starts to request, then [a politician] has to help Marcelo – if not, Marcelo may switch."[54] Overall, the threat of losing political support applies pressure on many politicians to fulfill requests, so much so that several even complained of being held "hostage" by citizen requests.[55]

In sum, qualitative evidence from Bahia comports with the logic of screening elaborated in Chapter 3. Within clientelist relationships, an important function of requesting benefits is acquiring information about whether politicians are trustworthy, even though their primary purpose is typically obtaining help amidst adversity. When citizens vote, they typically lack complete information about whether a given politician is a "trustworthy" type who will follow through on promises to provide assistance during shocks. However, citizens can mitigate this information asymmetry by screening against politicians with tarnished reputations – that is, refusing to vote for those who have denied their own requests in the past. In this way, citizen requests help to alleviate the problem of politician credibility that threatens the stability of relational clientelism.

6.4.2 Quantitative Evidence of Screening

Quantitative evidence is also consistent with the screening logic, which yields several predictions about how requests affect the beliefs and actions of citizens in contexts with relational clientelism. With respect to beliefs, if politicians' responsiveness transmits information about their hidden characteristics, one would expect citizens to have worse perceptions of mayors and councilors who deny their requests. In line with this prediction, analyses show that citizens with unfulfilled requests perceive that their politicians will return less money to others in hypothetical trust games. Moreover, citizens with unfulfilled requests have worse perceptions of incumbents when asked directly in survey questions.

---

[53] Author's interview, municipality in Bahia with 50,000 citizens (November 13, 2008).
[54] Author's interview, municipality in Bahia with 30,000 citizens (December 3, 2008).
[55] For example: Author's interview, municipality in Bahia with 10,000 citizens (November 5, 2008).

6.4 Requests and Screening

With respect to actions, if citizen requests serve a screening function, one would expect citizens whose requests are not fulfilled to be more likely to turn against politicians they had supported in the past. Consistent with this prediction, analyses suggest that citizens with unfulfilled requests are less likely to vote for politicians they voted for in a previous election. While it is important to recognize that these analyses do not establish causality, systematic differences in citizens' perceptions and behavior comport with predictions of the screening mechanism.

First, consider citizens' perceptions about politicians. In both hypothetical trust games and direct questions, citizens whose requests had been fulfilled by politicians (during election or non-election years) exhibited more positive perceptions about their politicians. In 2013, one year after Brazil's municipal elections, the Rural Clientelism Survey asked respondents how they expected the councilor for whom they voted in 2012 to behave in a series of hypothetical trust games. In each trust game, an unidentified random citizen ("Ana," for ease of exposition) from the municipality was paired with the respondent's councilor. To paraphrase, each respondent was asked: "If Ana sends your councilor R$2, and we triple that money so your councilor receives R$6, how much would your councilor send back to Ana?" As shown in Figure 6.4, the amount of money respondents expected their councilors to return differed significantly between citizens with fulfilled and unfulfilled requests. Citizens whose requests for private assistance from local politicians had been fulfilled in 2013 expected their councilor to return R$1.58, versus just R$1.17 for citizens whose requests had not been fulfilled (a difference significant at the 5 percent level). As with all analyses in this section, a limitation is that the Rural Clientelism Survey did not probe about which specific politician respondents had asked for help, as that line of inquiry was considered relatively sensitive. However, qualitative evidence about self-selection discussed earlier suggests that citizens tend to direct requests to politicians they supported in the past.

This striking difference is similarly observed when repeating the hypothetical trust games with higher values. If their councilor was sent R$4 (tripled to R$12), respondents with fulfilled requests in 2013 expected their councilor to return R$2.87, versus R$2.12 for respondents with unfulfilled requests. If their councilor was sent R$6 (tripled to R$18), respondents with fulfilled requests predicted their councilor would return R$3.80, versus R$2.91 for respondents with unfulfilled requests. And finally, if their councilor was sent R$8 (tripled to R$24), respondents with fulfilled requests predicted their councilor would return R$4.75, versus R$3.95 for respondents with unfulfilled requests. These substantial differences between citizens with fulfilled and unfulfilled requests are significant at the 5 percent level when the councilor was sent R$2, R$4, or R$6 (but not R$8).

One might be concerned that citizens with fulfilled requests systematically differ from those with unfulfilled requests, and such characteristics account for the trust game results shown in Figure 6.4. This possibility cannot be entirely

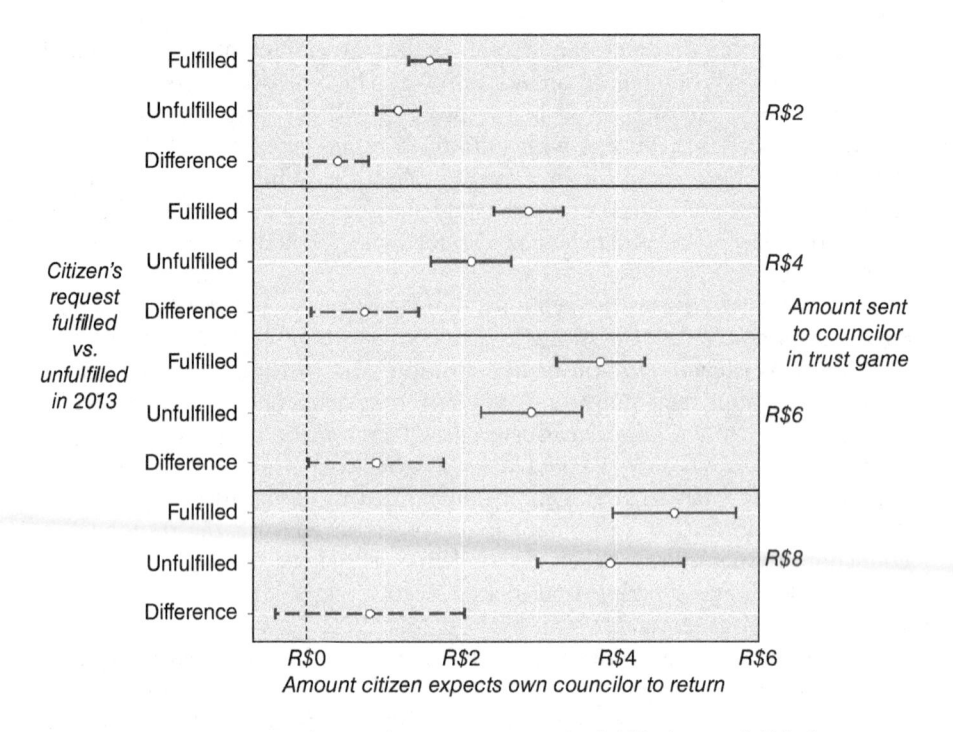

FIGURE 6.4 Perception of councilor in trust game, by fulfilled vs. unfulfilled request, rural Northeast Brazil, 2013

Note: Figure shows how much respondents expect the councilor they voted for in 2012 to return in four hypothetical trust games. Each game, with initial sent values on the right axis, paired an unidentified random citizen ("Ana," for ease of exposition) in the municipality with the respondent's councilor. To paraphrase, the first game asked: "If Ana sends your councilor R$2, and we triple that money so your councilor receives R$6, how much would your councilor send back to Ana?" "Fulfilled" indicates the mean response for the subset of respondents who had requested *and* received private assistance in 2013 from an elected politician in their municipality. "Unfulfilled" indicates the mean response for those who had requested such private assistance but *did not* receive it. "Difference" shows the difference in means (*t*-test) between "Fulfilled" and "Unfulfilled." Confidence intervals shown at 95 percent level. Analysis excludes respondents without requests in 2013. Regression tables in Appendix E show robustness to various controls and municipal fixed effects.

Source: Author's analysis of the Rural Clientelism Survey. Data collected by Gustavo Bobonis, Paul Gertler, Marco Gonzalez-Navarro, and Simeon Nichter.

ruled out; for instance, the analysis does not involve an experiment that randomly assigned whose requests were fulfilled and denied. However, regressions in Appendix E partially address this concern by confirming that citizens with unfulfilled requests expect their councilors to return significantly less money (at the 5 percent level) when controlling for various political and socioeconomic

6.4 Requests and Screening

variables as well as municipal fixed effects. Moreover, the inclusion of these controls provides additional evidence consistent with the mechanism elaborated in Chapter 5: citizens who declared support for a councilor in the prior year's municipal campaign expect their councilor to return more money (significant at the 1 percent level, except in specifications with fixed effects). More important for the present analysis, results from these hypothetical trust games are consistent with the theoretical prediction that citizens update their perceptions of politicians based on whether their requests are fulfilled.

Beyond trust games, direct questions in the Rural Clientelism Survey also provide evidence about the informational role of citizen requests. As described in Chapter 5, the 2012 wave asked respondents about several characteristics of that year's mayoral candidates.[56] Regression analyses suggest that citizens with unfulfilled requests for private assistance from incumbents perceived the incumbent mayor to be significantly less competent than those with fulfilled requests (not shown).[57] This result is important to the extent that respondents consider the performance of delivering clientelist benefits in their assessment of a politician's competence. On a four-point scale, citizens whose requests had not been fulfilled rated the incumbent mayor 0.33 points lower on competence. This finding, which includes municipal fixed effects to compare perceptions across the same mayor, is significant at the 5 percent level. One might be concerned that this relationship runs in the reverse direction, in that mayors refuse to fulfill requests of citizens who think poorly of them. To some extent mitigating this concern, the result remains significant when including various controls, including ex-ante level of satisfaction with the mayor (provided by household heads in the 2011 baseline survey).[58] The finding is also robust and comparable in magnitude when examining perceptions of the incumbent party's mayoral candidate, rather than just perceptions of the incumbent mayoral candidate. This approach expands the sample, as not all mayors were eligible or chose to run for reelection in 2012. With respect to other perceptions captured by the survey (accessibility, experience and honesty), findings are similarly negative and significant in some specifications, but are less robust. While these specifications cannot entirely rule out the influence of unobserved factors, findings nevertheless lend empirical support to the argument that citizens update their perceptions based on politicians' responsiveness to requests.

---

[56] Higher values indicate more favorable assessments on a four-point scale ("very good," "good," "bad" or "very bad").

[57] Requests of incumbents include those of the mayor and of city councilors. Recall that most requests are channeled to councilors, who often serve as intermediaries for the mayor. This finding is also significant if excluding requests of councilors. The survey did not ask about perceptions of councilors.

[58] Mayoral satisfaction in 2011 is unavailable at the individual level as only household heads were interviewed at baseline. Data from 2012 show a substantial correlation between views of household heads and average responses of their household members; e.g., a correlation coefficient of 0.51 for perceptions of incumbent competence (significant at the 1 percent level).

The logic of screening described earlier not only involves citizens learning about politicians' underlying characteristics through requests, but also predicts refusals to vote for politicians who denied their requests. In line with this theoretical prediction, citizens with unfulfilled requests are far more likely to switch their votes than those with fulfilled requests. The 2013 wave of the Rural Clientelism Survey asked respondents which mayoral candidate they had voted for during the 2008 and 2012 elections. To assess the prediction, consider all respondents who both requested assistance from incumbents and could have switched in 2012 – that is, those having voted for a mayoral candidate in 2008 who ran for mayor again in 2012.[59] Among this subset, only 28.8 percent of those with fulfilled requests voted against their prior choice, versus 50 percent of those with unfulfilled requests (difference significant at the 5 percent level). Figure 6.5 summarizes regression results in Appendix E, which include various controls and municipal fixed effects. As shown in the most inclusive specification, citizens with unfulfilled requests were 26.5 percentage points less likely to vote again for the same candidate (significant at the 5 percent level). In the bottom row of Figure 6.5, observe that findings are similar when examining whether respondents voted again for either the same candidate or the same party. This latter specification reveals citizens' voting consistency when their 2008 vote choice did not personally run again (e.g., second-term mayors);[60] the point estimate is 20 percentage points when including controls and municipal fixed effects ($p = 0.056$). It should be noted that endogeneity remains a possibility, even though the more inclusive specifications in Figure 6.5 include a wide range of controls and municipal fixed effects. For example, a politician may deny a request if she senses a given citizen is no longer a supporter and will thus likely switch. Although results in Figure 6.5 are not dispositive, they once again provide additional evidence consonant with the argument that citizens screen against politicians who have denied their requests.

As with interviews, quantitative evidence from rural Northeast Brazil is thus consistent with the screening logic elaborated in Chapter 3. Beyond providing sustenance, a politician's responsiveness to citizen requests transmits information about the credibility of his or her promises to help in the future. Both hypothetical trust games and direct questions reveal a robust association between politicians' responsiveness and citizens' beliefs and behavior. While causality has not been established, evidence corroborates the argument that citizens use information garnered from requests to screen untrustworthy politicians. Citizens with denied requests have worse perceptions of their politicians and are more likely to switch their votes away from candidates they have

---

[59] For 43.2 percent of respondents, their 2008 candidate ran again in 2012 (either as an incumbent or as a defeated candidate).

[60] For 65.3 percent of respondents, their 2008 candidate or party ran again in 2012.

6.4 Requests and Screening

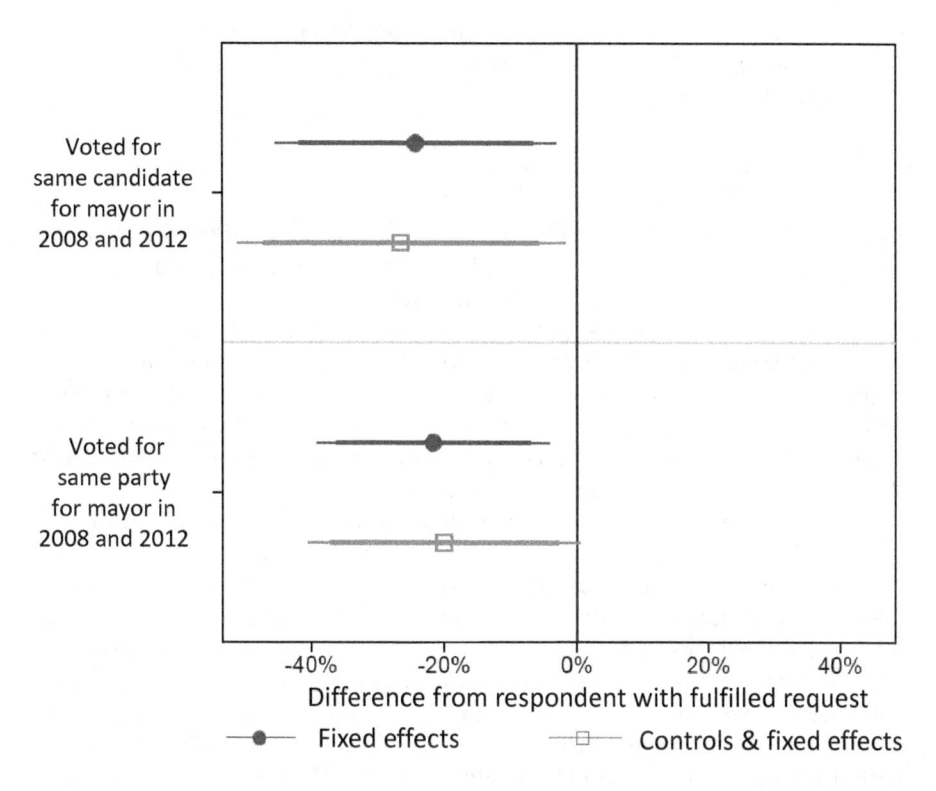

FIGURE 6.5 Consistency of voting, by unfulfilled vs fulfilled request, rural Northeast Brazil, 2012

Note: Figure summarizes regression specifications in which outcome variables are listed on the left axis. Markers correspond to regression coefficients for an explanatory variable that is coded 1 if citizen's request for private assistance of an incumbent politician was unfulfilled; 0 if it was fulfilled. Outcome variable in Row 1 (2) is coded 1 if the respondent voted for the same candidate (candidate or party) in 2008 and 2012; 0 if the respondent voted otherwise or did not vote. Analysis in Row 1 (2) excludes respondents whose chosen candidate (candidate and party) in 2008 did not re-run in 2012, as well as those who did not request assistance from incumbents. Thin whiskers on confidence intervals indicate 95 percent level; thicker whiskers indicate 90 percent level. Confidence intervals based on standard errors clustered at the neighborhood level. Linear probability models are employed; results are robust using logit specifications. Appendix E reports regression tables. Control variables, which are described in Appendix B, are: Declared support, talks with politicians, association membership, age, party supporter (DEM, PMDB, PSDB and PT dummies), gender, education, wealth, risk aversion, reciprocity, time preference, has piped water, has own cistern, and has access to other's cistern. Number of observations for the most inclusive specifications are 101 (Row 1) and 146 (Row 2).
Source: Author's analysis of the Rural Clientelism Survey. Data collected by Gustavo Bobonis, Paul Gertler, Marco Gonzalez-Navarro, and Simeon Nichter.

supported in the past. By alleviating an important information asymmetry, citizen requests tackle the problem of politician credibility that threatens relational clientelism.

6.5 SUMMARY

Given their substantial vulnerability, many citizens are motivated to buttress the stability of ongoing exchange relationships, and requesting benefits serves as a key mechanism in this regard. As elaborated in Chapter 3, citizens not only procure sustenance, but also glean information about politicians' credibility when they demand help. Politicians who vow to provide assistance, only to deny requests when adversity strikes, reveal that their promises are untrustworthy. By screening against politicians who have poor track records of fulfilling their requests, citizens can thus alleviate their own concerns about opportunistic defection in ongoing exchange relationships.

Evidence from Brazil corroborates this theoretical mechanism. Although most studies focus on the supply side of clientelism, many Brazilians are not merely passive recipients of handouts. Even in Northeast Brazil, a region often depicted as having a paucity of autonomous voters, the majority of citizens who received benefits had *asked* for help, often motivated by their vulnerability. Most requests pertain to life necessities, such as water and medicine, and they spike when adversity strikes. Consistent with relational clientelism, requesters disproportionately receive help during both election and non-election years, with declared supporters as more likely recipients. Moreover, many Brazilians draw inferences and screen against politicians, based on whether they fulfilled their requests. Interviews provide insight about the screening role of requests in clientelist relationships, and regressions show that survey respondents often espouse negative perceptions of politicians who deny their requests and refuse to vote for them.

More broadly, requesting benefits is a purposive action that alleviates one side of the dual credibility problem that threatens ongoing exchange relationships. Just as declared support tackles the issue of whether citizens' promises of support are credible, requesting benefits addresses the issue of whether politicians' promises of assistance are credible. Both mechanisms reveal how citizens – who are often motivated by vulnerability in contexts with inadequate welfare states – play an instrumental role in the survival of relational clientelism.

PART III

EXTENSIONS

7

Citizen Strategies in Comparative Context

Over the past few decades, the standard of living in many countries has increased markedly. But despite rising incomes, an expanding middle class, and improved health indicators, most of the world's population remains vulnerable to unemployment, illness, droughts, and other adverse shocks. Many nations continue to introduce or expand programs to mitigate citizens' vulnerability, yet social safety nets remain incomplete in most of the world. Social insurance fails to protect against the full range of risks facing citizens, and a substantial share of the population in many countries is excluded from coverage (e.g., informal and self-employed workers). Given this pronounced insecurity, many citizens depend on ongoing exchange relationships with politicians to cope with risks.

As demonstrated in this book, vulnerability motivates many citizens to help sustain such patterns of relational clientelism in Brazil, a context where various challenges threaten diverse forms of contingent exchanges. Brazilians undertake at least two actions that underpin the survival of ongoing exchange relationships – they *declare support* to signal the credibility of their vote promises, and they *request benefits* to screen the credibility of politicians' promises of assistance. Evidence in the present chapter suggests that these mechanisms extend beyond the case of Brazil. While clientelism is commonly observed in much of the world, its survival is under continual assault by a panoply of factors, including structural changes, institutional reforms, legal enforcement and partisan strategies. Even though relational clientelism is relatively resilient to many of these factors, its viability is threatened by the dual credibility problem elaborated in Chapter 3. The two mechanisms that enable many Brazilians to alleviate these credibility problems and thereby fortify relational clientelism – declared support and requesting benefits – are similarly observed in numerous other countries where contingent exchanges also face challenges. More specifically, this chapter presents evidence of both citizen actions in Argentina and Mexico, as well as cross-national evidence of citizen requests in Africa and Latin America. In addition, it discusses more limited evidence of these mechanisms in Ghana, India, Lebanon, and Yemen. While this comparative chapter provides less extensive analyses than the preceding chapters focused on Brazil, it nevertheless offers considerable evidence that the book's central argument travels to other contexts.

7.1 MEXICO

The case of Mexico provides a relatively rich array of evidence to investigate the mechanisms elaborated in Part II. Before examining declared support and requesting benefits, I briefly discuss clientelism and some challenges it faces in Mexico, and document substantial vulnerability that can motivate citizens to sustain ongoing exchange relationships with politicians.

7.1.1 Clientelism and its Challenges

Clientelism has long persisted in Mexico's evolving political arena.[1] Prominent studies emphasize its important role, along with broader forms of distributive politics, in sustaining the PRI's dominance during most of the twentieth century (e.g., Greene, 2007; Magaloni, 2006). During and after the country's pivotal 2000 election, national surveys have suggested the continued existence of clientelist exchanges (Cornelius, 2003; Diaz-Cayeros et al., 2009). For example, the 2012 Mexico Panel Study found that 63 percent of respondents believed that politicians often buy votes in their communities, with 7.7 percent reporting that they had themselves received clientelist offers during that year's presidential campaign. Estimates using a list experiment, which as discussed later mitigates social desirability bias, suggest even higher rates: 22.1 percent reported receiving offers in a survey wave just before the 2012 election. The PRI continues to have the most extensive clientelist network across Mexico, and while it is by no means the only party to offer contingent benefits, national surveys suggest that it does so more frequently than the PAN and PRD combined. Accusations of clientelism commanded substantial attention during the 2012 presidential campaign, as second-place finisher Andrés Manuel López Obrador claimed that vote buying and other violations clinched Enrique Peña Nieto's victory. Although the national electoral tribunal (TEPJF) deemed such allegations to be unfounded – and researchers contend it is highly unlikely that the PRI bought off enough voters to account for Peña Nieto's margin of victory (Greene, 2012; Simpser, 2012) – most observers concur that clientelism is alive and well in Mexico.

Despite the persistence of clientelism in Mexico, the phenomenon has encountered major challenges over the years. In fact, Diaz-Cayeros et al. (2012,

---

[1] This paragraph is adapted from Nichter and Palmer-Rubin (2015).

7.1 Mexico

165, 190–192) argue that various factors, including the 1995–1996 peso crisis and growing voter disaffection with the PRI, led to the "partial dismantling of clientelism." Whereas the PRI once used benefits from social programs such as Pronasol to reward its supporters, the party shifted towards non-discretionary social policy in the late 1990s (Diaz-Cayeros et al., 2012, 36, 165). Moreover, the PAN made a broad strategic decision to favor programmatic over clientelist policies (Hagopian, forthcoming), and while in power took strides to insulate social programs from political interference (Diaz-Cayeros et al., 2012, 36, 165).[2] A key example is Prospera (formerly Progresa and Oportunidades), a conditional cash transfer (CCT) program that reaches over a quarter of Mexico's population (6.8 million families in 2016).[3] De la O (2015, ch. 1) explains that this CCT program is not only insulated from political interference, but also undercuts clientelism by raising incomes of the poor, informing citizens about their entitlements, and decreasing brokers' discretion. As such, both partisan strategies and anti-poverty programs pose important challenges to clientelism in Mexico.

Another challenge is increased legal scrutiny by Mexico's independent electoral governance body. The recently renamed Federal Electoral Institute (IFE), founded in 1990 and granted autonomy from the executive after 1994 reforms, held both power and resources to reduce partisan malfeasance during elections (Eisenstadt, 2003, 33; Magaloni, 2010, 762).[4] During the 2012 presidential elections, IFE and other agencies investigated López Obrador's allegations of vote buying and other infractions by Peña Nieto.[5] However, after an extensive investigation, the national electoral tribunal (TEPJF) unanimously refused to annul the 2012 election due to inconclusive evidence of the alleged violations. Despite this outcome, greater legal scrutiny likely increases the potential costs of clientelism during elections.

Heightened ballot secrecy is another challenge for clientelism. In the 1980s and 1990s, it became far tougher for the PRI to violate the secret ballot as the opposition grew strong enough to install party representatives in many precincts (Diaz-Cayeros et al., 2012, 59). Whereas monitors observed ballot secrecy violations in 38.6 percent of all precincts in 1994 (cf. Fox, 2007, 122), about 97 percent of surveyed voters reported voting in secret during the 2000 presidential election (cf. Schedler, 2004, 62). IFE took many actions to promote the secret ballot, such as enclosing voting booths with curtains emblazoned with the statement, "Your vote is free and secret," and launching advertisements to increase awareness of voting secrecy (IRI, 2000, 36, 80). As discussed in Chapter 2, ballot secrecy facilitates opportunistic defection with some forms of clientelism. Indeed, a 2006 campaign slogan urged voters to

---

[2] See also Hagopian (2014, 142–144).
[3] Figure from Prospera's official web site, www.gob.mx/prospera.
[4] As a result of reforms under Peña Nieto, IFE transformed into the National Electoral Institute (INE) in 2014.
[5] "Pide IFE a Soriana Datos de Tarjetas," *El Universal*, July 5, 2012.

"take the dough and vote for PAN" (Diaz-Cayeros et al., 2016, 24). Given the substantial difficulty of monitoring how Mexicans vote, Larreguy et al. (2016) argue that the PRI and PAN are often motivated to use turnout buying instead of vote buying.

In sum, clientelism persists in Mexico, but faces various challenges, including partisan strategies, anti-poverty programs, increased legal scrutiny, and heightened ballot secrecy.

7.1.2 Vulnerability

In the context of such challenges facing clientelism, many Mexicans have a pressing motivation to ensure the survival of ongoing exchange relationships with politicians – their substantial vulnerability. Analogously to Chapter 4's discussion of Brazil, the present section documents the vulnerability that many Mexicans face in the spheres of employment, health, and water.

First, consider vulnerability in the arena of employment. Despite an expanding middle class, Mexico is the only OECD country without national unemployment insurance (OECD, 2015, 328), an issue the nation is attempting to rectify with proposed reforms. Exacerbating vulnerability, a third of salaried employees lack a contract, and over half of their positions provide no benefits (de la Fuente et al., 2015, 23). Furthermore, employment is especially precarious for the 60 percent of Mexican workers in the informal sector (Olaberría and Dugain, 2015, 15). Although Mexico offers some employment assistance – e.g., Programa de Empleo Temporal (PET) provided temporary employment at roughly the minimum wage to 1.1 million citizens in 2011 – such social programs typically fail to cover many vulnerable citizens (de la Fuente et al., 2015, 18–19). Job losses are one reason why many Mexicans are vulnerable to broader economic shocks; during the nation's peso crisis, the poverty rate (at $2.50 per capita) increased from 20 percent in 1994 to 34 percent in 1996 (Birdsall et al., 2014, 133). A lack of employment motivates some citizens to turn to clientelism in Mexico (Schedler, 2002, 18), where jobs have historically been doled out to loyal supporters (Cornelius, 2003, 48; Greene, 2007, 99–101; Grindle, 2012, 170–171, 190).

Notwithstanding substantial improvements in recent years, health care is another domain of vulnerability for many Mexicans. Until the national introduction of Seguro Popular in 2003, health insurance in Mexico was primarily limited to salaried employees in the formal sector (Knaul et al., 2012, 1266). Seguro Popular provides health insurance to formerly excluded citizens, and by 2012 had reached nearly universal coverage.[6] Despite various successes of the program, many Mexicans remain vulnerable to health shocks. Issues with health care access and quality often drive the poor to pay with their own funds.[7] For instance, approximately one-third of prescriptions issued under

---

[6] Knaul et al., 2012, 1267.
[7] Knaul et al., 2012, 1271–1272.

Seguro Popular cannot be filled – often due to a lack of medicine – so the poor must frequently turn to private pharmacies using their own funds (Nigenda et al., 2015, 224; Olaberría and Dugain, 2015, 34). Out-of-pocket spending continues to account for about half of Mexico's health care expenditures and is a leading reason why families fall into poverty (Bonilla-Chacín and Aguilera, 2013, 15; Olaberría and Dugain, 2015, 33). Unmet health needs motivate even some otherwise reluctant citizens to turn to clientelism in Mexico (Schedler, 2002, 18), a country where politicians have historically used medicine as a type of handout distributed to voters (Diaz-Cayeros et al., 2012, 289).

In addition to unemployment and illness, water issues also compound the vulnerability of many Mexicans. In 2012, Mexico experienced its most severe drought in seventy-one years, with millions of citizens lacking adequate food or water despite massive governmental relief efforts.[8] One factor complicating distribution: approximately 18.8 percent of poor Mexicans lacked piped water in 2012 (de la Fuente et al., 2015, 12).[9] Citizens who work in agriculture are especially prone to drought, as three-fourths of the country's cultivated land is rain-fed (de la Fuente et al., 2015, 26). Another key concern is water quality; Mexico confirmed over 45,000 cases of cholera in 1991–2001, followed by another minor outbreak in 2013 (CDC, 2014). Partially due to problematic water quality and access, Mexicans consume the most bottled water per capita in the world, with expenditures on this product averaging $11 per month and accounting for over 10 percent of some families' income.[10] To cope with vulnerability stemming from water problems, many Mexicans rely on relationships with local politicians and their operatives, who frequently dispatch water trucks or pay water bills on behalf of clients in exchange for political support (de Alba and Gamboa, 2014, 126,137; Townsend and Eyles, 2004, 81–82).

Given that Mexico fails to provide an adequate welfare state to mitigate the vulnerability of much of its population, this book suggests that many citizens in ongoing exchange relationships will undertake actions to help ensure the survival of relational clientelism. Consistent with this argument, the next two sections reveal that the key citizen actions examined in Part II – declared support and requesting benefits – are also linked to clientelism in Mexico.

7.1.3 Declared Support

My collaborative work with Brian Palmer-Rubin (Nichter and Palmer-Rubin, 2015) demonstrates that citizens who declared support were

---

[8] "Mexico Withers Under Worst Drought in 71 Years," *The Christian Science Monitor*, March 9, 2012.
[9] "Poor" defined as earning under $4 a day.
[10] "Mexicans Struggle to Kick Bottled-Water Habit," *New York Times*, July 17, 2012; "Latin America's Other Water Infrastructure," Inter-American Development Bank, November 10, 2011.

significantly more likely to experience clientelism during Mexico's 2012 presidential campaign.[11] This evidence is congruous with the mechanism of declared support elaborated in Chapter 3, as well as the overall argument of this book. Because ongoing exchange relationships provide benefits that are not exclusively limited to campaigns, a preferable test would examine whether declarers are more likely to receive both campaign handouts and post-election benefits (as conducted for Brazil). However, all quantitative analyses in this comparative chapter only consider campaign handouts, given the dearth of surveys that inquire about post-election benefits as well as declared support or citizen requests.

To provide broader context about declared support in Mexico, parties' expenditures on print advertisements (e.g., posters and billboards), rallies, and other campaign activities increased markedly in 2012, as an unintended consequence of IFE's new restrictions on mass media advertising. For example, a plastics producer association reported a 30 percent increase in the amount of plastics used in campaign advertisements between the 2006 and 2012 presidential campaign.[12] Most relevant for the present analysis, many Mexicans displayed such political advertising on their homes. This phenomenon was directly observed by enumerators in the Mexico 2012 Panel Study, who coded whether they observed advertisements for any political party or organization on respondents' residences. Such advertisements were visible on 16.7 percent of respondents' homes. The most common advertisements were for the PRI (8.2 percent of respondents), followed by the PAN (3.3 percent), and the PRD (2.8 percent).

If declared support is linked to clientelism as argued in Chapter 3, we would expect citizens with political advertisements on their homes (declarers) to be more likely to experience clientelism than citizens without such advertisements (non-declarers). Even before controlling for important factors, Figure 7.1 suggests that declarers had a greater tendency to be offered – and to actually receive – campaign handouts. When asked directly whether they had been offered benefits, 9.4 percent of declarers answered affirmatively, versus just 5.2 percent of non-declarers ($p = 0.057$). Use of a list experiment, which as described in Section 6.3 offers an unobtrusive measure of whether respondents actually received handouts, reveals an even starker difference. Applying this methodology, almost 57 percent of declarers reported receiving handouts, compared to just 16 percent of non-declarers (difference significant at the 5 percent level).

While these differences are consistent with the mechanism of declared support examined in Chapter 3, they do not control for important factors that may be correlated with both declaration and clientelism (e.g., partisanship).

---

[11] This section on declared support in Mexico is adapted from Nichter and Palmer-Rubin (2015).
[12] "Más de 2 mil Toneladas de Propaganda Electoral Invadirán a México," *Vanguardia*, March 6, 2012.

7.1 Mexico

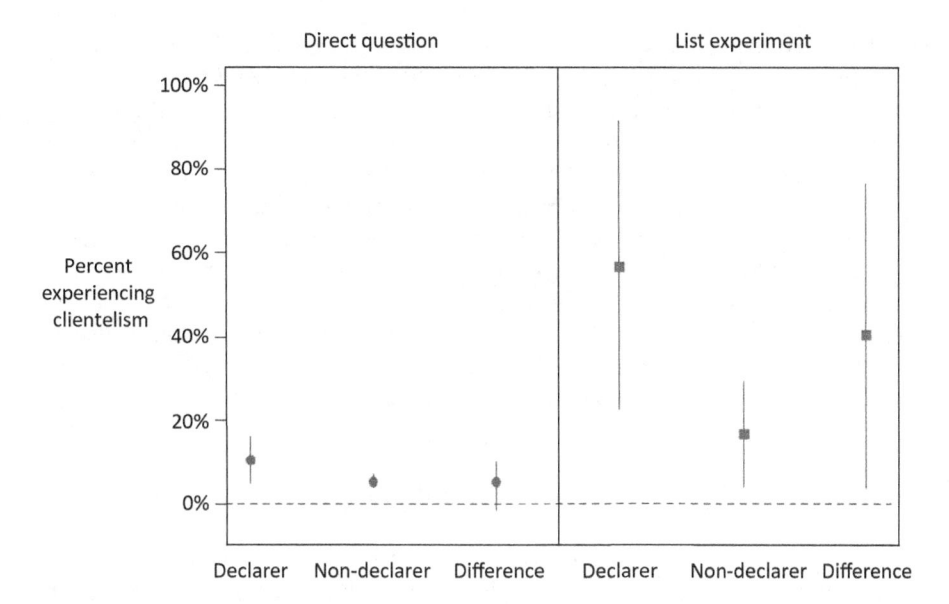

FIGURE 7.1 Mexico: Declared support and clientelism during campaign (2012)
Note: "Declarer" includes respondents with a political advertisement on home during Wave 1 or 2 (as observed by enumerator). Level of clientelism in Wave 2 shown with 95 percent confidence intervals. Direct question asked about offers of campaign handouts. List experiment asked about receipt of campaign handouts. $N = 128$ for declarer, 795 for non-declarer (includes respondents participating in both Waves 1 and 2).
Source: Adapted from Nichter and Palmer-Rubin (2015). Data from 2012 Mexico Panel Study.

To address this issue, Nichter and Palmer-Rubin (2015) conducted logistic regressions of the direct clientelism question, which include political and socioeconomic controls, as well as municipal fixed effects.[13] Respondents with political advertisements on their homes were 8.3 percentage points more likely to report clientelist offers than their counterparts without advertisements (significant at the 5 percent level).[14] In addition, we included controls to the list experiment measure by using Blair and Imai's (2012) item count regression method.[15] This approach suggests that declarers are 35.8 percentage points more likely to receive handouts than non-declarers ($p = 0.065$). Altogether, these results suggest that declarers were more likely to be offered and to receive clientelist benefits during Mexico's 2012 campaign.

---

[13] For consistency with our study, all analyses in the present chapter employ logistic regressions.
[14] As shown in Nichter and Palmer-Rubin (2015), omitting municipal fixed effects decreases the point estimate to 4 percentage points (significant at the 5 percent level).
[15] This method predicts each covariate's effect on the likelihood of responding affirmatively to the list experiment's sensitive item, as if it were measured for each respondent independently.

To test the robustness of this relationship, we also conducted matching using Sekhon's (2011) genetic search algorithm. Although this method does not offer a rigorous test of causality, it strives to improve inference given the lack of a counterfactual through the construction of an artificial comparison group. Genetic matching pairs our treatment units ("declarers") with control units ("non-declarers") who are comparable on a set of observable characteristics. In line with the earlier analyses, this approach also finds a significant difference in clientelist offers between declarers and non-declarers (at the 5 percent level).[16]

Overall, this evidence suggests a link between declared support and clientelism in Mexico. While these analyses of campaign handouts cannot distinguish between relational and electoral clientelism (e.g., spot-market payments for declarations), observed patterns of declared support corroborate the mechanism elaborated in Chapter 3.

7.1.4 Requesting Benefits

A second mechanism by which citizens help to sustain relational clientelism – requesting benefits – is also observed in Mexico. First, consider anthropologist Hector Tejera's (2000) study of Mexico City during the 1997 elections. In line with my central premise, Tejera notes that Mexico often fails to meet the basic needs of poor voters, who frequently rely on clientelist relationships and demand assistance from politicians (69–70). Many voters requested help from local politicians during the 1997 campaign, ranging from water cistern maintenance to construction materials (60–62). Although citizens requested benefits from all parties, Tejera argues that the PRI had a particular focus on collecting and fulfilling requests of its core supporters (60, 68). According to the campaign report of the PRI's mayoral candidate in Mexico City, his campaign received 270,000 citizen requests and resolved 27.5 percent of them. When reporting these figures, Tejera (2000, 61) cautions that they are likely inflated to emphasize responsiveness; an analysis of a subsample of the requests suggests that just 8.5 percent were actually resolved before the election. Regardless of the precise figures, Tejera's study underscores the importance of citizen requests in a Mexican election.

More broadly, a national study of Mexico's 2000 elections by FLACSO/IFE provides further evidence about the role of citizen requests.[17] Many citizens reportedly initiated requests from politicians in 2000 – especially for assistance with employment, construction, and personal favors – and about a third of requests were fulfilled.[18] Poor citizens disproportionately requested help,

---

[16] These analyses were conducted using the direct clientelism measure.
[17] The study was conducted by FLACSO (Latin American Faculty for Social Sciences) and funded by IFE. It surveyed 1,200 citizens and conducted qualitative research.
[18] "El Precio de los Votos," Francisco Ortiz Pardo, *El Universal*, May 12, 2002.

7.1 Mexico

and requests were predominantly directed towards the PRI.[19] An interesting observation by del Pozo and Aparicio (2001, 36) is that although a substantial share of respondents perceived that *others* demanded benefits in exchange for their political support, very few respondents admitted to doing so themselves. Schedler (2002, 10–11) provides additional insights from interviews conducted as part of the FLACSO/IFE study. He finds that citizens often request help from politicians, in part because the state fails to meet their needs. As one interviewee explains, because "of the needs that exist in the region, everybody asks for help" (11). In addition, Schedler (2002) finds that substantial evidence of clientelism coexists with anti-clientelist attitudes among many voters. All in all, these studies point to citizen requests in the context of clientelist exchanges in Mexico.

Survey data enable further investigation into the link between citizen requests and clientelism. Whereas the 2012 Mexico Panel Study discussed earlier does not inquire about citizen requests, the 2010 LAPOP AmericasBarometer survey captures information about requests (but not declared support).[20] More specifically, the survey asked respondents whether they had "sought assistance from or presented a request" from municipal officials during the last year. LAPOP's question about respondents' experience with clientelism, which asks whether politicians offered them handouts, would preferably have asked whether respondents *received* benefits. Nevertheless, the survey provides a unique opportunity to explore whether a link exists between citizen requests and clientelism in Mexico.

In the LAPOP survey, Mexicans who requested help from municipal officials were over twice as likely as non-requesters to experience clientelism (28.9 versus 14.2 percent).[21] Figure 7.2 summarizes the results of logistic regressions examining this relationship in Mexico as well as other cases discussed later; regression tables are provided in Appendix F. As shown in the bottom row, this difference remains significant at the 1 percent level when including various controls and/or state fixed effects. In the "Controls" and "Controls & fixed effects" specifications, citizens who request help from municipal officials are 13.8 and 12.1 percentage points more likely to experience clientelism, respectively. While such analyses in this chapter do not imply causality, they reveal a strong association between citizen requests and clientelism, similar to findings for Brazil in Chapter 6.

Altogether, evidence from Mexico is broadly consistent with the two mechanisms elaborated in Chapter 3, though available information does not facilitate testing the logic as thoroughly as for the case of Brazil. Clientelism in Mexico endures, but faces substantial challenges such as partisan strategies, anti-poverty programs, increased legal scrutiny and heightened ballot secrecy.

---

[19] "El Precio de los Votos."
[20] This survey included 1,562 citizens in 27 states and the Federal District.
[21] $N = 1,547$.

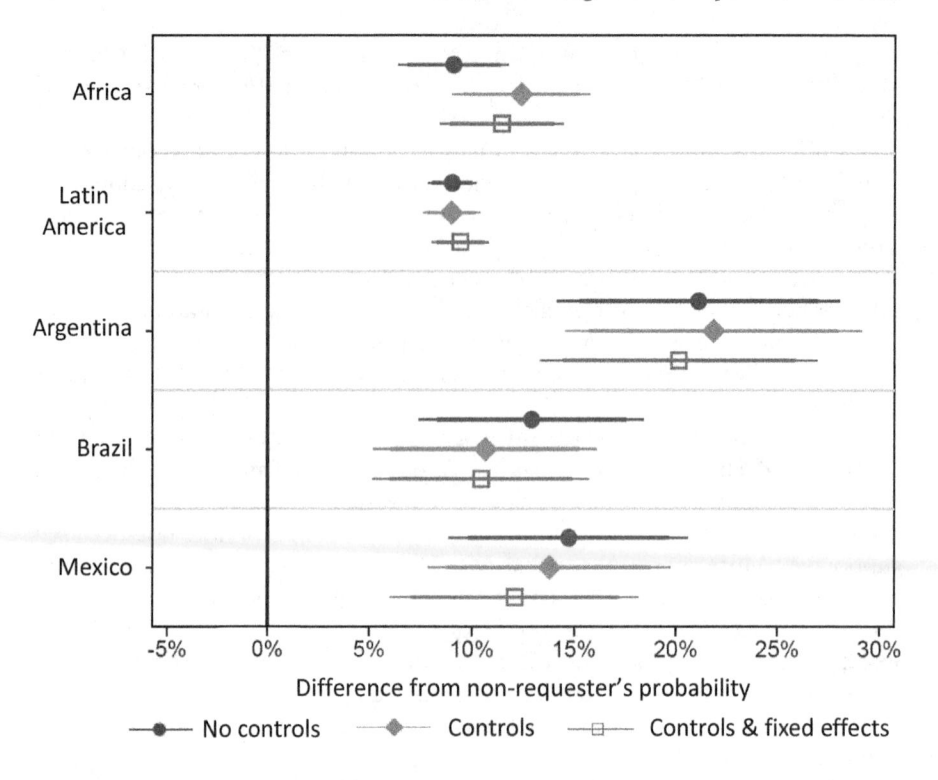

FIGURE 7.2 Citizen requests and clientelism during campaigns (2005–2010)
Note: Markers correspond to regression coefficients for a variable coded 1 if the citizen requested assistance from municipal officials in past year; 0 otherwise. Outcome variable coded 1 if the respondent reported that candidates or political parties "sometimes" or "often" offered them benefits during campaigns; 0 otherwise. Circles shown for bivariate regressions, diamonds with controls, and squares with controls and fixed effects (country for Africa and Latin America, province for Argentina, and state for Brazil and Mexico). Point estimates are marginal effects from logistic regressions; robust standard errors are employed. Thin whiskers on confidence intervals indicate 95 percent level; thicker lines indicate 90 percent level. Control variables are: Machine supporter, turnout, income, age, education, gender, and urban. Appendix F reports regression tables. Observations in bivariate specifications: Africa, 23,936; Latin America, 36,784; Argentina, 1,332; Brazil, 2,338; Mexico, 1,547.
Source: LAPOP AmericasBarometer (2010) and Afrobarometer Round 3 surveys (2005–2006). Estimates for Argentina, Brazil, and Mexico are from author's own analysis. Estimates for Africa and Latin America are adapted from Nichter and Peress (2016). Coding of machine parties based on Kitschelt (2013) dataset.

Nevertheless, many citizens have an important motivation to sustain ongoing exchange relationships – given the nation's inadequate welfare state, many Mexicans remain vulnerable to shocks including unemployment, illness, and drought. Amidst these factors, evidence from Mexico reveals patterns consistent

7.2 Argentina

with two mechanisms that citizens employ to bolster relational clientelism in Brazil. In the context of Mexico, citizens who declare support, as well as those who request benefits, are significantly more likely to experience clientelism.

7.2 ARGENTINA

The case of Argentina also offers considerable evidence consistent with the mechanisms of declared support and requesting benefits. As with the previous case, before examining these citizen actions, I first briefly discuss clientelism and some challenges it faces in Argentina, and then document vulnerability that can motivate citizens to sustain relational clientelism.

7.2.1 Clientelism and Its Challenges

In recent years, many studies have investigated the important role of clientelism in Argentina, so many, in fact, that it ranks as the most studied country in the latest wave of research on the topic (Weitz-Shapiro, 2014, 18). As Steven Levitsky (2003b) argues, the Peronist party transformed from a labor-based party to a clientelist party in the early 1990s, and providing sustenance to its lower-class base helped shore up support for Menem's neoliberal reforms. The Peronist party delivered social assistance, often clientelist in nature (Levitsky, 2003a, 8–9; 2003b, 187–188), through vast networks of *unidades básicas* (UBs, or "base units") and brokers. Javier Auyero (2000a, 14, 27) emphasizes that ongoing clientelist relationships – which he calls "Peronist problem-solving networks" – have helped many poor Argentines cope with substantial adversity. For instance, UBs serve as "centers from which food and medicine are distributed, and brokers can be approached for small favors all year around" (Auyero 2000a, 83). Although both the Peronist and Radical parties distribute contingent benefits, the Peronist party continues to be Argentina's dominant clientelist party: by a large margin, it distributes the most handouts and has the most operatives of any party in the nation (Calvo and Murillo, 2013; Stokes, 2005, 322).

Even though substantial clientelism persists in many parts of Argentina, it encounters numerous challenges. As in Brazil, rising incomes and declining poverty are sources of headwinds for contingent exchanges. According to a World Bank study, Argentina experienced strong economic growth after the 2001–2002 crisis (notwithstanding its recent deceleration), and this growth was more pro-poor than that of most countries in the region (Cord et al., 2015, 57). As many families' incomes increased, urban poverty (per-capita income below $4 per day) declined from 31.0 percent in 2004 to 10.8 percent in 2012.[22] This poverty decline was mostly due to an improving labor market,[23] with

---

[22] Cord et al., 2015, 53.
[23] Cord et al., 2015, 59.

real wages increasing 46 percent between 2003 and 2012 along with aggregate employment growth (Beccaria et al., 2015, 685). Research on Argentina emphasizes effects of standard-of-living improvements on contingent exchanges; for example, Cleary and Stokes (2006, 160–164) argue that rising income has "undermined clientelism" in the nation, partially because the diminishing marginal utility of income decreases the value of handouts to recipients.

Another related challenge for clientelism involves the rise of the middle class. Over the past decade, the middle class grew faster in Argentina than any other country in Latin America,[24] and by 2011 it accounted for over half the nation's population (Cord et al., 2015, 53). Weitz-Shapiro (2012, 2014) argues that some Argentine mayors refrain from distributing contingent benefits because middle-class citizens frequently punish clientelist candidates by voting against them. She suggests that this "audience cost" of clientelism is most severe in contexts with high levels of political competition and a large middle class (2012, 572; 2014, 5, 53). Consistent with her broader argument, Calvo and Murillo (2012, 153) discuss how some middle-class voters abandon the Peronist party due to its clientelist activities, raising the example of the 2009 midterm elections. Given the substantial level of political competition in many (but by no means all) provinces and municipalities (Gervasoni, 2014, 54–57; Szwarcberg, 2015, 8), Argentina's growing middle class likely hinders clientelism in some parts of the country.

Changes in voting technology pose yet another challenge to clientelist strategies that involve monitoring vote choices, most prominently vote buying. To see why, consider that some researchers contend that Argentina's voting procedures have enabled parties to observe citizens' vote choices.[25] For example, Stokes (2005, 318) and Stokes et al. (2013, 100–104) emphasize that monitoring is facilitated by Argentina's lack of an Australian ballot, because citizens can be shepherded to the polls with ballots provided to them by party operatives (see also Weitz-Shapiro, 2014, 18–19).[26] However, enacted and proposed electoral reforms threaten to undercut such monitoring by introducing different forms of the Australian ballot. The provinces of Córdoba and Santa Fe already employ a unified paper ballot, while Salta province and the capital city of Buenos Aires employ electronic voting.[27] In addition, monitoring could be further thwarted if the overall nation adopts the proposed "Single Electronic Ballot." During his

---

[24] "Latin America's Middle Class Grows, but in Some Regions More than Others," Pew Research Center, July 20, 2015.

[25] By contrast, Zarazaga (2014, 25) argues that ballot secrecy is strong in Argentina, so monitoring is "unlikely" to secure voter compliance. None of the 120 brokers he interviewed indicated they observed vote choices, even though they readily admitted to various other infractions (2014, 38).

[26] Note that citizens can still use ballots typically available in the voting booth, weakening this monitoring mechanism.

[27] A broader shift towards electronic voting has been underway for some time (Alvarez et al., 2013, 120–121), and more provinces were slated to use this methodology in 2017. See "En 2017 Habrá Boleta Electrónica sólo en 8 Provincias," *Clarín*, August 31, 2016.

7.2 Argentina

presidential campaign, Mauricio Macri had pledged to extend across Argentina this form of electronic voting, which he had already implemented in Buenos Aires as mayor in 2015. A key official involved with President Macri's proposed electoral reform, Adrián Pérez of the Ministry of the Interior claimed that the Single Electronic Ballot would even put an end to clientelism.[28] This reform was approved by the Chamber of Deputies and remained a stated priority of the Macri administration; however, it was blocked by the Senate in late 2016 so a unified paper ballot may be implemented as a temporary measure.[29] Regardless of the reform's outcome at the national level, the shifts noted at the subnational level suggest that changes in voting technology already pose a challenge for clientelism in Argentina.

Overall, clientelism encounters important challenges in Argentina, stemming from sources such as rising income, a growing middle class, and changes in voting technology.

7.2.2 Vulnerability

Amidst such challenges, many citizens in Argentina have a pressing motivation to reinforce ongoing exchange relationships. Just as in Brazil and Mexico, the state fails to shield much of its population from various life risks, so many Argentines rely on politicians to mitigate their vulnerability. This section documents three key arenas of vulnerability: unemployment, illness, and water.

A major source of vulnerability is job loss, the primary reason families enter poverty in Argentina (Beccaria et al., 2013, 575). While various programs have aimed to help poor unemployed Argentines – such as Plan Trabajar, Plan Jefes y Jefas de Hogar Desocupados, and Argentina Trabaja – these efforts have often involved the clientelist distribution of benefits. Poor Argentines who become unemployed often grow increasingly reliant on relationships with politicians for survival (Auyero, 2000a, 60–62), and Peronist networks frequently provided jobs as well as other benefits to the poor in the 1990s (Levitsky, 2003b, 140). In more recent work on clientelism, Stokes et al. (2013, 104–105) discuss citizens' employment requests, and Zarazaga (2014, 26–27) reports that 59 percent of interviewed brokers distribute temporary employment or workfare programs. These benefits are "ideally suited" for clientelism, Zarazaga (2014, 27) notes, because operatives influence whether clients receive and keep their jobs (see also Robinson and Verdier, 2013). Vulnerability to unemployment is often closely related to other sources of income shocks. For instance, the 2001–2002 crisis cut real incomes by at least a fifth in over 60 percent of households, disproportionately afflicting the poor (Cord et al., 2015, 54). This income

---

[28] "La Ley y la Trampa de la Reforma Electoral," *Clarín*, November 13, 2016.
[29] "El Peronismo Frenó en el Senado la Reforma Electoral del Gobierno," *La Nacion*, November 25, 2016; "Macri Analiza Utilizar la Boleta Única de Papel en las Elecciones 2017," *La Nacion*, December 2, 2016.

shock thrust many families into penury, with the poverty rate (at per-capita income of $2.50 per day) increasing from 14 percent in 2000 to 30 percent in 2002 (Birdsall et al., 2014, 133). Overall, unemployment and other sources of income shocks are a major source of vulnerability for many Argentines, who not uncommonly turn to politicians for jobs.

Illness is another source of vulnerability for many Argentines. On the one hand, the nation's recent health care improvements are impressive: it continues to expand health care coverage through Plan Sumar (which replaced predecessor Plan Nacer in 2012), and Argentina's health expenditures per capita are the highest in Latin America (Dmytraczenko and Almeida, 2015, 33).[30] But even though the country's health care reforms have substantially cut out-of-pocket expenditures on health care,[31] many citizens become impoverished each year due to medical expenses (Wagstaff et al., 2015, 1709). One indicator of vulnerability to health shocks is that nearly a tenth of Argentine households had catastrophic health expenditures in 2005 (Dmytraczenko and Almeida, 2015, 125).[32] When facing illness, poor Argentines often turn to party operatives who provide ongoing "problem-solving networks" (Auyero, 1999, 2000a; see also Levitsky, 2003b, 140). For instance, Auyero (2000b, 63, 67) reports that 11 percent of citizens surveyed in his field site turned to a Peronist grassroots committee or a broker for help with medicine, and provides the example of a broker who used his hospital contacts and own health insurance to procure medicine during emergencies. More recent work also suggests that citizens rely on clientelism during health shocks: Zarazaga (2014, 34) ranks health care as one of the most important benefits provided by brokers, and Stokes et al. (2013, 102, 104–105) include several mentions of voter requests for medicines during times of need. Overall, many Argentines remain vulnerable to illness, and often depend on politicians and their operatives for help when they become sick.

Many Argentines are also vulnerable to shortages of clean drinking water. Despite infrastructure investments, piped connections are by no means universal: 83 percent of households had service to the drinking water network in 2012, a figure reaching as low as 72 percent in Misiones province.[33] Argentina experienced its worst drought in many decades in 2009, which not only decimated agricultural production and livestock on which many poor families depend,[34] but also left many families scrambling for drinking water. A community in Córdoba province, for instance, struggled to supply water to over a thousand families during that drought through the use of just two

---

[30] Plan Sumar provides health care to the uninsured; initially to women and children, with an expansion to include men in 2015.
[31] Dmytraczenko and Almeida, 2015, 33.
[32] "Catastrophic" defined as at least 25 percent of nonfood consumption spent on out-of-pocket health care expenditures.
[33] Data from 2010 INDEC Census and Consejo Federal de Entidades de Servicios Sanitarios.
[34] "In Parched Argentina, Worries Over Economy Grow," *New York Times*, February 20, 2009.

7.2 Argentina

available water trucks.[35] And even when water is available, its quality remains a crucial issue. The National Ombudsman's Office found that a lack of clean drinking water (along with pollutants and poor sanitation) threatens the health of many Argentine children,[36] and researchers point to a link between poor water quality and a rise in infectious diarrhea in specified areas of Argentina (Rajal et al., 2010, 359–360). When clean drinking water is lacking, many poor Argentines rely on clientelism. For instance, Auyero discusses how clients demand help from Peronist councilors and other brokers at any time of day, including when there is a "lack of drinkable water in the block and hence the need to bring in the municipal water truck" (Auyero, 2000a, 125, 168; see also Auyero, 2000b, 66). More recently, Zarazaga (2014, 29) similarly finds a link between water and clientelism, and Landini (2013, 120) finds that Argentine peasants expect mayors and councilors to deliver water to their wells during droughts, through direct clientelist assistance rather than by way of "institutionalized" channels. In sum, water is an important source of vulnerability for many Argentines, who often rely on clientelism when water shortages arise.

In sum, clientelism persists in Argentina but encounters substantial challenges. Many Argentines have an important motivation to sustain clientelist linkages: the state fails to protect them from various shocks including unemployment, illness and water shortages. This book suggests that such vulnerability provides a powerful motivation for citizens to undertake actions that help sustain ongoing exchange relationships. While evidence on relational clientelism in Argentina is more limited than in the case of Brazil, findings explored next are consistent with this argument and with the two mechanisms elaborated in Chapter 3 – declared support and requesting benefits.

7.2.3 Requesting Benefits

My collaborative research with Michael Peress (Nichter and Peress, 2016) suggests that citizen requests in Argentina are both prevalent and linked to clientelism.[37] Even studies that focus on elite strategies of clientelism in Argentina mention how often citizens request benefits. For example, Stokes et al. (2013, 105–106) point out that most clientelist exchanges are initiated by citizen requests. More specifically, their survey of approximately 800 Argentine councilors and other brokers included the following two questions:[38]

---

[35] "La Sequía Arrasa Argentina," *El Pais*, November 16, 2009.
[36] "Proyecto: Los Efectos de la Contaminación Ambiental en la Niñez. Una Cuestión de Derechos," Presentation by Ombudsman Nacional, Defensor del Pueblo, October 14, 2010.
[37] This section on requesting benefits in Argentina is adapted from our article in *Comparative Political Studies* (Nichter and Peress, 2016).
[38] City councilors comprise 300 of the 800 brokers in their survey (Stokes et al., 2013, 261, 268).

(1) "Out of every 10 voters that you have ever helped, how many asked for help directly?"
(2) "Out of every 10 voters that you have ever helped, to how many have you extended help without them asking for it?"

Based on responses to both questions, Stokes et al. (2013, 105) report: "More brokers identify requests as originating with voters than the other way around." The authors do not investigate requests further, but they do note that brokers respond to requests in a clientelist manner, as they "mete out their time and assistance preferentially" (106).

Qualitative evidence also reveals the prevalence of citizen requests in the context of Argentine clientelism. Weitz-Shapiro explains that mayors often receive many citizen requests each day – with one mayor spending an estimated 80 percent of his time receiving requests – and these demands are fulfilled through clientelism in some municipalities (2014, 30–31, 38). Similarly, Szwarcberg (2015, 58) discusses how citizens ask clientelist brokers for medicine and other assistance, as does Auyero (2000a, 94) who explains that citizens "contact a broker when problems arise or when a special favor is needed (a food package, some medicine, a driver's license, the water truck, getting a friend out of jail, etc.)." Particularly telling is that one-third of Rodrigo Zarazaga's 120 interviews of brokers were interrupted by clients requesting help.[39] One of his interviewees conveyed the intense pressure to respond to citizen requests:

"I know I always have to have something ... food handouts, because at any time they knock on the door of my house. I know that when they bang on the door they come hungry, so I have to have food to give. When you don't have a response they go with another. It is a lot of pressure one feels to respond."[40]

Qualitative studies demonstrate the ongoing nature of citizen requests, which become even more prevalent during campaigns. For instance, Landini (2012, 210) reports that farmers are particularly keen to request help from politicians at that time, and a broker nicknamed *El Tigre* (Tiger) bemoaned to Zarazaga about the spike in demands during campaigns:

"Now the elections make me crazy. They know I have a lot of resources. Everyone comes and requests and I fulfill. There is a funeral and they come looking for me. They need money, El Tigre. They need zinc sheets, El Tigre. They need food handouts, El Tigre. Everything is El Tigre."[41]

Overall, this evidence suggests that citizens frequently demand benefits in the context of clientelism in Argentina.

Survey data also point to a link between citizen requests and the distribution of clientelist handouts in Argentina. The survey developed and analyzed by Stokes (2005), which focuses on campaign handouts but not citizen requests,

---

[39] Personal communication, September 25, 2013.
[40] Unpublished interview by Rodrigo Zarazaga, Conurbano, Argentina, December 7, 2010.
[41] Unpublished interview by Rodrigo Zarazaga, Conurbano, Argentina, June 27, 2009.

7.2 Argentina

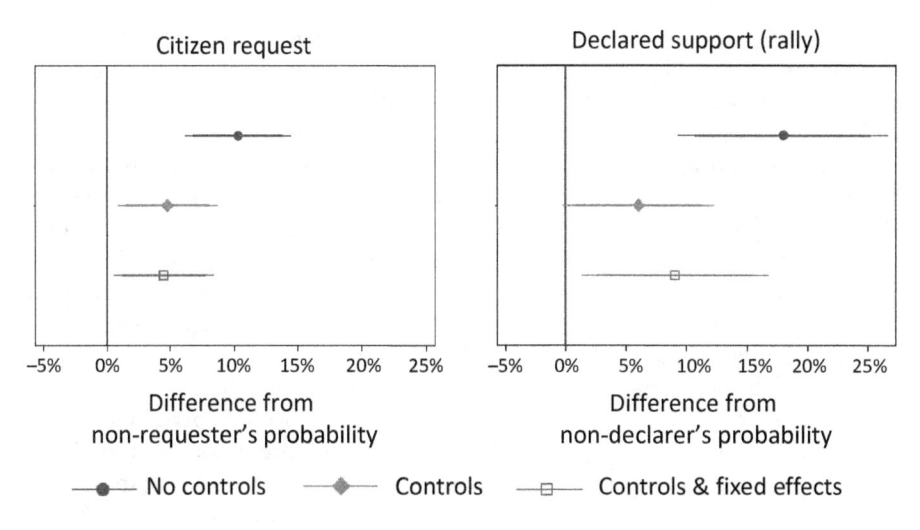

FIGURE 7.3 Argentina: citizen strategies and campaign handouts (2001)
Note: Outcome Variable: "Did you receive goods distributed by a party in the last campaign?"; coded 1 if yes, 0 if no. In (a), markers correspond to regression coefficients for a "Citizen request" variable coded 1 if citizen turned to a broker or local party patron for help in the past year; 0 otherwise. In (b), they correspond to a "Declared support" variable coded 1 if the citizen attended a rally; 0 otherwise. Circles shown for bivariate regressions, diamonds with controls, and squares with controls and fixed effects for the four study locations. Point estimates are marginal effects from logistic regressions. Whiskers indicate 95 percent confidence intervals based on robust standard errors. Control variables are: rally attendance (a), requested help (b), opinion of Peronist party, income, education, housing quality, log population, age, gender, party activist, Radical sympathizer, and ballot type. Appendix F reports regression tables. Observations in bivariate specifications are 1,860 and 1,747, respectively.
Source: Data from Stokes (2005). Estimates for (a) are adapted from Nichter and Peress (2016). Estimates for (b) are from the author's own analysis.

includes a question about whether respondents had turned to local political patrons or brokers for help in the past year. Citizens who made such requests were nearly three times as likely to receive handouts than non-requesters (16.1 versus 5.7 percent).

The left panel of Figure 7.3 shows that this difference between requesters and non-requesters remains statistically significant, albeit smaller in magnitude, when controlling for other factors. This figure summarizes the logistic regressions reported in Appendix F, which adapt analyses by Nichter and Peress (2016). Even with the inclusion of various controls and/or provincial fixed effects, respondents who requested help were 4.5–4.8 percentage points more likely to receive benefits (significant at the 5 percent level). This magnitude is substantial, given that the baseline probability of receiving a campaign handout is just 7.4 percent. The patterns do not merely reflect constituency service; consistent with clientelism, citizens who indicate support for the Peronist party – the predominant distributor of clientelist benefits in Argentina – are significantly more likely to receive handouts. As examined more thoroughly in Nichter and Peress (2016), this association is robust to multiple measures of Peronist support: whether respondents identified the party as their favorite without prompting, their evaluation of the party on a four-point scale, and whether they voted for the Peronist candidate in previous elections.[42] Given that respondents reported their support for the Peronist party concurrently with reporting the receipt of handouts, endogeneity is an important issue. To mitigate this concern, we show that strong supporters are the most likely to receive handouts, and also show robustness to an alternate approach that is arguably better insulated from potential endogeneity.[43]

This link between citizen requests and clientelism is also observed in Argentine data from the 2010 LAPOP survey. Whereas Section 7.1.4 employed Mexican data in the same year's LAPOP survey, the present section analyzes data on 1,410 Argentines.[44] Recall that the survey asks whether respondents had "sought assistance from or presented a request" from municipal officials during the last year, and inquires whether respondents had been offered handouts from politicians. Argentines who requested help in this manner were over twice as likely to experience clientelism (35.7 versus 14.6 percent).[45] As shown in Figure 7.2, this difference remains significant (at the 1 percent level) in regressions with various controls and provincial fixed effects. Citizens who asked for help were 21.9 and 20.2 percentage points more likely to experience clientelism in the "Controls" and "Controls & fixed effects" specifications, respectively.

Overall, in line with this book's argument and the mechanism examined in Chapter 3, qualitative evidence as well as analyses of two prominent surveys suggest a strong link between citizen requests and clientelism in Argentina.

7.2.4 Declared Support

Evidence from Argentina is also consistent with the mechanism of declared support, another action by which citizens can help to sustain relational clientelism. Several studies of clientelism in Argentina – which do not investigate the role of citizens quantitatively or formally – emphasize the role of rallies in conveying political support. To be sure, not all citizens who attend rallies are revealing such support; for this reason, analyses of Brazil in Chapter 5 only consider attendance to be a form of declaration if

---

[42] Results are robust to including only requests of local political patrons, or alternatively including only requests of brokers.
[43] This alternate approach uses a logistic regression to determine the predicted probability that each respondent supports the Peronist party, based on only socioeconomic, demographic, and geographic variables.
[44] Survey conducted in twenty-one provinces and the Autonomous City of Buenos Aires.
[45] $N = 1,332$.

7.2 Argentina

a citizen also reports displaying political paraphernalia while at the rally.[46] This point notwithstanding, Javier Auyero's (2000a) prominent qualitative study discusses rally attendance in the context of "problem-solving networks," long-term relationships in which the poor receive assistance from councilors and other political brokers. Many of Auyero's observations are consistent with the logic of declared support presented in this book, though he explains that factors other than self-interest also motivate citizens (2000, 12–13, 158). For instance, Auyero explains that rallies provide "an opportunity to declare one's intentions" (99). By attending a rally, citizens show that they are loyal and willing to offer political support, which in turn demonstrates that they are "deserving" of employment opportunities (163). Furthermore, Auyero cites an interviewee who suggests that receiving benefits from her councilor is contingent on rally attendance: "If I do not go to her rally, then, when I need something, she won't give it to me" (Auyero, 1999, 309–310).

Other work on Argentine clientelism similarly provides evidence about rallies that is consistent with declared support. Mariela Szwarcberg (2014, 2015) primarily focuses on how rally turnout provides information to party leaders about their brokers, but her work also suggests why clientelist payoffs motivate some citizens to attend rallies. She explains that voters understand that they will be rewarded for participation in political activities (if they are patient), and also realize that future benefits may be jeopardized if they do not participate (2015, 66–67). Szwarcberg also demonstrates one way that candidates monitor whether citizens attend rallies: 46 percent of candidates – and 61.2 percent of Peronist candidates – take attendance at rallies, some even using Excel spreadsheets (2015, 33, 63).[47] Also consistent with my argument that citizens' declarations transmit information, Brusco et al.'s (2004, 76) study on vote buying in Argentina posits that rally attendance enables operatives to "make good guesses" about citizens' vote choices. Additionally, they explain that operatives can observe whether citizens "make public pronouncements in favor of the party" (2004, 76). It deserves emphasis that none of these studies elaborate a mechanism by which declarations help to sustain ongoing clientelist relationships, nor do they employ regressions or formal analysis to examine citizen actions. Nevertheless, they provide evidence consistent with the mechanism of declared support presented in Chapter 3.

Survey data also suggest a link between declared support and clientelism in Argentina. The Stokes (2005) survey discussed in the preceding section includes a previously unanalyzed question about whether respondents attended a rally for a candidate. While this question does not hone in on whether a respondent displayed political paraphernalia at the rally – unlike the Rural Clientelism

---

[46] Furthermore, recall that findings about declared support in Chapter 5 are robust to the exclusion of rallies altogether as a form of declaration.

[47] These figures are based on Szwarcberg's coding of 137 councilor candidates in Buenos Aires and Córdoba in 2005–2006.

Survey analyzed in Chapter 5 – it nevertheless provides suggestive evidence regarding declared support. Argentines who attended a rally were over three times more likely than non-attendees to receive campaign handouts (24.7 versus 6.8 percent).[48] As shown in the right panel of Figure 7.3, the relationship between this citizen action and clientelism holds when using logistic regressions to control for other factors that may influence results. The specifications, which are fully reported in Appendix F, add a rally attendance variable to analyses in Stokes (2005). Respondents who attended a rally were 6.0 and 9.0 percentage points more likely to receive a campaign handout in the "Controls" and "Controls & fixed effects" specifications, respectively.[49] In addition, another survey by Stokes in 2003 provides information about the link between rally attendance and help received outside of electoral campaigns, a period when relational clientelism continues. Over 22.3 percent of citizens who attended rallies during the 2003 presidential campaign reported receiving help outside of campaigns over the past four years, compared to just 8.3 percent of citizens who had not attended rallies.[50] In short, both surveys by Stokes suggest that citizens who attended rallies disproportionately receive benefits.

As with Mexico, evidence from Argentina is broadly consistent with the argument of this book, though further research would be required to test mechanisms as thoroughly as in the case of Brazil. A rich literature documents the prevalence of clientelism in Argentina, yet the phenomenon encounters various challenges such as rising income, a growing middle class, and changes in voting technology. Many Argentines are motivated to sustain ongoing exchange relationships because the state fails to protect them from various shocks, such as unemployment, sickness, and drought. Empirical materials in this section have underscored this vulnerability and provided evidence consistent with the two key mechanisms elaborated in Chapter 3 – declared support and requesting benefits. In accordance with predictions, both citizen actions are significantly associated with clientelism in the Argentine case.

7.3 OTHER COUNTRIES

As explored in Chapter 1, clientelism faces major global challenges but endures in most of the world. One important reason is that the majority of countries inadequately protect their citizens from life risks, motivating many individuals to undertake actions that reinforce ongoing exchange relationships. The present section reveals that the mechanisms investigated in this book are observed in various parts of the world, though evidence is more limited than for the cases of Brazil, Mexico, and Argentina examined thus far.

Cross-national surveys reveal the remarkable prevalence of clientelism around the world. For instance, nearly 18 percent of Africans and 12 percent

---

[48] $N = 1,747$.
[49] These findings are significant at the 10 and 5 percent level, respectively.
[50] Author's analysis of Stokes's (2003) survey, which does not ask about citizen requests.

7.3 Other Countries

of Latin Americans surveyed "sometimes" or "always" received offers of handouts in exchange for their votes. Yet as argued in Chapter 1, four broad categories of challenges threaten the existence of clientelism: structural changes (e.g., rising income), institutional reforms (e.g., the secret ballot), heightened legal enforcement, and partisan strategies against clientelism. While the particular combination of threats to clientelism tends to vary across countries, a considerable share of the world's population has an important motivation for sustaining ongoing exchange relationships – their continued vulnerability.

7.3.1 Vulnerability of Citizens

Substantial vulnerability persists in most of the world, even where incomes are rising. In many countries, social insurance fails to cover significant portions of the population, either because programs simply do not exist, they exclude major groups of citizens, or they are poorly implemented (ILO, 2015, 73). For instance, less than a third of the world's workers in 2013 were legally covered by unemployment benefits (ILO, 2015, 79),[51] a devastating blow to many of the world's 204 million people who were unemployed in 2015 (UN, 2015, 17). Furthermore, nearly half of workers across the globe – and three-quarters of workers in Sub-Saharan Africa and South Asia – are categorized by the ILO as having "vulnerable employment" because they are either self-employed or work for their family's firm, and are thus less likely to have social insurance (ILO, 2015, 28; UN, 2015, 19). Of course, this vulnerability extends far beyond employment. Many nations provide insufficient basic health care to their populations, with poor and rural citizens especially likely to suffer from both incomplete access to services and low-quality care (WHO, 2015, 45). In low- and middle-income countries, residents are often unable to obtain generic medicines in public health clinics, partially explaining why in such contexts between 50 and 80 percent of all medicine expenditures are out-of-pocket (WHO, 2015, 56). Water scarcity is another problem that afflicts much of the world and exacerbates the vulnerability of the poor (UN, 2016, 14). Although 42 percent of the global population now has piped drinking water to their premises (UN, 2015, 58), billions of people continue to lack access to water deemed safe for consumption (UN, 2016, 19). In short, vulnerability afflicts much of the world's population, which as argued in this book provides a pressing motivation for citizens to undertake actions that sustain ongoing exchange relationships.

7.3.2 Requesting Benefits

Given this substantial vulnerability across the world, do individuals in other countries also engage in the mechanisms elaborated in this book? Qualitative and quantitative evidence suggests that many citizens do indeed request benefits and declare support and that these actions are linked to clientelism.

---

[51] Unemployment protection as defined by the ILO as "periodic cash benefits."

With respect to requests, for example, research on Ghana emphasizes both their prevalence and their relationship to clientelism. For instance, Members of Parliament (MPs) interviewed by Staffan Lindberg (2010, 123) ranked requests for clientelist benefits as the most common types of demands received from citizens. Requests most frequently involved financial assistance for bills, school fees, food, funerals, weddings, starting a business or farm, and roofing sheets; though less frequent, employment requests were also considered important (2010, 123). Similarly, Asante et al. (2011, 17) observed Ghanaian MPs receiving requests for private benefits, with each MP fielding such demands from about twenty citizens each day. Some MPs even avoid returning to their home districts during recesses to limit interactions with their constituencies, for fear of being inundated with requests (17, 20). In the words of one MP interviewed, one would have to "carry huge sums of money to meet the [personal] demands of constituents" (17). In Lindberg's (2010, 133) discussion of various nuances of clientelism in Ghana, he emphasizes that MPs strive to be reelected and their behavior is "largely demand-driven, defined by the accountability pressures they face at the micro-level," which primarily involve requests for private assistance. He notes that fulfilling clients' requests is a more advantageous political strategy in rural areas, as young urban residents are more likely to make requests of multiple candidates without providing political support (124). While these studies emphasize a link between requests and clientelism, they do not test to what extent benefits are contingent on political support. Nevertheless, they point to the importance of requests in a context with substantial clientelism.

Citizens in India also frequently request help from politicians and party operatives (e.g., Berenschot, 2010, 886–887; Jensenius, 2013, 56–58). A recent study by Jennifer Bussell (n.d., 24, 29) reports that many politicians in three Indian states receive hundreds or even thousands of visits from citizens each day – many involving requests for private assistance – and they spend 24 to 35 percent of their time in meetings with these constituents. Fulfilling these requests involves both clientelism, in which the receipt of benefits is contingent on providing political support, as well as non-partisan constituency service. With respect to clientelism, Berenschot describes citizens requesting help from their councilor in the Gujarat state, who "rewards loyal supporters" as part of his budget (2010, 893). More broadly, he emphasizes that politicians often provide water, jobs, and medical assistance in exchange for political support, in many cases responding to citizen demands (Berenschot, 2010, 893–896). It should be emphasized that not all requests involve clientelism; for example, Bussell (n.d., 5, 36) argues that many requests directed at higher-level politicians involve constituency service, though she notes some evidence regarding *local* politicians may be consistent with contingent exchanges. Overall, evidence from India suggests that citizen requests are prevalent, and elite responsiveness to some (but not all) of these demands involves clientelism.

7.3 Other Countries

In addition to this evidence from Ghana and India, cross-national survey data also suggest a link between citizen requests and clientelism. Two prominent surveys include questions about both clientelism and requests (but not declared support): the 2010 LAPOP AmericasBarometer survey, which includes 43,990 respondents in 26 countries, and the Afrobarometer Round 3 survey, which includes 25,397 respondents in 18 countries.[52] A drawback already discussed about LAPOP also extends to Afrobarometer: both surveys only ask if campaign handouts were offered, not if they were received.

Just as with the Argentine and Mexican LAPOP data analyzed earlier, overall, LAPOP data from across the Americas also reveals a strong link between requests and clientelism, in line with analyses in Chapter 6. Over 13.3 percent of LAPOP respondents reported that they had "sought assistance from or presented a request" from municipal officials during the last year. Once again, requesters were about twice as likely as non-requesters to experience clientelism (20.0 versus 11.0 percent). Analyses in Nichter and Peress (2016), which are summarized in Figure 7.2, show that this difference remains significant at the 1 percent level when including a broad range of control variables and country fixed effects. In the most inclusive specification, requesting help is associated with a 9.4 percentage point increase in the probability of experiencing clientelism. Appendix F reports full regression results.

Similar results are observed using data from eighteen African countries (Nichter and Peress, 2016). Afrobarometer inquires whether respondents contacted political party officials for "help to solve a problem or to give them your views," with a follow-up question about whether the primary reason for this contact was a "personal problem." African respondents who contacted party officials about personal problems disproportionately received clientelist offers. Whereas 26.7 percent of requesters experienced clientelism, only 17.6 percent of non-requesters did. Figure 7.2 demonstrates that the difference between requesters and non-requesters remains significant (at the 1 percent level) when including various controls and country fixed effects. In the most inclusive specification, requesting help is associated with an 11.5 percentage point increase in the probability of experiencing clientelism. Overall, cross-national data from both Africa and Latin America point to a robust association between requests and clientelism, again indicative of the mechanism in Chapter 3.

Moreover, evidence suggests this link does not simply reflect constituency service, in which politicians deliver benefits citizens without regard to political criteria. Instead, both Afrobarometer and LAPOP data show that citizens who support clientelist parties disproportionately receive contingent offers. In Nichter and Peress (2016), we adapt the core vs. swing test of Stokes et al. (2013), which uses as a proxy for supporters whether respondents identify with any political party. To examine whether citizens who identify

---

[52] Canada and the United States are excluded from LAPOP analyses. Afrobarometer's Round 3 survey was fielded in 2005 and 2006.

with *clientelist* parties are more likely to receive benefits, data are employed from Kitschelt's (2013) expert survey about clientelist activities by parties in eighty-eight nations.[53] In particular, we coded whether respondents identified with a party that experts described as engaging in "moderate" or "major" clientelist efforts.[54] In both Africa and Latin America, citizens who identify with a clientelist party have a higher likelihood of experiencing clientelism (at the 1 percent significance level). This finding suggests a political logic of benefits flowing to machine supporters, which is congruent with relational clientelism.

In sum, both qualitative and quantitative evidence from various countries across the world suggest a link between citizen requests and clientelism, consistent with the key theoretical mechanism elaborated in Chapter 3.

7.3.3 Declared Support

Compared to the previous section on citizen requests, evidence about a link between declared support and clientelism is more limited outside of Brazil, Argentina, and Mexico.[55] Nevertheless, research from Lebanon, Yemen, and Ghana provides suggestive evidence outside of Latin America that is broadly consistent with the role of declarations examined in Chapter 3.

In Lebanon, Melani Cammett (2011, 2014) examines the distribution of social assistance by sectarian political parties. While the role of citizens in clientelism is not her primary focus, Cammett reveals that Lebanese citizens who demonstrate their commitment to a party through various actions are more likely to receive benefits, and those who do so more extensively receive a greater value of benefits (2011, 75, 84–87; 2014, 128–129). She creates an index of forms of citizen participation that demonstrate partisan commitment (e.g., voting, party membership, and volunteering), which specifically includes citizens "signaling their political preferences" by displaying posters, symbols and other party materials at home (2011, 75, 95; 2014, 118). Regressions using a national survey reveal that citizens who engage in more of these actions receive more social assistance such as food, health care, and education (2011, 84–87; 2014, 128–129). While Cammett's analysis reflects actions broader than declared support, her findings are consistent with the mechanism elaborated in the present book.

In Lebanon and Yemen, Daniel Corstange (2016) also reveals patterns consistent with declared support. As part of his broader argument that intra-ethnic competition affects how elites distribute patronage, Corstange suggests

---

[53] Survey fielded in 2008–2009 in all democratic polities with at least two million citizens.
[54] Analysis employs the subset of nations in Kitschelt's survey (81 percent of LAPOP countries and 67 percent of Afrobarometer countries). Results are also consistent when a party identifier variable is used, which includes all countries in Afrobarometer and LAPOP (except for Canada and the United States).
[55] For example, to the best of my knowledge, no cross-national survey includes questions about both declared support and clientelism.

that many voters engage in "public sycophancy" – displays of political iconography – to demonstrate how intensely they are committed to leaders (10, 198–203). In line with the signaling model in the present book, Corstange reasons that public sycophancy sends a costly signal because "it imposes opportunity, psychological, and social costs on clients which are easier for committed supporters to bear than for the uncommitted" (200). To investigate the link between these displays and patronage, he analyzed a survey question about whether a respondent believed connections or merit is more important to obtain a government job. Regressions suggest that citizens who answered "connections" were significantly more likely to display political posters and flags than those who answered "merit" (219). This pattern is only observed in constituencies dominated by a single leader, consistent with his argument that voters compete for patronage in politically dominated communities (16, 219). Overall, findings in Corstange (2016) suggest that declarations may influence patronage in both Lebanon and Yemen.

In addition, recent work on Ghana identifies patterns consistent with declared support. Kristin Michelitch (2013, 109–111) briefly reports that many Ghanaians believe that public expressions of partisan support – including rally attendance and the use of flags, posters, shirts, hats, or even hair weavings – will enhance their ability to obtain future benefits from elected officials. Moreover, they perceive that "the *more they show party loyalty* in these very public ways, the *more likely they will be able to access* favorable services and goods if their party obtains power" (2013, 110, italics in original). Post-election benefits may include funds for medical expenses, weddings, funerals, and even employment offers; in addition, Ghanaians who engage in these public displays also tend to receive small handouts before the election (110–111). Michelitch (2011, 36) mentions that displays are observed by parties' dense network of operatives, and thereby facilitate clientelism even as Ghana strengthens ballot secrecy. Once again, these observations are consistent with the logic of declared support presented in Chapter 3.

In sum, clientelism faces major challenges across the world, but pervasive vulnerability provides an important motivation for citizens to reinforce relational clientelism. This brief discussion of several countries, as well an analysis of cross-national data, provide suggestive evidence of declared support and requesting benefits in the broader global context.

7.4 SUMMARY

As explored in this chapter, citizens play an important role in clientelism far beyond Brazil. In many countries, clientelism confronts serious threats to its existence, such as rising income, institutional reforms, heightened legal enforcement, and partisan strategies. Yet clientelism endures, in part because many citizens are motivated to help sustain ongoing exchange relationships that mitigate their vulnerability. Evidence from Argentina and Mexico documents various challenges threatening clientelism, as well as the substantial vulnerability facing many citizens. While data limitations inhibit analyses of post-election benefits in countries other than Brazil, a strong link is observed in both countries between clientelism and the two key mechanisms explored in this book. Citizens who declare support publicly for candidates – and those who ask politicians and their representatives for benefits – are more likely to experience clientelism in Argentina and Mexico. Similar findings are observed for one or both mechanisms in Ghana, India, Lebanon, and Yemen, and cross-national data from Africa and Latin America reveal a robust association between requesting benefits and clientelism. To be sure, evidence from these countries is suggestive rather than dispositive, but it nevertheless corroborates the more thorough testing of mechanisms in Part II using empirical materials from Brazil. When considered holistically, such patterns across the world add credence to the book's argument that citizens undertake both actions – declared support and requesting benefits – and thereby often play an important role in sustaining relational clientelism.

8

Conclusion

This book has explored an important phenomenon observed in much of the world – the contingent exchange of material benefits for political support. Many journalists and scholars assume that these exchanges always involve vote buying, a campaign strategy that rewards citizens who vote for candidates they do not prefer. In recent years, however, a growing number of observers have become increasingly attentive to several other campaign strategies that also distribute contingent benefits. For example, elites often induce supporters to show up at the polls (turnout buying), and in some contexts reward opposing voters for staying home on Election Day (abstention buying). Over the past decade, a vibrant research agenda has greatly advanced our understanding of such strategies of "electoral clientelism," which exclusively provides benefits during campaigns. Unfortunately, this recent strand of research has generally remained silent about the role, and sometimes even about the existence, of benefits distributed during non-campaign periods.

This recent fixation on electoral clientelism diverges from generations of studies focused on what I call "relational clientelism" – ongoing exchange relationships in which contingent benefits extend beyond election campaigns. Decades of ethnographic work on patron-client ties documented how a variety of elites, ranging from politicians to village notables, provided sustenance to the poor within the context of enduring relationships. Much of this work emphasized the asymmetry of relationships between patrons and clients; for instance, land tenure contracts often restricted citizens' exit options, thereby hindering voter autonomy. While no longer the predominant focus of research, some influential studies investigated how and why elites in various contemporary societies maintain long-term clientelist relationships with citizens. A limitation of such studies, in part stemming from the contexts they examined, is that they tend to pay minimal attention to the ways in which citizen choices may also shape ongoing exchange relationships. By contrast, the present book puts the choices of citizens into stark relief and argues that they often play an instrumental role in the survival of relational clientelism.

Increased voter autonomy has empowered many citizens to play this important role in ongoing exchange relationships. Unlike many of their historical counterparts, citizens in the modern world frequently have sufficient independence to undertake political actions of their own volition. Furthermore, a shift from monopolistic to competitive clientelism in many countries expanded the potential scope for citizen choice because a single machine often no longer serves as the exclusive distributor of benefits. Coupled with this heightened voter autonomy, citizens often have a pressing motivation – their own vulnerability to adverse shocks – to undertake actions that fortify relational clientelism. Despite various countries' efforts to develop welfare states, social policies often inadequately protect citizens from the full range of risks that threaten their livelihoods. And even though GDP per capita has risen substantially in much of the world, income gains alone are often insufficient to enable voters to self-insure against risks. Amid such vulnerability, many citizens rely on ongoing relationships with politicians who provide material assistance when adversity strikes. In short, many citizens have both the autonomy and motivation to undertake purposive actions to buttress the stability of relational clientelism.

Citizens' choices to undertake such actions often underpin the survival of relational clientelism because ongoing exchange relationships are particularly susceptible to the threat of opportunistic defection. More specifically, this book has elaborated and tested two key mechanisms – declared support and requesting benefits – by which citizens help to alleviate a dual-sided credibility problem inherent in relational clientelism. By declaring support publicly, citizens mitigate the concern that they will renege on their promises to vote for politicians with whom they have ongoing exchange relationships. And by screening out politicians who have denied their requests, citizens reduce their own concerns that entrusted politicians will defect on promises to help during adverse shocks. Declared support and requesting benefits are by no means the only important actions that citizens undertake in ongoing exchange relationships, but evidence of both mechanisms underscores how citizens can play an instrumental role in sustaining relational clientelism.

Substantial evidence suggests that citizens employ both mechanisms in Brazil. With regards to declared support, many Brazilians publicly pledge allegiance to political candidates, and are more likely to do so amidst adverse shocks. While citizens have various reasons to declare support, the practice is strongly linked to relational clientelism. Two original surveys, as well as many interviews, reveal the widely shared perception that declaring support can influence the benefits one receives. Beyond perceptions, quantitative analyses suggest that citizens who declare for victorious candidates are more likely recipients of benefits. As expected with relational clientelism, this finding is observed during both election and non-election years, even when controlling for various other factors. Quantitative and qualitative evidence is also consistent with a signaling model of declared support, which elucidates how and why declarations can mitigate concerns that citizens will renege on their vote promises. In further corroboration of this important mechanism, citizens overwhelmingly vote and hold perceptions in accordance with their declarations.

Just as for declared support, evidence from Brazil also points to the mechanism of requesting benefits. Even in rural Northeast Brazil, an area not traditionally known for voter autonomy, the majority of citizens who received material benefits from politicians had requested it. Vulnerability is frequently a motivating factor: requests increase during adverse shocks and typically involve life necessities. As expected with relational clientelism, requesters disproportionately receive benefits during both election and non-election years, and declared supporters are more likely to be recipients through bottom-up demands. Qualitative and quantitative evidence suggests that citizens screen out politicians with poor track records of fulfilling their requests; for instance, they tend to hold negative perceptions of candidates who are unresponsive to their demands and refuse to vote for them. Overall, empirical materials from Brazil elucidate how citizens can play an important role in sustaining relational clientelism, as both mechanisms mitigate credibility problems that threaten ongoing exchange relationships.

Comparative evidence suggests that this role of citizens in bolstering clientelism extends beyond Brazil. In both Argentina and Mexico, survey respondents who declare support – as well as those who demand benefits – are more likely to experience clientelism. Qualitative evidence likewise suggests the role of both declared support and requesting benefits in these countries. In addition, one or both mechanisms are observed in Ghana, India, Lebanon, and Yemen. Moreover, cross-national surveys from Africa and Latin America reveal a strong association between citizen requests and clientelism. To be sure, the mechanisms elaborated in the present study warrant additional investigation outside Brazil; for instance, quantitative analyses of comparative cases examined only patterns during campaigns, due to data availability. Notwithstanding such limitations, evidence of declared support and requesting benefits in other countries points towards the role of citizens in the wider global context.

By broadening its analytical lens to encompass voter choice, this book has revealed an important explanation for the survival of clientelism. As mentioned, the choices of citizens can mitigate the dual credibility problem that challenges the viability of ongoing exchange relationships. Aside from this problem that citizens mitigate, relational clientelism is relatively more resilient than electoral clientelism to numerous key challenges. For instance, income gains from economic development frequently reduce citizens' willingness to accept vote-buying offers, but are often insufficient to eliminate voters' reliance on clientelist relationships to cope with adverse shocks. Institutional factors such as ballot secrecy and compulsory voting are also less damaging for relational clientelism, in part because it does not channel benefits to swing voters (as with vote buying and abstention buying) or to those unlikely to participate in elections (as with turnout buying). Furthermore, ongoing exchange relationships provide benefits extending beyond campaign periods (unlike electoral clientelism), so they have a greater ability to withstand heightened legal enforcement focused on the months preceding elections. The broader point is that relational clientelism is better able to withstand the onslaught of challenges facing clientelism, once citizens' choices help to alleviate its dual credibility problem. Relational clientelism is by no means a new phenomenon, but its resilience to growing challenges often makes it a more efficacious political strategy than electoral clientelism. In such contexts, machines are expected to rely relatively more heavily on ongoing exchange relationships than on electoral clientelism. However, both forms of contingent exchanges often coexist because clientelism is typically most effective when employing a diverse portfolio (Magaloni et al., 2007; Diaz-Cayeros et al., 2016; Gans-Morse et al., 2014).[1]

This book emphasizes that vulnerability often motivates citizens to help sustain relational clientelism, and thus clarifies an important reason why the phenomenon often persists in contexts with low poverty. Many studies underscore that clientelism flourishes when poverty is rife. A common explanation invokes the diminishing marginal utility of income, which suggests that poor citizens place relatively greater value on material benefits than ideological preferences (Dixit and Londregan, 1996, 1114; Stokes, 2005, 315). However, an unresolved question in the literature is why clientelism often remains remarkably resilient when poverty declines. An important explanation emerges when broadening the focus to vulnerability – a concept that encompasses poverty as well as risk, which both reduce citizens' well-being (Ligon and Schechter, 2003). The present book's focus on vulnerability clarifies that *either* poverty or risk may be sufficient to motivate citizens to undertake actions that sustain relational clientelism.[2] Therefore, nonexistent and inadequate welfare states often contribute to the perpetuation of clientelism. In much of the world, welfare states are underdeveloped and truncated, reaching only narrow subset of the population such as formal employees. Ongoing exchange relationships often help unprotected citizens cope with adverse shocks. This book thereby provides important microfoundations for the longstanding observation that relational clientelism tends to erode as welfare states are developed (e.g., Banfield and Wilson 1963; Scott, 1969). Even if poverty declines, clientelism may persist until a welfare state is developed that adequately mitigates shocks in an institutionalized manner, or until alternative mechanisms emerge that enable citizens to cope with risks without relying on politicians. These insights help to explain why mere income transfers, such as those offered by conditional cash transfer (CCT) programs burgeoning across the developing world, often

---

[1] Formal analyses in Magaloni et al. (2007) and Diaz-Cayeros et al. (2016) predict machines diversify their portfolios across both clientelism and public goods. The model in Gans-Morse et al. (2014) suggests machines optimally mix several strategies of electoral clientelism.

[2] Risk may be an insufficient condition on its own to motivate citizens to sustain clientelism, if their income is high enough to self-insure.

Conclusion

do not lead to the demise of clientelism. For example, this book has documented the resilience of clientelism in Brazil, where Bolsa Família – one of the world's largest CCT programs – serves about a quarter of the country's population (see Chapter 4). Given the pronounced vulnerability of many citizens across world, future research should investigate the relative importance of economic development versus welfare state development to the trajectory of clientelism in various settings. In addition to relational clientelism, such research should consider how these factors influence electoral clientelism, which does not necessarily decline in all contexts with high income levels and comprehensive welfare states.[3]

If vulnerability motivates citizen choices that bolster clientelism, as this book argues, then reductions in vulnerability should decrease such choices. A field experiment in Northeast Brazil (Bobonis, Gertler, Gonzalez-Navarro and Nichter, 2018) reveals precisely this effect on one of the mechanisms examined in the present book: decreased vulnerability cuts requests by citizens likely to be in clientelist relationships. In that project, we randomly assigned households in rural Northeast Brazil without piped water to receive 16,000-liter water cisterns. These concrete tanks collect and store rainwater, thereby decreasing households' vulnerability to droughts. The study finds that the intervention not only reduced vulnerability, but also reduced requests for private benefits by 3.2 percentage points (significant at the 5 percent level). These treatment effects were entirely concentrated among respondents likely to be in ongoing exchange relationships – those who had talked to a politician at least monthly before the start of the 2012 municipal campaign. For such citizens, the cisterns intervention reduced requests by 11.1 percentage points (significant at the 1 percent level). By contrast, the intervention had negligible and statistically insignificant effects on other respondents. Evidence suggests that the impact of the cisterns treatment, which reduced citizens' vulnerability, extended beyond the campaign period: the decline in requests during the 2013 non-election year is comparable to the decline in requests during the 2012 election year. The study also reveals electoral effects on incumbent politicians. If vulnerability weakens ongoing exchange relationships through a decrease in requests, one might expect incumbents – who tend to have a competitive advantage at clientelism – to suffer a loss in electoral support. Indeed, the cisterns treatment reduced the number of votes cast for incumbent mayors during their reelection campaigns.[4] Overall, these experimental findings from Northeast Brazil are consistent with the present book's argument that vulnerability motivates citizens to undertake actions (such as requesting benefits) that help sustain clientelism. Futhermore,

---

[3] For example, although analyses in Chapter 4 show that citizens' willingness to accept clientelist offers during campaigns decreases as incomes rise, substantial electoral clientelism remains in some developed nations.

[4] Our analysis compares voting machines within the same voting location. Machines with a greater number of voters randomly assigned to the cisterns treatment had fewer votes for the incumbent mayoral candidate, conditional on the number of voters in the experiment.

they suggest that curbing vulnerability may have important political ramifications by undercutting the electoral prospects of clientelist politicians.

Given that citizens often play an instrumental role in sustaining relational clientelism, why is the phenomenon not even more widespread? As discussed in the Introduction, both demand-side and supply-side factors help to explain why some citizens do not undertake actions to fortify ongoing exchange relationships. With regard to demand-side factors, citizens are unlikely to play this role unless their circumstances meet two scope conditions: voter autonomy and vulnerability. Citizens with insufficient autonomy, such as those in contexts with substantial coercion, may be unable to engage in various political actions of their own volition. In addition, voters who experience neither poverty nor unprotected risk may lack motivation to buttress the stability of exchange relationships. Moreover, not all citizens who meet both scope conditions are involved with relational clientelism. While much of the world's population relies on enduring exchange relationships to cope with adversity, other voters express aversion to clientelism and refuse to promise political support in return for assistance. In the case of Brazil, numerous interviewed politicians emphasized the distinction between "voters of conscience," who vote purely on programmatic grounds, and "clientelist voters," who are responsive to contingent benefits. Likewise, experimental evidence from Benin suggests that clientelism is not universally appealing to all impoverished citizens (Wantchekon 2003, 422); reasons for such variation are frequently multifaceted and context-specific. Citizens may also be less likely to undertake actions to bolster relational clientelism in contexts where viable candidates offer credible policy proposals, underscoring the importance of supply-side factors. While this book aims to tilt the focus of research on clientelism towards the understudied role of citizens, a wide body of scholarship emphasizes various ways in which elites shape contingent exchanges. Politicians may eschew clientelism under numerous conditions, such as if they are able to make credible campaign promises about programmatic benefits (Keefer, 2007), or if middle-class voters penalize candidates who distribute handouts (Weitz-Shapiro, 2012). Other supply-side constraints on relational clientelism include resources, discretion, and organizational structure. In some contexts, local politicians only cultivate long-term relationships with a small subset of voters due to the sheer level of resources available. The discretion of politicians to channel existing resources to supporters may also be limited to varying degrees by institutional factors, such as statutory requirements regarding municipal expenditures as well as randomized federal audits in Brazil. In addition, politicians may not have sufficient organizational infrastructure to observe clients' declarations and fulfill their requests reliably. In short, both demand-side and supply-side factors help to explain why relational clientelism is not even more prevalent than observed.

While relational clientelism is by no means ubiquitous, its prevalence is often underappreciated, in part because analysts rarely consider the broader duration of exchange relationships. When contingent benefits are distributed during campaigns, this practice is commonly depicted as vote buying or other forms of electoral clientelism. But most studies fail to distinguish whether a citizen's receipt of contingent benefits also extends beyond campaigns. Thus, much of what scholars interpret as electoral clientelism is actually relational clientelism. Notwithstanding this important point, many contingent exchanges across the world are indeed restricted to campaign periods. Strategies such as vote buying and turnout buying persist in many countries, even in the face of challenges from structural changes, institutional reforms, legal enforcement and partisan strategies. For example, this book demonstrated that a reduced level of electoral clientelism continues in Brazil, in part because some politicians "gamble" on these relatively unreliable strategies as a secondary measure in competitive elections. In addition, evidence suggests that a small share of Brazilians targeted with electoral clientelism may well be influenced by its rewards.[5] But in Brazil and beyond, many campaign handouts are distributed not in isolation, but rather as part of ongoing relationships in which benefits extend beyond campaigns.

Considering the broader duration of exchange relationships also helps to resolve an outstanding puzzle in the clientelism literature: Why do politicians often distribute campaign handouts to their own voting supporters? From the vantage point of electoral clientelism, such behavior is wasteful. As emphasized by the typology in Chapter 2, politicians who employ electoral clientelism target citizens who are unlikely to vote for them or participate in an imminent election, in exchange for promising to act as instructed. An influential study by Stokes et al. (2013) suggests that due to a principal-agent problem, voting supporters are the unintended recipients of electoral clientelism: party leaders strive to target swing voters with campaign handouts, but their resources are misdirected by brokers who find it easier to target supporters instead. By contrast, the present book argues that providing benefits to supporters who face adverse shocks is part and parcel of relational clientelism, regardless whether an election is a week or a year away. And crucially, supporters often receive benefits during campaigns because they demand them, not because they are targeted with offers. In the context of ongoing exchange relationships, denying supporters' requests during a campaign tends to be counterproductive, as it tarnishes the credibility of a politician's promises to continue providing help to supporters during times of need. And such credibility often takes years to cultivate, as shown in Chapter 6. Hence, broadening the analytical lens to consider citizen actions in relational clientelism provides an alternative explanation for otherwise puzzling behavior by elites.

---

[5] As discussed in Chapter 2, 18 percent of respondents who received vote-buying offers in the nationally representative Brazilian Electoral Panel Study said they were more likely to vote for the specified candidate (Ames et al., 2013). In the Rural Clientelism Survey, 18 percent of respondents indicated they would choose a candidate who provided them a large campaign handout over one who repeatedly provided them more modest help over time (see Chapter 6).

Even though many citizens rely on relational clientelism to cope with vulnerability, it deserves emphasis that these ongoing exchange relationships are an inferior substitute for a universal, comprehensive welfare state. Relational clientelism provides assistance in contingent exchange for political support, and generally withholds benefits from citizens who fail to provide such support. This contingency frequently distorts the allocation of public resources. For instance, when a mayor leverages the municipal hospital to provide supporters with preferential access to costly medicines or expedited surgeries, such actions often exacerbate the difficulties other patients face when seeking similar health care. Another concern is that unlike social insurance enshrined in legislation, relational clientelism bestows clients with no formal rights to benefits. Even when citizens undertake actions to reinforce ongoing exchange relationships, elites maintain broad discretion to rejigger their clientelist networks as is deemed politically advantageous. Such considerations may lead politicians to adjust their provision of benefits and terminate ongoing relationships with particular clients. These issues of exclusivity and discretion, as well as other concerns discussed next, render relational clientelism a troubling and imperfect substitute for an adequate welfare state. As a stopgap in countries with patchy social insurance, however, relational clientelism often serves an important role in mitigating citizens' vulnerability.

More broadly, it is also important to emphasize the wide array of other potential negative consequences of clientelism. To name a few, Hicken (2011, 302–304) summarizes numerous studies suggesting that clientelism can contribute to the under-provision of public goods, undermine political institutions, bloat and politicize bureaucracies, weaken political parties, increase rent seeking, expand public deficits, and heighten corruption. Furthermore, by protecting their clients from risks, clientelist politicians are often able to secure electoral victories while they enact policies against the broader interests of poor voters (Anderson et al., 2015, 1786). As such, they may have incentives to undermine the implementation of social policies that reduce the vulnerability of the poor. Research on Brazil also finds various negative consequences of clientelism, such as the weakening of legislators' incentives to work collaboratively with copartisans on policy (Desposato, 2007), hindering policy reforms that would otherwise benefit the poor (Weyland, 1996), and fostering the use of illegal funds obtained from corrupt activities (Gingerich, 2014). While such findings should be considered neither definitive nor exhaustive, they do collectively emphasize that clientelism can impose substantial costs. Notwithstanding these consequences, the present book suggests that interventions combating clientelism should pay close attention to the role of ongoing exchange relationships in alleviating citizens' vulnerability. To enhance such interventions, a crucial step is to improve alternative means of risk mitigation. As suggested by the cisterns experiment in Brazil, providing other mechanisms that insulate citizens from shocks will likely reduce their actions that serve to reinforce clientelism. Perhaps even more important, this step can help shield citizens from unintended consequences, as anti-clientelism interventions may otherwise aggravate citizens' vulnerability by undercutting the informal insurance provided by ongoing exchange relationships.

It is important to emphasize that not all consequences of clientelism are uniform across subtypes of the phenomenon. One key distinction, for example, involves consequences for democracy. The predominant form of electoral clientelism in many contexts, vote buying, is often viewed to be especially pernicious for democracy. One key reason is that vote buying undermines democratic accountability by enabling politicians to buy the votes of citizens who are unsatisfied with their performance in office (Stokes et al., 2013, 254). Instead, Susan Stokes (2005) argues that vote buying only involves "perverse accountability," in which rewarded citizens are punished if they do not vote as instructed. By contrast, this book's focus on relational clientelism emphasizes that politicians are indeed accountable to their clients, though in a manner that diverges from how many observers expect democracy to function. As shown in Chapter 6, citizens who request help systematically vote against politicians who are unresponsive to them, as they deem such politicians untrustworthy promisers of assistance. Such findings dovetail with Kitschelt's (2000, 851–852) argument that "clientelist politics establishes very tight bonds of accountability and responsiveness. ... Politicians who refuse to be responsive to their constituents' demands for selective incentives will be held accountable by them and no longer receive votes and material contributions." Undeniably, vote buying and relational clientelism also share some negative consequences for democracy; for instance, both subtypes of clientelism tend to undermine political equality by enabling those with resources to attract votes of the poor, and they often weaken representation by distorting the link between citizens' preferences and voting behavior. Despite such similarities, their divergent implications for democratic accountability suggest the need to investigate potential differences across a host of other consequences.

Another fruitful area for future research involves the role that citizens play in clientelism in authoritarian contexts, particularly in non-democratic regimes that allow some form of limited electoral politics. Although the present study focuses on democratic settings, numerous prominent studies have explored elite strategies of clientelism in various authoritarian regimes. For instance, Blaydes (2006, 5–8) documents how some Egyptian candidates not only engage in vote buying during electoral campaigns, but also cultivate longer-term relationships through the distribution of particularistic benefits to citizens. In the cases of Brazil and Mexico explored in this book, clientelism was extensively employed in both countries during recent authoritarian periods (e.g., Hagopian, 1996; Magaloni, 2006). Citizens may have substantially less autonomy to undertake political actions that sustain clientelism in non-democratic polities. Furthermore, politicians in such contexts may be more likely to employ negative inducements, such as threats of physical and economic sanctions, which are used for clientelism in various countries and likely have different implications for citizens' behavior (Mares and Young, 2016, 269–271). The mechanisms examined in this book are expected to be applicable even with negative inducements; as discussed in Chapter 3, Nichter and Nunnari (2017) show experimentally that patterns of declared support persist with some level of punishment. Nevertheless, given this book's focus on Brazil – a democracy where incentives are by far predominantly used – the role of citizens in clientelism under authoritarianism deserves further investigation.

An additional line of inquiry involves the formation of clientelist relationships. This book presupposes the existence of ongoing exchange relationships, as it argues that citizens' actions help to ensure their continued survival. Although it is commonly assumed that elites initiate these relationships, citizens also often approach potential patrons – with whom they may or may not have existing personal or economic ties – when in dire need of assistance (e.g., Powell, 1970, 412–413; Silverman, 1965, 176–177). In the case of Brazil, interviewees suggest that both citizens and politicians can take the first step in forming clientelist linkages. Given the understudied role of citizens in contingent exchanges, further research should investigate the extent to which voters not only fortify clientelist relationships, but also help to create them. Citizens' proclivity to do so is likely influenced by various individual and contextual characteristics, including their ability to mitigate adverse shocks through self-insurance, kinship, or social networks; the degree to which entitlement programs provide adequate risk protection; and the existence of viable political candidates who offer credible policy proposals. When citizens seek to form clientelist relationships, an additional research question involves how they choose which elites to approach. For example, numerous factors discussed in this book may influence citizens' decisions, such as politicians' probability of winning, incumbency status, available resources, and number of existing clients. Also worthy of further investigation are the diverse ways in which citizens can seek to initiate clientelist relationships; for instance, some citizens may first request help from prospective benefactors, while others may first declare support to signal the trustworthiness of their vote promises. Such questions would further understanding of the phenomenon, but it deserves emphasis that this book's argument and mechanisms do not depend on how a clientelist relationship was initially formed. As demonstrated, citizens often play an instrumental role in the survival of relational clientelism, as their actions foster a mutually reinforcing cycle: ongoing patterns of both declared support and fulfilled requests buttress the stability of established exchange relationships, which may originate from various sources.

This book has focused on municipal-level politics, and has shown that citizens' actions often help to sustain their ongoing exchange relationships with local politicians. In turn, these actions can have important consequences for higher levels of political systems because local politicians often serve as brokers for state, provincial, and national politicians in various countries. In Brazil, Novaes (2017, 4–5) argues that mayoral candidates often serve as brokers by mobilizing their established clienteles on behalf of congressional candidates, who in return provide money and other benefits to these local politicians. In Argentina, Stokes et al. (2013, 261, 268) emphasize that elected city councilors – who comprise three hundred of the eight hundred brokers they survey – frequently serve as intermediaries for higher-level politicians. And in the Philippines, Ravanilla, Haim, and Hicken (2017, 8) describe a "chain of patron-broker relationships" connecting local and higher-level politicians, including mayors who receive resources from national candidates and mobilize votes for them in return. When local politicians have enduring clientelist relationships with voters, their ability to mobilize votes on behalf of other politicians in this manner is often heightened. As such, citizens who fortify relational clientelism may help to perpetuate a cascade of exchanges across different tiers of government. By strengthening the capacity of local politicians to serve as brokers, citizen actions can also influence the political strategies of higher-level politicians, with potentially important policy effects. For example, a model by Keefer and Vlaicu (2008, 371–373, 395) predicts that when there are low costs to obtaining votes through intermediaries with established clienteles, politicians will underprovide public goods and make fewer broad policy appeals through programmatic linkages. Such potential effects underscore the importance of further research about how citizens' role in sustaining ongoing exchange relationships with local politicians may also influence higher spheres of politics. One important question involves how these broader effects are shaped by contextual factors. For example, citizens' actions to reinforce relational clientelism are likely to have greater effects on state and national politics when many local politicians serve as brokers, which Novaes (2017, 1–4) argues is more likely if political parties have weak brands and few linkages to voters.[6] As researchers explore such questions, they should pay close attention to the effects of citizens' relationships with various types of brokers, which can include a broad range of actors beyond local politicians.[7] This investigation will require expanded data and analyses, given that existing work on brokers tends to focus almost exclusively on electoral clientelism (e.g., Stokes et al., 2013; Larreguy et al., 2016).

The demand side of clientelism is relatively understudied, presenting numerous additional directions for future research. One direction involves how citizens may collectively shape relational clientelism. Although the present book has focused on the role of individuals in sustaining ongoing exchange relationships, clientelism in some contexts may involve groups of citizens, such as neighborhoods or organizations (Kitschelt and Wilkinson, 2007, 11–12). For instance, Gay (1990, 106–107) discusses how a neighborhood association in

---

[6] Such conditions pertain in Brazil. Only a third of respondents in the Brazil 2010 Panel Study expressed a preference for any party. In Datafolha polls, comparable figures are about 40–45 percent (Samuels and Zucco Jr., 2014, 214). Parties other than the PT and PMDB tend to have minimal infrastructure in most municipalities (Braga and Pimentel Jr., 2013, 19).

[7] For an excellent overview, see Mares and Young (2016).

Rio de Janeiro exchanged its political support for road paving. Under what conditions and how do such groups help to sustain relational clientelism? Extending the mechanisms examined in this book, citizens may declare support jointly to signal the credibility of their vote promises. Likewise, they may collectively ask for private or club goods, and screen against politicians who fail to meet their demands. Conversely, under what conditions and how do groups of citizens undermine relational clientelism? Shifting away from clientelism involves a coordination problem (e.g., Diaz-Cayeros et al., 2016, 34; Lyne, 2008, 37). If many citizens jointly abandon a clientelist candidate, they can elect a programmatic competitor; however, if a citizen acts alone, she is unlikely to affect the election outcome and may lose contingent benefits. While analyses in this book employ controls to hone in on the role of individual citizens, future work should investigate how and why the actions of collective actors may also fortify or undercut relational clientelism. Another important direction involves exploring how citizens' choices about clientelism influence politicians' actions. Whereas this book strives to call attention to the undertheorized role of citizens in clientelism, the extant literature generally emphasizes the pivotal role of elites. As such, the strategic interaction between citizens and politicians is an important research frontier. A recent study that begins to tackle this research agenda is Nichter and Peress (2016), which as discussed in Chapter 3, develops and tests a formal model of how politicians respond when citizens demand clientelist benefits during campaigns. Within this agenda, future work should consider how citizens' actions affect the relative effectiveness of relational versus electoral clientelism, as well as how they influence the allure of clientelism to politicians vis-á-vis many other tools for obtaining votes (ranging from electoral fraud to campaign advertising). More broadly, such questions suggest that the demand side of clientelism presents intriguing opportunities for additional scholarly inquiry.

Stepping back, the present book suggests three overarching directions for the study of clientelism. First, it underscores the need to take more seriously the independent role of citizens in the survival of clientelism. Second, it emphasizes that analysts must consider how vulnerability, and not just poverty, shapes contingent exchanges. And finally, it calls for renewed attention to ongoing exchange relationships, which have been given short shrift compared to electoral clientelism in recent years.

Overall, this study has shifted the dominant analytical lens to consider the logic, mechanisms, and motivations behind citizens' actions in clientelist exchanges. A broad array of evidence from numerous countries reveals how and why voters often play an instrumental role in the survival of clientelism. Despite income gains in much of the world, vulnerability frequently motivates citizens to help sustain ongoing exchange relationships with politicians who mitigate risks.

Appendix A

Description of Qualitative Fieldwork

Fieldwork on clientelism was conducted by the author for more than eighteen months in Brazil. During and after the 2008 municipal campaign, I conducted a total of 110 formal interviews on clientelism in Bahia state. These interviews were conducted of both citizens (55 interviews) and elites (55 interviews). Each interview was conducted in Portuguese, lasting an average of 70 minutes. In addition, I conducted informal interviews of another 350 citizens and elites, and three focus groups of citizens.

This fieldwork was supplemented in Pernambuco in mid-2012 with additional interviews of sixteen elites and six rural citizens. These supplementary interviews specifically focused on clientelism in water delivery, and therefore did not employ the same interview protocol as the Bahia research. I conducted the Pernambuco interviews in collaboration with Gustavo Bobonis and Marco Gonzalez-Navarro.

Interviews were conducted in municipalities with 100,000 citizens or fewer. Municipalities of this size account for approximately 45 percent of Brazil's population (IBGE, 2010). They also comprise about 95 percent of the country's municipalities. The primary field site, Bahia, is the most populous state in the Northeast region of Brazil with 14 million citizens (IBGE, 2010). Pernambuco is also in the Northeast region with 8.8 million citizens. The Northeast is the poorest region of Brazil and one of the most unequal regions in the world. Approximately 29 percent of Bahia's population lives in households below the poverty level, and the state has amongst the lowest social indicators in Brazil (UNDP, 2017). The Gini coefficient of income inequality in Bahia is 0.62 (UNDP, 2017).

In order to identify potential themes, develop interview questions, and field-test the citizen and elite interview protocols, I commenced this qualitative research in a municipality of ten thousand citizens in central Bahia, where I lived for approximately five months. During this time, I selected a stratified

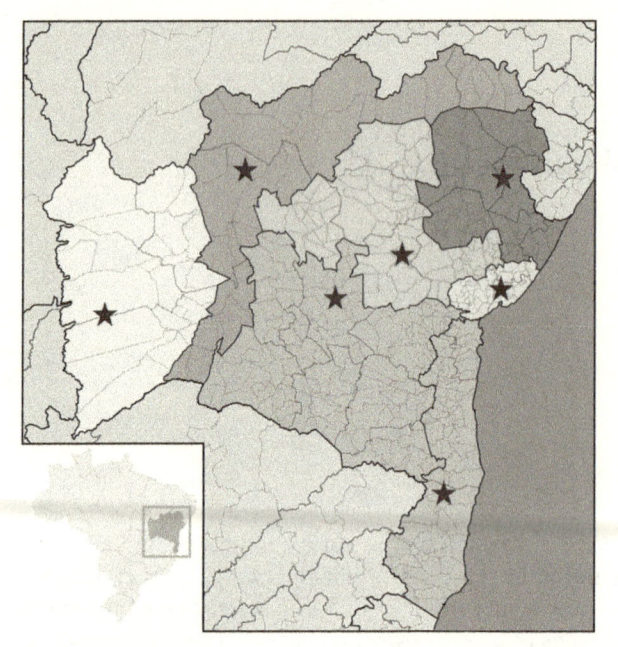

FIGURE A.1 *Map of research sites in Bahia (Northeast Brazil)*

random sample of six additional municipalities to conduct further interviews. Altogether, the municipalities spanned each of Bahia's seven "mesoregions," which are defined by Brazil's national census bureau (IBGE) as areas that share common geographic characteristics. Figure A.1 shows the geographical distribution of interview locations across the state of Bahia. The population sizes of the seven municipalities selected were approximately: 10,000; 15,000; 30,000; 45,000; 60,000; 80,000; and nearly 100,000.

Within each selected municipality, individuals for community member interviews were selected randomly using quota sampling in multiple rural and urban areas. Criteria for participation were as follows: (1) interviewees were at least sixteen years of age (the voting age in Brazil), (2) they had lived in the municipality since the previous mayoral election, and (3) they were not a household member of any other interviewee. The sample was stratified to ensure balanced representation across gender, age, and urban/rural mix.

In Bahia, with respect to elites, a range of perspectives were obtained by interviewing ten mayors and former mayors, twenty-eight city councilors, three vice-mayors, six party heads, five heads of social services, and several other elites. These interviews were balanced to include a combination of elites both allied and opposed to the current municipal administration. Given that mayors may face different incentives if ineligible for reelection, the random sample of municipalities was stratified to include municipalities with both first-term and second-term mayors.[1]

Informed consent was obtained from all community members and elites before initiating each interview. The citizen and elite interview protocols consisted of both open-ended and closed-ended questions. An iterative research design was employed; pertinent themes emerging during thematic analysis were investigated during ongoing interviews. While the original, core questions in the interview protocols were asked of all respondents, probes about emerging themes were included in later interviews.

When combined with later Pernambuco interviews, total interviews included seventy-one elites (primarily mayors and councilors) and sixty-one citizens (both urban and rural residents). Altogether, interviewed elites included fourteen mayors and former mayors, thirty-four city councilors, three vice-mayors, six party heads, five heads of social services, and several others.

---

[1] The prior three paragraphs and map are adapted from Nichter (2014a).

Appendix B

Description of Surveys

RURAL CLIENTELISM SURVEY

The Rural Clientelism Survey was collected by Gustavo Bobonis, Paul Gertler, Marco Gonzalez-Navarro, and Simeon Nichter in 2011–2013. This panel survey conducted face-to-face interviews across rural Northeast Brazil. Altogether, the Rural Clientelism Survey was fielded in 654 rural neighborhood clusters in 40 municipalities across 9 states. These surveys were collected in conjunction with a randomized control trial involving a water cisterns treatment. Results from that study, which focused on an experimental subsample of the Rural Clientelism Survey, are summarized briefly in Chapter 8.

The population for this study is rural households in the semi-arid zone of Brazil that do not have reliable access to drinking water. The semi-arid zone is almost entirely located in the Northeast region, with an area exceeding one million square kilometers in 1,262 contiguous municipalities. The zone has much less precipitation than the rest of Brazil, and its twenty-eight million residents are primarily poor and rural. The following inclusion criteria were used for households in our study: (a) no water cistern or piped drinking water, (b) sufficient physical space on the household's property to build a cistern, and (c) a roof no less than forty square meters, made of metal sheeting or tile (to allow for rainfall collection).

For the purpose of household sample selection, administrative data from the Brazilian federal government's *Cadastro Único* were first employed. We randomly selected municipalities employing weights proportional to the number of households without access to cisterns and piped water. Next, clusters of neighboring households (*logradouros* in the federal database) were randomly chosen within the sample municipalities. Per cluster, up to six eligible households were interviewed. Clusters were required to be at least two kilometers away from each other, to avoid spillovers. A localization survey was conducted

Description of Surveys 221

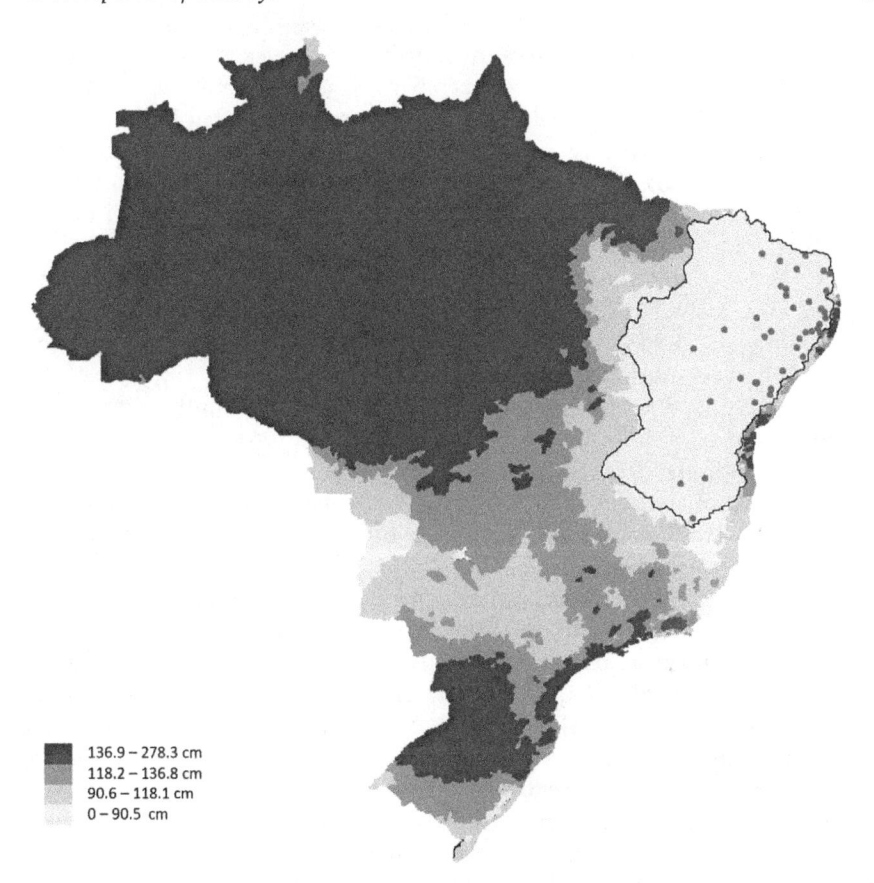

```
■ 136.9 – 278.3 cm
▨ 118.2 – 136.8 cm
▨ 90.6 – 118.1 cm
□ 0 – 90.5 cm
```

FIGURE B.1 Municipalities in rural clientelism survey, Brazil's semi-arid region, and rainfall levels
Note: Each dot indicates the location of a sampled municipality. Brazil's semi-arid region is circumscribed by a black line in the figure. Shading reflects average annual rainfall levels (1986–2013) as specified in the legend, with darker colors reflecting more rainfall.
Source: Bobonis, Gertler, Gonzalez-Navarro and Nichter (2018).

in May–July 2011 for the purpose of obtaining household characteristics and identifying families eligible for the study. In October–December 2011, a first wave collected a more detailed baseline survey with information about household characteristics and family members.

Whereas those two waves interviewed only household heads, the next two waves interviewed all household members present who were at least eighteen years old. These latter waves provide many variables analyzed in this book, as they include extensive modules related to clientelism. To learn about patterns around a municipal campaign, the second wave (with 3,685 respondents) was conducted in November–December 2012, just after the municipal elections in

October 2012. To learn about patterns during a non-election year, the third wave was conducted in November–December 2013 (with 3,761 respondents). A subset of respondents in the third wave had not participated in the second wave for two primary reasons: (a) different family members were present during household visits in 2012 and 2013, and (b) we obtained additional funding to add households to the sample in 2013 (such households are not used in the experimental analysis).

In the survey, attrition was relatively low. Bobonis, Gertler, Gonzalez-Navarro, and Nichter (2018) provide an analysis of attrition across rounds in the experimental sample: 9.1 percent of households identified for study participation were not successfully interviewed in Wave 1, 5.4 percent of households identified for study participation were not successfully interviewed in Wave 2, and 14.5 percent of households identified for study participation were not successfully interviewed in Wave 3.

This low rate of attrition did not affect the core characteristics across waves. Following Fitzgerald et al. (1997), attrition probits were employed to assess whether variables analyzed in this book were significantly associated with future nonresponse. With respect to key dependent variables, household heads who reported receiving benefits, requesting benefits, or declaring support in the 2012 wave were no more or less likely to drop out before the 2013 wave than those that did not. In addition, the vast majority of control variables were also not significantly associated with attrition. Moreover, the R-squared was very small even in the most inclusive specifications (less than 0.05), suggesting their low explanatory power with regards to attrition.

All dependent and independent variables from the Rural Clientelism Survey employed in the present book are now described. This list employs the names that are shown in regression tables and figures, in alphabetical order.

Dependent Variables

Amount Citizen Expects Own Councilor to Return (Log Reais)
The amount of money (in log Reais) the respondent expects his or her own councilor to return in a hypothetical trust game. The hypothetical trust game was played between a random citizen and the councilor for whom the respondent voted in the previous election. Responses were recorded for four rounds asked consecutively, in which the citizen sends R$2, R$4, R$6, and R$8 (respectively) to the councilor. Questions in 2013. For example, for the R$2 round: "Think of the councilor candidate that you voted for in the last election. Our team doesn't want to know the name of that candidate and is not going to talk to any politician from here. Suppose that someone named Fulano is chosen to be your councilor's partner in the game. Suppose that our team gives R$10 to Fulano. If Fulano gives R$2 to your candidate, we give R$4 more, so now your candidate gets R$6. Of that R$6, how much money (or nothing) do you think your candidate will send back to Fulano? Your candidate will never know who Fulano is or where he lives."

Description of Surveys

Benefit from Municipality
Respondent reports receiving a private benefit or service from the municipality in 2013. Coded 1 if answered yes to receiving a benefit or service from the municipality, unless specifying in a follow-up question that it was a non-private good or service; 0 otherwise. Questions in 2013: (a) "In 2013, did you receive any benefit or service from the municipality?"; (b) "What did you receive?"

Benefit from Politician
Respondent reports receiving a private benefit or service from a politician in 2013. Coded 1 if answered yes to receiving a benefit or service from a politician, unless specifying in a follow-up question that it was a non-private good or service; 0 otherwise. Questions in 2013: (a) "Now I'm going to ask about help from politicians. I don't want to know anyone's name. In 2013, did you receive help from a city councilor?"; (b) "What did you receive?"; (c) "In 2013, did you receive help from the mayor?"; (d) "What did you receive?"

No Benefit Due to Vote Choice
Respondent reports that his or her family did not receive help from a politician in 2013 due to vote choice. Coded 1 if answered that did not receive help from a politician in 2013 due to vote choice; 0 otherwise. Question in 2013: "In 2013, do you think that your family didn't receive help from a politician because it didn't vote for him?"

Perceptions of Defeated (Victorious) Mayoral Candidate's Competence, Experience, Accessibility, and Honesty
Respondent's opinion about 2012 mayoral candidates' attributes. Four characteristics (competence, experience, accessibility, and honesty) were each coded on a four-point scale: "Very good," "Good," "Bad," and "Very Bad." Questions in 2012: "I am going to ask you about these politicians, whether they are good or not, your opinion about them. I would just like to remind you that I have no connection with any of them and that your answers will be kept secret. What do you think of [name of victorious or defeated mayoral candidate] in relation to: (a) capacity to do things; (b) experience; (c) is it easy to find him?; (d) honesty?"

Politician Helped Get Job
Respondent reports that in 2013, a family member received help obtaining a job from an elected politician. Coded 1 if answered that he or she received such help in 2013 from a candidate who won the election; 0 otherwise. Questions in 2013: (a) "In 2013, did any of the last election's candidates help you or someone in your family to get a job?"; (b) "Did this candidate, the one that helped getting a job, win or lose the last election?"

Post-Election Benefit by Request
Respondent reported receiving private benefits or services requested from a politician in 2013. Coded 1 if answered yes to receiving a requested benefit or

service; 0 otherwise. This variable is generated from a question asked directly after the questions described next in the "Post-Election Request" variable. Question in 2013: "Did you receive it?"

Post-Election Request
Respondent requested private benefits or services from a politician in 2013. Coded 1 if answered yes to requesting from politician, unless specifying in a follow-up question that the request was for a non-private good or service; 0 otherwise. Questions in 2013: (a) "Now, I am going to ask about requests for help. It doesn't matter if you received it or not, but I want to know if you asked for any help. In 2013, did you ask a city councilor for help?"; (b) If yes: "What did you ask for?"; (c) "In 2013, did you ask the mayor for help?"; (d) If yes: "What did you ask for?"

Pre-Election Benefit by Request
Respondent reported receiving private benefits or services requested from a politician in 2012. Coded 1 if answered yes to receiving a requested benefit or service; 0 otherwise. This variable is generated from a question asked directly after the questions described next in the *Pre-Election Request* variable. Question in 2012: "Did you receive it?"

Pre-Election Request
Respondent requested private benefits or services from a politician in 2012. Coded 1 if answered yes to a question about making a request, unless specifying it was for a non-private good or service; 0 otherwise. Questions in 2012: (a) "This year, did you ask a city councilor candidate for help?"; (b) If yes: "What did you ask for?"; (c) "This year, did you ask a mayor candidate for help?"; (d) If yes: "What did you ask for?"

Received Campaign Handout
Respondent reported receiving private benefits or services from a campaign visit in 2012. Coded 1 if answered yes to having received, prior to the 2012 election, a private benefit or service during or through promises made in a campaign visit; 0 otherwise. Question in 2012, asked during module about campaign visits by representatives of politicians: (a) "Did you receive any help? For example, help can be goods (like bricks), services (like medical exams), money, food or beverages"; (b) If yes: "What help was this?", (c) "Did you receive the help before or after the election?"

Voted for Same Candidate / Party
Respondent reported voting for same mayoral candidate (party) in the 2008 and 2012 elections. Coded 1 if vote choice for candidate (party) was identical in both years; 0 otherwise. Questions in 2013: (a) "In the 2012 election, for which mayoral candidate did you vote?" [List of 2012 mayoral candidates provided];

Description of Surveys

(b) "In the election 5 years ago, for which candidate did you vote? [List of 2008 mayoral candidates provided]. Choices also included not voting and casting a blank or invalid ballot.

Independent Variables

Access to Cistern
Respondent has access to, but does not own, a cistern. Coded 1 if answered yes to accessing a cistern but does not own a cistern; 0 otherwise. Question in 2012 and 2013: "Do you usually fetch water from any cistern?"

Age
Respondent's age, in years.

Any Declaration
Respondent publicly declared support for any political candidate during the 2012 election. For analyses of the 2012 wave, coded 1 if answered yes to any of the following four questions asked in 2012; 0 otherwise: (a) "Let's talk about this year's political campaign: about the last 3 months before the election. Did you wear a candidate's sticker or shirt?"; (b) Asked of rally attendees: "In this rally, did you use a flag, shirt or anything else to show your support?"; (c) "During the electoral campaign, did you put a flag or a poster on your house?"; (d) "Was the wall of your house painted with the name of a candidate?" For analyses of the 2013 wave, coded 1 if answered yes to the following question asked in 2013, 0 otherwise: "Let's talk about 2012's political campaign: about the 3 months before the election. Some people declared their support for a candidate by using stickers or shirts, going to rallies or placing flags or posters on their houses. Did you declare your support for any candidate during the campaign?"

Association Member
Respondent or someone in household is member of an association. Coded 1 if answered yes to both of the following questions, 0 otherwise. Questions in 2012 and 2013 waves: (a) "We heard that, in some neighborhoods, people get together to solve problems in the community, forming a kind of association. Are there any associations in this neighborhood?"; (b) "Are you or is someone in this house a member of the association?"

Declared for Councilor
Respondent publicly declared support for any councilor candidate during the 2012 political campaign. This variable is used as a control in the hypothetical trust games involving councilors, which were included in the 2013 wave. Question in 2013 wave: "For whom did you declare your support?" Coded 1 if selected either of these answers; 0 otherwise: (a) "For a city councilor

candidate who won the election"; (b) "For a city councilor candidate who lost the election." This question was asked of all declarers; i.e., respondents who answered affirmatively to the 2013 question in the *Any Declaration* variable description earlier. Multiple answer choices could be selected.

Declared for Loser
Respondent publicly declared support for a defeated candidate during the 2012 political campaign. Question in 2013 wave: "For whom did you declare your support?" Coded 1 if either of these responses, 0 otherwise: (a) "For a mayoral candidate who lost the election"; (b) "For a city councilor candidate who lost the election." This question was asked of all declarers; i.e., respondents who answered affirmatively to the 2013 question in the *Any Declaration* variable description earlier. Multiple answer choices could be selected.

Declared for Winner
Respondent publicly declared support for a victorious candidate during the 2012 political campaign. Question in 2013 wave: "For whom did you declare your support?" Coded 1 if either of these responses, 0 otherwise: (a) "For a mayoral candidate who won the election"; (b) "For a city councilor candidate who won the election." This question was asked of all declarers; i.e., respondents who answered affirmatively to the 2013 question in the *Any Declaration* variable description earlier. Multiple answer choices could be selected.

Declared on Body
Respondent publicly declared support on body during the 2012 political campaign. Coded 1 if answered yes to the following question; 0 otherwise. Question in 2012 wave: "Let's talk about this year's political campaign: about the last three months before the election. Did you wear a candidate's sticker or shirt?"

Declared on House
Respondent publicly declared support on house during the 2012 political campaign. Coded 1 if answered yes to the following question; 0 otherwise. Question in 2012 wave: "During the electoral campaign, did you put a flag or a poster on your house?"

Declared at Rally
Respondent publicly declared support at a political rally during the 2012 political campaign. Coded 1 if answered yes to the following question; 0 otherwise. Question in 2012 wave: Asked of rally attendees: "In this rally, did you use a flag, shirt or anything else to show your support?"

Description of Surveys 227

DEM, PMDB, PSDB, or PT Supporter
Respondent spontaneously indicates preference for DEM, PMDB, PSDB, or PT parties (respective dummy variables for each party). Questions in 2011 (household head only) and 2013 (all respondents). Coded 1 if both conditions apply; 0 otherwise: (a) answered yes to the question "Do you have a preference for any political party?"; and (b) spontaneously mentions DEM, PMDB, PSDB or PT, respectively, when asked in an immediate follow-up question, "Which party?"

Education
Level of education attained by respondent, twenty-point scale ranging from No Education to Post-Graduate. Question in 2011.

Female
Gender of respondent, coded 1 if female. Coded by enumerator in 2011.

Has Own Cistern
Respondent's house has own water cistern. Question in 2012 and 2013: "Does your house have a cistern?"

Has Piped Water
Respondent has piped water. Question in 2012 and 2013: "Do you have piped water?"

Log Amount Sent to Councilor
As described more extensively earlier, respondents were asked about four rounds of a hypothetical trust game, in which a random citizen sends money to the respondent's own councilor. This variable indicates whether in the round analyzed, the question specified that the citizen had sent R$2, R$4, R$6, or R$8 to the councilor. Variable is logged.

Neighborhood Collaboration
Respondent indicates that his or her neighborhood worked collaboratively to solve a problem in past year. Coded 1 if answered yes to the following question; 0 otherwise. Question in 2013: "In the last 12 months, did your neighborhood work together to solve any problem?"

Public Goods
Amount of money (in R$) that respondent would contribute in a hypothetical, non-incentivized public goods game. Question in 2013, with a diagram and examples: "You are in a group with 4 people; you and 3 other neighbors. Suppose that our research team will give R$5 to each person in the group. You can keep the R$5 or put a part of it, or everything, in the community savings pot. The research team will double the money in the pot. It doesn't matter how

much you will put in the pot, you will receive an equal share of any amount that ends up in the pot. Would you like to put some of the R$5 to the savings pot?"

Reciprocity
Measure of reciprocity based on experimental games (with differing values) and analyses in Finan and Schechter (2012). Questions in 2012 (non-incentivized) and 2013 (incentivized); for example: "If your secret partner sends you R$2, we'll add R$4 more, so now you have R$6. You can give some, all or none of this money back to your secret partner. Do you want to send any money back? If yes, how much?"

Requested Assistance
Respondent requested private benefits or services from a politician. For 2012, variable coded as described in "Pre-Election Request" in the dependent variables section earlier. For 2013, variable coded as described in "Post-Election Request" in the dependent variables section earlier.

Requested Job Assistance
Respondent requested job assistance from an elected politician in 2013. Coded 1 if answered yes to requesting from politician, if specifying in a follow-up question that the request was employment; 0 otherwise. Questions in 2013: (a) "Now, I am going to ask about requests for help. It doesn't matter if you received it or not, but I want to know if you asked for any help. In 2013, did you ask a city councilor for help?"; (b) If yes: "What did you ask for?"; (c) "In 2013, did you ask the mayor for help?"; (d) If yes: "What did you ask for?"

Risk Aversion
Measure of risk aversion based on experimental games with differing values. Questions in 2012 (non-incentivized) and 2013 (incentivized); for example (with image and example): "Tell me which of the bags you'd like to choose. Bag A has a R$2 coin. Bag B has a coin worth R$0.20 and a coin worth R$5. Which of the two bags do you choose?"

Satisfaction with Mayor
Household head's satisfaction with current mayor in 2011. Question in 2011 wave (asked of household heads): "Regarding the current mayor of your municipality, would you say that you are 'Very Unsatisfied,' 'Unsatisfied,' 'Satisfied,' or 'Very Satisfied?'"

Talks with Politicians
Respondent reports conversing with a politician at least monthly. Coded 1 if answered yes to having spoken with politician at least monthly; 0 otherwise. Questions in 2012 refer to conversations with political candidates before

Description of Surveys

the campaign began: (a) "This year, did you speak with any city councilor candidate?"; (b) If yes: "How often before the political campaign (before June)?"; (c) "This year, did you speak with any mayor candidate?"; (d) If yes: "How often before the political campaign (before June)?" Questions in 2013 refer to conversations with office-holders during that year: (a) "In 2013, did you speak with a councilor?"; (b) If yes: "How often?"; (c) "In 2013, did you speak with the mayor?"; (d) If yes: "How often?"

Time Preference
Measure of time preference based on experimental games with differing values. Questions in 2012 and 2013 (both non-incentivized); for example: "Let's now think of a situation that isn't real but that I'd like you to answer as if it were true. Suppose that you won a money prize. You can receive this prize in two ways. Do you prefer a prize of R$100 tomorrow or a guaranteed prize of R$110 in three months? Don't worry because in the game, you are sure to receive the prize."

Voted for Elected Councilor
Respondent reported voting for a victorious city councilor candidate in 2012. Questions asked of citizens who reported voting in 2012; coded 1 if answered "win"; 0 otherwise. Question in 2012: "In this election, did the city councilor candidate, for whom you voted, win or lose?" Question in 2013: "In the 2012 election, did the city councilor candidate, for whom you voted, win or lose?"

Voted for Mayor
Respondent reported voting for the victorious mayoral candidate in 2012. Questions asked of citizens who reported voting in 2012. Question in 2012; coded 1 if answered "win"; 0 otherwise: "In this election, did the mayoral candidate, for whom you voted, win or lose?" Question in 2013; coded 1 if selected name of victorious candidate in the following question; 0 otherwise: "In the 2012 election, for which mayoral candidate did you vote?" (Names of all 2012 mayoral candidates provided).

Voted in 2008
Reported voting in 2008 municipal election. Coded 1 if voted; 0 otherwise. Question in 2011 (asked of household heads only): "Did you vote for mayor in the last elections that took place in 2008?" Question in 2013: "In the election 5 years ago, for which candidate did you vote?" [In 2013, coded as 0 if selecting "did not vote" as answer choice].

Voted in 2012
Respondent reported voting in 2012 municipal election. Coded 1 if voted; 0 otherwise. Question in 2012: "Did you vote in the last election?" Question in 2013: "Did you vote in the 2012 election?"

Wealth

Wealth of respondent's household, based on numerous household assets and using a principal-components analysis (see Filmer and Pritchett, 2001). Household heads were asked in 2011 about accumulated household wealth rather than flows such as income and expenditures. Questions asked about financial assets, property, household assets, animals, debts, and remittances.

ONLINE CLIENTELISM SURVEY

The Online Clientelism Survey was collected by Simeon Nichter and Salvatore Nunnari in August–December 2016. This survey recruited participants through Facebook advertisements displayed in all Brazilian municipalities with 250,000 or fewer residents. Municipalities of this size comprise 98.2 percent of Brazil's municipalities and 59.7 percent of the nation's population. Overall, 2,286 citizens from 1,210 municipalities commenced the survey, and 1,859 citizens from 1,065 municipalities completed it.

According to 2016 estimates, Facebook had 90.1 million registered users in Brazil, compared to an overall population of about 200 million.[1] In terms of users, Brazil is Facebook's third largest market, after India and the United States. Our Facebook recruitment strategy builds on research in Brazil by Samuels and Zucco (2013, 2014) and Boas (2014), as well as additional information provided by those authors. Facebook allows advertisers to target specific demographic groups; we targeted Brazilians at least eighteen years of age. Our advertisement offered an equal opportunity drawing for an iPhone 5S; four phones were awarded in total. Facebook users who clicked on the advertisement were redirected to a separate web page. Informed consent was obtained for all participants. Consenting participants commenced a fifteen-minute survey including both experimental and observational questions on Qualtrics.

Although online participants were not randomly selected from a sampling frame, their characteristics are fairly representative of Brazil with respect to gender, age, and geographic region. With respect to gender, 47.8 percent of the online surveys were completed by women. By comparison, women comprised 51 percent of Brazil's population in the 2010 IBGE census. With respect to age, 33.5 percent of the online surveys were completed by the youngest quartile of Brazilian adults (ages 18–28), 17.7 percent were completed by the second quartile (ages 29–39), 27.4 percent were completed by the third quartile (ages 40–53), and 20.8 percent were completed by the oldest quartile (age fifty-four and greater). Age quartiles are based on 2013 IBGE projections. With respect to geographic region, 37.4 percent of the online surveys were completed by citizens in the Southeast, 30.9 percent in the Northeast, 18.6 percent in the South,

---

[1] Estimate of Facebook users retrieved from: www.statista.com/statistics/268136/top-15-countries-based-on-number-of-facebook-users/

Description of Surveys

6.6 percent in the Center-West, and 6.5 percent in the North. By comparison, IPEA reported in 2014 that 33.5 percent of Brazilians in municipalities with 250,000 or fewer residents live in the Southeast, 33 percent live in the Northeast, 17.1 percent live in the South, 7.1 percent live in the Center-West, and 9.2 percent live in the North. To obtain this balance, advertisements were shown with greater frequency to certain groups, such as women and older citizens.

The survey included both observational and experimental components. The present book primarily employs the observational component, which had more participants and includes questions about respondents' experiences with declared support and clientelism. The experimental component is analyzed in Nichter and Nunnari (2017), which is discussed in Section 5.4. The experimental questions elicited participants' willingness to declare support for fictitious candidates, while using actual incentives (iPhone drawing tickets) to change rewards, penalties, and preferences for fictitious candidates. To control for the level of participant attentiveness, the survey included two screener questions inserted in different points of the survey, following the work of Berinsky et al. (2014).

All dependent and independent variables from the Online Clientelism Survey employed in the present book are described next. This list employs the names that are shown in regression tables and figures in alphabetical order.

Dependent Variables

Benefit from Municipality
Respondent reports that his or her family received a benefit or service from the municipality between January 2013 and June 2016. Coded 1 if answered yes to the following question; 0 otherwise. Question: "Between January 2013 and June 2016, did you or your family receive some benefit or service from the municipality?"

Benefit from Politician
Respondent reports that his or her family received a benefit or service from a politician or politician's representative between January 2013 and June 2016. Coded 1 if answered yes to the following question; 0 otherwise. Question: "Now, think about any help that your family received in recent years, between January 2013 and June 2016. During this time, did you or your family receive some benefit or service from the mayor, a councilor, or their representatives?"

Denied Benefit Due to Vote Choice
Respondent reports that his or her family did not receive help from the municipality between January 2013 and June 2016 due to vote choice. Coded 1 if answered that did not receive help from the municipality during this period due to vote choice; 0 otherwise. Question: "Between January 2013 and June 2016, do you think that someone from your family didn't receive some benefit

or service from the municipality because he didn't vote for a candidate who won?"

Received Campaign Handout in 2012
Respondent reported receiving a benefit or service from a politician or politician's representative during the 2012 municipal campaign. Coded 1 if answered yes to receiving; 0 otherwise. Question: "Think about the political campaign four years ago for mayors and councilors. During the 2012 political campaign, did you or someone in your family receive some benefit or service from the mayor, a councilor, or their representatives?"

Received Campaign Handout in 2016
Respondent reported receiving a benefit or service from a politician or politician's representative during the 2016 municipal campaign. Coded 1 if answered yes to receiving; 0 otherwise. Question: "Now, think about the political campaign this year. In last few months, did you or someone in your family receive some benefit or service from the mayor, a councilor, or their representatives?"

Independent Variables

Age
Respondent's age, in years. Question: "What is your age?"

Declared for Loser
Respondent publicly declared support for a defeated candidate during the 2012 political campaign. Immediately following the question in the "Declared Support in 2012" variable description, respondents who answered affirmatively were asked: "For whom did you declare your support? Mark all answers that apply." Coded 1 if either of these responses; 0 otherwise: (a) "For a mayoral candidate who lost the election"; (b) "For a city councilor candidate who lost the election."

Declared for Winner
Respondent publicly declared support for a victorious candidate during the 2012 political campaign. Immediately following the question in the "Declared Support in 2012" variable description, respondents who answered affirmatively were asked: "For whom did you declare your support? Mark all answers that apply." Coded 1 if either of these responses; 0 otherwise: (a) "For a mayoral candidate who won the election"; (b) "For a city councilor candidate who won the election."

Declared Support in 2012
Respondent publicly declared support for any candidate during the 2012 political campaign. Coded 1 if answered yes to declaring support; 0 otherwise.

Description of Surveys 233

Question: "Think about the political campaign in 2012 for mayors and councilors. Some people showed their support for a candidate publicly. For example, they used stickers or T-shirts, went to rallies, placed flags or banners on their homes, or painted their houses. Did you show your support publicly for some candidate during the 2012 municipal campaign?"

Declared Support in 2016

Respondent publicly declared support for any candidate during the 2016 political campaign. Coded 1 if answered yes to declaring support; 0 otherwise. Question: "Think about the political campaign this year. Some people showed their support for a candidate publicly. For example, they used stickers or T-shirts, went to rallies, placed flags or banners on their homes, or painted their houses. In the past few months, did you show your support publicly for some candidate?"

DEM, PMDB, PSDB, or PT Supporter

Respondent indicates a preference for DEM, PMDB, PSDB, or PT parties. Coded 1 for each respective dummy variables if indicating preference for that party; 0 otherwise. Question: "Currently, do you sympathize with some political party? If yes, please indicate which party. If not, choose 'no party.'"

Education

Level of education attained by respondent, on a seven-point scale ranging from "no education" to "post-graduate." Question: "What is your level of education?"

Female

Gender of respondent, coded 1 if female.

Income

Monthly family income of respondent, measured on a ten-point scale. Question: "What is the monthly income of your family?"

Risk Aversion

Measure of risk aversion based on experimental game with increasing values. Coded on a four-point scale based on responses to several questions. Example of question (with images): "Suppose that you have to choose between two bags. In bag 1, there is a R$20 bill. In bag 2, there is a R$2 bill and a R$50 bill. After you choose the bag, you can put your hand inside your chosen bag and take out only one of the bills of money. It doesn't matter which bill you take out, you win that one. Which of the two bags do you choose?"

Rural

Respondent lives in a rural area. Code 1 if rural; 0 otherwise. Question: "Do you live in the rural zone of your municipality?"

Screener
As described earlier, the survey included two screener questions to control for the level of participant attentiveness (see Berinsky et al., 2014). Coded on a three-point scale, with 0, 1, or 2 screeners answered correctly.

Voted for Mayor in 2012
Respondent reported voting for the victorious mayoral candidate in 2012. Question: "In 2012, did the mayoral candidate you voted for win or lose?" Coded 1 if answered that candidate "won"; 0 otherwise.

Voted in 2012
Respondent reported voting in 2012. Question: "In 2012, did the mayoral candidate you voted for win or lose?" Coded 0 if answered "did not vote"; 1 if selecting a different answer choice.

Appendix C

Signaling Model of Declared Support

This model examines the conditions under which declared support signals that a citizen's promise to vote for a politician is credible. In this way, declared support helps to sustain relational clientelism in contexts where the politician cannot observe citizens' vote choices and does not know citizens' underlying preferences. This game examines the subset of citizens in a district who meet two conditions: (1) they promise to vote for politician P in an upcoming election in exchange for future benefits if P wins, and (2) their vote choices and preferences are not perfectly known by P (i.e., there is incomplete information).

Given incomplete information, the politician is uncertain whether a citizen who promises a vote will actually fulfill that promise. To simplify the analysis, I assume that two types of citizens promise to vote for P in exchange for future benefits: *supporting promisers* and *opposing promisers*. Supporting promisers prefer to vote for P in the upcoming election, whereas opposing promisers prefer to vote against P in the election.

For the subset of the population under analysis, the politician cannot observe whether a promiser prefers to vote for her. And with effective ballot secrecy, she cannot monitor voting decisions. The politican observes, however, whether the citizen declares support for her during the campaign. A citizen declares support during the campaign by displaying political paraphernalia on his home, on his body, or at a rally. After the declaration action, the citizen votes according to his type, and then nature decides the election winner. If elected, the politician then decides whether to deliver benefits to the citizen.

The following formal analysis examines the separating conditions under which declared support serves as an informational signal distinguishing between citizen types. As such, it reveals how declared support can be a mechanism to facilitate relational clientelism in contexts in which citizens have asymmetric information. It is not guaranteed that such conditions will exist in every political context. A fuller characterization of the model would examine pooling conditions, under which both citizen types declare or do not declare.[1] It would also examine possible conditions under which equilibria are nonexistent.

Timing of the Game

- Nature chooses if citizen is a supporting or opposing promiser, $x \in \{s, n\}$.
- Citizen chooses whether to declare for politician, $d \in \{d, nd\}$.
- Citizen votes according to his type.
- Nature chooses the election outcome.
- If elected, politician chooses whether to provide benefits to citizen, $r \in \{0, r\}$.
- Utilities are allocated.

The signaling game is examined under the assumption that a citizen prefers to vote for or against P strictly due to expressive utility from the act of voting. Furthermore, to simplify the analysis, it is assumed the citizen does not influence the election outcome.

Model Parameters

Citizen

$x_t \in (-\infty, \infty)$: expressive utility gain/loss from voting for politician P
$d(x_t) \in (-\infty, \infty)$: expressive utility gain/loss from declaring for P. The function d is assumed to be a positive monotonic transformation of x_t (i.e., if $x > y$, then $d(x) > d(y)$)
$r \geq 0$: reward for declaring for P, when P wins election
$z \geq 0$: punishment for declaring for P, when P loses election
$c \geq 0$: material cost of declaring

Politician

$p \in [0, 1]$: probability P wins election
$v \geq 0$: utility to politician of a citizen's vote (0 if does not vote for P)
$f \geq 0$: utility to politician of a citizen's future votes (net of any future costs).
0 if citizen does not provide future votes to P

Citizen Utility

The citizen receives an expressive utility gain/loss of x_t from voting for politician P. This assumption – that voting provides only expressive utility, not utility from the possibility of influencing the election outcome – follows other models of clientelism such as Stokes (2005), Nichter (2008), Morgan and Vardy (2012), and Gans-Morse, Mazzuca, and Nichter (2014).[2]

---

[1] A previous version of this model examined pooling conditions.
[2] See Morgan and Vardy (2012) for a formal defense of the use of expressive utility.

Signaling Model of Declared Support

The citizen receives r if P provides her a reward, which is assumed to be a possible action only if P wins the election. P's probability of winning is p, which is not influenced by the citizen's voting or declaration decision.

If the citizen declares for P during the campaign, he also receives expressive utility $d(x_t)$, which is assumed to be a positive monotonic transformation of x_t – that is, if he obtains expressive (dis)utility from voting for P, he also obtains expressive (dis)utility from declaring for P, respectively. If he declares, the citizen also incurs a direct material cost of c.

By assumption, supporting promisers (citizen type S) prefer to vote for P in the election, whereas opposing promisers (citizen type N) prefer that P loses. Given that the model assumes voting only provides expressive utility, this implies that $x_s \geq 0$ and $x_n < 0$. Therefore, it follows that $x_s > x_n$.

If elected, the opposition candidate is assumed to impose a punishment of z if a citizen declared for P during the campaign. This punishment is realized only if P loses, so the probability is $1 - p$.

Politician Utility

Politician P receives utility v if the citizen votes for her and 0 otherwise. P incurs cost r if she wins and she decides to provide a reward to the citizen. The politician also receives utility $f \geq 0$ from future votes in subsequent elections not analyzed in this game. Under the shroud of ballot secrecy, a promiser who opposes P will never vote for P, so $v = 0$ and $f = 0$. On the other hand, if P follows through with her promise to provide benefits once elected, a supporting promiser may once again promise to provide votes in a subsequent election. But if P defects once elected, then the citizen is assumed not to commit to provide votes in subsequent elections.[3] For simplification, I assume that the politician prefers to continue to receive the promiser's votes in the future, which implies $f \geq r$. This assumption is similar to that in Stokes (2005), who assumes one-sided uncertainty in which citizens but not machines can defect. Such credible commitment by the politician can be derived as the cooperative equilibrium of a repeated game involving a grim trigger strategy by citizens. With this grim trigger strategy, citizens never vote again for a politician who defects on providing promised benefits. Chapter 6 more extensively examines the issue of politician credibility and how citizens respond to defecting politicians.

Separating Equilibria

The section examines conditions necessary for a separating equilibrium, in which declaring provides meaningful information about whether a citizen is a supporting promiser. In a separating equilibrium, voter types undertake different actions: the supporting promiser declares support and the opposing

---

[3] Recall that P never rewards if she loses, so in this case a lack of rewards does not affect the citizen's subsequent actions.

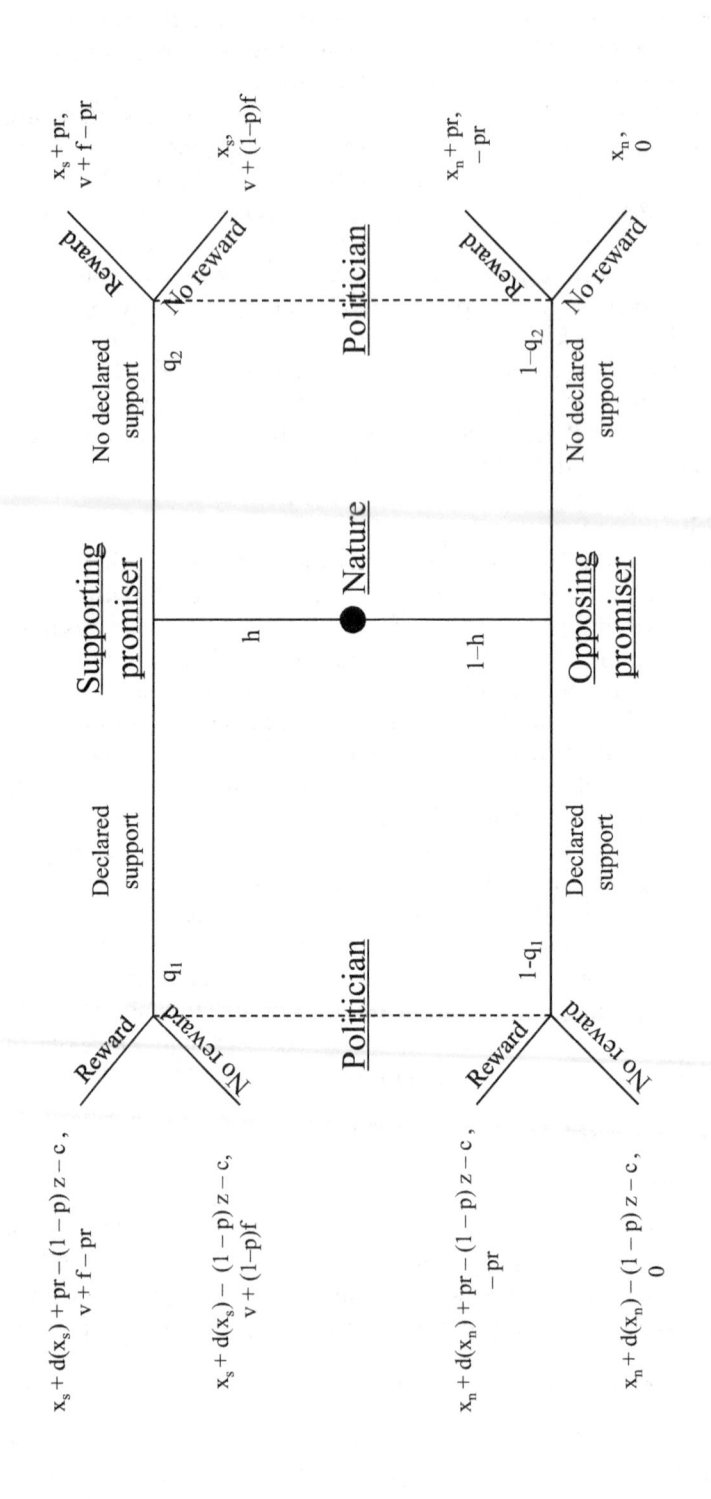

Top payoff: citizen's utility,
Bottom payoff: politician's utility

FIGURE C.1 *Signaling credibility through declared support*

Signaling Model of Declared Support

promiser does not declare support. The politician's updated beliefs are $q_1 = 1$ and $q_2 = 0$, so he has complete information when she decides whether to provide a reward to the citizen (i.e., the fifth bullet in the game's timing).

Examining the bottom right half of the game tree, P's best response is not to reward if she does not observe declaration, because $0 > -pr$. Turning to the top left of the game tree, if the politician observes declaration, her best response is to reward the promiser if the cost of doing so is less than the value of future votes he expects to receive from complying. That is:

$$v + f - pr \geq v + (1-p)f$$
$$-pr \geq -pf$$
$$r \leq f$$

This condition holds, given the previously discussed assumption that the citizen's future votes are more valuable than the reward a politician pays (i.e., $r \leq f$).

Turning to the citizen's incentive compatibility constraints, the supporting promiser will declare if the utility of declaring (in which case P provides a reward) is weakly greater than the utility of not declaring (in which case P does not provide a reward):

$$x_s + d(x_s) + pr - (1-p)z - c \geq x_s$$
$$d(x_s) + pr - (1-p)z \geq c \qquad (C.1)$$

On the other hand, the opposing promiser will remain undeclared if the utility of not declaring (in which case P withholds the reward) is weakly greater than the utility of declaring (in which case P provides a reward):

$$x_n \geq x_n + d(x_n) + pr - (1-p)z - c$$
$$c \geq d(x_n) + pr - (1-p)z \qquad (C.2)$$

Thus, in order for separation, the following condition must hold:

$$d(x_n) + pr - (1-p)z \leq c \leq d(x_s) + pr - (1-p)z$$
$$d(x_n) \leq c - pr + (1-p)z \leq d(x_s) \qquad (C.3)$$

If the condition in Inequality C.3 holds, then supporting promisers declare and opposing promisers do not declare. Under such conditions, separating equilibria exist. First, as discussed above, $x_s > x_n$, and given that $d(x_t)$ is a positive monotonic function of x_t, then $d(x_s) > d(x_n)$. Thus, the right side of Inequality C.3 is strictly greater than the left side. In a separating equilibrium, the politician updates her beliefs as indicated, and provides a reward if and only if she observed a declaration in the second step of the game. For the existence of a separating Perfect Bayesian Equilibrium, the condition provided by Equation C.3 is necessary as well as sufficient. In words, the center portion of the inequality, $c - pr + (1-p)z$, refers to the material cost (or benefit, if negative) that either citizen type receives if he declares. The terms in left and right portions of the inequality, $d(x_t)$, are the expressive utility gain or loss for each citizen type from the act of declaring itself.

Inequality C.3 also reveals the conditions under which declaration provides an especially informative signal. When the politician observes a citizen declaring, each of the following conditions render the declaration more informative about the citizen's type: smaller clientelist rewards (r), larger punishments (z), higher declaration costs (c), and a lower probability (p) that the politician will win. But if these conditions are too extreme, pooling is observed as supporters opt not to declare. Likewise, pooling conditions exist in which all citizen types declare, rendering declaration non-informative.

In sum, this analysis shows conditions under which separating equilibria exist, such that declared support provides a mechanism for citizens to signal that their promises of votes are credible (i.e., they are supporting promisers). Again, a fuller characterization of the model would analyze pooling conditions as well as any conditions under which equilibria are nonexistent.

Appendix D

Regression Tables for Declared Support

TABLE D.1 *Declared support and post-election benefits, rural Northeast Brazil, 2013 – Regressions in Figure 5.1, rows 1 and 2*

	Benefit from politician			Benefit from municipality		
	(1)	(2)	(3)	(4)	(5)	(6)
Declared for winner	0.077***	0.073***	0.071***	0.042**	0.044**	0.044**
	(0.02)	(0.02)	(0.02)	(0.02)	(0.02)	(0.02)
Declared for loser	0.007	0.003	−0.000	0.015	0.005	−0.016
	(0.02)	(0.02)	(0.02)	(0.02)	(0.02)	(0.02)
Voted for mayor		−0.010	−0.008		−0.012	−0.003
		(0.01)	(0.01)		(0.01)	(0.01)
Voted in 2012		0.005	0.005		0.042***	0.041***
		(0.01)	(0.01)		(0.01)	(0.01)
Talks with politicians		0.142***	0.132***		0.028	0.025
		(0.03)	(0.03)		(0.02)	(0.02)
Association member		−0.003	−0.002		0.005	0.010
		(0.01)	(0.01)		(0.01)	(0.01)
Neighborhood collaboration		0.009	0.006		0.005	0.007
		(0.01)	(0.01)		(0.01)	(0.01)
PT supporter		−0.001	0.006		−0.007	0.013
		(0.02)	(0.02)		(0.01)	(0.01)
PSDB supporter		−0.045***	−0.042**		−0.043***	−0.029**
		(0.01)	(0.01)		(0.01)	(0.01)
PMDB supporter		0.035	0.015		−0.007	−0.026
		(0.07)	(0.07)		(0.04)	(0.04)
DEM supporter		−0.030**	−0.034+		−0.046***	−0.047**
		(0.01)	(0.02)		(0.01)	(0.02)
Wealth		0.002	−0.004		0.005+	0.007**
		(0.00)	(0.00)		(0.00)	(0.00)
Education		−0.001	−0.001		0.002+	0.001
		(0.00)	(0.00)		(0.00)	(0.00)
Female		0.010	0.010		0.008	0.006
		(0.01)	(0.01)		(0.01)	(0.01)
Age		−0.000	−0.000		0.000	0.000
		(0.00)	(0.00)		(0.00)	(0.00)
Reciprocity		0.052	0.064		0.094+	0.101*
		(0.05)	(0.05)		(0.05)	(0.05)
Risk aversion		−0.003	−0.003		0.005	0.004
		(0.00)	(0.00)		(0.00)	(0.00)
Public goods		0.005	0.003		0.012***	0.006*
		(0.00)	(0.00)		(0.00)	(0.00)
Time preference		−0.003*	−0.003*		−0.002	−0.001
		(0.00)	(0.00)		(0.00)	(0.00)
Has piped water		−0.026*	−0.018		−0.001	0.011
		(0.01)	(0.01)		(0.01)	(0.01)
Has own cistern		0.004	0.004		0.015+	0.014
		(0.01)	(0.01)		(0.01)	(0.01)
Access to cistern		−0.006	−0.014		0.001	−0.002
		(0.01)	(0.01)		(0.01)	(0.01)
Constant	0.039***	0.049*	0.060**	0.040***	−0.076**	−0.054*
	(0.00)	(0.02)	(0.02)	(0.00)	(0.02)	(0.02)
Municipal fixed effects	No	No	Yes	No	No	Yes
Observations	3714	3218	3218	3749	3247	3247
R^2	0.014	0.049	0.075	0.005	0.026	0.113

Note: + $p < 0.10$, * $p < 0.05$, ** $p < 0.01$, *** $p < 0.001$. Linear probability model with robust standard errors clustered at neighborhood level. Results are robust using logit specifications.
Source: Author's analysis of the Rural Clientelism Survey. Data collected by Gustavo Bobonis, Paul Gertler, Marco Gonzalez-Navarro, and Simeon Nichter.

Regression Tables for Declared Support

TABLE D.2 *Declared support and post-election benefits, rural Northeast Brazil, 2013 – Regressions in Figure 5.1, rows 3 and 4*

	Politician helped get job			No benefit due to vote choice		
	(1)	(2)	(3)	(4)	(5)	(6)
Declared for winner	0.031**	0.030**	0.030*	0.003	0.003	0.002
	(0.01)	(0.01)	(0.01)	(0.01)	(0.01)	(0.01)
Declared for loser	0.009	0.011	0.009	0.094***	0.089***	0.083***
	(0.01)	(0.01)	(0.01)	(0.02)	(0.02)	(0.02)
Voted for mayor		0.002	0.002		−0.027***	−0.027***
		(0.00)	(0.00)		(0.01)	(0.01)
Voted in 2012		−0.004	−0.003		0.013	0.010
		(0.01)	(0.01)		(0.01)	(0.01)
Talks with politicians		0.029*	0.029*		0.021	0.020
		(0.01)	(0.01)		(0.02)	(0.02)
Association member		−0.001	0.000		0.000	0.003
		(0.00)	(0.00)		(0.01)	(0.01)
Neighborhood collaboration		0.006	0.003		0.006	−0.005
		(0.01)	(0.01)		(0.01)	(0.01)
PT supporter		0.001	−0.000		0.002	0.002
		(0.01)	(0.01)		(0.01)	(0.01)
PSDB supporter		−0.013*	−0.011		0.053	0.047
		(0.01)	(0.01)		(0.07)	(0.07)
PMDB supporter		−0.019**	−0.021**		−0.022	−0.018
		(0.01)	(0.01)		(0.03)	(0.03)
DEM supporter		−0.015**	−0.015*		0.157	0.131
		(0.01)	(0.01)		(0.12)	(0.10)
Wealth		−0.001	−0.001		−0.002	−0.001
		(0.00)	(0.00)		(0.00)	(0.00)
Education		0.002*	0.002*		0.001	0.001
		(0.00)	(0.00)		(0.00)	(0.00)
Female		−0.001	−0.000		0.005	0.003
		(0.00)	(0.00)		(0.01)	(0.01)
Age		0.000	0.000		−0.000	−0.000
		(0.00)	(0.00)		(0.00)	(0.00)
Reciprocity		0.016	0.020		0.024	0.030
		(0.02)	(0.02)		(0.04)	(0.04)
Risk aversion		0.004*	0.003*		0.001	0.000
		(0.00)	(0.00)		(0.00)	(0.00)
Public goods		−0.001	−0.002		0.002	0.002
		(0.00)	(0.00)		(0.00)	(0.00)
Time preference		0.000	0.000		−0.001	−0.001
		(0.00)	(0.00)		(0.00)	(0.00)
Has piped water		−0.006	−0.006		−0.000	−0.004
		(0.00)	(0.01)		(0.01)	(0.01)
Has own cistern		0.008*	0.008*		0.000	0.001
		(0.00)	(0.00)		(0.01)	(0.01)
Access to cistern		−0.001	−0.001		0.006	0.006
		(0.01)	(0.01)		(0.01)	(0.01)
Constant	0.007***	−0.022+	−0.022+	0.026***	0.016	0.020
	(0.00)	(0.01)	(0.01)	(0.00)	(0.02)	(0.02)
Municipal fixed effects	No	No	Yes	No	No	Yes
Observations	3742	3243	3243	3647	3158	3158
R^2	0.010	0.027	0.045	0.018	0.033	0.063

Note: + $p < 0.10$, * $p < 0.05$, ** $p < 0.01$, *** $p < 0.001$. Linear probability model with robust standard errors clustered at neighborhood level. Results are robust using logit specifications.
Source: Author's analysis of the Rural Clientelism Survey. Data collected by Gustavo Bobonis, Paul Gertler, Marco Gonzalez-Navarro, and Simeon Nichter.

TABLE D.3 *Declared support and post-election benefits, rural Northeast Brazil, 2013 – Regressions in Figure 5.1, row 5*

	Club good from politician		
	(1)	(2)	(3)
Declared for winner	0.003	0.002	0.002
	(0.00)	(0.00)	(0.01)
Declared for loser	0.003	0.002	0.001
	(0.01)	(0.01)	(0.01)
Voted for mayor		−0.006	−0.005
		(0.00)	(0.00)
Voted in 2012		0.003	0.003
		(0.01)	(0.00)
Talks with politicians		0.010	0.009
		(0.01)	(0.01)
Association member		0.002	0.007+
		(0.00)	(0.00)
Neighborhood collaboration		0.015*	0.014*
		(0.01)	(0.01)
PT supporter		0.008	0.010
		(0.01)	(0.01)
PSDB supporter		−0.009*	−0.007
		(0.00)	(0.00)
PMDB supporter		−0.012***	−0.021**
		(0.00)	(0.01)
DEM supporter		−0.003	−0.010
		(0.00)	(0.01)
Wealth		0.003**	0.002*
		(0.00)	(0.00)
Education		−0.001*	−0.001+
		(0.00)	(0.00)
Female		−0.003	−0.002
		(0.00)	(0.00)
Age		−0.000	−0.000
		(0.00)	(0.00)
Reciprocity		−0.015	−0.013
		(0.02)	(0.02)
Risk aversion		0.000	0.000
		(0.00)	(0.00)
Public goods		−0.000	−0.001
		(0.00)	(0.00)
Time preference		−0.000	−0.001
		(0.00)	(0.00)
Has piped water		0.000	0.003
		(0.01)	(0.01)
Has own cistern		0.003	0.003
		(0.00)	(0.00)
Access to cistern		−0.004	−0.007+
		(0.00)	(0.00)
Constant	0.007***	0.016	0.016
	(0.00)	(0.01)	(0.01)
Municipal fixed effects	No	No	Yes
Observations	3714	3218	3218
R^2	0.000	0.013	0.029

Note: + $p < 0.10$, * $p < 0.05$, ** $p < 0.01$, *** $p < 0.001$. Linear probability model with robust standard errors clustered at neighborhood level. Results are robust using logit specifications.
Source: Author's analysis of the Rural Clientelism Survey. Data collected by Gustavo Bobonis, Paul Gertler, Marco Gonzalez-Navarro, and Simeon Nichter.

TABLE D.4 *Declared support and post-election water delivery, rural Northeast Brazil, 2013*

	Months with water delivery			Total liters of water delivered		
	(1)	(2)	(3)	(4)	(5)	(6)
Declared for winner	0.578**	0.481*	0.444*	3382.6*	2894.4+	2589.9+
	(0.19)	(0.20)	(0.19)	(1422.1)	(1531.9)	(1478.1)
Declared for loser	0.377	0.383	0.275	1895.7	2160.2	1320.8
	(0.25)	(0.28)	(0.26)	(1972.5)	(2184.4)	(2087.5)
Rainfall in municipality	−1.999***	−1.866***		−15778.3***	−14826.5***	
	(0.44)	(0.46)		(3512.2)	(3733.2)	
Has piped water	−0.861***	−0.983***	−1.031***	−7047.6***	−7785.7***	−7779.1***
	(0.11)	(0.14)	(0.20)	(871.9)	(1100.2)	(1522.0)
Voted for mayor		0.104	0.065		694.8	316.4
		(0.14)	(0.14)		(1168.6)	(1135.5)
Voted in 2012		0.015	0.074		100.2	657.7
		(0.19)	(0.17)		(1592.6)	(1406.9)
Talks with politicians		0.233	0.297		1501.1	1851.3
		(0.28)	(0.27)		(2168.9)	(2045.0)
Association member		0.292+	0.011		1736.9	−231.6
		(0.17)	(0.17)		(1350.0)	(1346.1)
Neighborhood collaboration		0.374+	0.195		2765.9	1335.4
		(0.21)	(0.19)		(1652.2)	(1495.6)
PT supporter		0.505+	0.199		3767.9	1478.9
		(0.30)	(0.30)		(2414.0)	(2404.4)
PSDB supporter		−0.168	−0.387		−1436.1	−3454.7
		(0.60)	(0.59)		(4712.7)	(4610.5)
PMDB supporter		0.152	0.234		−1055.0	−146.4
		(0.63)	(0.51)		(4421.3)	(3629.8)
DEM supporter		0.208	0.311		9794.1	10742.4
		(0.49)	(0.47)		(9786.0)	(8495.1)
Wealth		0.015	0.038		78.2	234.3
		(0.05)	(0.05)		(402.2)	(440.3)
Education		−0.015	−0.017		−106.8	−142.2
		(0.02)	(0.02)		(136.3)	(126.1)
Female		−0.121	−0.111		−1002.2	−874.4
		(0.08)	(0.08)		(638.2)	(624.9)
Age		−0.002	−0.006		−15.6	−40.7
		(0.00)	(0.00)		(32.3)	(30.7)
Reciprocity		−0.347	−0.085		−4013.8	−1930.0
		(0.57)	(0.54)		(4485.3)	(4273.2)
Risk aversion		−0.042	−0.054		−177.2	−246.8
		(0.04)	(0.04)		(329.0)	(317.2)
Public goods		−0.049	0.001		−384.7	−31.8
		(0.04)	(0.04)		(355.9)	(357.1)
Time preference		0.063**	0.039+		481.9*	308.0+
		(0.02)	(0.02)		(187.3)	(178.65)
Has own cistern		−0.141	−0.186		−1141.2	−1629.1
		(0.19)	(0.21)		(1555.2)	(1660.1)
Access to cistern		0.523*	0.441+		5164.4**	4485.3*
		(0.24)	(0.25)		(1967.1)	(2032.7)
Constant	0.944***	0.939**	1.266***	7768.4***	7538.5**	10069.1***
	(0.09)	(0.35)	(0.35)	(753.1)	(2885.4)	(2837.9)
Municipal fixed effects	No	No	Yes	No	No	Yes
Observations	3160	2822	2967	3147	2809	2954
R^2	0.031	0.053	0.121	0.028	0.050	0.114

Note: + $p < 0.10$, * $p < 0.05$, ** $p < 0.01$, *** $p < 0.001$. OLS specifications with robust standard errors clustered at neighborhood level. Data are reported by respondents and reflect deliveries from *Operação Carro-Pipa* (Operation Water Truck), which was by far the principal source of water deliveries in the Rural Clientelism Survey. Given outliers, liters of water delivery are Winsorized at the 95 percent level. Rainfall control variable is standardized using historical municipal data, as described in Chapter 4.
Source: Author's analysis of the Rural Clientelism Survey. Data collected by Gustavo Bobonis, Paul Gertler, Marco Gonzalez-Navarro, and Simeon Nichter.

TABLE D.5 *Declared support and post-election benefits, Brazil, online survey, 2016 – Regressions in Figure 5.2, rows 1 and 2*

	Benefit from politician			Benefit from municipality		
	(1)	(2)	(3)	(4)	(5)	(6)
Declared for winner	0.181***	0.166***	0.158***	0.201***	0.165***	0.155***
	(0.02)	(0.02)	(0.02)	(0.02)	(0.03)	(0.02)
Declared for loser	−0.093**	−0.059	−0.061	−0.074*	−0.041	−0.043
	(0.03)	(0.04)	(0.04)	(0.03)	(0.04)	(0.05)
Voted for mayor		0.045*	0.046*		0.070*	0.075*
		(0.02)	(0.02)		(0.03)	(0.03)
Voted in 2012		0.043	0.032		−0.012	−0.020
		(0.03)	(0.03)		(0.04)	(0.04)
Age		−0.003***	−0.003**		−0.003**	−0.003**
		(0.00)	(0.00)		(0.00)	(0.00)
Income		−0.000	0.002		−0.005	−0.002
		(0.01)	(0.01)		(0.01)	(0.01)
Education		−0.014*	−0.015*		0.004	0.004
		(0.01)	(0.01)		(0.01)	(0.01)
Female		−0.025	−0.017		−0.019	−0.011
		(0.02)	(0.02)		(0.02)	(0.02)
DEM supporter		−0.030	0.006		−0.011	0.012
		(0.07)	(0.07)		(0.06)	(0.05)
PSDB supporter		0.015	0.022		0.054	0.062
		(0.03)	(0.03)		(0.05)	(0.05)
PMDB supporter		−0.006	0.008		−0.019	−0.009
		(0.04)	(0.04)		(0.04)	(0.04)
PT supporter		−0.005	−0.005		0.055	0.056
		(0.02)	(0.02)		(0.04)	(0.04)
Rural		0.055+	0.050+		0.028	0.027
		(0.03)	(0.03)		(0.03)	(0.03)
Risk aversion		−0.004	−0.004		−0.015+	−0.015
		(0.01)	(0.01)		(0.01)	(0.01)
Screener		0.010	0.010		0.015	0.014
		(0.01)	(0.01)		(0.01)	(0.01)
Constant	0.120***	0.228***	0.222***	0.165***	0.282***	0.275***
	(0.01)	(0.05)	(0.05)	(0.01)	(0.05)	(0.06)
State fixed effects	No	No	Yes	No	No	Yes
Observations	1837	1466	1466	1843	1470	1470
R^2	0.053	0.087	0.109	0.051	0.069	0.088

Note: + $p < 0.10$, * $p < 0.05$, ** $p < 0.01$, *** $p < 0.001$. Linear probability model with robust standard errors clustered at state level. Results are robust using logit specifications.
Source: Author's analysis of the Online Clientelism Survey. Data collected by Simeon Nichter and Salvatore Nunnari.

TABLE D.6 *Declared support and post-election benefits, Brazil, online survey, 2016 – Regressions in Figure 5.2, row 3*

	Denied benefit due to vote choice		
	(1)	(2)	(3)
Declared for winner	0.046+	0.030	0.027
	(0.02)	(0.03)	(0.03)
Declared for loser	0.055+	0.051+	0.038
	(0.03)	(0.03)	(0.02)
Voted for mayor		−0.034	−0.037+
		(0.02)	(0.02)
Voted in 2012		0.065*	0.069**
		(0.02)	(0.02)
Age		−0.002**	−0.001*
		(0.00)	(0.00)
Income		−0.015**	−0.015**
		(0.00)	(0.00)
Education		0.009	0.008
		(0.01)	(0.01)
Female		−0.043*	−0.035*
		(0.02)	(0.02)
DEM supporter		−0.061	−0.058
		(0.06)	(0.06)
PSDB supporter		−0.023	−0.016
		(0.03)	(0.03)
PMDB supporter		0.066+	0.064+
		(0.04)	(0.03)
PT supporter		0.024	0.023
		(0.03)	(0.03)
Rural		0.045	0.048
		(0.03)	(0.03)
Risk aversion		−0.012+	−0.010+
		(0.01)	(0.01)
Screener		−0.017+	−0.016
		(0.01)	(0.01)
Constant	0.145***	0.279***	0.251***
	(0.02)	(0.05)	(0.05)
State fixed effects	No	No	Yes
Observations	1884	1493	1493
R^2	0.008	0.038	0.074

Note: + $p < 0.10$, * $p < 0.05$, ** $p < 0.01$, *** $p < 0.001$. Linear probability model with robust standard errors clustered at state level. Results are robust using logit specifications.
Source: Author's analysis of the Online Clientelism Survey. Data collected by Simeon Nichter and Salvatore Nunnari.

TABLE D.7 *Declared support and campaign handouts, rural Northeast Brazil, 2012 – Regressions in Figure 5.3*

	\multicolumn{6}{c}{Received campaign handout}
	(1)	(2)	(3)	(4)	(5)	(6)
Any declaration	0.032***	0.030**	0.025*			
	(0.01)	(0.01)	(0.01)			
1 declaration method				0.014	0.011	0.006
				(0.01)	(0.01)	(0.01)
2 declaration methods				0.049**	0.050**	0.047**
				(0.02)	(0.02)	(0.02)
3 declaration methods				0.061**	0.061**	0.057**
				(0.02)	(0.02)	(0.02)
Voted for mayor		−0.023+	−0.022+		−0.021+	−0.019
		(0.01)	(0.01)		(0.01)	(0.01)
Voted in 2012		0.031	0.039+		0.028	0.035
		(0.02)	(0.02)		(0.02)	(0.02)
Talks with politicians		0.044**	0.046**		0.040**	0.043**
		(0.01)	(0.02)		(0.01)	(0.02)
Association member		−0.014	−0.009		−0.015	−0.009
		(0.01)	(0.01)		(0.01)	(0.01)
PT supporter		−0.028*	−0.019+		−0.030**	−0.022*
		(0.01)	(0.01)		(0.01)	(0.01)
PSDB supporter		0.122	0.120		0.119	0.116
		(0.08)	(0.08)		(0.08)	(0.08)
PMDB supporter		−0.018	−0.036		−0.019	−0.038
		(0.03)	(0.03)		(0.03)	(0.03)
DEM supporter		0.012	0.011		0.010	0.010
		(0.05)	(0.04)		(0.05)	(0.04)
Wealth		−0.007*	−0.010**		−0.007*	−0.011**
		(0.00)	(0.00)		(0.00)	(0.00)
Education		−0.002	−0.002		−0.002	−0.002
		(0.00)	(0.00)		(0.00)	(0.00)
Female		0.008	0.006		0.009	0.006
		(0.01)	(0.01)		(0.01)	(0.01)
Age		−0.001*	−0.001+		−0.000	−0.000
		(0.00)	(0.00)		(0.00)	(0.00)
Reciprocity		−0.063	−0.039		−0.064	−0.042
		(0.04)	(0.04)		(0.04)	(0.04)
Risk aversion		0.003	0.002		0.003	0.002
		(0.00)	(0.00)		(0.00)	(0.00)
Time preference		0.001	0.002		0.001	0.002
		(0.00)	(0.00)		(0.00)	(0.00)
Piped water		−0.012	−0.002		−0.011	−0.000
		(0.01)	(0.02)		(0.01)	(0.02)
Own cistern		0.010	0.010		0.008	0.010
		(0.01)	(0.01)		(0.01)	(0.01)
Access to cistern		0.010	−0.008		0.009	−0.008
		(0.01)	(0.01)		(0.01)	(0.01)
Constant	0.047***	0.047	0.040	0.047***	0.045	0.036
	(0.01)	(0.03)	(0.03)	(0.01)	(0.03)	(0.03)
Municipal fixed effects	No	No	Yes	No	No	Yes
Observations	3167	2725	2725	3167	2725	2725
R^2	0.004	0.023	0.070	0.008	0.027	0.074

Note: + $p < 0.10$, * $p < 0.05$, ** $p < 0.01$, *** $p < 0.001$. Linear probability model with robust standard errors clustered at neighborhood level. Results are robust using logit specifications.
Source: Author's analysis of the Rural Clientelism Survey. Data collected by Gustavo Bobonis, Paul Gertler, Marco Gonzalez-Navarro, and Simeon Nichter.

Regression Tables for Declared Support

TABLE D.8 *Declared support and campaign handouts, Brazil, online survey, 2012 – Regressions in Figure 5.4, rows 1 and 2*

	Received campaign handout in 2012			Received campaign handout in 2016		
	(1)	(2)	(3)	(4)	(5)	(6)
Declared support in 2012	0.133***	0.129***	0.120***			
	(0.01)	(0.02)	(0.02)			
Declared support in 2016				0.139***	0.117***	0.103***
				(0.02)	(0.02)	(0.03)
Voted for mayor in 2012		0.064**	0.065**		0.079***	0.083***
		(0.02)	(0.02)		(0.01)	(0.01)
Voted in 2012		0.005	−0.005		0.009	0.003
		(0.02)	(0.02)		(0.03)	(0.03)
Age		−0.003***	−0.003***		−0.002**	−0.002*
		(0.00)	(0.00)		(0.00)	(0.00)
Income		0.002	0.006		−0.005	−0.002
		(0.00)	(0.00)		(0.01)	(0.01)
Education		−0.016**	−0.017***		−0.013*	−0.015**
		(0.00)	(0.00)		(0.00)	(0.01)
Female		−0.003	0.007		−0.039	−0.030
		(0.01)	(0.01)		(0.02)	(0.02)
DEM supporter		0.012	0.031		0.048	0.076
		(0.05)	(0.05)		(0.09)	(0.09)
PSDB supporter		0.048	0.060		−0.001	0.013
		(0.04)	(0.04)		(0.04)	(0.04)
PMDB supporter		0.032	0.048*		0.039	0.052
		(0.03)	(0.02)		(0.04)	(0.04)
PT supporter		0.008	0.004		−0.005	−0.004
		(0.03)	(0.02)		(0.03)	(0.03)
Rural		0.015	0.009		0.018	0.016
		(0.03)	(0.03)		(0.03)	(0.02)
Risk aversion		−0.015**	−0.016***		−0.009	−0.009
		(0.00)	(0.00)		(0.01)	(0.01)
Screener		−0.005	−0.003		0.019+	0.018+
		(0.01)	(0.01)		(0.01)	(0.01)
Constant	0.077***	0.242***	0.241***	0.072***	0.220***	0.207***
	(0.01)	(0.04)	(0.04)	(0.01)	(0.05)	(0.04)
State fixed effects	No	No	Yes	No	No	Yes
Observations	1769	1451	1451	1789	1447	1447
R^2	0.037	0.081	0.110	0.040	0.076	0.109

Note: + $p < 0.10$, * $p < 0.05$, ** $p < 0.01$, *** $p < 0.001$. Linear probability model with robust standard errors clustered at state level. Results are robust using logit specifications.
Source: Author's analysis of the Online Clientelism Survey. Data collected by Simeon Nichter and Salvatore Nunnari.

TABLE D.9 *Declared support and perceptions of victorious mayoral candidate, rural Northeast Brazil, 2012–2013 – Regressions in Figure 5.6, rows 1–3*

	Perceptions of victorious mayoral candidate					
	Composite		Competence		Honesty	
	(1)	(2)	(3)	(4)	(5)	(6)
Declared for winner	0.239***	0.236***	0.303***	0.291***	0.203***	0.209***
	(0.04)	(0.04)	(0.05)	(0.05)	(0.05)	(0.05)
Declared for loser	−0.441***	−0.502***	−0.397**	−0.495***	−0.329*	−0.414**
	(0.13)	(0.13)	(0.14)	(0.15)	(0.15)	(0.14)
Satisfaction w/ mayor		0.026		0.057+		0.015
		(0.03)		(0.03)		(0.03)
Voted in 2012		−0.076		−0.043		0.011
		(0.06)		(0.07)		(0.08)
Talks with politicians		0.018		0.120**		−0.017
		(0.04)		(0.04)		(0.04)
Association member		0.028		0.028		0.029
		(0.04)		(0.04)		(0.04)
PT supporter		0.056		0.075		0.005
		(0.05)		(0.05)		(0.06)
PSDB supporter		−0.140		−0.377		−0.235
		(0.22)		(0.24)		(0.26)
PMDB supporter		0.123		0.090		0.048
		(0.10)		(0.09)		(0.08)
DEM supporter		−0.013		0.082		0.077
		(0.13)		(0.21)		(0.13)
Wealth		0.008		0.004		0.001
		(0.01)		(0.01)		(0.01)
Education		0.007		0.004		−0.002
		(0.00)		(0.00)		(0.01)
Female		−0.009		−0.016		0.003
		(0.03)		(0.03)		(0.03)
Age		0.002		−0.002		−0.000
		(0.00)		(0.00)		(0.00)
Reciprocity		0.105		−0.047		0.149
		(0.16)		(0.17)		(0.15)
Risk aversion		0.003		−0.005		0.001
		(0.01)		(0.01)		(0.01)
Time preference		0.012+		0.014*		0.004
		(0.01)		(0.01)		(0.01)
Piped water		−0.009		−0.021		−0.042
		(0.05)		(0.06)		(0.05)
Own cistern		0.021		−0.005		−0.028
		(0.05)		(0.06)		(0.05)
Access to cistern		−0.048		−0.008		−0.099
		(0.06)		(0.06)		(0.06)
Constant	2.845***	2.678***	2.954***	2.821***	2.923***	2.905***
	(0.02)	(0.13)	(0.02)	(0.15)	(0.02)	(0.15)
Municipal fixed effects	Yes	Yes	Yes	Yes	Yes	Yes
Observations	1213	1066	1570	1375	1435	1255
R^2	0.181	0.225	0.142	0.189	0.103	0.134

Note: + $p < 0.10$, * $p < 0.05$, ** $p < 0.01$, *** $p < 0.001$. OLS specification with robust standard errors clustered at neighborhood level. All specifications include municipal fixed effects to compare across same politician.
Source: Author's analysis of the Rural Clientelism Survey. Data collected by Gustavo Bobonis, Paul Gertler, Marco Gonzalez-Navarro, and Simeon Nichter.

TABLE D.10 *Declared support and perceptions of victorious mayoral candidate, rural Northeast Brazil, 2012–2013 – Regressions in Figure 5.6, rows 4 and 5*

	Perceptions of victorious mayoral candidate			
	Experience		Accessibility	
	(1)	(2)	(3)	(4)
Declared for winner	0.204***	0.202***	0.362***	0.372***
	(0.05)	(0.05)	(0.06)	(0.06)
Declared for loser	−0.654***	−0.717***	−0.344*	−0.376*
	(0.13)	(0.13)	(0.15)	(0.15)
Satisfaction w/ mayor		0.055+		0.005
		(0.03)		(0.03)
Voted in 2012		−0.047		−0.075
		(0.07)		(0.11)
Talks with politicians		−0.004		−0.003
		(0.04)		(0.05)
Association member		−0.011		0.061
		(0.04)		(0.05)
PT supporter		0.058		0.153*
		(0.06)		(0.07)
PSDB supporter		−0.087		0.017
		(0.23)		(0.18)
PMDB supporter		0.190+		0.189
		(0.11)		(0.14)
DEM supporter		−0.052		0.042
		(0.13)		(0.19)
Wealth		0.010		0.009
		(0.01)		(0.01)
Education		0.009+		0.004
		(0.01)		(0.01)
Female		0.004		−0.085*
		(0.03)		(0.03)
Age		0.000		0.005***
		(0.00)		(0.00)
Reciprocity		0.280+		−0.194
		(0.15)		(0.24)
Risk aversion		−0.011		−0.017
		(0.01)		(0.01)
Time preference		0.017*		−0.002
		(0.01)		(0.01)
Piped water		−0.075		0.021
		(0.07)		(0.08)
Own cistern		−0.008		0.041
		(0.05)		(0.06)
Access to cistern		0.007		−0.058
		(0.05)		(0.07)
Constant	2.914***	2.716***	2.380***	2.269***
	(0.02)	(0.14)	(0.02)	(0.16)
Municipal fixed effects	Yes	Yes	Yes	Yes
Observations	1591	1397	1671	1459
R^2	0.106	0.144	0.181	0.217

Note: + $p < 0.10$, * $p < 0.05$, ** $p < 0.01$, *** $p < 0.001$. OLS specification with robust standard errors clustered at neighborhood level. All specifications include municipal fixed effects to compare across same politician.
Source: Author's analysis of the Rural Clientelism Survey. Data collected by Gustavo Bobonis, Paul Gertler, Marco Gonzalez-Navarro, and Simeon Nichter.

TABLE D.11 *Declared support and perceptions of defeated mayoral candidate, rural Northeast Brazil, 2012–2013 – Regressions in Figure 5.6, rows 6 - 8*

	Perceptions of defeated mayoral candidate					
	Composite		Competence		Honesty	
	(1)	(2)	(3)	(4)	(5)	(6)
Declared for winner	−0.355***	−0.312***	−0.387***	−0.345***	−0.308***	−0.265**
	(0.07)	(0.08)	(0.08)	(0.08)	(0.09)	(0.09)
Declared for loser	0.435***	0.453***	0.386***	0.429***	0.368**	0.415***
	(0.10)	(0.10)	(0.11)	(0.11)	(0.12)	(0.10)
Satisfaction w/ mayor		0.059+		0.063+		0.058+
		(0.03)		(0.04)		(0.03)
Voted in 2012		−0.085		−0.098		0.014
		(0.07)		(0.09)		(0.09)
Talks with politicians		0.046		0.003		−0.015
		(0.05)		(0.06)		(0.06)
Association member		−0.011		−0.012		−0.056
		(0.04)		(0.05)		(0.05)
PT supporter		0.065		0.063		0.086
		(0.07)		(0.08)		(0.08)
PSDB supporter		−0.072		−0.302		−0.264
		(0.24)		(0.24)		(0.26)
PMDB supporter		0.036		−0.028		0.143
		(0.13)		(0.16)		(0.16)
DEM supporter		0.163		0.201		0.023
		(0.14)		(0.16)		(0.15)
Wealth		0.005		0.014		0.005
		(0.01)		(0.02)		(0.02)
Education		0.008		0.013*		0.009
		(0.01)		(0.01)		(0.01)
Female		0.011		0.019		0.016
		(0.04)		(0.04)		(0.04)
Age		0.007***		0.008***		0.008***
		(0.00)		(0.00)		(0.00)
Reciprocity		−0.039		−0.131		−0.328
		(0.25)		(0.24)		(0.30)
Risk aversion		0.007		0.005		0.005
		(0.01)		(0.01)		(0.01)
Time preference		−0.003		0.002		−0.008
		(0.01)		(0.01)		(0.01)
Piped water		−0.066		−0.102		0.037
		(0.06)		(0.07)		(0.07)
Own cistern		0.056		0.021		0.091
		(0.06)		(0.06)		(0.06)
Access to cistern		0.034		−0.009		0.075
		(0.06)		(0.07)		(0.06)
Constant	2.612***	2.170***	2.671***	2.182***	2.691***	2.149***
	(0.02)	(0.15)	(0.02)	(0.17)	(0.02)	(0.17)
Municipal fixed effects	Yes	Yes	Yes	Yes	Yes	Yes
Observations	1214	1067	1555	1362	1364	1191
R^2	0.185	0.229	0.162	0.198	0.115	0.156

Note: + $p < 0.10$, * $p < 0.05$, ** $p < 0.01$, *** $p < 0.001$. OLS specification with robust standard errors clustered at neighborhood level. All specifications include municipal fixed effects to compare across same politician.
Source: Author's analysis of the Rural Clientelism Survey. Data collected by Gustavo Bobonis, Paul Gertler, Marco Gonzalez-Navarro, and Simeon Nichter.

Regression Tables for Declared Support

TABLE D.12 *Declared support and perceptions of defeated mayoral candidate, rural Northeast Brazil, 2012–2013 – Regressions in Figure 5.6, rows 9 and 10*

	\multicolumn{4}{c}{Perceptions of victorious mayoral candidate}
	\multicolumn{2}{c}{Experience}	\multicolumn{2}{c}{Accessibility}
	(1)	(2)	(3)	(4)
Declared for winner	−0.276***	−0.242**	−0.387***	−0.398***
	(0.08)	(0.08)	(0.08)	(0.08)
Declared for loser	0.341***	0.383***	0.553***	0.566***
	(0.10)	(0.09)	(0.14)	(0.13)
Satisfaction w/ mayor		0.068*		0.044
		(0.03)		(0.03)
Voted in 2012		−0.200*		−0.079
		(0.08)		(0.09)
Talks with politicians		0.013		0.103+
		(0.05)		(0.06)
Association member		0.046		−0.008
		(0.05)		(0.05)
PT supporter		0.015		−0.008
		(0.07)		(0.07)
PSDB supporter		−0.089		0.009
		(0.27)		(0.16)
PMDB supporter		−0.058		0.054
		(0.13)		(0.14)
DEM supporter		0.234		0.239
		(0.16)		(0.22)
Wealth		0.017		0.000
		(0.01)		(0.02)
Education		0.004		0.003
		(0.01)		(0.01)
Female		0.048		−0.059
		(0.04)		(0.04)
Age		0.005***		0.003+
		(0.00)		(0.00)
Reciprocity		0.153		−0.085
		(0.24)		(0.28)
Risk aversion		0.010		−0.000
		(0.01)		(0.01)
Time preference		−0.014+		−0.001
		(0.01)		(0.01)
Piped water		−0.025		0.005
		(0.07)		(0.07)
Own cistern		0.043		0.049
		(0.06)		(0.06)
Access to cistern		−0.007		0.002
		(0.06)		(0.06)
Constant	2.690***	2.447***	2.289***	2.116***
	(0.02)	(0.16)	(0.02)	(0.18)
Municipal fixed effects	Yes	Yes	Yes	Yes
Observations	1555	1367	1644	1438
R^2	0.150	0.188	0.192	0.221

Note: $+ p < 0.10$, $* p < 0.05$, $** p < 0.01$, $*** p < 0.001$. OLS specification with robust standard errors clustered at neighborhood level. All specifications include municipal fixed effects to compare across same politician.

Source: Author's analysis of the Rural Clientelism Survey. Data collected by Gustavo Bobonis, Paul Gertler, Marco Gonzalez-Navarro, and Simeon Nichter.

Appendix E

Regression Tables for Requesting Benefits

Regression Tables for Requesting Benefits

TABLE E.1 *Citizen requests and post-election benefits, rural Northeast Brazil, 2013 – Regressions in Figure 6.2, rows 1 and 2*

	Benefit from politician			Benefit from municipality		
	(1)	(2)	(3)	(4)	(5)	(6)
Requested assistance	0.398***	0.384***	0.377***	0.109***	0.102***	0.092***
	(0.03)	(0.03)	(0.03)	(0.02)	(0.03)	(0.02)
Declared for winner		0.043**	0.042**		0.036*	0.035*
		(0.02)	(0.02)		(0.02)	(0.02)
Declared for loser		0.003	−0.001		0.005	−0.015
		(0.02)	(0.02)		(0.02)	(0.02)
Voted for mayor		−0.009	−0.009		−0.012	−0.004
		(0.01)	(0.01)		(0.01)	(0.01)
Voted in 2012		−0.008	−0.007		0.039***	0.039***
		(0.01)	(0.01)		(0.01)	(0.01)
Talks with politicians		0.082***	0.079**		0.012	0.012
		(0.02)	(0.02)		(0.02)	(0.02)
Association member		−0.007	−0.006		0.004	0.009
		(0.01)	(0.01)		(0.01)	(0.01)
Neighborhood collaboration		0.001	0.001		0.003	0.005
		(0.01)	(0.01)		(0.01)	(0.01)
PT supporter		−0.011	−0.008		−0.010	0.010
		(0.01)	(0.01)		(0.01)	(0.01)
PSDB supporter		−0.036+	−0.037+		−0.042***	−0.028*
		(0.02)	(0.02)		(0.01)	(0.01)
PMDB supporter		0.033	0.016		−0.008	−0.027
		(0.06)	(0.06)		(0.04)	(0.04)
DEM supporter		−0.011	−0.019		−0.041***	−0.044**
		(0.01)	(0.01)		(0.01)	(0.02)
Wealth		0.001	−0.002		0.005+	0.007**
		(0.00)	(0.00)		(0.00)	(0.00)
Education		−0.000	−0.000		0.002*	0.002
		(0.00)	(0.00)		(0.00)	(0.00)
Female		0.007	0.007		0.007	0.006
		(0.01)	(0.01)		(0.01)	(0.01)
Age		−0.000	−0.000		0.000+	0.000
		(0.00)	(0.00)		(0.00)	(0.00)
Reciprocity		0.063	0.068+		0.097+	0.102*
		(0.04)	(0.04)		(0.05)	(0.05)
Risk aversion		−0.002	−0.002		0.005	0.004
		(0.00)	(0.00)		(0.00)	(0.00)
Public goods		0.003	0.002		0.011***	0.005+
		(0.00)	(0.00)		(0.00)	(0.00)
Time preference		−0.003*	−0.003+		−0.002	−0.001
		(0.00)	(0.00)		(0.00)	(0.00)
Has piped water		−0.016+	−0.014		0.002	0.012
		(0.01)	(0.01)		(0.01)	(0.01)
Has own cistern		0.003	0.002		0.015+	0.013
		(0.01)	(0.01)		(0.01)	(0.01)
Access to cistern		−0.010	−0.014		−0.000	−0.002
		(0.01)	(0.01)		(0.01)	(0.01)
Constant	0.018***	0.031	0.039+	0.037***	−0.081***	−0.060**
	(0.00)	(0.02)	(0.02)	(0.00)	(0.02)	(0.02)
Observations	3693	3195	3195	3727	3223	3223
R^2	0.244	0.271	0.283	0.019	0.043	0.127
Municipal fixed effects	No	No	Yes	No	No	Yes

Note: + $p < 0.10$, * $p < 0.05$, ** $p < 0.01$, *** $p < 0.001$. Linear probability model with robust standard errors clustered at neighborhood level. Results are robust using logit specifications.
Source: Author's analysis of the Rural Clientelism Survey. Data collected by Gustavo Bobonis, Paul Gertler, Marco Gonzalez-Navarro, and Simeon Nichter.

TABLE E.2 *Citizen requests and post-election benefits, rural Northeast Brazil, 2013 – Regressions in Figure 6.2, row 3 (and club goods)*

	Politician helped get job			Club good from politician		
	(1)	(2)	(3)	(4)	(5)	(6)
Requested job assistance	0.212*	0.153+	0.152			
	(0.10)	(0.09)	(0.09)			
Requested club good				0.225**	0.223**	0.221**
				(0.07)	(0.08)	(0.08)
Declared for winner		0.029**	0.028*		0.000	0.000
		(0.01)	(0.01)		(0.00)	(0.00)
Declared for loser		0.010	0.009		0.002	0.001
		(0.01)	(0.01)		(0.01)	(0.01)
Voted for mayor		0.001	0.001		−0.004	−0.003
		(0.00)	(0.00)		(0.00)	(0.00)
Voted in 2012		−0.004	−0.004		−0.000	0.001
		(0.01)	(0.01)		(0.00)	(0.00)
Talks with politicians		0.028*	0.028*		0.010	0.009
		(0.01)	(0.01)		(0.01)	(0.01)
Association member		−0.000	0.001		0.002	0.006
		(0.00)	(0.00)		(0.00)	(0.00)
Neighborhood collaboration		0.006	0.003		0.014*	0.013*
		(0.01)	(0.01)		(0.01)	(0.01)
PT supporter		0.002	−0.000		0.008	0.009
		(0.01)	(0.01)		(0.01)	(0.01)
PSDB supporter		−0.012*	−0.011		−0.006+	−0.004
		(0.01)	(0.01)		(0.00)	(0.00)
PMDB supporter		−0.018**	−0.020**		−0.022*	−0.031**
		(0.01)	(0.01)		(0.01)	(0.01)
DEM supporter		−0.014*	−0.015+		−0.000	−0.007
		(0.01)	(0.01)		(0.00)	(0.01)
Wealth		−0.000	−0.001		0.003**	0.002+
		(0.00)	(0.00)		(0.00)	(0.00)
Education		0.002*	0.002*		−0.001+	−0.001+
		(0.00)	(0.00)		(0.00)	(0.00)
Female		−0.001	−0.000		0.000	0.001
		(0.00)	(0.00)		(0.00)	(0.00)
Age		0.000	0.000		−0.000	−0.000
		(0.00)	(0.00)		(0.00)	(0.00)
Reciprocity		0.014	0.019		−0.019	−0.018
		(0.02)	(0.02)		(0.02)	(0.02)
Risk aversion		0.004*	0.003*		0.001	0.001
		(0.00)	(0.00)		(0.00)	(0.00)
Public goods		−0.001	−0.001		0.000	−0.001
		(0.00)	(0.00)		(0.00)	(0.00)
Time preference		0.000	0.000		−0.000	−0.000
		(0.00)	(0.00)		(0.00)	(0.00)
Has piped water		−0.007	−0.007		0.001	0.003
		(0.00)	(0.01)		(0.00)	(0.01)
Has own cistern		0.008*	0.008*		0.005+	0.005+
		(0.00)	(0.00)		(0.00)	(0.00)
Access to cistern		−0.001	−0.001		−0.002	−0.004
		(0.01)	(0.01)		(0.00)	(0.00)
Constant	0.011***	−0.022+	−0.022+	0.005***	0.009	0.009
	(0.00)	(0.01)	(0.01)	(0.00)	(0.01)	(0.01)
Observations	3721	3220	3220	3692	3194	3194
R^2	0.019	0.037	0.056	0.086	0.087	0.100
Municipal fixed effects	No	No	Yes	No	No	Yes

Note: + $p < 0.10$, * $p < 0.05$, ** $p < 0.01$, *** $p < 0.001$. Linear probability model with robust standard errors clustered at neighborhood level. Results are robust using logit specifications.
Source: Author's analysis of the Rural Clientelism Survey. Data collected by Gustavo Bobonis, Paul Gertler, Marco Gonzalez-Navarro, and Simeon Nichter.

Regression Tables for Requesting Benefits

TABLE E.3 *Citizen requests and campaign benefits, rural Northeast Brazil, 2012 – Regressions in Figure 6.2, row 4*

	\multicolumn{3}{c}{Received campaign benefit from politician}		
	(1)	(2)	(3)
Requested help	0.171***	0.162***	0.153***
	(0.02)	(0.02)	(0.02)
Any declaration		0.023*	0.020*
		(0.01)	(0.01)
Voted for mayor		−0.020+	−0.019
		(0.01)	(0.01)
Voted in 2012		0.014	0.021
		(0.02)	(0.02)
Talks with politicians		0.026+	0.032*
		(0.01)	(0.01)
Association member		−0.008	−0.007
		(0.01)	(0.01)
PT supporter		−0.021*	−0.018+
		(0.01)	(0.01)
PSDB supporter		0.119	0.110
		(0.07)	(0.07)
PMDB supporter		−0.032	−0.044
		(0.03)	(0.03)
DEM supporter		−0.011	−0.008
		(0.04)	(0.03)
Wealth		−0.006+	−0.008*
		(0.00)	(0.00)
Education		−0.001	−0.001
		(0.00)	(0.00)
Female		−0.003	−0.005
		(0.01)	(0.01)
Age		−0.000	−0.000
		(0.00)	(0.00)
Reciprocity		−0.050	−0.031
		(0.04)	(0.04)
Risk aversion		0.004	0.003
		(0.00)	(0.00)
Time preference		0.000	0.001
		(0.00)	(0.00)
Piped water		−0.008	−0.002
		(0.01)	(0.02)
Own cistern		0.000	0.005
		(0.01)	(0.01)
Access to cistern		−0.005	−0.014
		(0.01)	(0.01)
Constant	0.024***	0.031	0.026
	(0.00)	(0.03)	(0.03)
Observations	3160	2720	2720
R^2	0.087	0.096	0.132
Municipal fixed effects	No	No	Yes

Note: + $p < 0.10$, * $p < 0.05$, ** $p < 0.01$, *** $p < 0.001$. Linear probability model with robust standard errors clustered at neighborhood level. Results are robust using logit specifications.
Source: Author's analysis of the Rural Clientelism Survey. Data collected by Gustavo Bobonis, Paul Gertler, Marco Gonzalez-Navarro, and Simeon Nichter.

TABLE E.4 *Citizen requests and campaign benefits, rural Northeast Brazil, 2012 – Regressions in Figure 6.2, row 5*

	\multicolumn{3}{c}{Received campaign benefit from politician}	
	(1)	(2)	(3)
Requested help	0.432***	0.469***	0.496***
	(0.10)	(0.11)	(0.10)
Any declaration		−0.047	−0.041
		(0.08)	(0.08)
Voted for mayor		−0.073	−0.124
		(0.09)	(0.09)
Voted in 2012		−0.158	−0.126
		(0.14)	(0.14)
Talks with politicians		−0.054	−0.053
		(0.12)	(0.12)
Association member		0.040	0.033
		(0.09)	(0.09)
PT supporter		0.198	0.177
		(0.13)	(0.12)
PMDB supporter		0.003	−0.121
		(0.30)	(0.31)
PSDB supporter		0.230	0.135
		(0.57)	(0.53)
DEM supporter		−0.140	−0.169
		(0.30)	(0.32)
Wealth		0.008	0.001
		(0.03)	(0.03)
Education		0.004	0.003
		(0.01)	(0.01)
Female		0.118	0.119
		(0.08)	(0.08)
Age		−0.003	−0.004
		(0.00)	(0.00)
Reciprocity		0.463	0.460
		(0.41)	(0.40)
Risk aversion		0.031	0.030
		(0.03)	(0.03)
Time preference		0.000	0.001
		(0.02)	(0.02)
Piped water		−0.200+	−0.206+
		(0.11)	(0.11)
Own cistern		−0.198	−0.202+
		(0.12)	(0.12)
Access to cistern		−0.173	−0.198
		(0.13)	(0.12)
Constant	2.378***	1.868***	1.722***
	(0.04)	(0.18)	(0.18)
Observations	3616	3085	3085
R^2	0.024	0.081	0.134
Municipal fixed effects	No	No	Yes

Note: $+ p < 0.10$, $* p < 0.05$, $** p < 0.01$, $*** p < 0.001$. Analyses are OLS regressions with the list experiment count as the outcome variable. Coefficients reflect interactions between each independent variable and the treatment variable. The treatment variable is coded 1 if the respondent was exposed to a fifth item in the list (regarding a campaign benefit); 0 otherwise. Robust standard errors clustered at the neighborhood level.
Source: Author's analysis of the Rural Clientelism Survey. Data collected by Gustavo Bobonis, Paul Gertler, Marco Gonzalez-Navarro, and Simeon Nichter.

TABLE E.5 *Correlates of post-election benefits by request, rural Northeast Brazil, 2013 – Regressions in Figure 6.3, row 1*

	Post-election benefit by request			
	(1)	(2)	(3)	(4)
Declared for winner	0.056*** (0.02)		0.047** (0.02)	0.046** (0.02)
Talks with politicians		0.128*** (0.03)	0.126*** (0.03)	0.119*** (0.03)
Declared for loser			0.009 (0.02)	0.007 (0.02)
Voted for mayor			0.000 (0.01)	0.000 (0.01)
Voted in 2012			0.005 (0.01)	0.007 (0.01)
Association member			0.002 (0.01)	0.002 (0.01)
Neighborhood collaboration			0.012 (0.01)	0.012 (0.01)
PT supporter			0.009 (0.02)	0.017 (0.02)
PSDB supporter			0.009 (0.05)	0.016 (0.05)
PMDB supporter			0.013 (0.05)	0.000 (0.06)
DEM supporter			−0.029** (0.01)	−0.033 (0.02)
Wealth			0.003 (0.00)	−0.002 (0.00)
Education			−0.002+ (0.00)	−0.002* (0.00)
Female			0.010 (0.01)	0.010 (0.01)
Age			−0.000+ (0.00)	−0.001* (0.00)
Reciprocity			0.045 (0.05)	0.054 (0.05)
Risk aversion			−0.001 (0.00)	−0.001 (0.00)
Public goods			0.005 (0.00)	0.004 (0.00)
Time preference			−0.003+ (0.00)	−0.003* (0.00)
Has piped water			−0.024* (0.01)	−0.016 (0.01)
Has own cistern			0.006 (0.01)	0.007 (0.01)
Access to cistern			−0.010 (0.01)	−0.016 (0.01)
Constant	0.039*** (0.00)	0.038*** (0.00)	0.045+ (0.02)	0.052* (0.02)
Observations	3722	3724	3225	3225
R^2	0.008	0.021	0.037	0.063
Municipal fixed effects	No	No	No	Yes

Note: + $p < 0.10$, * $p < 0.05$, ** $p < 0.01$, *** $p < 0.001$. Linear probability model with robust standard errors clustered at neighborhood level. Results are robust using logit specifications.
Source: Author's analysis of the Rural Clientelism Survey. Data collected by Gustavo Bobonis, Paul Gertler, Marco Gonzalez-Navarro, and Simeon Nichter.

TABLE E.6 *Correlates of post-election requests, rural Northeast Brazil, 2013 – Regressions in Figure 6.3, row 2*

	Post-election request			
	(1)	(2)	(3)	(4)
Declared for winner	0.091***		0.078***	0.081***
	(0.02)		(0.02)	(0.02)
Talks with politicians		0.169***	0.157***	0.143***
		(0.04)	(0.04)	(0.04)
Declared for loser			0.001	0.001
			(0.02)	(0.02)
Voted for mayor			−0.001	0.003
			(0.01)	(0.01)
Voted in 2012			0.033**	0.032**
			(0.01)	(0.01)
Association member			0.011	0.009
			(0.01)	(0.01)
Neighborhood collaboration			0.022	0.017
			(0.01)	(0.01)
PT supporter			0.026	0.037
			(0.02)	(0.02)
PSDB supporter			−0.020	−0.012
			(0.05)	(0.05)
PMDB supporter			0.004	−0.007
			(0.06)	(0.07)
DEM supporter			−0.048***	−0.037
			(0.01)	(0.02)
Wealth			0.002	−0.004
			(0.00)	(0.00)
Education			−0.004*	−0.004**
			(0.00)	(0.00)
Female			0.008	0.008
			(0.01)	(0.01)
Age			−0.000	−0.001
			(0.00)	(0.00)
Reciprocity			−0.026	−0.010
			(0.06)	(0.06)
Risk aversion			−0.001	−0.002
			(0.00)	(0.00)
Public goods			0.004	0.004
			(0.00)	(0.00)
Time preference			−0.001	−0.001
			(0.00)	(0.00)
Has piped water			−0.032*	−0.022
			(0.01)	(0.02)
Has own cistern			−0.000	−0.001
			(0.01)	(0.01)
Access to cistern			0.012	0.001
			(0.02)	(0.02)
Constant	0.066***	0.067***	0.052+	0.063*
	(0.01)	(0.00)	(0.03)	(0.03)
Observations	3720	3722	3224	3224
R^2	0.012	0.023	0.043	0.073
Municipal fixed effects	No	No	No	Yes

Note: + $p < 0.10$, * $p < 0.05$, ** $p < 0.01$, *** $p < 0.001$. Linear probability model with robust standard errors clustered at neighborhood level. Results are robust using logit specifications.
Source: Author's analysis of the Rural Clientelism Survey. Data collected by Gustavo Bobonis, Paul Gertler, Marco Gonzalez-Navarro, and Simeon Nichter.

Regression Tables for Requesting Benefits

TABLE E.7 *Correlates of pre-election benefits by request, rural Northeast Brazil, 2012 – Regressions in Figure 6.3, row 3*

	\multicolumn{4}{c}{Pre-election benefit by request}
	(1)	(2)	(3)	(4)
Any declaration	0.050***		0.040**	0.035*
	(0.01)		(0.01)	(0.01)
Talks with politicians		0.082***	0.074***	0.062***
		(0.02)	(0.02)	(0.02)
Voted for mayor			−0.015	−0.016
			(0.02)	(0.02)
Voted in 2012			0.040+	0.052*
			(0.02)	(0.02)
Association member			−0.023	0.005
			(0.01)	(0.02)
PT supporter			−0.050**	−0.032+
			(0.02)	(0.02)
PSDB supporter			0.060	0.081
			(0.08)	(0.08)
PMDB supporter			0.034	0.026
			(0.06)	(0.06)
DEM supporter			0.110	0.099
			(0.10)	(0.10)
Wealth			−0.000	−0.007
			(0.00)	(0.01)
Education			−0.005*	−0.005*
			(0.00)	(0.00)
Female			0.059***	0.058***
			(0.01)	(0.01)
Age			−0.000	−0.000
			(0.00)	(0.00)
Reciprocity			−0.047	−0.032
			(0.06)	(0.06)
Risk aversion			−0.003	−0.004
			(0.00)	(0.00)
Time preference			0.006**	0.007**
			(0.00)	(0.00)
Piped water			−0.028+	−0.012
			(0.02)	(0.02)
Own cistern			0.047**	0.031+
			(0.02)	(0.02)
Access to cistern			0.037*	0.002
			(0.02)	(0.02)
Constant	0.103***	0.113***	0.046	0.035
	(0.01)	(0.01)	(0.03)	(0.03)
Observations	3660	3659	3111	3111
R^2	0.006	0.009	0.038	0.082
Municipal fixed effects	No	No	No	Yes

Note: + $p < 0.10$, * $p < 0.05$, ** $p < 0.01$, *** $p < 0.001$. Linear probability model with robust standard errors clustered at neighborhood level. Results are robust using logit specifications.
Source: Author's analysis of the Rural Clientelism Survey. Data collected by Gustavo Bobonis, Paul Gertler, Marco Gonzalez-Navarro, and Simeon Nichter.

TABLE E.8 *Correlates of pre-election requests, rural Northeast Brazil, 2012 – Regressions in Figure 6.3, row 4*

	Pre-election request			
	(1)	(2)	(3)	(4)
Any declaration	0.059***		0.036*	0.027+
	(0.01)		(0.02)	(0.02)
Talks with politicians		0.119***	0.115***	0.104***
		(0.02)	(0.02)	(0.02)
Voted for mayor			−0.020	−0.020
			(0.02)	(0.02)
Voted in 2012			0.065*	0.083**
			(0.03)	(0.03)
Association member			−0.031+	0.000
			(0.02)	(0.02)
PT supporter			−0.044+	−0.009
			(0.02)	(0.02)
PSDB supporter			−0.017	0.021
			(0.08)	(0.08)
PMDB supporter			0.079	0.050
			(0.06)	(0.06)
DEM supporter			0.168	0.143
			(0.12)	(0.11)
Wealth			−0.002	−0.012+
			(0.01)	(0.01)
Education			−0.008***	−0.009***
			(0.00)	(0.00)
Female			0.072***	0.071***
			(0.01)	(0.01)
Age			−0.001+	−0.001+
			(0.00)	(0.00)
Reciprocity			−0.054	−0.035
			(0.08)	(0.08)
Risk aversion			−0.006	−0.006
			(0.00)	(0.00)
Time preference			0.007*	0.009**
			(0.00)	(0.00)
Piped water			−0.034	−0.006
			(0.02)	(0.03)
Own cistern			0.058**	0.035
			(0.02)	(0.02)
Access to cistern			0.082***	0.033
			(0.02)	(0.03)
Constant	0.186***	0.193***	0.136**	0.121**
	(0.01)	(0.01)	(0.05)	(0.04)
Observations	3660	3659	3111	3111
R^2	0.005	0.013	0.047	0.092
Municipal fixed effects	No	No	No	Yes

Note: + $p < 0.10$, * $p < 0.05$, ** $p < 0.01$, *** $p < 0.001$. Linear probability model with robust standard errors clustered at neighborhood level. Results are robust using logit specifications.
Source: Author's analysis of the Rural Clientelism Survey. Data collected by Gustavo Bobonis, Paul Gertler, Marco Gonzalez-Navarro, and Simeon Nichter.

TABLE E.9 *Perception of councilor in trust game, unfulfilled vs. fulfilled request, rural Northeast Brazil, 2013 – Regressions in Figure 6.4*

	Amount citizen expects own councilor to return (log reais)					
	(1)	(2)	(3)	(4)	(5)	(6)
Unfulfilled request	−0.601+	−0.705+	−0.897*	−0.585+	−0.701+	−0.909*
	(0.34)	(0.39)	(0.37)	(0.34)	(0.39)	(0.37)
Log amount sent to councilor	0.702***	0.684***	0.684***	0.700***	0.684***	0.684***
	(0.09)	(0.10)	(0.10)	(0.09)	(0.10)	(0.10)
Declared for councilor				1.134**	1.286**	0.673
				(0.40)	(0.46)	(0.41)
Voted for elected councilor		−0.454	−0.456		−0.588	−0.486
		(0.40)	(0.38)		(0.41)	(0.38)
Voted for mayor		0.060	0.403		−0.011	0.338
		(0.41)	(0.41)		(0.40)	(0.42)
Voted in 2012		0.036	−0.961		0.002	−0.914
		(0.85)	(0.80)		(0.88)	(0.80)
Talks with politicians		−0.202	0.224		−0.308	0.147
		(0.50)	(0.46)		(0.48)	(0.46)
Association member		−0.543	−0.708		−0.481	−0.643
		(0.37)	(0.46)		(0.36)	(0.46)
Neighborhood collaboration		0.228	0.422		0.149	0.390
		(0.45)	(0.45)		(0.44)	(0.45)
PT supporter		1.383*	1.504*		1.285*	1.438*
		(0.59)	(0.61)		(0.59)	(0.61)
PSDB supporter		2.674***	1.338		3.095***	1.664+
		(0.70)	(0.81)		(0.73)	(0.85)
PMDB supporter		−0.092	2.341		−0.361	2.132
		(1.63)	(2.11)		(1.63)	(2.19)
Wealth		−0.101	−0.141		−0.105	−0.144
		(0.11)	(0.11)		(0.11)	(0.11)
Education		−0.016	0.003		−0.035	−0.009
		(0.06)	(0.05)		(0.06)	(0.05)
Female		0.225	−0.102		0.185	−0.111
		(0.38)	(0.36)		(0.37)	(0.36)
Age		−0.006	0.002		−0.005	0.002
		(0.02)	(0.01)		(0.02)	(0.01)
Reciprocity		2.261	4.034*		2.767	4.119*
		(2.08)	(2.00)		(2.05)	(2.01)
Risk aversion		−0.107	−0.069		−0.147	−0.090
		(0.15)	(0.15)		(0.15)	(0.15)
Public goods		−0.076	−0.213		−0.069	−0.198
		(0.17)	(0.17)		(0.16)	(0.17)
Time preference		0.039	0.066		0.017	0.048
		(0.08)	(0.07)		(0.07)	(0.07)
Has piped water		−0.981	−0.635		−0.675	−0.517
		(0.68)	(0.80)		(0.69)	(0.81)
Has own cistern		−0.637	0.505		−0.465	0.514
		(0.46)	(0.44)		(0.47)	(0.44)
Access to cistern		−0.552	0.306		−0.493	0.287
		(0.47)	(0.47)		(0.47)	(0.48)
Constant	−2.045***	−0.583	−0.971	−2.275***	−0.622	−0.976
	(0.23)	(1.33)	(1.32)	(0.25)	(1.35)	(1.31)
Observations	1137	988	988	1137	988	988
R^2	0.023	0.082	0.315	0.045	0.108	0.321
Municipal fixed effects	No	No	Yes	No	No	Yes

Note: + $p < 0.10$, * $p < 0.05$, ** $p < 0.01$, *** $p < 0.001$. OLS model with robust standard errors clustered at neighborhood level.
Source: Author's analysis of the Rural Clientelism Survey. Data collected by Gustavo Bobonis, Paul Gertler, Marco Gonzalez-Navarro, and Simeon Nichter.

TABLE E.10 *Voting for same mayoral candidate/party in 2008 and 2012, unfulfilled vs. fulfilled request, rural Northeast Brazil, 2012 – Regressions in Figure 6.5*

	Voted for same candidate		Voted for same candidate/party	
	(1)	(2)	(3)	(4)
Unfulfilled request	−0.243*	−0.265*	−0.217*	−0.200+
	(0.11)	(0.12)	(0.09)	(0.10)
Declared support		0.109		0.064
		(0.11)		(0.09)
Talks with politicians		0.143		0.232*
		(0.11)		(0.09)
Association member		−0.058		−0.146
		(0.14)		(0.11)
PT supporter		−0.020		0.142
		(0.16)		(0.19)
PMDB supporter		0.088		0.116
		(0.18)		(0.15)
DEM supporter		0.493**		0.583***
		(0.16)		(0.15)
Wealth		0.032		−0.002
		(0.03)		(0.03)
Education		0.014		0.017
		(0.01)		(0.01)
Female		−0.094		−0.107
		(0.10)		(0.08)
Age		0.000		−0.003
		(0.00)		(0.00)
Reciprocity		0.576		−0.200
		(0.69)		(0.53)
Risk aversion		−0.022		0.001
		(0.04)		(0.03)
Time preference		0.035+		0.030+
		(0.02)		(0.02)
Piped water		0.036		0.048
		(0.18)		(0.18)
Own cistern		0.093		0.104
		(0.22)		(0.14)
Access to cistern		0.128		0.194
		(0.19)		(0.13)
Constant	0.723***	0.366	0.678***	0.462*
	(0.05)	(0.24)	(0.04)	(0.22)
Observations	113	101	161	146
R^2	0.434	0.597	0.370	0.501
Municipal fixed effects	Yes	Yes	Yes	Yes

Note: + $p < 0.10$, * $p < 0.05$, ** $p < 0.01$, *** $p < 0.001$. Linear probability model with robust standard errors clustered at neighborhood level. Results are robust using logit specifications.
Source: Author's analysis of the Rural Clientelism Survey. Data collected by Gustavo Bobonis, Paul Gertler, Marco Gonzalez-Navarro, and Simeon Nichter.

Appendix F

Regression Tables for Comparative Chapter

TABLE F.1 *Citizen requests and clientelism during campaigns – Regressions in Figure 7.2 – Africa (Afrobarometer Round 3, 2005–2006)*

	(1)	(2)	(3)
Requested help	0.091***	0.124***	0.115***
	(0.014)	(0.017)	(0.015)
Machine supporter		−0.004	0.046***
		(0.006)	(0.007)
Voter		0.048***	0.048***
		(0.007)	(0.007)
Income		−0.028***	−0.018***
		(0.002)	(0.002)
Education		0.003	0.004*
		(0.002)	(0.002)
Age		−0.001***	−0.001**
		(0.000)	(0.000)
Gender		−0.033***	−0.026***
		(0.006)	(0.006)
Urban		−0.020**	−0.005
		(0.006)	(0.006)
Country fixed effects	No	No	Yes
Observations	23936	15701	15701

Robust standard errors in parentheses. Logit specifications with marginal effects shown.
+ $p < 0.10$, * $p < 0.05$, ** $p < 0.01$, *** $p < 0.001$

TABLE F.2 *Citizen requests and clientelism during campaigns – Regressions in Figure 7.2 – Latin America (LAPOP, 2010)*

	(1)	(2)	(3)
Requested help	0.090***	0.090***	0.094***
	(0.006)	(0.007)	(0.007)
Machine supporter		0.043***	0.031***
		(0.006)	(0.006)
Voter		0.030***	0.027***
		(0.005)	(0.005)
Income		−0.007**	−0.008**
		(0.003)	(0.003)
Education		−0.000	−0.000
		(0.001)	(0.001)
Age		−0.002***	−0.001***
		(0.000)	(0.000)
Gender		−0.021***	−0.020***
		(0.004)	(0.004)
Urban		0.001	−0.003
		(0.005)	(0.005)
Country fixed effects	No	No	Yes
Observations	36784	27606	27606

Standard errors in parentheses. Logit specifications with marginal effects shown.
+ $p < 0.10$, * $p < 0.05$, ** $p < 0.01$, *** $p < 0.001$

TABLE F.3 *Citizen requests and clientelism during campaigns – Regressions in Figure 7.2 – Argentina (LAPOP, 2010)*

	(1)	(2)	(3)
Requested help	0.211***	0.219***	0.202***
	(0.036)	(0.037)	(0.035)
Machine supporter		0.063	0.030
		(0.039)	(0.037)
Voter		0.004	−0.021
		(0.025)	(0.026)
Income		−0.019	−0.030**
		(0.012)	(0.011)
Education		−0.007*	−0.003
		(0.003)	(0.003)
Age		0.000	0.001
		(0.001)	(0.001)
Gender		−0.012	−0.004
		(0.021)	(0.020)
Urban		−0.066+	−0.016
		(0.038)	(0.039)
Province fixed effects	No	No	Yes
Observations	1332	1240	1229

Standard errors in parentheses. Logit specifications with marginal effects shown.
+ $p < 0.10$, * $p < 0.05$, ** $p < 0.01$, *** $p < 0.001$

TABLE F.4 *Citizen requests and clientelism during campaigns – Regressions in Figure 7.2 – Brazil (LAPOP, 2010)*

	(1)	(2)	(3)
Requested help	0.129***	0.107***	0.104***
	(0.028)	(0.028)	(0.027)
Machine supporter		0.021	0.003
		(0.032)	(0.029)
Voter		0.026	0.026
		(0.020)	(0.021)
Income		−0.015	−0.015
		(0.010)	(0.010)
Education		0.002	0.003
		(0.002)	(0.002)
Age		−0.003***	−0.003***
		(0.001)	(0.001)
Gender		−0.012	−0.011
		(0.016)	(0.015)
Urban		−0.067*	−0.129***
		(0.026)	(0.037)
State fixed effects	No	No	Yes
Observations	2388	2240	2240

Standard errors in parentheses. Logit specifications with marginal effects shown.
+ $p < 0.10$, * $p < 0.05$, ** $p < 0.01$, *** $p < 0.001$

TABLE F.5 *Citizen requests and clientelism during campaigns – Regressions in Figure 7.2 – Mexico (LAPOP, 2010)*

	(1)	(2)	(3)
Requested help	0.147***	0.138***	0.121***
	(0.030)	(0.030)	(0.031)
Machine supporter		0.013	0.022
		(0.025)	(0.028)
Voter		0.018	0.017
		(0.023)	(0.024)
Income		−0.038**	−0.040**
		(0.013)	(0.014)
Education		0.004	0.003
		(0.003)	(0.003)
Age		−0.001	−0.001
		(0.001)	(0.001)
Gender		−0.006	−0.007
		(0.019)	(0.020)
Urban		0.011	0.010
		(0.023)	(0.026)
State fixed effects	No	No	Yes
Observations	1547	1492	1436

Standard errors in parentheses. Logit specifications with marginal effects shown.
+ $p < 0.10$, * $p < 0.05$, ** $p < 0.01$, *** $p < 0.001$

TABLE F.6 *Argentina: citizen strategies and campaign handouts, 2001 – Regressions in Figure 7.3*

	(1)	(2)	(3)	(4)
Requested help	0.103***		0.048*	0.045*
	(0.021)		(0.020)	(0.020)
Attended rally		0.180***	0.060+	0.090*
		(0.044)	(0.032)	(0.039)
Opinion of peronists			0.020*	0.022*
			(0.010)	(0.009)
Voter			0.020	0.018
			(0.020)	(0.021)
Income			−0.015**	−0.016**
			(0.005)	(0.005)
Education			−0.014*	−0.016*
			(0.006)	(0.006)
Housing quality			−0.008	−0.013
			(0.010)	(0.010)
Log population			−0.008*	−0.003
			(0.004)	(0.004)
Age			−0.001*	−0.001*
			(0.001)	(0.001)
Gender			−0.015	−0.017
			(0.015)	(0.015)
Ballot			0.026	0.028
			(0.021)	(0.021)
Radical sympathizer			−0.032+	−0.033+
			(0.019)	(0.019)
Location fixed effects	No	No	No	Yes
Observations	1860	1747	1293	1293

Standard errors in parentheses. Logit specifications with marginal effects shown.
+ $p < 0.10$, * $p < 0.05$, ** $p < 0.01$, *** $p < 0.001$

Bibliography

Abers, Rebecca. 2000. *Inventing Local Democracy: Grassroots Politics in Brazil*. Boulder: Lynne Rienner Publishers.

Afrobarometer. 2005–2006. Data available at www.afrobarometer.org.

Agência Nacional de Águas ANA. 2014. *Conjuntura dos Recursos Hídricos do Brasil*. Tech. rept.

Aidt, Toke S., and Jensen, Peter S. 2017. From Open to Secret Ballot: Vote Buying and Modernization. *Comparative Political Studies*, 50(5), 555–593.

Alvarez, R. Michel, Levin, Ines, Pomares, Julia, and Leiras, Marcelo. 2013. Voting Made Safe and Easy: The Impact of e-Voting on Citizens' Perceptions. *Political Science Research and Methods*, 1(1), 117–137.

Alves, Jorge Antonio and Wendy Hunter. 2017. From Right to Left in Brazil's Northeast: Transformation, or "Politics as Usual"? *Comparative Politics*, 49(4), 437–455.

Alwang, Jeffrey, Paul B. Siegel and Steen L. Jørgensen. 2001. Vulnerability: A View from Different Disciplines. Social Protection Discussion Paper Series, Number 115. Washington, DC: World Bank.

Amaral, Oswaldo E. do, and Power, Timothy J. 2016. The PT at 35: Revisiting Scholarly Interpretations of the Brazilian Workers' Party. *Journal of Latin American Studies*, 48(1), 147–171.

Ames, Barry. 1995. Electoral Strategy under Open-List Proportional Representation. *American Journal of Political Science*, 39(2), 406–433.

Ames, Barry. 2002. *The Deadlock of Democracy in Brazil*. Ann Arbor, MI: University of Michigan Press.

Ames, Barry, Machado, Fabiana, Renno, Lucio, Samuels, David, Smith, Amy Erika, and Zucco, Cesar, Jr. 2013. *The Brazilian Electoral Panel Studies (BEPS): Brazilian Public Opinion in the 2010 Presidential Elections*. Tech. rept. 508. Inter-American Development Bank.

Amitrano, Claudio Roberto. 2015. *Um Mapa Setorial do Emprego e dos Salários a partir dos Dados da RAIS*. IPEA, Texto para Discussão, 2033.

Anderson, Siwan, Francois, Patrick, and Kotwal, Ashok. 2015. Clientelism in Indian Villages. *The American Economic Review*, 105(6), 1780–1816.

Andrade, Maria Antonia Alonso de. 1997. Coronelismo × Clientelismo. Pages 99–110 of: Siqueira, Deis E (ed), *Relacoes de Trabalho, Relacoes de Poder*. Editora Universidade de Brasília.

Asante, Kojo R., Brobbey, Victor, and Ofosu, George. 2011. Responding to Constituents' Demands: Survival Strategies of Legislators in Ghana's Fourth Republic. *Available at SSRN 2353296*.

Auyero, Javier. 1999. From the Client's Point of View: How Poor People Perceive and Evaluate Political Clientelism. *Theory and Society*, 28, 297–224.

Auyero, Javier. 2000a. *Poor People's Politics: Peronist Survival Networks and the Legacy of Evita*. Durham: Duke University Press.

Auyero, Javier. 2000b. The Logic of Clientelism in Argentina: An Ethnographic Account. *Latin American Research Review*, 35(3), 55–81.

Baker, Andy, Barry Ames, Anand E. Sokhey, and Lucio R. Renno. 2016. The Dynamics of Partisan Identification When Party Brands Change: The Case of the Workers Party in Brazil, *Journal of Politics* 78(1): 197–213.

Banfield, Edward C., and Wilson, James Q. 1963. *City Politics*. Cambridge, MA: Harvard University Press.

Barone, Leonardo Sangali. 2010. *Emprego Público e Política: Uma Radiografia da Gestão 2005/2008 nos Municípios Brasileiros*. III Congresso Consad de Gestão Pública.

Barreto, Joslene Lacerda, and do Carmo Lessa Guimarães, Maria. 2010. Avaliação da Gestão Descentralizada da Assistência Farmacêutica Básica em Municípios Baianos, Brasil. *Cadernos da Saúde Pública*, 26(6), 1207–1220.

Barrientos, Armando. 2013. *Social Assistance in Developing Countries*. New York: Cambridge University Press.

Barros, Aluísio J. D., João Luiz Bastos and Andréa H. Dâmaso. 2011. Gasto Catastrófico com Saúde no Brasil: Planos Privados de Saúde não Parecem ser a Solução. *Caderno Saúde Pública*, 27, S254–S261.

Barros, Ricardo, de Carvalho, Mirela, Franco, Samuel, and Mendonça, Rosane. 2010. *Markets, the State and the Dynamics of Inequality: The Case of Brazil*. Discussion Paper, United Nations Development Programme Bureau for Development Policy.

Beccaria, Luis, Maurizio, Roxana, Fernández, Ana Laura, Monsalvo, Paula, and Álvarez, Mariana. 2013. Urban Poverty and Labor Market Dynamics in Five Latin America Countries: 2003–2008. *The Journal of Economic Inequality*, 11(4), 555–580.

Beccaria, Luis, Maurizio, Roxana, and Vázquez, Gustavo. 2015. Recent Decline in Wage Inequality and Formalization of the Labor Market in Argentina. *International Review of Applied Economics*, 29(5), 677–700.

Berenschot, Ward. 2010. Everyday Mediation: The Politics of Public Service Delivery in Gujarat, India. *Development and Change*, 41(5), 883–905.

Berinsky, Adam J, Margolis, Michele F, and Sances, Michael W. 2014. Separating the Shirkers from the Workers? Making Sure Respondents Pay Attention on Self-Administered Surveys. *American Journal of Political Science*, 58(3), 739–753.

Bernal, Cleide. 2001. Sobre o Projeto Nacional, Depois das Eleições 2000. *Cadernos do Nordeste*, 8–11.

Bertoldi, Andréa Dâmaso, Helfer, Ana Paula, Camargo, Aline L, Tavares, Noêmia UL, and Kanavos, Panos. 2012. Is the Brazilian Pharmaceutical Policy Ensuring Population Access to Essential Medicines? *Globalization and Health*, 8(6), 1–10.

Bibliography

Birdsall, Nancy, Lustig, Nora, and Meyer, Christian J. 2014. The Struggers: The New Poor in Latin America? *World Development*, 60, 132–146.

Blair, Graeme, and Imai, Kosuke. 2012. Statistical Analysis of List Experiments. *Political Analysis*, 20, 47–77.

Blaydes, Lisa. 2006. Who Votes in Authoritarian Elections and Why? Determinants of Voter Turnout in Contemporary Egypt. In: *Annual Meeting of the American Political Science Association. Philadelphia, PA.*

Boas, Taylor. 2014. Pastor Paulo vs. Doctor Carlos: Professional Titles as Voting Heuristics in Brazil. *Journal of Politics in Latin America*, 6(2), 39–72.

Bobonis, Gustavo, Gertler, Paul, Gonzalez-Navarro, Marco, and Nichter, Simeon. 2018. Vulnerability and Clientelism.

Bonilla-Chacín, M. E., and Aguilera, Nelly. 2013. The Mexican Social Protection System in Health. UNICO Studies Series 1. World Bank.

Borges, André. 2007. Rethinking State Politics: The Withering of State Dominant Machines in Brazil. *Brazilian Political Science Review*, 1(2), 108–156.

Borges, André. 2011. The Political Consequences of Center-Led Redistribution in Brazilian Federalism: The Fall of Subnational Party Machines. *Latin American Research Review*, 46(3), 21–45.

Boto, Carlota. 1994. Nacionalidade, Escola e Voto: A Liga Nacionalista de São Paulo. *Perspectivas: Revista de Ciências Sociais*, 17–18, 145–163.

Bratton, M. 2008. Vote Buying and Violence in Nigerian Election Campaigns. *Electoral Studies*, 27(4), 621–632.

Brinks, Daniel and Abby Blass. 2013. "Beyond the Façade: Institutional Engineering and Potemkin Courts in Latin America, 1975–2009." In Conference "Ruling Politics: the Formal and Informal Foundations of Power in New Democracies," University of Chicago.

Brooks, Sarah M. 2009. *Social Protection and the Market in Latin America: The Transformation of Social Security Institutions*. New York: Cambridge University Press.

Brunazo Filho, Amílcar, and Cortiz, Maria Aparecida. 2006. *Fraudes e Defesas no Voto Eletrônico*. São Paulo: All Print Editora.

Brusco, Valeria, Nazareno, Marcelo, and Stokes, Susan C. 2004. Vote Buying in Argentina. *Latin American Research Review*, 39(2), 66–88.

Bursztyn, Marcel, and Chacon, Suely Salgueiro. 2013. Ligações Perigosas: Proteção Social e Clientelismo no Semiárido Nordestino. *Estudos Sociedade e Agricultura*, 19(1), 30–61.

Bussell, Jennifer. *Clients or Constituents? Distribution between the Votes in India.* Prepared for presentation at the Berkeley Comparative Politics Colloquium, April 2, 2015.

Calheiros, Lelio Bringel, de Castro, Antonio L. C., and Dantas, Maria Cristina. 2007. *Apostila sobre Implantação e Operacionalização de COMDEC*. Tech. rept. Departamento de Minimização de Desastres, Secretaria Nacional de Proteção e Defesa Civil, Ministério da Integração Nacional.

Calvo, Ernesto, and Murillo, Maria Victoria. 2013. When Parties Meet Voters Assessing Political Linkages through Partisan Networks and Distributive Expectations in Argentina and Chile. *Comparative Political Studies*, 46(7), 851–882.

Calvo, Ernesto, and Murillo, Victoria. 2012. Argentina: The Persistence of Peronism. *Journal of Democracy*, 23(2), 148–161.

Câmara dos Deputados. 1999. *Combatendo a Corrupção Eleitoral: Tramitação do Primeiro Projeto de Lei de Iniciativa Popular Aprovado pelo Congresso Nacional.* Brasília: Biblioteca Digital da Câmara dos Deputados.
Camerer, Colin. 2003. *Behavioral Game Theory: Experiments in Strategic Interaction.* Princeton: Princeton University Press.
Cammack, Paul. 1982. "Clientelism and Military Government in Brazil." In Christopher Clapham, ed. *Private Patronage and Public Power: Political Clientelism in the Modern State.* London: Pinter, pp 53–75.
Cammett, Melani. 2014. *Compassionate Communalism: Welfare and Sectarianism in Lebanon.* Ithaca: Cornell University Press.
Cammett, Melani Claire. 2011. Partisan Activism and Access to Welfare in Lebanon. *Studies in Comparative International Development,* 46(1), 70–97.
Campello, Tereza, and Neri, Marcelo Côrtes. 2013. *Programa Bolsa Família: Uma Década De Inclusão e Cidadania.* Brasília: IPEA.
Campos, André Gambier. 2015. *Bem-estar Social nos Anos 1990 e 2000: Traços Estilizados da História Brasileira.* IPEA, Texto para Discussão, 2025.
Carey, John M, and Shugart, Matthew Soberg. 1995. Incentives to Cultivate a Personal Vote: A Rank Ordering of Electoral Formulas. *Electoral Studies,* 14(4), 417–439.
Carvalho, José Murilo de. 1997. Mandonismo, Coronelismo, Clientelismo: Uma Discussão Conceitual. *Dados,* vol. 40 no. 2.
Centers for Disease Control and Prevention (CDC). 2014. Morbidity and Mortality Weekly Report. *U.S Department of Health and Human Services. Centers for Disease Control and Prevention,* 63(25).
Cepaluni, Gabriel and F. Daniel Hidalgo. 2016. Compulsory Voting Can Increase Political Inequality: Evidence from Brazil. *Comparative Political Studies,* 24(2), 273–280.
Chandra, Kanchan. 2004. *Why Ethnic Parties Succeed: Patronage and Ethnic Head Counts in India.* New York: Cambridge University Press.
Chubb, Judith. 1982. *Patronage, Power, and Poverty in Southern Italy: A Tale of Two Cities.* Cambridge, MA: Cambridge University Press.
Cleary, Matthew R., and Stokes, Susan. 2006. *Democracy and the Culture of Skepticism: The Politics of Trust in Argentina and Mexico.* New York: Russell Sage Foundation.
Coelho, Jorge. 1985. *As Secas do Nordeste e a Indústria das Secas.* Petrópolis: Vozes.
Collier, Ruth Berins, and Collier, David. 1991. *Shaping the Political Arena.*
Comissão Brasileira da Justiça e Paz (CBJP). 2000. *Vamos Acabar com a Corrupção Eleitoral.* São Paulo: Editora Paulinas.
Confederação Nacional de Municípios (CNM). 2013. *Análise Sobre a Seca Do Nordeste.* Tech. rept.
Conselho Federal de Medicina, and Conselho Regional de Medicina do Estado de São Paulo (CFM). 2013. *Demografia Médica no Brasil.* Volume 2: Cenários e Indicadores de Distribuição.
Controladoria-Geral da Unio (CGU). 2014. *Auditoria Integrada de Acompanhamento na Operação Carro-Pipa, Relatório de Auditoria No. 201318217.* Tech. rept.
Coppedge, Michael, John Gerring, Staffan I. Lindberg, Svend-Erik Skaaning, Jan Teorell, David Altman, Michael Bernhard, M. Steven Fish, Adam Glynn, Allen Hicken, Carl Henrik Knutsen, Joshua Krusell, Anna Lührmann, Kyle L. Marquardt, Kelly McMann, Valeriya Mechkova, Moa Olin, Pamela Paxton, Daniel Pemstein, Josefine Pernes, Constanza Sanhueza Petrarca, Johannes von Römer, Laura Saxer, Brigitte

Seim, Rachel Sigman, Jeffrey Staton, Natalia Stepanova, and Steven Wilson. 2017. "V-Dem Dataset v7." Varieties of Democracy (V-Dem) Project.

Cord, Louise, Genoni, Maria Eugenia, and Rodriguez-Castelán, Carlos. 2015. Shared Prosperity and Poverty Eradication in Latin America and the Caribbean. World Bank Group.

Cornelius, Wayne. 2003. Mobilized Voting in the 2000 Elections: The Changing Efficacy of Vote Buying and Coercion in Mexican Electoral Politics. In: Dominguez, Jorge I., and Lawson, Chappell (eds), *Mexico's Pivotal Democratic Elections: Candidates, Voters, and the Presidential Campaign of 2000*. Stanford, CA: Stanford University Press.

Corstange, Daniel. 2016. *The Price of a Vote in the Middle East: Clientelism and Communal Politics in Lebanon and Yemen*. New York: Cambridge University Press.

Corstange, Daniel. 2018. Clientelism in Competitive and Uncompetitive Elections. *Comparative Political Studies* 51(1), 76–104.

Cox, Gary. 2009. Swing Voters, Core Voters, and Distributive Politics. In: Shapiro, Ian, Stokes, Susan, Wood, Elisabeth, and Kirshner, Alexander S. (eds), *Political Representation*. Cambridge, MA: Cambridge University Press.

Cox, Gary W., and Kousser, J. Morgan. 1981. Turnout and Rural Corruption: New York as a Test Case. *American Journal of Political Science*, 25(4), 646–663.

Cureau, Sandra. 2010. *A Captação Ilícita de Sufrágio*. Presentation at Congresso Nacional da Escola Judiciária Eleitoral, Brasília.

da Costa, Adriano Soares. 2009. *Instituições de Direito Eleitoral*. Rio de Janeiro: Editora Lumen Juris.

da Silva, Francisco Carlos Teixeira. 2005. A Presença de Vargas na República Brasileira. *Senatus*, 4(1), 14–17.

Davalle, Regina. 2011. Federalismo, Política dos Governadores, Eleições e Fraudes Eleitorais na República Velha. *Métis: História & Cultura*, 2(4).

de Alba, Felipe, and Gamboa, Hugo Hernández. 2014. Intermediarios, Usos Políticos en una Metrópolis en Stress Hídrico en México. *Provincia*, 31, 121–145.

de Figueiredo, Miguel F. P., Hidalgo, F. Daniel, and Kasahara, Yuri. 2013. When Do Voters Punish Corrupt Politicians? Experimental Evidence from Brazil. Typescript.

de la Fuente, Alejandro, Ortiz-Juarez, Eduardo, and Rodriguez-Castelán, Carlos. 2015. *Living on the Edge: Vulnerability to Poverty and Public Transfers in Mexico*. Policy Research Working Paper 7165. Word Bank Gorup.

de la O, Ana L. 2015. *Crafting Policies to End Poverty in Latin America: The Quiet Transformation*. Cambridge: Cambridge University Press.

De León, Juan Carlos Villagrán. 2006. "Vulnerability: A Conceptual and Methodological Review." Studies of the University: Research, Counsel, Education Publication Series, No. 4, Bonn, Germany: United Nations University – Institute for Environment and Human Security.

de Souza, Pedro Herculano Guimarães Ferreira, and Osorio, Rafael Guerreiro. 2013. O Perfil da Pobreza no Brasil e suas Mudanças entre 2003 e 2011. In: Campello, Tereza, and Neri, Marcelo Côrtes (eds), *Programa Bolsa Família: Uma Década de Inclusão e Cidadania*, 139–155. Brasília: IPEA.

Dedecca, Claudio Salvadori. 2015. *A Redução da Desigualdade e seus Desafios*. IPEA, Texto para Discussão, 2031.

Delgado, José Augusto. 2010. Reflexões Doutrinárias e Jurisprudenciais sobre o Art. 41-A da Lei N. 9.504/97. In: Coêlho, Marcus Vinícius Furtado, and Agra, Walber de Moura (eds), *Direito Eleitoral e Democracia: Desafios e Perspectivas*. Brasília: Conselho Federal da OAB: TSE, Escola Judiciria Eleitoral (EJE).

del Pozo, Blanca Elena, and Aparicio, Ricardo. 2001. Estudio Sobre la Participación Ciudadana y las Condiciones del Voto Libre y Secreto en las Elecciones Federales del Año 2000. *México, FLACSO-IFE*.

Departamento Intersindical de Estatística e Estudos Socioeconômicos (DIEESE). 2011. Anuário do Sistema Público de Emprego, Trabalho e Renda 2010/2011: Mercado de Trabalho, 3rd Edition. São Paulo: DIEESE.

Departamento Intersindical de Estatística e Estudos Socioeconômicos (DIEESE). 2014a. *O Mercado de Trabalho Assalariado Rural Brasileiro*. Estudos e Pesquisas. Número 74.

Departamento Intersindical de Estatística e Estudos Socioeconômicos (DIEESE). 2014b. *Rotatividade e Políticas Públicas para o Mercado de Trabalho*. São Paulo: DIEESE.

Departamento Intersindical de Estatística e Estudos Socioeconômicos (DIEESE). 2015. *Política de Valorização do Salário Mínimo: Salário Mínimo de 2015 Fixado em R$788,00*. Tech. rept. 143. DIEESE.

Desposato, Scott. 2002. *How Vote Buying Shapes the Political Arena*. Paper prepared for the Comparative Politics of Vote Buying Conference, Massachusetts Institute of Technology.

Desposato, Scott. 2007. How Does Vote Buying Shape the Legislative Arena? In: Schaffer, Frederic C. (ed), *Elections for Sale: The Causes and Consequences of Vote Buying*. Boulder, CO: Lynne Rienner Publishers.

Diaz-Cayeros, Alberto, Estévez, Federico and Magaloni, Beatriz. 2009. "Welfare Benefits, Canvassing, and Campaign Handouts." In Jorge I. Domínguez, Chappell H. Lawson, and Alejandro Moreno. Consolidating Mexico's Democracy: The 2006 Presidential Campaign in Comparative Perspective. Baltimore: Johns Hopkins University Press.

Diaz-Cayeros, Alberto, Estévez, Frederico, and Magaloni, Beatriz. 2016. *The Political Logic of Poverty Relief: Electoral Strategies and Social Policy in Mexico*. Cambridge: Cambridge University Press.

Diaz-Cayeros, Alberto, Estévez, Frederico, and Magaloni, Beatriz. 2012. "Strategies of Vote Buying: Democracy, Clientelism, and Poverty Relief in Mexico." Unpublished typescript.

Diniz, Eli. 1982. *Voto e Máquina Política: Patronagem e Clientelismo no Rio de Janeiro*. Vol. 59. São Paulo: Paz e Terra.

Dixit, Avinash, and Londregan, John. 1996. The Determinants of Success of Special Interests in Redistributive Politics. *The Journal of Politics*, 58(4), 1132–1155.

Dmytraczenko, Tania, and Almeida, Gisele. 2015. *Toward Universal Health Coverage and Equity in Latin America and the Caribbean: Evidence from Selected Countries*. World Bank Group.

Dollar, David. 2005. Globalization, Poverty, and Inequality since 1980. *The World Bank Research Observer*, 20(2), 145–175.

Dunning, Thad, and Stokes, Susan. 2009. *Persuasion vs. Mobilization*. Typescript.

Eaton, Kent, and Chambers-Ju, Christopher. 2014. Teachers, Mayors and the Transformation of Clientelism in Colombia. In: Brun, D.A., and Diamond, L. (eds), *Clientelism, Social Policy, and the Quality of Democracy*. Johns Hopkins University Press.

Eiró, Flávio and Diego Lindoso. 2015. Reinvenção de Práticas Clientelistas no Programa um Milhão de Cisternas - P1MC. *Ciência e Sustentabilidade*, 1(1), 62–76.

Eisenstadt, Todd A. 2003. Thinking Outside the (Ballot) Box: Informal Electoral Institutions and Mexico's Political Opening. *Latin America Politics and Society*, 45(1), 25–54.

Esping-Andersen, Gøsta. 1990. *The Three Worlds of Welfare Capitalism*. Princeton University Press.

Esping-Andersen, Gøsta. 1996. *Welfare States in Transition: National Adaptations in Global Economies*. Sage.

Falcón, Gustavo. 1995. *Os Coronéis do Cacau*. Salvador: Centro Editorial e Didático, Edições Ianamá.

Faughnan, Brian M, and Zechmeister, Elizabeth J. 2011. Vote Buying in the Americas. *Americas Barometer Insights*, 57.

Federação Brasileira de Bancos (Febraban). 2007. *Projeto Cisternas Transformando Possibilidades em Realidade*. Cartilha.

Federação Brasileira de Bancos (Febraban). 2008. *Participação da Febraban no Projeto Cisternas: Programa de Formação e Mobilização para a Convivência com o Semiárido*.

Fenno, Richard F. 1978. *Home Style: House Members in Their Districts*. Boston, MA: Little Brown.

Fernandes, Carla Montuori. 2015. O Coronelismo Ficcional e os Desmandos da Política Brasileira na Telenovela Meu Pedacinho de Chão. *Comunicação e Sociedade*, v. 37, n. 1, p. 213–235.

Ferreira, Francisco H. G., Messina, Julian, Rigoli, Jamele, López-Calva, Luis-Felipe, Lugo, Maria Ana, and Vakis, Renos. 2013. *Economic Mobility and the Rise of the Latin American Middle Class*. Washington, D.C.: World Bank.

Figuereido, Marcus. 1991. *A Decisão do Voto: Democracia e Racionalidade*. São Paulo: Sumaré.

Filmer, Deon, and Pritchett, Lant H. 2001. Estimating Wealth Effects without Expenditure Data – or Tears: An Application to Educational Enrollments in States of India. *Demography*, 38(1), 115–132.

Finan, Frederico, and Schechter, Laura. 2012. Vote-Buying and Reciprocity. *Econometrica*, 80(2), 863–881.

Fiszbein, Ariel, and Schady, Norbert. 2009. *Conditional Cash Transfer: Reducing Present and Future Poverty*. Washington D.C.: A World Bank Policy Research Report.

Fox, Jonathan A. 2007. *Accountability Politics: Power and Voice in Rural Mexico*. Oxford: Oxford University Press.

Frey, Anderson. 2017. "Reelection and Manipulation in Cash Transfers." Unpublished typescript.

Fukumoto, Kentaro, and Horiuchi, Yusaku. 2011. Making Outsiders' Votes Count: Detecting Electoral Fraud through a Natural Experiment. *American Political Science Review*, 105(3), 586–603.

Fukuyama, Francis. 2013. The Politics of Latin America's New Middle Class. Pages 26–33 of: *The Americas in Motion: Looking Ahead, 30th Anniversary Sol M. Linowitz Forum Commemorative Volume*. Washington, DC: Inter-American Dialogue.

Gallego, Jorge and Leonard Wantchekon. 2012. "Experiments on Clientelism and Vote-Buying." In Danila Serra and Leonard Wantchekon (ed.), *New Advances in Experimental Research on Corruption* Research in Experimental Economics, Vol. 15. Bingley, UK: Emerald Group Publishing Limited, pp. 177–212.

Gans-Morse, Jordan, Mazzuca, Sebastian, and Nichter, Simeon. 2014. Varieties of Clientelism: Machine Politics during Elections. *American Journal of Political Science*, 58(2), 415–432.

Garcia, Leila Posenato, Sant'Anna, Ana Cláudia, de Magalhães, Luís Carlos Garcia, and Aurea, Adriana Pacheco. 2013. Gastos com Saúde das Famílias Brasileiras Residentes em Regiões Metropolitanas: Composição e Evolução no Período 1995–2009. *Ciência e Saúde Coletiva*, 18(1), 115–128.

Gastaldi, Helio, and Rosendo, Rosi. 2012. Urna Eletrônica no Brasil: Mudanças no Processo Eleitoral e no Comportamento do Eleitores. *Revista Latinoamericana de Opinión Pública*, 2, 73–108.

Gay, Robert. 1990. Neighborhood Associations and Political Change in Rio de Janeiro. *Latin American Research Review*, 25(1), 102–118.

Gerard, François, and Gonzaga, Gustavo. 2014. Informal Labor and the Efficiency Cost of Social Programs: Evidence from 15 Years of Unemployment Insurance in Brazil. Working Paper.

Gerber, Alan S, Huber, Gregory A, Doherty, David, and Dowling, Conor M. 2013. Is There a Secret Ballot? Ballot Secrecy Perceptions and Their Implications for Voting Behaviour. *British Journal of Political Science*, 43(01), 77–102.

Gervasoni, Carlos. 2014. Argentina's Democracy Four Decades after Modernization and Bureaucratic-Authoritarism. In: Brinks, Daniel, Leiras, Marcelo, and Mainwaring, Scott (eds), *Reflections on Uneven Democracies: The Legacy of Guillermo O'Donnell*. Baltimore: Johns Hopkins University Press.

Gingerich, Daniel. 2013. Can Institutions Cure Clientelism? Assessing the Impact of the Australian Ballot in Brazil. IDB Working Paper Series. Washington, DC: Inter-American Development Bank.

Gingerich, Daniel. 2014. Brokered Politics in Brazil: An Empirical Analysis. *Quarterly Journal of Political Science*, 9(3), 269–300.

Gonzalez-Ocantos, Ezequiel, de Jonge, Chad Kiewiet, Meléndez, Carlos, Osorio, Javier, and Nickerson, David W. 2012. Vote Buying and Social Desirability Bias: Experimental Evidence from Nicaragua. *American Journal of Political Science*, 56(1), 202–217.

Gonzalez-Ocantos, Ezequiel, de Jonge, Chad Kiewiet, and Nickerson, David W. 2014. The Conditionality of Vote-Buying Norms: Experimental Evidence from Latin America. *American Journal of Political Science*, 58(1), 197–211.

Greene, Kenneth F. 2007. *Why Dominant Parties Lose: Mexico's Democratization in Comparative Perspective*. Cambridge: Cambridge University Press.

Greene, Kenneth F. 2012. *Se compró la Elección Presidencial?* Presentación para el "Seminario Proceso Electoral 2012," El Tribunal Electoral del Poder Judicial de la Federación (TEPJF), México D.F., October 12.

Grindle, Merilee S. 2012. *Jobs for the Boys: Patronage and the State in Comparative Perspective*. Cambridge, MA: Harvard University Press.

Gutiérrez, Ana Paula A., Engle, Nathan L., Nys, Erwin De, Molejón, Carmen, and Martins, Eduardo Sávio. 2014. Drought Preparedness in Brazil. *Weather and Climate Extremes*, 3, 95–106.

Haggard, Stephan, and Kaufman, Robert R. 2008. *Development, Democracy, and Welfare States: Latin America, East Asia, and Eastern Europe*. Princeton: Princeton University Press.

Hagopian, Frances. 1996. *Traditional Politics and Regime Change in Brazil*. New York: Cambridge University Press.

Hagopian, Frances. 2014. Reorganizing Interests in Latin America in the Neo-Liberal Age. In: Hall, Peter A., Jacoby, Wade, Levy, Jonah, and Meunier, Sophie (eds), *The Politics of Representation in the Global Age: Identification, Mobilization, and Adjudication*. Cambridge, MA: Cambridge University Press.

Hagopian, Frances. Forthcoming. *Reorganizing Political Representation in Latin America: Parties, Program, and Patronage in Argentina, Brazil, Chile, and Mexico*. New York: Cambridge University Press.

Hall, Anthony. 1974. Patron-client relationships. *Journal of Peasant Studies*, 1 (4), 506–509.

Hartlyn, Jonathan, McCoy, Jennifer, and Mustillo, Thomas. 2008. Electoral Governance Matters: Explaining the Quality of Elections in Contemporary Latin America. *Comparative Political Studies*, 41(1), 73–98.

Heckelman, Jac C. 1998. Bribing Voters without Verification. *The Social Science Journal*, 35(3), 435–443.

Hicken, Allen. 2011. Clientelism. *Annual Review of Political Science*, 14, 289–310.

Hicken, Allen. 2007. Institutional Incentives: Do Candidate-Centered Electoral Rules Encourage Vote Buying? In: Schaffer, Frederic C. (ed), *Elections for Sale: The Causes and Consequences of Vote Buying*. Boulder, CO: Lynne Rienner Publishers.

Hidalgo, F Daniel, and Nichter, Simeon. 2016. Voter Buying: Shaping the Electorate through Clientelism. *American Journal of Political Science*.

Hochstetler, Kathryn. 2008. "Organized Civil Society in Lula's Brazil." In Peter Kingstone and Timothy Power, *Democratic Brazil Revisited*, Pittsburgh: University of Pittsburgh Press, pp 33–53.

Hoefle, Scott William. 1985. Harnessing the Interior Vote: The Impact of Economic Change, Unbalanced Development and Authoritarianism on the Local Politics of Northeast Brazil. Institute of Latin American Studies Research Papers. 14 1–43.

Hoff, Karla, and Stiglitz, Joseph E. 1990. Introduction: Imperfect Information and Rural Credit Markets: Puzzles and Policy Perspectives. *The World Bank Economic Review*, 4(3), 235–250.

Holston, James. 2008. *Insurgent Citizenship: Disjunctions of Democracy and Modernity in Brazil*. Princeton University Press.

Huckfeldt, Robert. 1979. "Political Participation and the Neighborhood Social Context." *American Journal of Political Science* 23(3): 579–592.

Huckfeldt, Robert and John Sprague. 1992. "Political Parties and Electoral Mobilization: Political Structure, Social Structure, and the Party Canvass." *American Political Science Review*, 86(1), 70–86.

Huckfeldt, Robert and John Sprague. 1995. *Citizens, Politics and Social Communication: Information and Influence in an Election Campaign*. New York: Cambridge University Press.

Hunter, Wendy. 2010. *The Transformation of the Workers' Party in Brazil, 1989–2009*. Cambridge: Cambridge University Press.

Hunter, Wendy, and Power, Timothy. 2005. Lula's Brazil at Midterm. *Journal of Democracy*, 16(3), 127–139.

Hyde, Susan D. 2011. Catch Us If You Can: Election Monitoring and International Norm Diffusion. *American Journal of Political Science*, 55(2), 356–369.
Ichino, Naomi, and Schündeln, Matthias. 2012. Deterring or Displacing Electoral Irregularities? Spillover Effects of Observers in a Randomized Field Experiment in Ghana. *Journal of Politics*, 74(1), 292–307.
Instituto Agropolos de Ceará. 2012. *O Caminho das Águas nas Rotas dos Carros-Pipa*. Tech. rept.
Instituto Brasileiro de Geografia e Estatística (IBGE). 1977. *Anuário Estatístico do Brasil – 1977*. Rio de Janeiro: IBGE.
Institutio Brasileiro de Geografia e Estatística (IBGE). 2010. *Censo Demográfico 2010*.
Instituto Brasileiro de Geografia e Estatística (IBGE). 2011. *Reflexões sobre os Deslocamentos Populacionais no Brasil*. Rio de Janeiro: IBGE.
Instituto Brasileiro de Geografia e Estatística (IBGE). 2012a. *Censo Demográfico 2010. Famílias e Domicílios. Resultados da Amostra*. Rio de Janeiro: IBGE.
Instituto Brasileiro de Geografia e Estatística (IBGE). 2012b. *Perfil dos Municípios Brasileiros: 2012*. Rio de Janeiro: IBGE.
Institute for Democracy and Electoral Assistance (IDEA). 2012. Data available at www.idea.int.
Instituto de Pesquisa Econômica Aplicada (IPEA). 2009. *Vinte Anos da Constituição Federal, Políticas Sociais: Acompanhamento e Análise, Volumes 1 and 2*. Brasília: IPEA.
Instituto de Pesquisa Econômica Aplicada (IPEA). 2010a. *Perspectivas da Política Social no Brasil*. IPEA, Série Eixos Estratégicos do Desenvolvimento Brasileiro; Livro 8. Brasília: IPEA.
Instituto de Pesquisa Econômica Aplicada (IPEA). 2010b. *Presença do Estado no Brasil: Federação, sua Unidades e Municipalidades*. Brasília: IPEA.
Instituto de Pesquisa Econômica Aplicada (IPEA). 2013a. *Duas Décadas de Desigualdade e Pobreza no Brasil*. Comunicado No. 159.
Instituto de Pesquisa Econômica Aplicada (IPEA). 2013b. *Programa Bolsa Família: Uma Década de Inclusão e Cidadania*. Brasília: IPEA.
Instituto de Pesquisa Econômica Aplicada (IPEA). 2015. *Políticas Sociais: Acompanhamento e Análise*. Vol. 23, Brasília: IPEA.
International Labour Office (ILO). 2013. *Brazil Unemployment Insurance*. ILO Notes on the Crisis. Geneva: ILO.
International Labour Office (ILO). 2015. *World Employment Social Outlook: The Changing Nature of Jobs*. Geneva: ILO Research Department.
International Republican Institute (IRI). 2000. *Mexico: Election Observation Mission Report*. International Republican Institute.
Jensen, Peter Sandholt, and Justesen, Mogens K. 2014. Poverty and Vote Buying: Survey-Based Evidence from Africa. *Electoral Studies*, 33, 220–232.
Jensenius, Francesca Refsum. 2013. *Power, Performance and Bias: Evaluating the Electoral Quotas for Scheduled Castes in India*. PhD thesis, University of California, Berkeley.
Justiça Eleitoral. 2007. *Instruções Para Preenchimento e Utilização do FASE*.
Keck, Margareth E. 1992. *The Workers' Party and Democratization in Brazil*. New Haven: Yale University Press.
Keefer, Philip. 2007. Clientelism, Credibility, and the Policy Choices of Young Democracies. *American Journal of Political Science*, 51(4), 804–821.

Keefer, Philip, and Vlaicu, Razvan. 2008. Democracy, Credibility, and Clientelism. *Journal of Law, Economics, and Organization*, 24(2), 371–406.

Kitschelt, Herbert. 2000. Linkages Between Citizens and Politicians in Democratic Polities. *Comparative Political Studies*, 33, 845–879.

Kitschelt, Herbert. 2011. *Clientelistic Linkage Strategies: A Descriptive Exploration*. Paper Prepared for the Workshop on Democratic Accountability Strategies, Duke University.

Kitschelt, Herbert. 2013. *Democratic Accountability and Linkages Project*. Durham, NC: Duke University.

Kitschelt, Herbert, and Wilkinson, Steven. 2007. *Patrons, Clients, and Policies: Patterns of Democratic Accountability and Political Competition*. Cambridge, MA: Cambridge University Press.

Knaul, Felicia Marie, González-Pier, Eduardo, Gómez-Dantés, Octavio, García-Junco, David, Arreola-Ornelas, Héctor, Bazarra-Lloréns, Mariana, Sandoval, Rosa, Caballero, Francisco, Hernandéz-Avila, Mauricio, Juan, Mercedes, Kershenobich, David, Nigenda, Gustavo, Ruelas, Enrique, Sepúlveda, Jaime, Tapia, Roberto, Soberón, Guillermo, Chertorivski, Salomón, and Frenk, Julio. 2012. The Quest for Universal Health Coverage: Achieving Social Protection for all in Mexico. *Health Policy*, 380(9849), 1259–1279.

Kuo, Joanna Dee. 2013. *Patron States: The Decline of Clientelism in the United States and Britain*. PhD thesis, Harvard University.

Lamounier, Bolivar, and Duarte, Celina Rabello. 1980. *Voto de Desconfiança: Eleições e Mudança Política no Brasil, 1970–1979*. Rio de Janeiro: Editora Vozes.

Landini, Fernando. 2012. Prácticas Clientelares y Control Político en la Experiencia Campesina de Argentina. *Perfiles Latinoamericanos*, 40, 205–226.

Landini, Fernando. 2013. Asistencialismo y Búsqueda de Ayudas como Estrategia de Supervivencia en Contextos Campesinos Clientelares. *Polis*, 12(34), 185–202.

Larreguy, Horacio A., Marshall, John, and Querubín, Pablo. 2016. When Do Parties Buy Turnout? How Monitoring Capacity Facilities Voter Mobilization in Mexico. *American Political Science Review* 110 (1), (February), 160–179.

Latin American Public Opinion Project (LAPOP). 2007–2014. The AmericasBarometer. Data available at www.LapopSurveys.org.

Lawson, Chappell, and Greene, Kenneth. 2014. Making Clientelism Work: How Norms of Reciprocity Increase Voter Compliance. *Comparative Politics*, 47(1), 61–85.

Levi-Moreira, Silvia. 1984. A Luta pelo Voto Secreto no Programa da Liga Nacionalista de São Paulo (1916–1924). *Revista Brasileira de História*, 72–80.

Levitsky, Steven. 2003a. From Labor Politics to Machine Politics: The Transformation of Party-Union Linkages in Argentine Peronism, 1983–1999. *Latin America Research Review*, 38(3), 3–36.

Levitsky, Steven. 2003b. *Transforming Labor-Based Parties in Latin America: Argentine Peronism in Comparative Perspective*. Cambridge University Press.

Ligon, Ethan, and Schechter, Laura. 2003. Measuring Vulnerability. *The Economic Journal*, 113(486), C95–C102.

Limongi, Fernando, Juliana Oliveira, Stefanie Schmitt, and Fernanda Machado. 2018. "Democratization via Mobilization: The Birth of the Brazilian 3rd Republic." Working paper.

Lindberg, Staffan I. 2010. What Accountability Pressures do MPs in Africa Face and How Do They Respond? Evidence from Ghana. *The Journal of Modern African Studies*, 48(1), 117–142.

Lloyd, Ryan Samuel. 2012. The Decline of Traditional Clientelist Parties: The Case of the Partido da Frente Liberal in Brazil. Thesis, University of Texas Austin.

Lucas, Kevin, and Samuels, David. 2010. The Ideological "Coherence" of the Brazilian Party System, 1990–2009. *Journal of Politics in Latin America*, 2(3), 39–69.

Lustig, Nora, Lopez-Calva, Luis F., and Ortiz-Juarez, Eduardo. 2013. Declining Inequality in Latin America in the 2000s: The Cases of Argentina, Brazil, and Mexico. *World Development*, 44, 129–141.

Lyne, Mona M. 2008. *The Voter's Dilemma and Democratic Accountability: Latin America and Beyond*. University Park: Penn State University Press.

Maddison, Angus. 2001. *The World Economy: A Millennial Perspective*. Organisation for Economic Co-Operation and Development.

Magaloni, Beatriz. 2006. *Voting for Autocracy: Hegemonic Party Survival and Its Demise in Mexico*. New York: Cambridge University Press.

Magaloni, Beatriz. 2010. The Game of Electoral Fraud and the Ousting of Authoritarian Rule. *American Journal of Political Science*, 54(3), 751–765.

Magaloni, Beatriz, Diaz-Cayeros, Alberto, and Estévez, Federico. 2007. Clientelism and Portfolio Diversification: A Model of Electoral Investment with Applications to Mexico. In: *Patrons, Clients, and Policies: Patterns of Democratic Accountability and Political Competition*, 182–205. New York: Cambridge University Press.

Mainwaring, Scott. 1986. *The Catholic Church and Politics in Brazil, 1916–1985*. Stanford, CA: Stanford University Press.

Mainwaring, Scott. 1991. Politicians, Parties, and Electoral Systems: Brazil in Comparative Perspective. *Comparative Politics* 24(1) (October), 21–43.

Mainwaring, Scott. 1999. *Rethinking Party Systems in the Third Wave of Democratization: The Case of Brazil*. Stanford: Stanford University Press.

Mainwaring, Scott, Meneguello, Rachel, and Power, Timothy. 1999. *Conservative Parties, Democracy, and Economic Reform in Contemporary Brazil*. Working Paper No. 264. University of Notre Dame, Helen Kellogg Institute for International Studies.

Marchetti, Vitor. 2008. Governança Eleitoral: O Modelo Brasileiro de Justiça Eleitoral. *Dados*, 51(4), 865–893.

Mares, Isabela, and Carnes, Matthew E. 2009. Social Policy in Developing Countries. *Annual Review of Political Science*, 12, 93–113.

Mares, Isabela, and Young, Lauren. 2016. Buying, Expropriating, and Stealing Votes. *Annual Review of Political Science*, 19, 267–288.

Mares, Isabela and Lauren E. Young. 2018. The Core Voter's Curse: Clientelistic Threats and Promises in Hungarian Elections. *Comparative Political Studies*, OnlineFirst.

Matijascic, Milko. 2015. *Política Social Brasileira: Conquistas e Desafios*. IPEA, Texto para Discussão, 2062.

Matijascic, Milko, and Kay, Stephen J. 2008. Pensions in Brazil: Reaching the Limits of Parametric Reform in Latin America. In: Kay, Stephen J., and Sinha, Tapen (eds), *Lessons from Pension Reform in the Americas*. Oxford: Oxford University Press.

Matos, Júlia Silveira and Elisabete Zimmer Ferreira. 2015. Telenovela: Um Elemento do Cotidiano como Fonte de Aprendizagem Histórica. *OPSIS*, 15(1), 117–135.

Medeiros, Marcelo, and de Souza, Pedro H. G. F. 2013. *Previdências dos Trabalhadores dos Setores Público e Privado e Desigualdade no Brasil*. IPEA, Texto para Discussão, 1876.
Mercuri, Rebecca. 2002. A Better Ballot Box? *Spectrum, IEEE*, 39(10), 46–50.
Merton, Robert K. 1968. *Social Theory and Social Structure*. New York: The Free Press.
Mesquita, Mario. 2010. Brasil 1961–1964: Inflação, Estagnação e Ruptura. *Department of Economics PUC-Rio (Brazil)*.
Michelitch, Kristin Grace. 2011. "Electoral Competition and Fluctuations in Partisan and Ethnic Discrimination: Theory and Evidence from Ghana." Working paper.
Michelitch, Kristin Grace. 2013. *Electoral Competition and Interpartisan Economic Discrimination*. PhD thesis, New York University.
Miguel, Edward, Satyanath, Shanker, and Sergenti, Ernest. 2004. Economic Shocks and Civil Conflict: An Instrumental Variables Approach. *Journal of Political Economy*, 112(4), 725–753.
Miller, F., H. Osbahr, E. Boyd, F. Thomalla, S. Bharwani, G. Ziervogel, B. Walker, J. Birkmann, S. Van der Leeuw, J. Rockström, J. Hinkel, T. Downing, C. Folke, and D. Nelson. 2010. Resilience and Vulnerability: Complementary or Conflicting Concepts? *Ecology and Society* 15(3): 11.
Ministério do Trabalho e Emprego MTE. 2015. *Histórico do Seguro-Desemprego Trabalhor Formal*. Departamento de Emprego e Salário, Coordenação Geral do Seguro-Desemprego e Abono Salarial, Brasilia.
Montero, Alfred P. 2012. A Reversal of Political Fortune: The Transitional Dynamics of Conservative Rule in the Brazilian Northeast. *Latin American Politics and Society*, 54(1), 1–36.
Moraes, Joysi. 2015. Clientelistic Organizational Practices in Northeast Brazil. *Revista de Administração FACES Journal*, 14(3).
Moreira, Marcelo Rasga, and Escorel, Sarah. 2009. Conselhos Municipais de Saúde do Brasil: Um Debate Sobre a Democratização da Política de Saúde nos Vinte Anos do SUS. *Ciência e Saúde Coletiva*, 14(3), 795–806.
Morgan, John, and Várdy, Felix. 2012. Negative Vote Buying and the Secret Ballot. *Journal of Law, Economics, and Organization*, 28(4), 818–849.
Movimento de Combate à Corrupção Eleitoral (MCCE). 2009. "Pesquisa Prefeitos e Vereadores Cassados por Corrupção Eleitoral (2000 a 2009)." Dataset collected on March 10–20, 2009 in collaboration with Corregedoria Geral, Tribunal Superior Eleitoral (TSE).
Movimento de Combate à Corrupção Eleitoral (MCCE). 2007. "Políticos Cassados por Corrupção Eleitoral." Tech. rept.
Movimento do Ministério Público Democrático (MPPD). 2006. *MPD Dialógico*, 3(9).
Nelson, Donald R., and Finan, Timothy J. 2009. Praying for Drought: Persistent Vulnerability and the Politics of Patronage in Ceará, Northeast Brazil. *American Anthropologist*, 111(3), 302–316.
Neri, Marcelo Côrtes. 2010. *The New Middle Class: The Bright Side of the Poor*. Rio de Janeiro: Fundação Getulio Vargas / Centro de Políticas Sociais.
Neri, Marcelo Côrtes. 2014. *Brazil New Middle Classes: The Bright Side of the Poor*. BRICs 6th Academic Forum, Palácio da Cidade, March 18–19.
Nichter, Simeon. 2008. Vote Buying or Turnout Buying? Machine Politics and the Secret Ballot. *American Political Science Review*, 102(1), 19–31.

Nichter, Simeon. 2010. *Politics and Poverty: Electoral Clientelism in Latin America*. PhD thesis, Department of Political Science, University of California, Berkeley.

Nichter, Simeon. 2014a. Political Clientelism and Social Policy in Brazil. In: Brun, Diego Abente, and Diamond, Larry J. (eds), *Political Clientelism, Social Policy, and the Quality of Democracy: Evidence from Latin America, Lessons from Other Regions*. Johns Hopkins University Press.

Nichter, Simeon. 2014b. Conceptualizing Vote Buying. *Electoral Studies* 35: 315–327.

Nichter, Simeon, and Nunnari, Salvatore. 2017. Declared Support: Citizen Strategies of Clientelism. Unpublished typescript.

Nichter, Simeon, and Palmer-Rubin, Brian. 2015. Clientelism, Declared Support and Mexico's 2012 Campaign. In: Domínguez, Jorge I., Greene, Kenneth G., Lawson, Chappell, and Moreno, Alejandro (eds), *Mexico's Evolving Democracy: A Comparative Study of the 2012 Elections*. Baltimore: Johns Hopkins University Press.

Nichter, Simeon, and Peress, Michael. 2016. Request Fulfilling: When Citizens Demand Clientelist Benefits. *Comparative Political Studies*, 50(8), pp. 1086–1117.

Nicolau, Jairo. 2002a. *História do Voto no Brasil*. Rio de Janeiro: Jorge Zahar.

Nicolau, Jairo. 2002b. *A Participação Eleitoral no Brasil*. Centre for Brazilian Studies, University of Oxford.

Nigenda, Gustavo, Wirtz, Veronika J., González-Robledo, Luz María, and Reich, Michael R. 2015. Evaluating the Implementation of Mexico's Health Reform: The Case of Seguro Popular. *Health Systems and Reform*, 1(3), 217–228.

Novaes, Lucas. 2017. Disloyal Brokers and Weak Parties. *American Journal of Political Science*, 62(1), 84–68.

Nunes, Edson. 1997. *A Gramática Política do Brasil*. Rio de Janeiro: Jorge Zahar.

Nunes Leal, Victor. 1949. *Coronelismo, Enxada e Voto: O Município e o Regime Representativo no Brasil*. Rio de Janeiro: Revista Forense.

OECD. 2015. Urban Policy Reviews: Mexico 2015: Transforming Urban Policy and Housing Finance. OECD Publishing.

OECD, IDB, and World Bank Group. 2014. Pensions at a Glance: Latin America and the Caribbean. Paris: OECD Publishing.

Olaberría, Eduardo, and Dugain, Valéry. 2015. Sharing the Fruits of Growth with all Mexicans. OECD Economics Department Working Papers, No. 1197, OECD Publishing.

Partido Democratico (PD). 1927. *O Voto Secreto: Collectanea de Opiniões, Discursos e Documentos Sobre O Assumpto*. São Paulo: Livraria Liberdade.

Pasotti, Eleonora. 2010. *Political Branding in Cities: The Decline of Machine Politics in Bogotá, Naples, and Chicago*. Cambridge, MA: Cambridge University Press.

Paxson, Christina H. 1992. Using Water Variability to Estimate the Response of Savings to Transitory Income in Thailand. *The American Economic Review*, 82(1), 15–33.

Pesquisa Mensal de Emprego (PME). 1996. Rio de Janeiro: Instituto Brasileiro de Geografia e Estatística.

Pesquisa Nacional por Amostra de Domicílios (PNAD). 1988. Rio de Janeiro: Instituto Brasileiro de Geografia e Estatística.

Peterson, Christopher. 1998. Medical Slang in Rio de Janeiro, Brazil. *Cadernos de Saúde Pública*, 14(4), 671–699.

Piattoni, Simona. 2001. *Clientelism, Interests, and Democratic Representation: The European Experience in Historical and Comparative Perspective*. Cambridge, MA: Cambridge University Press.

Pope, Clara Amanda. 1985. Human Rights and the Catholic Church in Brazil, 1970–1983: The Pontifical Justice and Peace Commission of the São Paulo Archdiocese. *Journal of Church and State*, 27(3), 429–452.
Powell, John Duncan. 1970. Peasant Society and Clientelist Politics. *American Political Science Review*, 64(2), 411–425.
Power, Timothy J. 2009. Compulsory for Whom? Mandatory Voting and Electoral Participation in Brazil, 1986–2006. *Journal of Politics in Latin America*, 1(1), 97–122.
Power, Timothy. 2010. *The Political Right in Postauthoritarian Brazil*. University Park, PA: Pennsylvania State University Press.
Power, Timothy J, and Zucco Cesar, Jr. 2009. Estimating Ideology of Brazilian Legislative parties, 1990–2005: A Research Communication. *Latin American Research Review*, 44(1), 218–246.
Przeworski, Adam. 2015. "Suffrage and Voting Secrecy in General Elections." *In Secrecy and Publicity in Votes and Debates*. Edited by Jon Elster. New York: Cambridge University Press.
Queiroz, Maria Isaura Pereira de. 1976. *O Mandonismo Local na Vida Política Brasileira e Outros Ensaios*. São Paulo: Editora Alfa-Omega.
Rajal, Veronica B., Cruz, Cindy, and Last, Jerold A. 2010. Water Quality Issues and Infant Diarrhoea in a South American Province. *Global Public Health*, 5(4), 348–363.
Ravallion, Martin. 2010. The Developing World's Bulging (but Vulnerable) "Middle Class." *World Development*, 38(4), 445–454.
Ravanilla, Nico, Dotan Haim and Allen Hicken. 2017. "Brokers, Social Networks, Reciprocity, and Clientelism." Paper presented at Annual Meeting of the American Political Science Association, San Francisco, CA.
Reis, Márlon Jacinto. 2006. *Uso Eleitoral da Máquina Administrativa e Captação Ilícita de Sufrágio*. Rio de Janeiro: FGV Editora.
Robinson, James A, and Verdier, Thierry. 2013. The Political Economy of Clientelism. *The Scandinavian Journal of Economics*, 115(2), 260–291.
Roniger, Luis. 1987. Caciquismo and Coronelismo: Contextual Dimensions of Patron Brokerage in México and Brazil. *Latin American Research Review*, 22(2), 71–99.
Rosas, Guillermo. 2010. Trust in Elections and the Institutional Design of Electoral Authorities: Evidence from Latin America. *Electoral Studies*, 29(1), 74–90.
Rosas, Guillermo, and Hawkins, Kirk. 2008. *Turncoats, True Believers, and Turnout: Machine Politics in the Absence of Vote Monitoring*. Manuscript.
Rueda, Miguel R. 2016. Small Aggregates, Big Manipulation: Vote Buying Enforcement and Collective Monitoring. *American Journal of Political Science*.
Rusk, Jerold G. 1974. Comment: The American Electoral Universe: Speculation and Evidence. *American Political Science Review*, 68(3), 1028–1049.
Sampaio, Consuelo Novais. 1979. *Crisis in the Brazilian-Oligarchic System: A Case Study on Bahia, 1889–1937*. Doctoral Dissertation, The Johns Hopkins University.
Sampaio, João. 1922. "Campanha do Voto Secreto: Conferencia do Dr. João Sampaio no Theatro Boa Vista, em 11 de Junho de 1922." São Paulo: Liga Nacionalista.
Samuels, David J., and Zucco, Cesar. 2013. *Using Facebook as a Subject Recruitment Tool for Survey-Experimental Research*. Available at SSRN: https://ssrn.com/abstract=2101458.
Schaffer, Frederic Charles. 2002. "What is Vote Buying? Empirical Evidence." Typescript, Massachusetts Institute of Technology.
Schaffer, Frederic Charles. 2008. *The Hidden Costs of Clean Electoral Reform*. Ithaca: Cornell University Press.

Schaffer, Frederic Charles, and Schedler, Andreas. 2007. What Is Vote Buying? In: Schaffer, Frederic Charles (ed), *Elections for Sale: The Causes and Consequences of Vote Buying*, 17–30. Lynne Reinner Publishers.

Schedler, Andreas. 2002. My Vote? Not for Sale. How Mexicans Citizens View Electoral Clientelism. Comparative Politics of Vote Buying Conference, Massachusetts Institute for Technology, Cambridge, Massachusetts.

Schedler, Andreas. 2004. "El Voto es Nuestro"; Cómo los Ciudadanos Mexicanos Perciben el Clientelismo Electoral. *Revista Mexicana de Sociología*, 66(1), 57–97.

Scott, James C. 1969. Corruption, Machine Politics, and Political Change. *American Political Science Review*, 63(4), 1142–1158.

Scott, James C. 1972. Patron-Client Politics and Political Change in Southeast Asia. *American Political Science Review*, 66(1), 91–113.

Shefter, Martin. 1977. *Patronage and Its Opponents: A Theory and Some European Cases*. Cornell: Cornell University Press.

Silverman, Sydel F. 1965. Patronage and Community-Nation Relationships in Central Italy. *Ethnology*, 4(2), 172–189.

Simpser, Alberto. 2012. *Could the PRI Have Bought Its Electoral Result in the 2012 Mexican Election? Probably Not*. The Monkey Cage (blog), July 10.

Sistema de Indicadores de Percepção Social (SIPS). 2011a. *Sistema de Indicadores de Percepção Social: Justiça*. Instituto de Pesquisa Econômica Aplicada in Brasília.

Sistema de Indicadores de Percepção Social (SIPS). 2011b. *Sistema de Indicadores de Percepção Social: Primeira Edição*. Brasília: Organizador: Fábio Schiavinatto. Instituto de Pesquisa Econômica Aplicada.

Sistema de Indicadores de Percepção Social (SIPS). 2011c. *Sistema de Indicadores de Percepção Social: Saúde*. Instituto de Pesquisa Econômica Aplicada in Brasília.

Sistema de Indicadores de Percepção Social (SIPS). 2011d. "Sistema de Indicadores de Percepção Social: Trabalho e Renda." Brasília: Instituto de Pesquisa Econômica Aplicada.

Sistema Nacional de Informações sobre Saneamento (SNIS). 2014. *Diagnóstico dos Serviços de Água e Esgotos – 2013*. Brasília: Secretaria Nacional de Saneamento Ambiental / Ministro de Estado das Cidades.

Soares, Fábio Veras, Ribas, Rafael Perez, and Osório, Rafael Guerreiro. 2010a. Evaluating the Impact of Brazil's Bolsa Familia: Cash Transfer Programs in Comparative Perspective. *Latin American Research Review*, 45(2), 173–190.

Soares, Sergei, de Souza, Pedro Herculano G. Ferreira, Osósio, Rafael Guerreiro, and Silveira, Fernando Gaiger. 2010b. Os Impactos do Benefício do Programa Bolsa Família sobre Desigualdade e a Pobreza. Pages 25–52 of: *Bolsa Família 2003–2010: Avanços e Desafios*, vol. 2. Brasília: IPEA.

Soares, Sergei, Ribas, Rafael Perez, and Soares, Fábio Veras. 2010c. Targeting and Coverage of the Bolsa Família Programme: Why Knowing what You Measure is Important in Choosing the Numbers. Working Paper, Number 71. Brasília: International Policy Centre for Inclusive Growth.

Sousa, Francisca Meire Silva. 2014. "Inobservância do Concurso para Aceso ao Serviço Público: O Caso do Município de São Domingos do Maranhão." *Revista e-Gaia Conhecimento Jurídico*, 1.1.

Speck, Bruno Wilhelm. 2003. A Compra de Votos: Uma Aproximação Empírica. *Opinião Pública*, 9(1), 148–169.

Spence, Michael. 1973. Job Market Signaling. *The Quarterly Journal of Economics*, 87(3), 355–374.

Stiglitz, Joseph E. 1975. The Theory of "Screening," Education, and the Distribution of Income. *The American Economic Review*, 65(3), 283–300.
Stiglitz, Joseph E., and Weiss, Andrew. 1983. Incentive Effects of Terminations: Applications to the Credit and Labor Markets. *The American Economic Review*, 73(5), 912–927.
Stokes, Susan, Dunning, Thad, Nazareno, Marcelo, and Brusco, Valeria. 2013. *Brokers, Voters and Clientelism*. New York: Cambridge University Press.
Stokes, Susan C. 2005. Perverse Accountability: A Formal Model of Machine Politics with Evidence from Argentina. *American Political Science Review*, 99(3), 315–325.
Sugiyama, Natasha Borges, and Hunter, Wendy. 2013. Whither Clientelism? Good Governance and Brazil's Bolsa Família Program. *Comparative Politics*, 46(1), 43–62.
Szwarcberg, Mariela. 2014. Political Parties and Rallies in Latin America. *Party Politics*, 20(3), 456–466.
Szwarcberg, Mariela. 2015. *Mobilizing Poor Voters: Machine Politics, Clientelism, and Social Networks in Argentina*. Cambridge: Cambridge University Press.
Tavares, André Ramos, and Moreira, Diogo Rais Rodrigues. 2011. O Voto Eletrônico no Brasil. *Estudos Eleitorais*, 6(3), 9–32.
Tejera, Héctor. 2000. Cultura de la Política, Campañas Electorales e Demandas Ciudadanas en la Cuidad de México. *Perfiles Latinoamericanos*, 53–75.
Tesliuc, Emil D. and Kathy Lindert. 2002. "Vulnerability: A Quantitative and Qualitative Assessment." Guatemala Poverty Assessment Program, Washington, DC: World Bank.
Thorp, Rosemary. 1998. *Progress, Poverty and Exclusion: An Economic History of Latin America in the 20th Century*. Washington, DC: Inter-American Development Bank.
Townsend, Kaya, and Eyles, John. 2004. Capacity and Transparency of Potable Water Regulation in Tijuana, Mexico: Challenges for Ensuring Water Quality at Community Level. *Health Promotion International*, 19(1), 77–83.
Tozzi, Leonel. 2008. *Ações, Impugnações e Procedimentos Recursais no Direito Eleitoral*. Porto Alegre: Editora Verbo Jurídico.
Trejo, Guillermo, and Neto, Fernando Bizzarro. 2014. *Religious Competition and the Rise of the Workers' Party in Brazil*. EDGS Working Paper. Paper prepared for presentation at the Comparative Politics Workshop, Northwestern University, May 27, 2014.
Tribunal de Contas da União (TCU). 2011. Document Number AC-1459-21/11-P. Processo 011.290/2010-2.
Tribunal de Contas da União (TCU). 2014a. *Relatório de Levantamento FiscSaúde*. TC 032.624/2013-1.
Tribunal de Contas da União (TCU). 2014b. *Secretaria de Controle Externo da Educação, da Cultura e do Desporto. Relatório de Auditoria Operacional Coordenada no Ensino Médio*. TC 007.081/2013-8.
Tribunal de Contas do Estado de Mato Grosso (TCE-MT). 2013 (Dezembro). *Cartilha de Orientação para Contratação por Tempo Determinado para Atender a Necessidade Temporária de Excepcional Interesse Público*. Comissão Permanente de Uniformização de Jurisprudência.
Tribunal Regional Eleitoral da Bahia (TRE-BA). 2012. *80 Anos Elegendo o Futuro*.
Tribunal Superior Eleitoral. 2013. *Eleições no Brasil: Uma História de 500 Anos*. Brasilia: Tribunal Superior Eleitoral.
United Nations (UN). 2015. *The Millennium Development Goals Report*.

United Nations World Water Assessment Programme. 2016. *The United Nations World Water Development Report 2015: Water for a Sustainable World*. Paris, UNESCO.

Vakis, Renos, Rigoli, Jamele, and Lucchetti, Leonardo. 2015. *Left Behind: Chronic Poverty in Latin America and Caribbean*. World Bank.

Verba, Sidney, Norman H. Nie, and Jae-On Kim. 1978. *Participation and Political Equality: A Seven-Nation Study*. Chicago, IL: University of Chicago Press.

Vicente, Pedro C. 2014. Is Vote Buying Effective? Evidence from a Field Experiment in West Africa. *The Economic Journal*, 124(574), F356–F387.

Vilaça, Marcos Vinicios and Albuquerque, Roberto Cavalcanti. 1965. *Coronel, Coronéis*. Rio de Janeiro: Tempo Brasileiro.

Wagstaff, Adam, Dmytraczenko, Tania, Almeida, Gisele, Buisman, Leander, Eozenou, Patrick Hoang-Vu, Bredenkamp, Caryn, Cercone, James A., Diaz, Yadira, Maceira, Daniel, Molina, Silvia, Paraje, Guillhermo, Ruiz, Fernando, Sarti, Flavia, Scott, John, Valdivia, Martin, and Werneck, Heitor. 2015. Assessing Latin America's Progress Toward Achieving Universal Health Coverage. *Health Affairs*, 34(10), 1704–1712.

Wantchekon, Leonard. 2003. Clientelism and Voting Behavior: Evidence from a Field Experiment in Benin. *World Politics*, 55(3), 399–422.

Weigelt, Keith, and Camerer, Colin. 1988. Reputation and Corporate Strategy: A Review of Recent Theor. *Strategic Management Journal*, 9(5), 443–454.

Weitz-Shapiro, Rebecca. 2012. What Wins Votes: Why Some Politicians Opt Out of Clientelism. *American Journal of Political Science*, 56(3), 568–583.

Weitz-Shapiro, Rebecca. 2014. *Curbing Clientelism in Argentina: Politics, Poverty, and Social Policy*. New York: Cambridge University Press.

Weyland, Kurt Gerhard. 1996. *Democracy Without Equity: Failures of Reform in Brazil*. Pittsburgh: University of Pittsburgh Press.

Woodward, James P. 2009. *A Place in Politics: São Paulo, Brazil, from Seigneurial Republicanism to Regionalist Revolt*. Durham, North Carolina: Duke University Press.

World Bank. 2015. *The State of Social Safety Nets 2015*. Washington, D.C.: World Bank Group.

World Development Indicators. 2017. Washington, DC: World Bank.

World Health Organization (WHO). 2015. Health in 2015: From Millennium Development Goals to Sustainable Development Goals. Geneva: WHO Publicationsma.

World Meteorological Organization. 2014. *WMO Statement on the Status of the Global Climate in 2013*. WMO-No. 1130.

World Meteorological Organization. 2015. *WMO Statement on the Status of the Global Climate in 2014*. WMO-No. 1152.

Yeung, Luciana, and Azevedo, Paulo. 2011. Measuring Efficiency of Brazilian Courts with Data Envelopment Analysis (DEA). *IMA Journal of Management Mathematics*, 22(4), 1–14.

Zarazaga, Rodrigo. 2014. Brokers beyond Clientelism: A New Perspective on Brokerage through the Argentine Case. *Latin American Politics and Society*, 56(3), 23–45.

Zucco, Cesar, Jr. 2008. The President's 'New' Constituency: Lula and the Pragmatic Vote in Brazil's 2006 Presidential Elections. *Journal of Latin American Studies*, 40(1), 29–49.

Author Index

Abers, Rebecca, 59
Aidt, Toke, 8
Almeida, Gisele, 192
Alvarez, R. Michael, 190
Ames, Barry, 17, 19, 28, 39, 95, 211
Amitrano, Claudio Roberto, 87
Anderson, Siwan, 212
Andrade, Maria Antonia Alonso de, 16, 17
Aparicio, Ricardo, 187
Archer, Ronald, 6
Asante, Kojo, 200
Auyero, Javier, 8, 189, 191–194, 197

Baker, Andy, 58
Banfield, Edward, 7, 15, 208
Barrientos, Armando, 91, 99
Barros, Ricardo, 86, 88
Beccaria, Luis, 190, 191
Berenschot, Ward, 200
Berinsky, Adam, 132, 231, 234
Bernal, Cleide, 21
Birdsall, Nancy, 99, 111, 182, 192
Blair, Graeme, 161, 185
Blaydes, Lisa, 213
Boas, Taylor, 230
Bobonis, Gustavo, 20, 22, 95, 96, 116, 125, 128, 136, 140, 142, 144, 155, 159, 163, 172, 175, 209, 217, 220–222, 242–264
Bonilla-Chacin, M., 183
Borges, Andre, 20, 92
Boto, Carlota, 35
Bratton, Michael, 8
Brobbey, Victor, 200

Brunazo Filho, Amilcar, 37
Brusco, Valeria, 2–4, 8, 14, 19, 30, 50, 93, 190–193, 197, 202, 211, 213, 215
Bursztyn, Marcel, 21
Bussell, Jennifer, 200

Calheiros, Lelio Bringel, 110
Calvo, Ernesto, 189
Camerer, Colin, 80, 81
Cammack, Paul, 16
Cammett, Melani, 7, 202
Campello, Tereza, 91, 99
Campos, Andre Gambier, 105
Carey, John, 4
Carnes, Matthew, 7, 73
Cepaluni, Gabriel, 44, 46
Chacon, Suely Salgueiro, 21
Chambers-Ju, Christopher, 4
Chandra, Kanchan, 40
Chubb, Judith, 7, 16, 73
Cleary, Matthew, 190
Coelho, Jorge, 108
Collier, David, 16
Collier, Ruth Berins, 16
Cord, Louise, 86, 189
Cornelius, Wayne, 6, 29, 180, 182
Corstange, Daniel, 146, 147, 203
Cox, Gary, 4, 8, 29, 36
Cureau, Sandra, 62

da Costa, Adriano Soares, 62
Davalle, Regina, 34
de Alba, Felipe, 183

Author Index

de Figueiredo, Miguel, 45
de Jonge, Chad Kiewiet, 2, 8, 160
de la Fuente, Alejandro, 182, 183
de la O, Ana, 181
de Souza, Pedro, 89, 92, 99
Dedecca, Claudio Salvadori, 106
del Pozo, Blanca Elena, 187
Desposato, Scott, 3, 93, 212
Diaz-Cayeros, Alberto, 7, 14, 30, 131, 180–183, 208, 216
Diniz, Eli, 16
Dixit, Avinash, 3, 92, 208
Dmytraczenko, Tania, 192
Doherty, David, 38
Dowling, Conor, 38
Duarte, Celina Rabello, 43
Dugain, Valery, 182, 183
Dunning, Thad, 2–4, 8, 14, 19, 29, 30, 50, 93, 190–193, 202, 211, 213, 215

Eaton, Kent, 4
Eisenstadt, Todd, 181
Esping-Andersen, Gøsta, 7
Estevez, Frederico, 7, 14, 30, 131, 180–183, 208, 216

Faughnan, Brian, 2
Fenno, Richard, 10
Ferreira, Francisco, 85–87, 99
Filmer, Deon, 229, 230
Finan, Frederico, 11, 39, 108
Fiszbein, Ariel, 91
Fleischer, David, 40, 72
Fox, Jonathan, 181
Francois, Patrick, 212
Frey, Anderson, 91
Fukumoto, Kentaro, 50
Fukuyama, Francis, 86, 87

Gans-Morse, Jordan, 4, 8, 21, 30–32, 41, 208, 236
Gastaldi, Helio, 39
Gay, Robert, 6, 215
Gerard, Francois, 104, 105
Gerber, Alan, 38
Gertler, Paul, 20, 22, 95, 96, 116, 125, 128, 136, 140, 142, 144, 152, 155, 159, 163, 172, 175, 209, 217, 220–222, 242–264
Gingerich, Daniel, 36, 212
Golden, Miriam, 9
Gonzaga, Gustavo, 104, 105

Gonzalez-Navarro, Marco, 20, 22, 95, 96, 116, 125, 128, 136, 140, 142, 155, 159, 163, 172, 175, 209, 217, 220–222, 242–264
Gonzalez-Ocantos, Ezequiel, 2, 8, 160
Greene, Kenneth, 11, 39, 180, 182
Grindle, Merilee, 107, 182

Haggard, Stephan, 7, 89
Hagopian, Frances, 2–5, 16, 19, 28, 43, 59, 72, 181, 213
Hall, Anthony, 6
Hanusch, Marek, 11
Hawkins, Kirk, 29
Heckelman, Jac, 29
Hicken, Allen, 2–4, 70, 212, 215
Hidalgo, F. Daniel, 19, 21, 29, 44–46, 49, 50, 52–54, 95
Hilgers, Tina, 6
Hochstetler, Kathryn, 58
Hoefle, Scott, 21
Hoff, Karla, 80, 81
Holston, James, 19, 44
Horiuchi, Yusaku, 50
Huber, Gregory, 38
Huckfeldt, R. Robert, 75, 146
Hunter, Wendy, 20, 58, 59, 91

Ichino, Nahomi, 50
Imai, Kosuke, 161, 185

Jensen, Peter, 8
Jensenius, Francesca, 200
Justesen, Mogens, 8

Kasahara, Yuri, 45
Kaufman, Robert, 7, 89
Keck, Margaret, 58
Keefer, Phil, 5, 15, 210, 215
Kitschelt, Herbert, 2–6, 9, 11, 16, 17, 70, 93, 131, 146, 152, 188, 202, 213, 215
Klašnja, Marko, 64
Knaul, Felicia, 182
Kotwal, Ashok, 212
Kousser, Morgan, 29
Kuo, Joanna, 2

Lamounier, Bolivar, 43
Landini, Fernando, 193, 194
Larreguy, Horacio, 8, 182, 215
Lawson, Chappell, 39
Leal, Victor Nunes, 16, 21, 35
Levi-Moreira, Silvia, 34

Author Index

Levitsky, Steven, 5, 7, 189, 191, 192
Ligon, Ethan, 7, 15, 73, 98, 111, 208
Limongi, Fernando, 43
Lindberg, Staffan, 200
Lloyd, Ryan, 2
Londregan, John, 3, 92, 208
Lucas, Kevin, 20
Lupia, Arthur, 11
Lustig, Nora, 99, 111, 182, 192
Lyne, Mona, 2, 216

Machado, Fabiana, 17, 39, 95, 211
Maddison, Angus, 3
Magaloni, Beatriz, 7, 14, 30, 131, 180–183, 208, 213, 216
Mainwaring, Scott, 16, 19, 56, 57, 59
Mares, Isabela, 7, 15, 73, 147, 165, 214, 215
Margolis, Michele, 132, 231, 234
Marshall, John, 8, 182, 215
Matijascic, Milko, 89, 90
Mazzuca, Sebastian, 4, 8, 21, 30–32, 41, 208, 236
McCrary, Justin, 52
McCubbins, Mathew, 11
Medeiros, Marcelo, 89
Meléndez, Carlos, 2, 8, 160
Mercuri, Rebecca, 19
Merton, Robert, 7
Mesquita, Mario, 44
Meyer, Christian, 99, 111, 182, 192
Michelitch, Kristin, 203
Miguel, Edward, 95
Montero, Alfred, 2, 20
Moraes, Joysi, 21
Morgan, John, 8, 29, 236
Murillo, Maria Victoria, 189, 190

Naidu, Suresh, 95
Nazareno, Marcelo, 2, 4, 8, 14, 19, 30, 50, 93, 190–193, 197, 202, 211, 213, 215
Neri, Marcelo, 86, 87, 91, 92, 99
Nickerson, David, 2, 8, 160
Nicolau, Jairo, 34, 35, 41–45, 52
Nigenda, Gustavo, 183
Novaes, Lucas, 214, 215
Nunnari, Salvatore, 21, 78, 119, 132, 138, 145–147, 214, 230, 231, 247–249

Ofosu, George, 200
Olaberria, Eduardo, 182, 183
Osorio, Javier, 2, 8, 160
Osorio, Rafael Guerreiro, 89, 92, 99

Palmer-Rubin, Brian, 21, 115, 141, 180, 185
Pasotti, Eleonora, 2
Paxson, Christina, 95
Peress, Michael, 14, 21, 82, 160, 188, 193, 195, 201, 216
Piattoni, Simona, 6, 15
Powell, John Duncan, 6, 214
Power, Timothy, 16, 20, 44, 46, 47, 58, 59
Pritchett, Lant, 229, 230
Przeworski, Adam, 4, 33

Querubin, Pablo, 8, 182, 215

Ravallion, Martin, 86, 99, 111
Ravanilla, Nico, 215
Reis, Marlon, 40, 55, 57, 61, 62
Renno, Lucio, 17, 39, 95, 211
Richardson, Neal, 95
Robinson, James, 8, 11, 191
Roniger, Luis, 21
Rosas, Guillermo, 29
Rueda, Miguel, 8, 40
Rusk, Jerold, 4

Sampaio, Consuelo Novais, 34–36, 49
Samuels, David, 17, 20, 39, 95, 211, 215, 230
Sances, Michael, 132, 231, 234
Satyanath, Shanker, 95
Schady, Norbert, 91
Schaffer, Frederic, 4, 29, 40
Schechter, Laura, 7, 11, 15, 39, 73, 98, 111, 208
Schedler, Andreas, 4, 40, 181–183, 187
Schündeln, Matthias, 50
Scott, James, 3, 6, 7, 15, 93, 208
Sekhon, Jasjeet, 186
Sergenti, Ernest, 95
Shefter, Martin, 4
Shugart, Matthew, 4
Simpser, Alberto, 180
Smith, Amy Erika, 17, 39, 95, 211
Soares, Sergei, 18, 92, 99
Speck, Bruno, 39
Spence, Michael, 13, 80
Sprague, John, 75
Stiglitz, Joseph, 80, 81
Stokes, Susan, 2–4, 8, 11, 14, 16, 19, 29, 30, 34, 50, 92, 93, 146, 189–193, 195, 197, 198, 202, 208, 211, 213, 215, 236, 237
Sugiyama, Natasha Borges, 91
Szwarcberg, Mariela, 190, 194, 197

Tavares, Andre Ramos, 37
Taylor-Robinson, Michelle, 6
Tejera, Hector, 186
Titiunik, Rocio, 64
Townsend, Kaya, 183
Tozzi, Leonel, 57
Trejo, Guillermo, 58

Vardy, Felix, 8, 29, 76, 236
Verba, Sidney, 75
Verdier, Thierry, 8, 11, 191
Vicente, Pedro, 8
Vlaicu, Razvan, 5, 215

Wantchekon, Leonard, 210
Weigelt, Keith, 80, 81
Weiss, Andrew, 80, 81
Weitz-Shapiro, Rebecca, 2, 15, 38, 86, 118, 189, 190, 194, 210
Weyland, Kurt, 16, 89, 100, 212
Whitaker, Francisco, 58
Wilkinson, Steven, 2, 3, 8, 11, 16, 70, 93, 131, 152, 215
Wilson, James Q., 7, 15
Woodward, James, 34

Young, Lauren, 15, 147, 165, 214, 215

Zarazaga, Rodrigo, 190–194
Zechmeister, Elizabeth, 2
Zucco Jr., Cesar, 17, 20, 39, 58, 59, 95, 211, 215, 230

Subject Index

9840 Committees, 61, 62, 154

absentee voting, 45
abstention, 42, 44, 46, 47, 72
   costs of, 31, 41, 45
   justified, 42, 44–46, 48
   penalties for, 4, 41, 44, 45, 47
abstention buying, *see also* electoral clientelism, 27, 29, 32, 33, 41, 43, 48, 55, 61, 63, 65, 72, 205, 207
accessibility, 143, 173, 223, 251, 253
accountability, *see also under* consequences, 213
Acre, 98
activists, *see* civil society
administrative constraints, 7, 73
adverse selection, 80, 81
advertising, 12, 75, 114, 181, 184, 185, 216
Africa, 2, 14, 24, 102, 180, 188, 201, 204, 207
Afrobarometer, *see* survey evidence
age, exemptions from compulsory voting, 48
Agua para Todos program, 108
Alagoas, 29, 45, 98
Amapa, 98
Amazon region, 104, 108
Amazonas, 50, 98
ambulances, 119, 121
animal husbandry, 109
anti-clientelism
   committees, *see* 9840 Committees
   effect of laws on electoral clientelism, 53–63
   enactment of laws, 57, 59
   initiative, 57

   intervention, 213
   laws, 19, 62
   task force, 57
anti-poverty programs, 181, 182, 187
appeals, 55, 62
Argentina, 2, 7, 14, 24, 27, 34, 78, 179, 188, 189, 198, 201, 202, 204, 207, 215, 266, 268
argument of book, 5–6
Army, 109, 110, 126
assistance, *see* benefits
associations, 129, 155, 215, 225
   membership, 128, 136, 144, 158, 159, 175
asymmetric information, *see under* information
attrition, 222
audits, 19, 22, 28, 33, 49, 52, 63, 72, 103, 110
   criteria for, 52
   effect on electoral clientelism, 49–53
   federal, 103, 130, 210
Australia, 36, 101
Australian ballot, 34, 36, 43, 190
authoritarianism, 15, 36, 43, 44, 57, 213, 214
authorities, *see also* enforcement and judiciary, 19
autonomy, *see under* citizens
Auxilio Gas, 90
aversion to clientelism, 210

Bahia, 20, 28, 29, 42, 43, 46–48, 59, 76, 91, 98, 102, 104, 116, 119, 121, 122, 126, 140, 154, 156, 165, 167, 170, 217

Subject Index

ballot secrecy, 4, 10, 19, 22, 24, 27, 30, 32–41, 49, 50, 63, 71, 74, 79, 113, 139, 145, 181, 187, 190, 199, 203, 207, 235, 237
  effect on electoral clientelism, 33–41
  perceptions of, 37, 38
  violations of, 4, 36, 37
ballots, 35, 36
  paper, 19, 36, 38, 190
  uniform, 34
Barbosa, Rui, 34, 35
base units, *see* unidades basicas
beliefs, 12, 13, 16, 17, 37, 93, 118, 140, 150, 165, 170, 174
Benefício de Prestação Continuada program, 89
benefits
  during and beyond campaigns, 8
  during campaigns, 2, 8, 10, 14, 17, 19, 22, 30, 47, 55, 59–65, 72, 84, 132, 134–139, 160, 162, 166, 184–186, 194, 198, 211, 224, 232, 248, 249, 257, 258, 261, 262, 265–268
  from municipality, 118, 129, 131, 161, 231
  non-excludable, 9
  non-negotiable, 8
  post-election, 8, 9, 117, 127–135, 139, 146, 148, 150, 155, 156, 158, 166, 203, 204, 208, 211, 242–260
  timing of, 8, 70
Benin, 2, 210
Bhutan, 33
Bismarckian approach, 89
Bolsa Alimentação program, 90
Bolsa Escola program, 90
Bolsa Família program, *see* conditional cash transfer
Brasil Carinhoso program, 91
Brasil Sem Miséria program, 86
Brazilian Electoral Study (ESEB), 17, 39, 76, 93, 94, 100, 101, 115, 211, 215
bricks, *see* building materials
Britain, 4
brokers, 6, 8, 12, 14, 24, 62, 78, 143, 152, 173, 181, 189–194, 197, 203, 211, 214, 215, 231
budget law violations, 58
building materials, 59, 93, 152, 154, 157, 186
Bulgaria, 1
bureaucracy, 7, 107
bureaucratic hassles, 44

Cadastro Único, 21, 91, 92, 220
camera phones, 40

campaigns, 1, 2, 8, 10, 55, 71, 78, 82, 114, 116, 126, 132, 134, 138, 139, 148, 150, 155–157, 160, 164, 168, 181, 185, 186, 194, 203, 209, 213, 216
  municipal, 61, 64
  office, 157
  presidential, 19
  visits, 74, 78, 142
campaign handouts, *see* benefits during campaigns
captação ilícita de sufrágio, 60, 61
Cartão Alimentação program, 90
Catholic Church, 57, 58
Comissão Brasileira Justiça e Paz (CBJP), 56, 58, 61
Ceará, 99, 108–110, 126
census, 18, 42, 151
Central Única dos Trabalhadores, 57
Chain of Love, 36
challenges, *see also under* electoral clientelism, relational clientelism, and clientelism, 2, 87, 111
Chamber of Deputies, 58
cheap talk, 12, 74, 114
churches, 155
cistern, *see under* water
citizen requests, *see* requesting benefits
citizens
  autonomy of, 6, 15, 16, 21, 23, 79, 83, 150, 176, 205–207, 210
  choices of, 6–8, 10–13, 15, 20, 70, 113, 205–207, 209, 216
  consistency of voting, 174, 175, 264
  demands of, *see* requesting benefits
  depicted as passive, 6, 8, 21, 150
  exclusion of, 182
  history of support by, 165
  motivation of, 12, 149, 176, 179, 180, 182, 189, 191, 193, 198, 199, 203, 206–208, 210, 216
  pressure from, 82, 157, 194
  role of, 5, 6, 9–11, 14, 15, 21, 24, 69–71, 78, 83, 112–114, 149, 153, 167, 176, 189, 199, 204, 206–208, 210, 214, 216
  terminating relationships, 13, 79, 81–83
  threats by, 169
  untrustworthy, 74
city councilors, *see* councilors
civil service, *see under* employment
civil society, 17, 56–59, 61, 103, 107

Subject Index

clientelism, *see also under* electoral clientelism and relational clientelism, 2
  acceptability of, 71, 94, 111, *see also under* poverty, 207
  aversion to, 57
  challenges for, 3–5, 10, 16, 18, 24, 98, 180, 182, 187, 189, 191, 193, 198, 203
  costs of, 3, 12, 19, 181
  decline of, 2, 84
  definition of, 2
  effectiveness of, 10, 216
  elite strategies of, 213
  in developed nations, 3
  in developing nations, 3, 198
  increase of, 2
  municipal vs national elections, 59
  persistence of, 2, 3, 16, 17, 180, 182, 187, 189, 198, 208
  resilience of, 208
  shifts away from, 216
  survival of, 2, 3, 5, 6, 10, 16, 18, 24, 207, 216
climactic variation, 96
club goods, 131, 134, 161, 216
coalition, 152
coercion, 15, 210
collaborative efforts with neighbors, 128, 158, 159
collective action, 215, 216
collective benefits, 131, 152
Colombia, 4
comparative evidence, 179–204
competence, 143, 173, 223, 252
competition, 5, 12, 31, 64, 72, 78, 146, 147, 152, 169, 190, 202, 211
competitive clientelism, 6, 78, 145, 147, 206
compliance, 43, 71
compulsory voting, 4, 10, 19, 22, 27, 28, 30, 32, 33, 41, 50, 63, 71, 207
  effect on electoral clientelism, 41–49
  exemptions, 44, 48
concursos públicos, *see under* employment
conditional cash transfers, 18, 23, 45, 87, 88, 90–92, 99, 111, 181, 208
conditionalities, 91, 92
Conferência Nacional dos Bispos do Brasil (CNBB), 56
Congress, 19, 34, 35, 56, 58, 59, 62, 104, 212, 215
consequences, 212, 213
  for democracy, 24, 83, 213
  for development, 24, 83
  for higher levels of political systems, 214, 215
conservative machines, 20, 59
consistency of voting, *see under* citizens
constituency service, 9, 10, 13, 70, 150, 161, 162, 164–166, 195, 200, 201
Constitution, 41, 56, 89, 100, 101, 103, 104
constitutional amendment, 43
constitutionality, 62
construction, *see* building materials
contingency, 2, 8–10, 13, 70, 74, 98, 160, 200, 205, 211, 212
coordination, *see* collective action
core, *see under* supporters
corruption, 20, 58, 72, 110, 212
costs, of voting, 31, 32
councilors, 14, 20, 29, 38, 39, 47, 48, 51, 59, 64, 72, 107, 109, 114, 120, 121, 124, 128, 140, 152–154, 157, 158, 160, 162, 165, 166, 168–173, 193, 197, 215, 218, 222, 225, 227, 229, 230, 263
courts, *see* judiciary
coverage
  exclusion from, 84, 89, 179, 199, 208, 212
  expansion of, 88, 90
  healthcare, 192
Cadastro de Pessoas Físicas (CPF), 45
credibility, *see also* promises and trust, 9–12, 14, 16, 22, 27, 70, 72, 74, 75, 77, 79, 113, 117, 131, 135, 147–149, 167, 174, 179, 207, 208, 210, 211, 216, 240
  dual credibility problem, 5, 11, 13, 14, 22, 65, 69, 71, 73, 74, 113, 149, 176, 179, 206, 207
  of citizens, 5, 12, 139, 141, 161, 235
  of politicians, 5, 11, 79, 81, 148–150, 155, 156, 170, 176, 210, 237
criminal charges, 57, 62
cross-national survey, *see under* survey evidence
currais eleitorais (electoral corrals), 21

decentralized expenditures, 103
declared support, 5, 9, 12, 13, 21–24, 70, 71, 73, 74, 78–80, 83, 85, 112–149, 154, 159, 161–164, 173, 175, 176, 179, 183, 184, 189, 193, 195–199, 202–204, 206, 207, 214, 216, 225, 226, 232, 233, 235–253
  campaign banners and posters, 12, 74, 75, 114, 115, 137, 140, 184, 202, 203, 233, 235

Subject Index

declared support (cont.)
　campaign flags, 12, 74, 78, 115, 118, 137, 141, 202, 203, 233, 235
　cost of declaration, 12, 75–78, 124, 135, 146, 240
　declared opposer, 119, 120, 122–125, 127, 130, 134, 165
　declared supporters, 156, 166, 170
　displays at rallies, 12, 74, 76, 114, 115, 125, 136, 137, 141, 184, 196, 197, 203, 226, 233, 235
　effect of contextual factors, 145
　election influence, 75–78
　expected utility, 78
　expressive costs, 12, 75
　expressive utility, 76
　geographic variation of, 115
　influence of neighborhood, 146
　intensity of, 116, 135, 137, 141, 142
　link to clientelism, 186
　link to employment, 122–125
　link to healthcare, 118–122
　link to relational clientelism, 23, 77, 117–139, 148
　link to vote choice, 23, 77, 114, 139–145, 148, 207
　link to water provision, 125–127
　monitoring of, 146
　non-clientelist reasons for, 12, 75, 114
　non-declarers, 119, 121–125, 127, 129, 130, 132, 133, 137, 138, 143, 145–147, 162, 164, 165, 184, 185
　on bodies, 62, 74, 114, 115, 136, 137, 141, 203, 226, 233, 235
　on homes, 114, 136, 137, 141, 226
　painted houses, 233
　political paraphernalia, 6, 71, 114, 115, 136, 137, 141, 197
　prevalence of, 114–117
　quantitative analysis of, 127–139, 141–145
　robustness to exclusion of rallies, 137, 195
　signaling mechanism, 5, 12, 22, 23, 70, 71, 74–78, 80, 113, 114, 117, 118, 131, 135, 139, 145, 147, 148, 161, 179, 202, 203, 206, 214, 216, 235–240
　social costs of, 146
　stickers, 114, 115, 126, 137, 140, 141, 161
　summary of logic, 74–79
　vs. private pledges, 12, 74
　willingness to declare, 145
defeated candidate, 118, 120, 122, 123, 125, 130, 134, 141, 143, 162, 174, 226, 232, 252, 253

defection, *see* opportunistic defection
Democratas (DEM), 227, 233
demand side, *see also under* factors, 215
　focus on, 149, 150
demanding benefits, *see* requesting benefits
demands, *see* requesting benefits
demobilization, 10, 33
democracy, *see under* consequences
Democratic Party, 35
democratization, 44, 45
dentists, 102, 121
dependence, 5
detection, 4
developed countries, 2, 7, 209
developing countries, 7
development, *see under* consequences
digitization, 44, 52, 72
diminishing marginal utility of income, 3, 92, 190, 208
discretion, 13, 16, 23, 70, 73, 74, 80, 85, 92, 98, 100, 103, 104, 106–109, 111, 112, 131, 210, 212
discrimination, 118, 120–127, 130, 131, 134, 165, 231
disenfranchisement, 41
disfavored treatment, *see* discrimination
distributive politics, 5, 9, 10, 70, 180
doctors, 101, 102, 168
domestic workers, 105
double persuasion, *see also* electoral clientelism, 30, 32
drought, *see under* water
dual credibility problem, *see under* credibility

Ecclesial Base Communities (CEBs), 58
economic development, *see also* income, increase of, 3, 4, 10, 18, 71, 84, 92, 207, 209
economic crisis, *see* recession
economic growth, 87
economies of scale, 3, 19, 152
education, 107, 131
Egypt, 213
El Salvador, 151
elderly, 46, 47, 89
election influence, 12, 147, 236
election, *see* campaign
electoral clientelism, *see also* vote buying, turnout buying, abstention buying, voter buying and double persuasion, 8–11, 15, 21, 22, 24, 27–65, 69, 71, 84, 113, 116,

Subject Index

135, 156, 160, 186, 205, 207, 209, 211, 213, 215, 216
challenges for, 10, 22, 27–65, 111
combining strategies of, 32, 63
contrast with traditional literature, 69
costs of, 27, 33
decline of, 22, 63, 94, 211
different strategies of, 27–30
effect of anti-clientelism legislation on, 53–63
effect of ballot secrecy on, 33–41
effect of compulsory voting on, 41–49
effect of contextual factors, 32
effects of audits on, 49–53
link to vote choice, 95
logic of, 30–33
persistence of, 30, 64
punishments for, see also Law 9840
relative cost of strategies, 41, 63
electoral
  campaign, see campaign
  court, see judiciary
  Electoral Code, 28, 34, 36, 41, 44, 52, 53, 55, 63
  governance body, 57, 181
  infractions, 57
  institutions, 19, 33, 34, 41
  officials, 36, 43, 45, 50–52
  reforms, see under reforms
  registration, see voter registration
  revision, see audit
electorate, 18, 46
  growth of, 19
electronic voting, 19, 27, 33, 36–40, 44, 63, 71, 147, 190
emergencies, 108, 112, 119, 121, 130, 192
emigration, 53
employment, see also unemployment and patronage, 74, 87, 100, 104, 105, 112, 118, 119, 122–125, 127, 129, 160, 182, 186, 191, 200, 202, 203, 223
  assistance in obtaining, 118, 124, 131, 160, 161, 228
  by municipalities, 51, 106, 110, 123
  civil service, 51, 107, 123, 124
  competitive exams for civil service (*concursos públicos*), 107, 123
  formal, 87, 89, 100, 104, 105, 112, 182
  growth in municipal employment, 107, 108
  informal, 73, 89, 105, 179, 182
  labor market, 105
  minimum wage, 88, 89
  opportunities, 88, 123
  political appointments, 107
  public, 107, 122–124
  self-employment, 73, 179, 199
  temporary public positions, 105, 107, 123, 182, 191
  unskilled labor, 88
enforcement, 4, 10, 19, 41, 43, 44, 55, 72
  lack of, 55
enfranchisement, 18, 43
entitlement programs, 214
Espírito Santo, 57, 107
evidence, longitudinal, 64
exclusion, see under coverage
exit options, 15
experience, 143, 173, 223, 251, 253
experiment, 145–147, 155, 172, 209, 210, 212, 214, 222, 231
  experimental games, 129, 158, 228
  field experiment, 21, 22, 24, 150, 209
  list experiment, 159, 160, 162, 180, 185, 258
  survey experiment, 119, 122, 125, 127
expressive utility, 31, 76, 121, 147, 236, 237

factors
  demand-side, 15, 16, 210
  supply-side, 15, 16, 210
family, 81, 152, 154, 155
friends, 81
favoritism, 7, 17, 70, 73, 74, 117, 119, 121, 122, 125–127, 130, 131, 134, 135, 139, 161, 186, 212
  non-binding, 10
federal accountability office, 103
federal government, 73, 101, 103, 107, 109
Ficha Limpa, 63
field experiment, see under experiment
fieldwork, 16, 20
  description of, 217–219
  interview protocols, 219
Fiscal Responsibility Law, 106, 107
food, 8, 17, 59, 153, 169, 183, 194, 200, 202, 203
formal analysis, 6, 12, 22, 30–32, 48, 75–78, 114, 139, 145–148, 207, 215, 216, 235–240
formality, see under employment
formiguinha, 36, 38
France, 108
fraud, 37, 52, 216
fulfilled requests, see under requesting benefits

gender, 43
geographic regions, *see* regions
Germany, 101, 108
Ghana, 24, 78, 180, 200–204, 207
goodwill, 10
governors, 20
gratitude, 75
grotões, 59
Guatemala, 151

handouts, *see* benefits
health, 131, 179, 182
    appointments, 101, 102, 119, 120, 153
    assistance, 120, 140, 153, 200
    clinics, 101, 104, 154, 165, 199
    exams, 101
    expenditures, 74, 84, 100–104, 203
    healthcare, 7, 23, 74, 84, 100, 102–104, 112, 118, 120–122, 124, 125, 127, 152, 154, 182, 192, 199, 202
    hospitals, 9, 101, 120, 165, 212
    illness, 5, 7, 13, 23, 69, 73, 80, 81, 92, 98, 101, 103, 105, 112, 113, 119, 149, 154, 179, 183, 188, 191–193, 198
    infant mortality, 100, 102
    insurance, 23, 101, 112, 182, 192
    medicine, 8, 23, 59, 80, 101–103, 119, 120, 152, 154, 155, 157, 168–170, 176, 183, 192, 194, 199, 212
    outcomes, 101
    pharmacies, private, 120, 183
    pharmacies, public, 103, 120, 154
    public healthcare system (SUS), 100, 101, 103, 112, 120, 154
    staffing, 101, 102
    surgeries, 119, 120
    treatments, 93, 102, 118, 119, 121, 154, 155, 157
help, *see* benefits
honesty, 143, 173, 223, 252
households, 152
    multigenerational, 89
human rights, 57
hypothetical, 118, 122
    offers, 96, 97
    questions, 93
    vignettes, 125, 154, 162, 168

IBGE, *see* census
identification cards, 44
illegality, 160

illiteracy, 45
    exemptions from compulsory voting, 48
illiterates, enfranchisement of, 43
illness, *see under* health
impeachment, 58, 72
implications, *see* consequences
importing voters, *see* voter buying
impunity, 19, 55, 57, 61, 63
incentives, 5, 12
    of politicians, 14
income, *see also* poverty, 3, 6, 18, 73, 105, 111
    household, 87, 88, 92
    increase of, 5, 15, 18, 23, 24, 71, 84–98, 111, 149, 179, 181, 189, 191, 198, 199, 203, 206, 207, 209, 216
    labor, 87, 88, 92, 111
    link to clientelism, 92
    transfers, 88, 208
    transitory, 97
incumbency, 30, 50–52, 152, 170, 173, 174, 209, 214
independence, *see under* citizens
Index of Social Vulnerability, 98
India, 24, 90, 180, 200, 204, 207
indirect transactions, prohibition of, 62
inducements, *see* benefits and favoritism
ineligibility, 63
inequality, *see also under* regions, 85, 89
inflation, 44, 88
informality, *see under* employment
information, 12, 14, 22, 77, 80, 81, 83, 114, 127, 131, 139, 140, 147, 149, 150, 170, 174, 176, 197
    asymmetric, 12–14, 75, 78–81, 170, 176, 235
infrastructure, 108, 215
insecurity, *see* vulnerability
institutional factors, 22, 27, 32, 33, 49, 51, 53, 63, 72, 207
institutional reforms, 3, 5, 10, 19, 71, 72, 179, 199, 203, 211
institutionalized channels, 7, 15, 154, 208
insulation, from clientelist influence, 91
insurance, *see also under* health, unemployment, and social
    informal, 22, 69, 213
    lack of, 105
intermediaries, *see* brokers
intertemporal tradeoffs, 82
interviews, *see* fieldwork
IPEA, 18
Iran, 33
Italy, 4, 7, 40, 73

Subject Index

Japan, 101
job, see employment
judiciary, 55, 57, 62
  delays, 55, 57
  electoral courts, see also Tribunal Superior Eleitoral, 29, 42, 51, 57, 60, 61, 170
  judges, 17
  prosecutors, 17, 51
justification, see under abstention

Kenya, 2
Kubitschek, Juscelino, 44

labor union, 57
land tenure contracts, 6, 205
LAPOP AmericasBarometer, see under survey evidence
Latin America, 14, 24, 85, 86, 89, 90, 99, 107, 180, 188, 190, 201, 202, 204, 207, 266
Law 9840, 19, 53–63, 72
  public awareness of, 62
  signatures for, 56, 57
Law Saraiva, 33
Lebanon, 24, 78, 180, 202–204, 207
legal enforcement, 3–5, 10, 18, 19, 71, 179, 199, 203, 208, 211
legal scrutiny, 24, 181, 182, 187
legislation, 7, 10, 19, 22, 28, 33, 55, 56, 170
legislative elections, 41, 42
legislators, see Congress
Liberal Alliance, 35
list experiment, see experiment
literacy, 43
literates, 18
loans, public, 44
local, see municipal
Luiz Inácio Lula da Silva, 20, 88, 90

machine, see under party
machine politics, see clientelism
Madagascar, 2
mandatory voting, see compulsory voting
Maranhão, 17, 39, 47–49, 98, 107
marcação, 120, 124
mass media, see also radio and television, 38, 62, 126, 184
  Rede Globo, 62
Mato Grosso, 40, 52, 107
mayor, 14, 20, 40, 48, 51–54, 59, 72, 76, 78, 91, 107, 109, 110, 118, 120, 124–126, 128, 131, 132, 138, 141, 143–145, 152, 154, 156, 158, 160, 162, 166, 168–170, 173, 174, 186, 190, 193, 194, 209, 212, 214, 215, 218, 228–230, 234, 252, 264
mechanisms, see under relational clientelism
media, see mass media
medical, see health
medicine, see health
Mensalão scandal, 58
Mexico, 2, 24, 27, 40, 78, 90, 101, 179, 180, 182, 185, 187, 188, 191, 198, 201, 202, 204, 207, 213, 267
Mexico Panel Survey, see under survey evidence
middle class, 15, 86, 99, 179, 182, 190, 191, 198, 210
Millennium Development Goals, 86
Minas Gerais, 37, 52, 57, 108
minimum wage, see under employment, 88, 89
Ministry of Health, 103
Ministry of Social Development, 45, 91
mismanagement, 103
mobilization, 4, 10, 14, 30, 33, 41, 49
model, see formal analysis
money, 59
monitoring, 3, 4, 10, 11, 16, 18, 19, 33, 34, 36, 40, 50, 61, 64, 71, 78, 103, 131, 140, 145–147, 181, 190, 197, 210, 235
  aggregate, 40
  cost of, 4
  of elections, 4, 19
monopolistic clientelism, 6, 15, 147, 206
Movimento de Combate à Corrupção Eleitoral (MCCE), 1, 59
municipal health councils, 103
municipality, see also under employment and benefits
  offices, 130, 132, 133, 151, 160
  revenues, 106
  role of, 51, 91, 92
mutually reinforcing cycle, 139, 166

national level, see also under consequences, 72, 132, 214
  candidates, 24, 215
  elections, 64
Nationalist League, 34
negative inducements, see punishments and discrimination
neighborhoods, 131, 215, 227
neighboring districts, 50, 51, 53
neoliberal reforms, 5, 20
Nepal, 1

Subject Index

offers of benefits, 1, 2, 8, 13, 39, 79, 83, 149, 157, 180, 184, 185, 187, 196, 199, 201
  refusal of, 55
Old Republic, 34, 35
ongoing exchange relationships, *see* relational clientelism
Online Clientelism Survey, *see under* survey evidence
open-list proportional representation, 19, 20, 28
Operação Carro Pipa, 108–110, 126, 130, 245
Operação Lava Jato, 20, 58, 72
opportunistic defection, 5, 10, 11, 22, 38–40, 69, 71, 79, 147, 150, 156, 176, 181, 206
opposition, 31
optional voting, 46, 47
Ordem dos Advogados do Brasil, 57
organizational infrastructure, 16, 78, 210
ousted politicians, *see under* politicians

Partido Acción Nacional (PAN), 180–182, 184
paper ballots, *see under* ballots
Pará, 51, 57, 98, 109
Paraíba, 126
Paraguay, 2
participation, *see* turnout
parties, 9, 10, 15, 19, 20, 30, 36, 58, 128, 129, 132, 136, 138, 144, 158, 159, 173–175, 180, 184, 186, 188, 189, 195, 196, 201–203, 212, 215, 224, 227, 233, 264
  clientelist (machines), 7, 27, 63
  conservative, 59
  leaders of, 197, 211
  left-of-center, 57, 58
  strategies of, 3–5, 10, 18, 19, 71, 72, 179, 181, 182, 187, 199, 203, 211
partisanship, 75, 117, 184
patronage, 5, 72, 107, 202
patron-client relations, 6, 7, 205
pensions, 45, 48, 87, 88, 92, 111
  rural, 89, 90
  social, 23, 89
perceptions, 114, 118, 121, 122, 124–127, 134, 143, 145, 148, 150, 170, 173, 174, 176, 187, 206, 223, 251–253, 263
Pernambuco, 20, 51, 98, 109, 119, 125, 126, 140, 217
Peronist Party, 7, 189, 191–193, 195, 197
persecution, *see* discrimination
persuasion, 14, 30, 124

petition against clientelism, *see also* Law 9840, 19, 55
Philippines, 4, 36, 215
Piauí, 45
Piauí, 51, 102, 110, 126
Partido do Movimento Democrático Brasileiro (PMDB), 215, 227, 233
poison pills, 35
political machine, *see under* parties
politicians, *see also under* credibility and promises
  characteristics of, 143, 173, 223
  control by, 6
  declining control by, 6
  hidden characteristics of, 13
  increase in removals of, 59
  removal of, 1, 19, 22, 55, 57, 59–63, 72
  role of, 6, 8, 15, 193, 210
  strategies of, 6
  types of, 79–81, 167, 170
  untrustworthiness of, 81, 167, 168, 174, 176, 213
politicization, 16
poor, *see* poverty
popular initiative, *see also* Law 9840, 19, 56, 57, 61, 63
population growth, 3, 18
pork-barrel politics, 9, 70, 73
portfolio of strategies, 208
poverty, 3, 6, 10, 15, 18, 40, 44, 56, 73, 84–86, 89, 90, 92, 93, 95, 98, 99, 101, 106, 111, 181, 182, 186, 189, 191, 197, 199, 205, 208, 210, 212, 216
  link to acceptance of clientelism, 85, 92, 93, 95–97, 111, 209
poverty reduction, 3, 84, 86
poverty, dynamic nature of, 99
poverty, programs against, 7
Partido Revolucionario Democrático (PRD), 180, 184
precincts, 40, 53
preferences, 3, 12, 16, 18, 31–33, 40, 75–78, 84, 92, 114, 121, 124, 128, 129, 132, 136, 142, 144, 145, 158, 159, 202, 205, 208, 215, 233
preferential access, *see* favoritism
Partido Revolucionario Institucional (PRI), 180–182, 184, 186, 187
probability of victory, 78, 145, 146, 214
Programa Farmácia Popular, 103
Programa Mais Médicos, 102

Subject Index

programmatic politics, 2, 3, 9, 19, 20, 70, 72, 75, 131, 145, 146, 181, 210, 214–216
promises, *see also* credibility and trust, 10
   by citizens, 2, 5, 8–10, 12, 22, 23, 69, 70, 73–75, 77, 79, 83, 113, 114, 117, 131, 135, 139, 147–149, 161, 179, 206, 207, 214, 216, 235
   by politicians, 5, 6, 9, 11, 13–15, 22, 55, 69, 70, 73, 74, 80, 83, 113, 149, 150, 155, 156, 166–168, 170, 174, 176, 179, 206, 211
   insincere, 12
   insincere promisers, 114
   opposing promisers, 235
   unfulfilled, 11
prosecutions, 19, 55, 59, 62
prosecutors, *see under* judiciary
Partido da Social Democracia Brasileira (PSDB), 19, 72, 227, 233
Partido dos Trabalhadores (PT), 19, 58, 59, 72, 76, 215, 227, 233
party brand, 58
public goods, 128, 129, 144, 158, 159, 212, 215, 227
public programs, 51
public services, 84, 100, 107
   incomplete provision of, 154
punishments, *see also* discrimination, 11, 39, 40, 45, 55, 57, 62, 63, 76–78, 147, 165, 190, 210, 213, 214, 237

qualitative evidence, *see* fieldwork

Radical Party, 189, 195
radio, 38, 62
rainfall, 96, 97, 108, 116, 125, 130, 221, 245
   rainfall shocks, 93, 95, 111, 116, 155
recession, 18, 85, 87, 111
reciprocity, 11, 39, 129, 136, 144, 158, 159, 175, 228
reelection, 52–54, 91, 153, 173, 209, 218
reforms, 4, 5, 34–37, 40, 43, 72, 212
   electoral, 37, 190
   neoliberal, 189
regions, 132
   disparities across, 101, 106
   North, 57, 62, 86, 98, 99, 107, 115
   Northeast, 16, 17, 20, 23, 24, 28, 29, 37, 38, 47, 49, 57, 62, 79, 83, 85, 86, 91, 98–102, 106–108, 110, 112, 115–117, 119, 122, 126, 127, 130, 139, 141, 150, 152, 174, 176, 207, 209, 220
   South, 57, 62, 86, 102, 104, 106, 115
   Southeast, 57, 62, 86, 101, 115
registration, *see* voter registration
regression discontinuity design, 46, 52, 54
relational clientelism, 5, 7–15, 24, 65, 176, 205, 213
   challenges for, 10, 70, 71, 79, 113, 148, 156, 170, 176, 179, 207
   defining attributes of, 8, 9, 70
   definition of, 5, 70, 156
   distinguishing from electoral clientelism, 8, 18, 135
   erosion as welfare states are developed, 208
   inferior substitute for welfare state, 83, 212
   mechanisms for sustaining, 5, 9, 11–13, 16, 22, 70, 74, 75, 79, 83, 112–176, 179, 180, 184, 186, 187, 189, 193, 196–198, 202, 204, 206, 207, 209, 235
   origination of, 139, 166, 214
   periodic claims for assistance, 9, 70
   resilience of, 22, 27, 65, 69–71, 73, 113, 207
   scope conditions, 15, 210
   self-reinforcing nature of, 13, 14
   shifts away from sustaining, 24
   survival of, 6, 8, 12, 13, 20, 22, 24, 69, 71, 73, 74, 79, 83, 85, 111–113, 147, 148, 150, 154, 176, 179, 182, 183, 204, 206, 214
removal of politicians, *see under* politicians
reputation, 6, 10, 13, 75, 79–83, 150, 156, 167–170, 176, 207
   collective aspect of, 81
   decay of, 82
requesting benefits, 5, 9, 12–14, 21–24, 70, 73, 74, 79–81, 83, 85, 112, 113, 148–176, 179, 183, 186, 189, 191, 193, 194, 198–200, 203, 204, 206, 207, 209, 211, 216, 223, 254–267
   denial of requests, 13, 24, 79, 82, 83, 156, 164, 166, 167, 169–172, 174, 176, 206, 211, 263, 264
   evidence of screening mechanism, 166–176
   fulfilled requests, 6, 14, 79, 81, 83, 150, 155, 156, 160, 165, 167, 168, 186, 200, 214
   increase during elections, 152
   initiation by citizens, 14
   link to relational clientelism, 156–166, 194
   link to vote choice, 24, 81–83, 167, 169–171, 174–176, 213
   link to vulnerability, 153–156
   non-requesters, 157, 158, 161, 187, 195, 201

requesting benefits (cont.)
  prevalence of, 150–153, 157
  requesters, 157, 158, 161, 166, 195, 201
  screening mechanism, 5, 9, 12, 13, 23, 70, 74, 79–83, 113, 150, 156, 166, 167, 169–171, 174, 176, 179, 206, 207, 216
  summary of logic, 79–83
  unfulfilled requests, 150, 157
  varied composition of requests, 153
resources, see also scarcity, 13, 15, 16, 23, 41, 49, 50, 70, 72, 74, 76, 80–82, 85, 98, 100, 103, 104, 109, 112, 146, 181, 210, 214
  constraints, 55
responsiveness, 12, 13, 79, 82, 150, 156–158, 160–162, 165, 166, 169, 173, 174, 186, 200, 213
retaliation, see discrimination
Revolution of 1930, 55
rewarding loyalists, 30
rewards, see benefits
  definition of, 28
Rio de Janeiro, 45, 57, 216
Rio Grande do Norte, 51, 106
Rio Grande do Sul, 102
risk, see also shocks and vulnerability, 15, 23, 71, 73, 84, 92, 98–100, 104, 105, 111, 113, 121, 124, 127, 154, 170, 179, 191, 198, 206, 208, 210, 212
  inadequate protection from, 74, 99
  of clientelism, 19
  risk aversion, 3, 92, 128, 129, 132, 136, 138, 144, 158, 159, 175, 228, 233
  risk-coping mechanism, 24, 73, 92, 104, 106, 109, 111, 116, 119, 149, 179, 191, 208, 212, 214, 216
roads, 9, 131
Rondonia, 98
Roraima, 107
Rousseff, Dilma, 20, 58, 72, 110
rural, 17, 20, 23, 36, 40, 79, 86, 93, 95, 100, 102, 105, 108, 109, 112, 115–117, 119, 129, 130, 132, 139, 150, 151, 155, 174, 199, 200, 207, 209, 218, 220, 233
Rural Clientelism Survey, see under survey evidence

Sales, Campos, 34
sampling, see under survey evidence and fieldwork
sanitary movement, 100
sanitation, 107
Santa Catarina, 99, 102, 106
São Paulo, 34, 35, 45, 49, 57, 58, 108

Saraiva Law, 35
scandals, 20, 58
scarcity, 16, 73
scope conditions, see under relational clientelism
screeners, 132, 133, 138, 234
screening, see under requesting benefits
secret ballot, see ballot secrecy
Seguro Popular, 182
selection, of beneficiaries, 91, 111
self-insurance, 15, 71, 98, 99, 206, 208, 214
self-selection, 123, 157, 165, 171
semi-arid zone, 108
Senators, see Congress
separation, 77
  separating equilibria, 77
shocks, see also risk and vulnerability, 10, 12, 13, 15, 23, 69–74, 79–81, 83, 84, 98, 99, 103, 104, 108, 113, 114, 116, 148, 149, 154–156, 170, 179, 182, 188, 191–193, 198, 206–208, 211, 212, 214
sickness, see under health
signaling, see under declared support
signatures, see Law 9840
signs, 12, 141
Sistema Único de Saúde (SUS), see under health
small towns, 20, 29, 40, 50, 52, 53, 59, 103, 105, 106, 110, 126, 151, 217
social assistance, 189, 202, 203
social desirability bias, 95, 160, 180
social insurance, 73, 84, 89, 99, 179, 199, 212
social pensions, see under pensions
social policy, 7, 69, 73, 84, 105, 181, 182, 206, 212
  exclusion from coverage, 7, 73
  inadequate, 7
  politicized, 7
social safety net, 5, 22, 69, 98, 104, 105, 111, 179
  incomplete, 149
South Africa, 1
Southeast Asia, 7
state, 5, 7, 22, 69, 73, 84, 98, 101, 103, 107, 111, 149, 154, 187, 191, 193, 198, 214
state government, 110
state of emergency, 108, 109
strategic interaction between citizens and politicians, 216
strategies of parties, see under parties
structural changes, 3, 5, 10, 18, 19, 71, 179, 199, 211

Subject Index

suffrage
　of illiterates, 41
　of women, 41
supply curve of clientelism, 97
supply side of clientelism, typical focus on, 149, 176
supply-side factors, *see under* factors
supporters
　core supporters, 14, 201
　nonvoting supporters, 41
　supporting promisers, 75, 235, 240
　voting supporters, 30, 211
Supreme Court, 56
survey evidence, 1, 53, 64, 87, 89, 94, 101, 109, 114, 115, 118, 126, 127, 132, 135, 141, 148, 150, 151, 166, 170, 180, 181, 184, 187, 197, 198, 201–203, 206, 207
　Afrobarometer, 2, 188, 201, 265
　Argentina, 14
　cross-national, 2, 16, 17, 24, 64, 179, 198, 201–204, 207
　LAPOP AmericasBarometer, 1, 2, 65, 93, 94, 115, 150, 151, 166, 167, 187, 188, 196, 201, 266, 267
　Mexico Panel Study, 180, 184, 185, 187
　Online Clientelism Survey, 17, 21, 39, 47–49, 119, 122, 132, 134, 138, 141, 145, 166, 247–249
　Online Clientelism Survey, description of, 230–234
　other Brazilian surveys, 11, 16, 20, 23, 38, 93, 95, 100, 115, 186
　Rural Clientelism Survey, 17, 20, 28, 29, 37, 39, 45, 47–49, 64, 76, 78, 95, 100, 102, 109, 115, 117, 119, 121, 122, 125, 127–129, 131–133, 135, 136, 138, 141, 143, 144, 152, 154–157, 159, 161, 163–165, 168, 171–175, 198, 211, 222, 242–264
　Rural Clientelism Survey, description of, 220–230
　sampling, 21, 220, 230
　Varieties of Democracy, 64
survival
　of citizens, *see* citizens, vulnerability, and risk-coping mechanism
　of clientelism, *see under* clientelism and relational clientelism
swing voters, 8, 14, 201, 207, 211

Taiwan, 4
targeting, 7, 8, 10, 14, 31, 41, 73, 82, 99, 149, 211

Tasmanian Dodge, 36
teachers, 107, 124
television, 38, 62, 126
　telenovelas, 62
temporary contracts, *see under* employment
term limits, 20, 52
Thailand, 1, 4
theoretical framework, 22, 27, 30, 40, 41, 47
threats, 13, 14, 24, 213
time preferences, 3, 92
track record, *see* reputation
transfers, *see also under* income
　between levels of government, 88, 99
　to municipalities, 103
transportation, 31, 120, 169
trust, *see also* credibility and promises, 10–12, 23, 24, 70, 71, 73–75, 77, 79, 81, 83, 113, 114, 139, 147–150, 156, 167, 168, 170, 214
　link to relationship length, 167, 168
trust games, 150, 170, 172–174, 222, 263
Tribunal Superior Eleitoral (TSE), 19, 29, 33, 36, 37, 40, 42, 43, 44, 52, 57, 61, 62
turnout, 19, 41–43, 45, 47, 132, 138, 144, 158, 159, 188
turnout buying, *see also* electoral clientelism, 27–30, 32, 33, 41, 43, 47, 48, 50, 55, 63, 64, 72, 182, 205, 208, 211
typology, 27, 29, 211

Uganda, 2
uncertainty, *see* risk
unemployment, 5, 7, 23, 69, 73, 81, 84, 88, 92, 98, 105, 107, 112, 113, 124, 149, 179, 183, 188, 191, 193, 198, 199
　benefits, 199
　insurance, 23, 84, 104, 105, 107, 112, 182
　lack of protection, 105
unidades basicas, 8, 189
United States, 4, 7, 38, 101, 104
urban, 36, 86, 88, 119, 151, 188, 189, 200, 218
urbanization, 3, 18

Vargas, Getúlio, 34, 35, 41, 55
Varieties of Democracy, *see under* survey evidence
Vatican, 56
vignettes, 119, 122, 125, 146, 168

vote buying, *see also* electoral clientelism, 19, 27, 28, 32–37, 39, 40, 49, 50, 55, 61–64, 71, 91, 93, 95, 97, 113, 180–182, 190, 197, 205, 207, 211, 213
  mechanism of, 37
vote choices, *see also under* citizens, declared support, and requesting benefits, 75, 132, 136, 138, 140–143, 158, 159, 166, 190, 197, 223
  switching, 8, 28, 50, 150, 170
vote promises, *see* promises by citizens
voter
  audits, *see* audits
  autonomy of, *see under* citizens
  choice, *see under* citizens and vote choices
voter buying, *see also* electoral clientelism, 19, 22, 27, 29, 49–53, 63, 64, 72
  cost of, 50
voter registration, 19, 42, 43, 45, 49, 51, 52, 72
  rolls, 44, 46
  transfers, 50, 51, 53
voting, *see also* turnout
  documents, 43–45, 47
  folders, 43, 44
  receipts, 37
  technology, 190, 191, 198
votos de cabresto, 21
vulnerability, *see also* shocks and risk, 10, 15, 22–24, 69, 71, 73, 79, 82–216
  concept of, 6
  definition of, 98
  link to declared support, *see under* declared support
  link to requesting benefits, *see under* requesting benefits
  motivating citizens to sustain relational clientelism, *see under* citizens
vulnerable class, 99

water, 7, 23, 59, 74, 80, 84, 100, 108, 112, 118, 125–127, 130, 152, 154, 155, 157, 176, 182, 183, 191–193, 199, 200
  cistern, 21, 24, 108, 119, 125, 126, 128, 129, 136, 144, 150, 153, 155, 156, 158, 159, 175, 186, 209, 212, 220, 225, 227
  clientelist provision, 109
  community, 131
  consumption, 130
  deliveries, 118, 130, 134, 217, 245
  drought, 5, 7, 13, 23, 69, 71, 73, 74, 80, 81, 84, 92, 98, 108, 109, 112–114, 116, 118, 127, 130, 148–150, 154, 155, 179, 183, 188, 192, 193, 198, 209
  drought list, 126
  municipal programs, 109, 130
  piped, 108, 109, 128, 129, 136, 144, 153, 158, 159, 175, 183, 192, 199, 209, 220, 227
  shortages, 108, 111, 112
  trucks, 109–111, 125, 126, 130, 183, 193, 194
welfare, 7, 73, 98, 111
welfare state, 7, 15, 24, 83, 183, 206, 212
  development of, 209
  effect of introduction, 15
  inadequate, 176, 187, 188, 191, 193, 198, 206, 208
  relational clientelism as imperfect substitute for, *see under* relational clientelism
  willingness to accept clientelism, *see under* clientelism
workers, *see* employment
World Bank, 85, 99, 189

Yemen, 24, 78, 180, 202–204, 207

Other Books in the Series (continued from page ii)

Laia Balcells, *Rivalry and Revenge: The Politics of Violence during Civil War*
Lisa Baldez, *Why Women Protest? Women's Movements in Chile*
Kate Baldwin, *The Paradox of Traditional Chiefs in Democratic Africa*
Stefano Bartolini, *The Political Mobilization of the European Left, 1860–1980: The Class Cleavage*
Robert Bates, *When Things Fell Apart: State Failure in Late-Century Africa*
Mark Beissinger, *Nationalist Mobilization and the Collapse of the Soviet State*
Pablo Beramendi, *The Political Geography of Inequality: Regions and Redistribution*
Nancy Bermeo, ed., *Unemployment in the New Europe*
Nancy Bermeo and Deborah J. Yashar, eds., *Parties, Movements, and Democracy in the Developing World*
Carles Boix, *Democracy and Redistribution*
Carles Boix, *Political Order and Inequality: Their Foundations and their Consequences for Human Welfare*
Carles Boix, *Political Parties, Growth, and Equality: Conservative and Social Democratic Economic Strategies in the World Economy*
Catherine Boone, *Merchant Capital and the Roots of State Power in Senegal, 1930–1985*
Catherine Boone, *Political Topographies of the African State: Territorial Authority and Institutional Change*
Catherine Boone, *Property and Political Order in Africa: Land Rights and the Structure of Politics*
Michael Bratton and Nicolas van de Walle, *Democratic Experiments in Africa: Regime Transitions in Comparative Perspective*
Michael Bratton, Robert Mattes, and E. Gyimah-Boadi, *Public Opinion, Democracy, and Market Reform in Africa*
Valerie Bunce, *Leaving Socialism and Leaving the State: The End of Yugoslavia, the Soviet Union, and Czechoslovakia*
Daniele Caramani, *The Nationalization of Politics: The Formation of National Electorates and Party Systems in Europe*
John M. Carey, *Legislative Voting and Accountability*
Kanchan Chandra, *Why Ethnic Parties Succeed: Patronage and Ethnic Headcounts in India*
Eric C. C. Chang, Mark Andreas Kayser, Drew A. Linzer, and Ronald Rogowski, *Electoral Systems and the Balance of Consumer-Producer Power*
José Antonio Cheibub, *Presidentialism, Parliamentarism, and Democracy*
Ruth Berins Collier, *Paths toward Democracy: The Working Class and Elites in Western Europe and South America*
Daniel Corstange, *The Price of a Vote in the Middle East: Clientelism and Communal Politics in Lebanon and Yemen*
Pepper D. Culpepper, *Quiet Politics and Business Power: Corporate Control in Europe and Japan*

Sarah Zukerman Daly, *Organized Violence after Civil War: The Geography of Recruitment in Latin America*
Christian Davenport, *State Repression and the Domestic Democratic Peace*
Donatella della Porta, *Social Movements, Political Violence, and the State*
Alberto Diaz-Cayeros, *Federalism, Fiscal Authority, and Centralization in Latin America*
Alberto Diaz-Cayeros, Federico Estévez, Beatriz Magaloni, *The Political Logic of Poverty Relief*
Jesse Driscoll, *Warlords and Coalition Politics in Post-Soviet States*
Thad Dunning, *Crude Democracy: Natural Resource Wealth and Political Regimes*
Gerald Easter, *Reconstructing the State: Personal Networks and Elite Identity*
Margarita Estevez-Abe, *Welfare and Capitalism in Postwar Japan: Party, Bureaucracy, and Business*
Henry Farrell, *The Political Economy of Trust: Institutions, Interests, and Inter-Firm Cooperation in Italy and Germany*
Karen E. Ferree, *Framing the Race in South Africa: The Political Origins of Racial Census Elections*
M. Steven Fish, *Democracy Derailed in Russia: The Failure of Open Politics*
Robert F. Franzese, *Macroeconomic Policies of Developed Democracies*
Roberto Franzosi, *The Puzzle of Strikes: Class and State Strategies in Postwar Italy*
Timothy Frye, *Building States and Markets After Communism: The Perils of Polarized Democracy*
Geoffrey Garrett, *Partisan Politics in the Global Economy*
Scott Gehlbach, *Representation through Taxation: Revenue, Politics, and Development in Postcommunist States*
Edward L. Gibson, *Boundary Control: Subnational Authoritarianism in Federal Democracies*
Jane R. Gingrich, *Making Markets in the Welfare State: The Politics of Varying Market Reforms*
Miriam Golden, *Heroic Defeats: The Politics of Job Loss*
Jeff Goodwin, *No Other Way Out: States and Revolutionary Movements*
Merilee Serrill Grindle, *Changing the State*
Anna Grzymala-Busse, *Rebuilding Leviathan: Party Competition and State Exploitation in Post-Communist Democracies*
Anna Grzymala-Busse, *Redeeming the Communist Past: The Regeneration of Communist Parties in East Central Europe*
Frances Hagopian, *Traditional Politics and Regime Change in Brazil*
Mark Hallerberg, Rolf Ranier Strauch, Jürgen von Hagen, *Fiscal Governance in Europe*
Henry E. Hale, *The Foundations of Ethnic Politics: Separatism of States and Nations in Eurasia and the World*
Stephen E. Hanson, *Post-Imperial Democracies: Ideology and Party Formation in Third Republic France, Weimar Germany, and Post-Soviet Russia*
Michael Hechter, *Alien Rule*
Timothy Hellwig, *Globalization and Mass Politics: Retaining the Room to Maneuver*
Gretchen Helmke, *Institutions on the Edge: The Origins and Consequences of Inter Branch Crises in Latin America*
Gretchen Helmke, *Courts Under Constraints: Judges, Generals, and Presidents in Argentina*
Yoshiko Herrera, *Imagined Economies: The Sources of Russian Regionalism*

Alisha C. Holland, *Forbearance as Redistribution: The Politics of Informal Welfare in Latin America*
J. Rogers Hollingsworth and Robert Boyer, eds., *Contemporary Capitalism: The Embeddedness of Institutions*
John D. Huber, *Exclusion by Elections: Inequality, Ethnic Identity, and Democracy*
John D. Huber and Charles R. Shipan, *Deliberate Discretion? The Institutional Foundations of Bureaucratic Autonomy*
Ellen Immergut, *Health Politics: Interests and Institutions in Western Europe*
Torben Iversen, *Capitalism, Democracy, and Welfare*
Torben Iversen, *Contested Economic Institutions*
Torben Iversen, Jonas Pontussen, and David Soskice, eds., *Unions, Employers, and Central Banks: Macroeconomic Coordination and Institutional Change in Social Market Economics*
Thomas Janoski and Alexander M. Hicks, eds., *The Comparative Political Economy of the Welfare State*
Joseph Jupille, *Procedural Politics: Issues, Influence, and Institutional Choice in the European Union*
Stathis Kalyvas, *The Logic of Violence in Civil War*
Stephen B. Kaplan, *Globalization and Austerity Politics in Latin America*
David C. Kang, *Crony Capitalism: Corruption and Capitalism in South Korea and the Philippines*
Junko Kato, *Regressive Taxation and the Welfare State*
Orit Kedar, *Voting for Policy, Not Parties: How Voters Compensate for Power Sharing*
Robert O. Keohane and Helen B. Milner, eds., *Internationalization and Domestic Politics*
Herbert Kitschelt, *The Transformation of European Social Democracy*
Herbert Kitschelt, Kirk A. Hawkins, Juan Pablo Luna, Guillermo Rosas, and Elizabeth J. Zechmeister, *Latin American Party Systems*
Herbert Kitschelt, Peter Lange, Gary Marks, and John D. Stephens, eds., *Continuity and Change in Contemporary Capitalism*
Herbert Kitschelt, Zdenka Mansfeldova, Radek Markowski, and Gabor Toka, *Post-Communist Party Systems*
David Knoke, Franz Urban Pappi, Jeffrey Broadbent, and Yutaka Tsujinaka, eds., *Comparing Policy Networks*
Ken Kollman, *Perils of Centralization: Lessons from Church, State, and Corporation*
Allan Kornberg and Harold D. Clarke, *Citizens and Community: Political Support in a Representative Democracy*
Amie Kreppel, *The European Parliament and the Supranational Party System*
David D. Laitin, *Language Repertoires and State Construction in Africa*
Fabrice E. Lehoucq and Ivan Molina, *Stuffing the Ballot Box: Fraud, Electoral Reform, and Democratization in Costa Rica*
Benjamin Lessing *Making Peace in Drug Wars: Crackdowns and Cartels in Latin America*
Mark Irving Lichbach and Alan S. Zuckerman, eds., *Comparative Politics: Rationality, Culture, and Structure*, 2nd edition
Evan Lieberman, *Race and Regionalism in the Politics of Taxation in Brazil and South Africa*
Richard M. Locke, *The Promise and Limits of Private Power: Promoting Labor Standards in a Global Economy*

Julia Lynch, *Age in the Welfare State: The Origins of Social Spending on Pensioner's Workers and Children*
Pauline Jones Luong, *Institutional Change and Political Continuity in Post-Soviet Central Asia*
Pauline Jones Luong and Erika Weinthal, *Oil is Not a Curse: Ownership Structure and Institutions in Soviet Successor States*
Karen Long Jusko, *Who Speaks for the Poor? Electoral Geography, Party Entry, and Representation*
Doug McAdam, John McCarthy, and Mayer Zald, eds., *Comparative Perspectives on Social Movements*
Lauren M. MacLean, *Informal Institutions and Citizenship in Rural Africa: Risk and Reciprocity in Ghana and Côte d'Ivoire*
Beatriz Magaloni, *Voting for Autocracy: Hegemonic Party Survival and Its Demise in Mexico*
James Mahoney, *Colonialism and Postcolonial Development: Spanish America in Comparative Perspective*
James Mahoney and Dietrich Rueschemeyer, eds., *Historical Analysis and the Social Sciences*
Scott Mainwaring and Matthew Soberg Shugart, eds., *Presidentialism and Democracy in Latin America*
Melanie Manion, *Information for Autocrats: Representation in Chinese Local Congresses*
Isabela Mares, *From Open Secrets to Secret Voting: Democratic Electoral Reforms and Voter Autonomy*
Isabela Mares, *The Politics of Social Risk: Business and Welfare State Development*
Isabela Mares, *Taxation, Wage Bargaining, and Unemployment*
Cathie Jo Martin and Duane Swank, *The Political Construction of Business Interests: Coordination, Growth, and Equality*
Anthony W. Marx, *Making Race, Making Nations: A Comparison of South Africa, the United States, and Brazil*
Bonnie M. Meguid, *Party Competition between Unequals: Strategies and Electoral Fortunes in Western Europe*
Joel S. Migdal, *State in Society: Studying How States and Societies Constitute One Another*
Joel S. Migdal, Atul Kohli, and Vivienne Shue, eds., *State Power and Social Forces: Domination and Transformation in the Third World*
Scott Morgenstern and Benito Nacif, eds., *Legislative Politics in Latin America*
Kevin M. Morrison, *Nontaxation and Representation: The Fiscal Foundations of Political Stability*
Layna Mosley, *Global Capital and National Governments*
Layna Mosley, *Labor Rights and Multinational Production*
Wolfgang C. Müller and Kaare Strøm, *Policy, Office, or Votes?*
Maria Victoria Murillo, *Political Competition, Partisanship, and Policy Making in Latin American Public Utilities*
Maria Victoria Murillo, *Labor Unions, Partisan Coalitions, and Market Reforms in Latin America*
Monika Nalepa, *Skeletons in the Closet: Transitional Justice in Post-Communist Europe*
Simeon Nichter, *Votes for Survival: Relational Clientelism in Latin America*
Richard A. Nielson, *Deadly Clerics: Blocked Ambition and the Paths to Jihad*

Ton Notermans, *Money, Markets, and the State: Social Democratic Economic Policies since 1918*
Aníbal Pérez-Liñán, *Presidential Impeachment and the New Political Instability in Latin America*
Roger D. Petersen, *Understanding Ethnic Violence: Fear, Hatred, and Resentment in 20th Century Eastern Europe*
Roger D. Petersen, *Western Intervention in the Balkans: The Strategic Use of Emotion in Conflict*
Simona Piattoni, ed., *Clientelism, Interests, and Democratic Representation*
Paul Pierson, *Dismantling the Welfare State? Reagan, Thatcher, and the Politics of Retrenchment*
Marino Regini, *Uncertain Boundaries: The Social and Political Construction of European Economies*
Kenneth M. Roberts, *Changing Course in Latin America: Party Systems in the Neoliberal Era*
Marc Howard Ross, *Cultural Contestation in Ethnic Conflict*
Roger Schoenman, *Networks and Institutions in Europe's Emerging Markets*
Ben Ross Schneider, *Hierarchical Capitalism in Latin America: Business, Labor, and the Challenges of Equitable Development*
Lyle Scruggs, *Sustaining Abundance: Environmental Performance in Industrial Democracies*
Jefferey M. Sellers, *Governing from Below: Urban Regions and the Global Economy*
Yossi Shain and Juan Linz, eds., *Interim Governments and Democratic Transitions*
Beverly Silver, *Forces of Labor: Workers' Movements and Globalization since 1870*
Theda Skocpol, *Social Revolutions in the Modern World*
Prerna Singh, *How Solidarity Works for Welfare: Subnationalism and Social Development in India*
Austin Smith et al, *Selected Works of Michael Wallerstein*
Regina Smyth, *Candidate Strategies and Electoral Competition in the Russian Federation: Democracy without Foundation*
Richard Snyder, *Politics after Neoliberalism: Reregulation in Mexico*
David Stark and László Bruszt, *Postsocialist Pathways: Transforming Politics and Property in East Central Europe*
Sven Steinmo, *The Evolution of Modern States: Sweden, Japan, and the United States*
Sven Steinmo, Kathleen Thelen, and Frank Longstreth, eds., *Structuring Politics: Historical Institutionalism in Comparative Analysis*
Susan C. Stokes, *Mandates and Democracy: Neoliberalism by Surprise in Latin America*
Susan C. Stokes, ed., *Public Support for Market Reforms in New Democracies*
Susan C. Stokes, Thad Dunning, Marcelo Nazareno, and Valeria Brusco, *Brokers, Voters, and Clientelism: The Puzzle of Distributive Politics*
Milan W. Svolik, *The Politics of Authoritarian Rule*
Duane Swank, *Global Capital, Political Institutions, and Policy Change in Developed Welfare States*
Sidney Tarrow, *Power in Movement: Social Movements and Contentious Politics*
Sidney Tarrow, *Power in Movement: Social Movements and Contentious Politics, Revised and Updated Third Edition*
Tariq Thachil, *Elite Parties, Poor Voters: How Social Services Win Votes in India*

Kathleen Thelen, *How Institutions Evolve: The Political Economy of Skills in Germany, Britain, the United States, and Japan*
Kathleen Thelen, *Varieties of Liberalization and the New Politics of Social Solidarity*
Charles Tilly, *Trust and Rule*
Daniel Treisman, *The Architecture of Government: Rethinking Political Decentralization*
Guillermo Trejo, *Popular Movements in Autocracies: Religion, Repression, and Indigenous Collective Action in Mexico*
Rory Truex, *Making Autocracy Work: Representation and Responsiveness in Modern China*
Lily Lee Tsai, *Accountability without Democracy: How Solidary Groups Provide Public Goods in Rural China*
Joshua Tucker, *Regional Economic Voting: Russia, Poland, Hungary, Slovakia and the Czech Republic, 1990–1999*
Ashutosh Varshney, *Democracy, Development, and the Countryside*
Yuhua Wang, *Tying the Autocrat's Hand: The Rise of the Rule of Law in China*
Jeremy M. Weinstein, *Inside Rebellion: The Politics of Insurgent Violence*
Stephen I. Wilkinson, *Votes and Violence: Electoral Competition and Ethnic Riots in India*
Andreas Wimmer, *Waves of War: Nationalism, State Formation, and Ethnic Exclusion in the Modern World*
Jason Wittenberg, *Crucibles of Political Loyalty: Church Institutions and Electoral Continuity in Hungary*
Elisabeth J. Wood, *Forging Democracy from Below: Insurgent Transitions in South Africa and El Salvador*
Elisabeth J. Wood, *Insurgent Collective Action and Civil War in El Salvador*
Deborah Yashar, *Homicidal Ecologies: Violence After War and Dictatorship in Latin America*
Daniel Ziblatt, *Conservative Parties and the Birth of Democracy*